Bunker

Practical Methods for the Social Studies

M. EUGENE GILLIOM
The Ohio State University

JAMES DICK
State University of New York College at Buffalo

JACK R. FRAENKEL
San Francisco State University

JAMES E. HARF
The Ohio State University

DONALD HETZNER
State University of New York College at Buffalo

J. COLIN MARSH
Murdoch University, Murdoch, Western Australia

ANNE R. PETERSON
Columbus Technical Institute

JOEL S. POETKER
State University of New York College at Buffalo

Wadsworth Publishing Company, Inc.
Belmont, California

Roger S. Peterson
Education Editor

ISBN 0-534-00486-5

L. C. Cat. Card No. 76-40606

Printed in the United States of America

1 2 3 4 5 6 7 8 9 10—81 80 79 78 77

Library of Congress Cataloging in Publication Data

Main entry under title:

Practical methods for the social studies.

Bibliography: p.
Includes index.
1. Social sciences--Study and teaching (Higher)--United States. 2. Social sciences--Study and teaching (Secondary)--United States. I. Gilliom, M. Eugene.
H62.P647 300'.7 76-40606
ISBN 0-534-00486-5

Contents

Preface, v

Introduction **What this book is about,** 1
M. Eugene Gilliom
What is inquiry? 2
What is inquiry-oriented teaching? 3
The role of the teacher, 4
Why our commitment to inquiry? 4
Yes, but—, 5
Finally—, 11

Chapter 1 **Case studies,** 14
M. Eugene Gilliom
Using case studies in the inquiry-oriented classroom, 16
Types of case studies, 17
Designing case studies, 42
The teacher's role in analyzing case studies, 47

2 **Inquiry into values,** 50
Jack R. Fraenkel
Values as standards, 52
Value indicators, 52
Studying values in social studies classrooms, 55

3 **Simulations,** 82
M. Eugene Gilliom
Terminology, 84
Examples of simulations, 88
Why all the excitement about simulations? 94
Designing your own simulations, 97
Using simulations in the classroom, 110
The role of the teacher in using simulations, 112
Words of caution, 114
Sources and descriptions of selected simulations, 116

Chapter 4 **The quantitative perspective on inquiry in the social studies,** 140
James E. Harf / Anne R. Peterson
Purpose of this chapter, 143
Quantitative data, 149
Inquiry learning using quantitative data, 161
The process of inquiry teaching using quantitative data, 165
Examples of data analysis techniques, 172

5 **Local community studies,** 204
J. Colin Marsh
What are local community studies? 206
Why the interest in local community studies? 207
Some illustrations of local community studies, 209
Resources for local community studies, 216
Some precautions, 223

6 **Media,** 228
Donald Hetzner
Slides, filmstrips, and photographs, 230
8mm films, 236
Audio experiences, 237
Videotape, 243
Broadsides and newspaper headlines, 246
Artifacts and material remains, 248
Transparencies, 255
Needle-sort data decks, 261
Interactive computer-based instruction, 265

7 **Assessing what has been learned,** 276
Joel S. Poetker
Evaluation and measurement, 277
Objectives and evaluation, 278
Constructing objective test questions, 286
Using essay questions, 304
Techniques of evaluation other than testing, 311
Assessing attitudes and values, 318
Pitfalls to avoid, 322

8 **Resources for social studies teachers,** 326
James Dick
Sources of free and inexpensive materials, 328
Professional organizations, 349
Magazines and journals, 354
Social studies curriculum projects, 362
Media, 370
Embassies, 375
Publishers, 383

Index, 388

Preface

Practical Methods for the Social Studies was written for both preservice and in-service teachers. For preservice teachers it can be used as either a basic or a supplementary text in college courses dealing with methods of teaching social studies. For in-service teachers it can serve as a rich source of practical ideas and materials for implementing inquiry strategies in the classroom. Although the book focuses on the teaching of the social studies in the secondary school, many of the methods discussed can be adapted for use at the elementary level.

The ideas presented in this book have grown out of the authors' accumulation of more than 125 years of teaching experience at the elementary, secondary, and university levels. The book represents our collective as well as our individual thinking. Whereas we all share a commitment to inquiry in the social studies, each of us has reserved the right to apply his or her unique interpretation of inquiry in the individual chapters. Our intent in joining forces has been to present a collection of classroom-tested teaching approaches that hold promise for enlivening the social studies through the nurturing of inquiry. If you, the reader, find in these pages the means for challenging your students to become independent thinkers, we will have achieved our purpose.

We would like to extend our appreciation to the following people whose insightful reviews of our manuscript at various stages of its development helped to sharpen our ideas and polish our writing: Jan Tucker of Florida International University; Ronald Helms of Wright State University and the Kettering, Ohio, city schools; Adolph Crew of the University of Alabama; John F. Bartlett of Indiana State University; Clark C. Gill of the University of Texas; John Lunstrum of Florida State University; James P. Shaver of Utah State University; Frank E. Bloomer of Texas Technological University; Richard C. Phillips of the University of North Carolina; David Lonsdale of the University of Northern Colorado; and Mark M. Krug of the University of Chicago. Special thanks are also extended to Joseph Cirrincione of the University of Maryland and Albert Ogren of the Edina, Minnesota, public schools for their help in conceptualizing the project in its early stages. Finally, we would like to express our gratitude to Roger Peterson, Education Editor of the Wadsworth Publishing Company, for his professional know-how and his commitment to excellence.

M.E.G.

Introduction

What this book is about

This book is based on some rather bold assumptions by the authors. Rather than viewing the readers as mere babes in the woods of education—persons who have given little or no thought to their motives for being social studies teachers and who have little notion of what they hope to accomplish in the classroom—we have chosen to view them as persons who have a clear sense of purpose, are professionally alive, and are either committed to or willing to try inquiry-oriented teaching. As a result of these assumptions, there are several things this book is not intended to do. It does not, for example, present an exhaustive discourse on the nature of history and the social sciences, deal with the full range of problems facing social studies teachers, or present a neatly packaged social studies program designed to assure success in the classroom. Such topics deserve to be dealt with in professional literature. Our purposes, however, are considerably more specific. What the book *is* intended to do is to treat in sufficient depth a limited number of teaching approaches, ideas, examples, leads, and sources that can help to translate inquiry from an abstraction in a textbook to reality in the classroom.

We have assumed that teachers and students themselves are the final designers of curriculum and teaching strategies; therefore, the book has very much a "do-it-yourself" flavor. When appropriate, commercially produced materials are described, discussed, and evaluated. Throughout the book, however, suggestions are included for producing homemade teaching materials and for designing different kinds of instructional strategies. Most of the illustrative materials presented are appropriate for direct adoption in many classes. In some cases, however, the materials will serve primarily as examples, with the challenge being left to individual teachers to add their unique stamps of creativity before ideas are tried out with students.

The book does not require the reader to work through it from beginning to end to find it useful. Rather, it is composed of complementary chapters that stand independently as well as contributing to the whole. If you need help in testing for growth in inquiry skills, for example, plunge into chapter 7 on evaluation. On the other hand, if you want to try your hand at writing case studies, turn to chapter 1.

Above all, it is our fondest hope that the book will be *used*. It is not the kind of publication one should purchase, read, and place on a shelf to gather dust. If it is not a rich and useful source of teaching ideas and practical help, we've missed our mark. The approaches dealt with in the book are included because they are practical, have been found by the authors to be effective, can be adapted to a wide variety of teaching situations, and in most instances can be worked into existing programs—even those operating on a shoestring budget.

What is inquiry?

The thread that ties the chapters together and that runs throughout the book is our basic commitment to inquiry. The term inquiry, as it relates to the social studies, means many things to many people—a fact made evident during the past decade or so in the writings of such notable authors as Hunt, Metcalf, Jewett, Massialas, Cox, Fenton, Oliver, Shaver, Neumann, Fraenkel, Beyer, and Goldmark. It would appear fruitless for us to retill the soil these authors have worked over so thoroughly and to present yet another elaborate interpretation of inquiry. Suffice it to say that to us inquiry refers to the process by which one goes about rationally resolving doubt. To inquire in the social studies implies that one confronts and attempts to deal with significant problems relating to people's interaction with other people and with their environment. To that end, we share with Jewett the conviction that a major goal of the social studies should be the development of the intellectually autonomous individual—the independent person who blends a commitment to rationality with skills, understandings, and attitudes requisite to thoughtful inquiry.

The genesis of all inquiry is perplexity—a contradiction, a dilemma, an issue, a problem. To inquire is to seek reasoned solutions to our perplexities. Although inquiry is not governed by absolute rules, it is disciplined thinking that is controlled by an end—the pursuit of warranted conclusions or beliefs. The process of resolving doubt through inquiry normally involves a series of mental operations beginning with the recognition of a problem, moving to the casting and testing of hypotheses designed to resolve the problem, and culminating with the emergence of a resolution best supported by the available evidence. At all points along the line, evidence must be gathered, subjected to analysis, and either accepted or cast aside. Sources of data must be analyzed and compared. Assumptions regarding data must be examined and inferences drawn. In the end, perplexity is disposed of only as supportable conclusions emerge.

A cornerstone of inquiry is healthy skepticism: a reluctance to accept simple solutions to complex problems; a willingness to question authoritative answers when evidence casts doubt on their viability; a desire to ferret out truth even though it may contradict one's own feelings and convictions. At the same time, successful inquiry demands a willingness to suspend judgment, a capacity to live with tentativeness while the search for valid answers continues.

To inquire is to bring rigor to thought. This suggests that successful inquiry requires more than a comprehension of the processes of problem solving or the development of a set of requisite skills. It implies further that the inquirer has made a commitment to reason, and that he is willing to act upon this conviction. In this sense, inquiry is an affective as well as an intellectual commitment to a way of life that is characterized by doubting and questioning, a persistent and objective search for truth.

What is inquiry-oriented teaching?

Inquiry-oriented teaching involves creating a setting within which students feel compelled to pursue solutions to problems that are meaningful to them. It falls largely on you, the teacher, to launch inquiry by surfacing and giving immediacy to the problem to be pursued, and to nurture the process by supporting and assisting the students in their search for warranted answers. Problems may assume many forms and can be triggered by a myriad of stimuli. They may, for example, grow out of content being studied (Why did New Englanders generally oppose the War of 1812?) or out of current social problems (Why is the rate of unemployment higher among blacks in the United States than among whites?). They may focus on personal conflict (Should I support proabortion legislation currently before the state legislature?) or on public issues (Should we have federal legislation regulating the sale of handguns?).

One thing seems certain. If the problem being studied is not of genuine concern to the students—if it fails to gnaw at them, begging for an answer—it is predictable that the inquiry will assume its place among other soon-to-be-forgotten academic exercises. Focusing on problems that grow out of the students' experiences and taking into account their needs, interests, maturity, and backgrounds will go a long way toward assuring viable and stimulating inquiry.

The number of techniques and the variety of materials that can be used for stimulating students to inquire must be astronomical. The common quality among them is that they raise questions, contradict our expectations, seem to defy logic, and bring to light inconsistencies in our thinking. Conflicting editorials in two local newspapers, for example, might present entirely different opinions of the qualifications of local candidates for public office. Which presents the more accurate view? What is the truth? Which candidate is best suited for office? A speaker questions the advisability of establishing a civilian police review board. Are his arguments legitimate? Do they square with the facts? Should a board be established? A simulation exercise raises questions about the use and abuse of power. Why do people in positions of power behave as they do? What, if anything, should be done to curb power in the political arena?

With springboards to inquiry at our fingertips in nearly every conceivable form, the creative teacher should have little difficulty identifying questions that can be perceived by the students as being provocative. In fact, as students become attuned to the inquiry method and as they sharpen their investigative skills, they themselves can be expected to suggest problems worthy of study.

The role of the teacher

Your role as the teacher during inquiry must to a large extent be dictated by conditions as they arise. At times you may best serve the students as a helpful consultant, directing them to needed sources of information or delivering a timely lecture. At other times you might assume the role of the devil's advocate—provoking, questioning, challenging. At all times, however, inquiry is likely to be carried out most effectively in a nonthreatening atmosphere that is conducive to a free interchange of ideas, an atmosphere in which doubt is prized and students' ideas are courteously and fairly entertained.

The task of creating a healthy climate for learning is largely your responsibility. Such a climate seldom develops overnight. It must be cultivated patiently and nurtured with trust and with a willingness to hear out the other person's point of view. The development of mutual respect among members of a group is not always easily achieved, as personal prejudices and animosities commonly stand as barriers to rationality. Yet the teacher committed to inquiry must do everything possible—including serving as a model—to create a setting in which students can enter discussions without the threat of ridicule or censure and can expect a fair and balanced hearing of their ideas.

Why our commitment to inquiry?

The advantages and disadvantages of any approach to teaching must be judged in light of the instructional purposes one has in mind and the options that are available. If, for example, you view the primary goals of social studies instruction as being the exposure of students to vast amounts of historical and social science content, the inculcation of predetermined beliefs, or the molding of students intellectually into carbon copies of yourself, the inquiry approach probably will fall far short of your expectations. Such goals predictably will be better achieved through a tightly organized, teacher-dominated expository approach to teaching. On the other hand, if you share our inclination to encourage students to develop into autonomous individuals, to think independently, and to develop skills with which they can continue to examine problems and issues reflectively, the inquiry approach would seem to hold considerable promise for you.

We realize full well that using inquiry techniques cannot guarantee that dull classrooms will suddenly spring to life or that uninterested students will magically be turned on by the social studies. We do believe, however, that the inquiry approach, carried out by a skillful teacher, holds promise for a variety of reasons. It appears to us that when students are engaged in inquiry the following is likely to occur:

- Interest will be stimulated as students become actively involved in learning.
- The fostering of independent thinking not only will lead to more creative problem solving, but also will increase the numbers of students participating in the process.
- Students will tend to view content in a more realistic and positive way as they analyze and apply data to the resolution of problems.
- Teacher-student relations will assume a healthier tone as the teacher becomes more a facilitator of learning and less a director of teacher-dominated activities.
- Students will increasingly master a powerful way of knowing, as well as developing a set of more adequately grounded beliefs.
- Students will develop into more self-directed, autonomous thinkers.

We're not suggesting that all teachers can or will teach for inquiry with equal effectiveness or that an inquiry orientation will guarantee a simple, easy path to teaching success. On the contrary, the approach requires a commitment on the part of both the teacher and students in terms of interest, time, and energy. We feel, however, that the potential payoff in terms of student growth and, consequently, teacher satisfaction warrants the extra effort that inquiry requires.

Yes, but—

A fair question at this point could be, "If inquiry offers so much promise, why don't all social studies teachers teach in this fashion?" The reasons are myriad, and we'll not attempt to discuss them all. There are, however, nine negative statements about the inquiry approach that we have come across time and time again. A response to any one of the statements could easily fill many pages, so it is at the risk of oversimplification that we react briefly.

1. In our community it is professionally hazardous to deal with problems and issues in the social studies. Parents regard such an approach suspiciously, and administrators don't want us to rock the boat.

Unfortunately, this sometimes appears to be the case. Although it is not necessarily so, inquiry often focuses on controversial and "unsafe" areas of society. In some communities such study might be considered dangerous and inappropriate. When this occurs, even an appeal to reason often falls on deaf ears, and community pressures can make it virtually impossible to inquire into sensitive problems. In such an instance, you may have little choice practically but to skirt particularly explosive problems until the climate is such that they can be dealt with in a constructive and rational fashion. It is a promising fact that many school districts have taken steps to protect the rights of teachers and students by establishing policies that guarantee the right to learn in an unbiased atmosphere with free access to all sources of relevant information. Professional teachers' organizations have also become much more vigorous during the past several years in protecting teachers' rights and in supporting teachers who have suffered harassment for attempting to deal with controversial issues.

If you are pressured to avoid sensitive issues or to teach a particular point of view, you ultimately must respond out of your own convictions and sense of professionalism. None of us would presume to impose on others our definitions of academic freedom and teachers' rights and responsibilities. Questions of professional survival are of a highly personal nature and can be dealt with realistically only in the context of a particular school setting. It is clear that any teacher who chooses to encourage students to inquire should develop a sense for the community's tolerance of autonomous thinking by its young people.

We believe that there is a place in the social studies for pursuing significant problems and for attempting to come to grips with important issues. On the other hand, we see no place in the social studies for propagandizing, indoctrinating, or sermonizing. We have found that a community's tolerance for inquiry in the secondary school is often greater than we may believe, and we have found that the fears of parents and administrators usually diminish when they realize that inquiry involves *responsible* investigation, a reliance on sound data, and a balanced presentation of various points of view.

2. My students prefer the traditional chapter-by-chapter approach to the social studies. They don't want to become involved in thinking.

Occasionally students do react negatively to the challenge to think independently. This is especially true if they have come through a system of education in which they have seldom been challenged to make decisions and have been required to do little more than uncritically memorize and recite collections of facts. Whether to perpetuate this approach to education or to challenge the students to stretch their thinking and to accept the rigors of inquiry is a decision all teachers must make for themselves.

Curiously, it is often the A students who initially resist inquiry. This seems largely due to their fear that high grades will be threatened if emphasis is shifted from traditional expectations, such as "covering" the textbook, memorizing information, and completing end-of-the-chapter true-and-false examinations, to inquiry-type activities, such as identifying problems, seeking out evidence, and testing hypotheses. Such fears, although real, are groundless and certainly should not serve as a basis for making decisions regarding one's approach to teaching. Shifting to an inquiry orientation, however, takes time. Students not only must learn a new set of investigative skills, but also must accept increasing responsibility for the quality of work carried on in the classroom. We have found that once students become convinced that they *can* think effectively and experience the satisfaction accompanying rigorous inquiry, their fear of moving away from the read-recite-review-regurgitate approach to the social studies tends to dissipate.

3. I don't have materials available to carry out inquiry. All I'm given is a single outdated textbook.

Each of us would like to have easy access to all conceivable sources of information, including fully stocked libraries, museums, and data banks. Such, of course, is not the case. To assume, however, that fruitful inquiry cannot occur in less than ideal surroundings is testimony to one's lack of creativity. Granted, the quality and depth of inquiry are limited by the availability of sound data, but that is inevitably the case—in the social studies classroom, in government, in industry, in any walk of life. It is essential that students realize that we always function with something less than complete data when attempting to resolve problems, and at the same time recognize the hazards of basing judgments on incomplete evidence. The availability of resource material necessarily will have a bearing on the types of problems to be studied and on the degree to which they can be resolved. If ready resources clearly fail to provide sufficient depth of understanding of a particular problem, the problem should be temporarily shelved until further data are available.

Even the single outdated textbook can serve a useful purpose in an inquiry-oriented class if it is viewed and analyzed as *one* interpretation of content written by an author who functioned within a frame of reference at a particular point in time. No teacher should feel limited, however, to using a single textbook as the students' sole source of information. Sources of useful data surround us in a wide variety of forms. Consider, for example, the information provided in easily available newspapers, magazines, government publications, industry reports, census analyses, and radio and television programs. Why not draw on local volunteers through such sources as government agencies, service organizations, universities, and industries? The inexpensive cassette tape recorder and the camera have become invaluable tools for the imaginative teacher who wants to bring data to the classroom in oral and visual form. The heat process duplicator now available in most schools, together with the overhead projector and the spirit duplicator, provides the means by which teachers can quickly and inexpensively create transparencies and handouts for use in inquiry lessons. In short, the problems of locating and presenting data often seem less severe than the problem of selecting from the masses of information available that which can be used most effectively.

4. If I turn students loose to debate issues and to challenge one another's ideas, my classroom will be the noisiest in the school. My discipline will disappear. I'll lose control.

Whereas students involved in debating issues sometimes do become a bit vigorous and noisy, we don't view that as being necessarily undesirable. If the rising noise level reflects student enthusiasm for the social studies, perhaps we should welcome it. Better a classroom alive with ideas and student activity than one in which peace and quiet are never disturbed by either. We're not suggesting that the social studies classroom be turned into a circus and that all the rules of behavior be abandoned, however. To equate freedom of thought and expression with rowdiness and chaos is to overlook the responsibilities attached to responsible inquiry. What better place for students to learn the courtesies of debate and to develop sensitivity to the rights of others than the social studies classroom?

5. We'll never be able to cover the content I feel we should if we become involved in discussing problems.

This statement implies that one *either* focuses on content *or* deals in problem solving—a distinction we are unwilling to accept. Sound inquiry simply cannot proceed without one's drawing on relevant data or content. Furthermore, when students use content in the resolution of problems, they tend to attach importance to it and to view it as evidence to be sought and used rather than as trivia to be endured and forgotten.

Obviously, it would be inconceivable to cover *all* content in any given subject even if it were desirable. Like it or not, all teachers are faced with the inevitability of selecting content on which to focus their students' attention. The social studies teacher feels the pressure of these decisions perhaps more than anyone else. After all, where does one begin and end a study of world history, for example, given the limited amount of time available? We are being deluged at an ever-increasing rate with new information in amounts beyond our capacity to comprehend and learn, let alone teach. The mind boggles at the idea of teaching thoroughly even a small sampling of the content on which one could focus. Complicate this circumstance by the fact that social studies teachers usually are expected to take an interdisciplinary approach, integrating history and the social sciences when possible.

Considering the utter impossibility of dealing with all the content in any subject, it would appear that we should be less concerned with textbook coverage and more concerned with developing insights and skills our students need in sorting, analyzing, and applying the vast amounts of information with which they are already faced. This is not to downgrade the importance of content in the social studies. After all, the quality of inquiry is largely dependent upon the soundness of data collected as evidence. It *is* to suggest that all content is not of equal importance, and that content most meaningful to students will be that used in their search for answers to relevant problems.

6. My students aren't capable of inquiry. They'll have to master the subject matter before they begin to think.

It is true that the students must have enough background to recognize the existence of conflict if a problem for study is to emerge. This could mean that the use of an appropriate film, readings, or a lecture in the early stages of inquiry would be advisable to bring focus to the problem. To assume, however, that students must have "mastered the subject matter" required to solve the problem before confronting it is to create a false dichotomy between a method of thinking and the product of thought. This position implies that subject matter should be viewed as a kind of commodity that is accumulated, filed away mentally for possible future use, and drawn out of storage when needed. We, too, want students to develop useful concepts and generalizations in the social studies, but we feel that this can be done more effectively when the students deal with the content and develop their insights *during* the course of inquiry. Psychologists tell us that material that is meaningful to students is learned more readily than material for which they can see no value or which they fail to understand. Surely, data that are located, analyzed, and applied in the resolution of puzzlement assume more meaning than data simply collected and put on the mental shelf. If we feel that subject matter *is* important, why not demonstrate that belief to the students by putting content to work in an attempt to resolve conflicts they consider significant?

7. Inquiry might be all right for college-bound students, but mine are not academically inclined.

This implies an elitism that bothers us. Obviously the solving of problems is not the sole province of any one segment of society. Each of us, from the most humble to the most powerful, is involved in the resolution of conflict every day, and each of us can benefit from efforts to sharpen our problem-solving skills. Granted, inquiry is carried on at different levels of sophistication, depending upon the nature of the problem and the inquirer's skills, past experience, motivation, and native ability. Students who are academically inclined and who have a rich background in a particular subject will likely deal with abstract problems in greater depth than students whose capabilities and experiences are more limited. By the same token, students not of an academic bent can draw on a wealth of less scholarly but nevertheless valid experiences as they inquire into problems of concern to them. In either case, we've found that the opportunity for students to exchange insights with peers from varying backgrounds and interests is one of the exciting features of inquiry in the social studies.

8. To involve students in inquiry, deludes them into thinking that they can solve problems that are far beyond their comprehension or beyond current solution.

If students do become convinced that all problems are within their capacity to solve, they have failed to grasp much of the essence of inquiry. After all, who among us can claim with certainty to know the resolution to such problems as these: What should be done to combat global hunger? How can the world's energy problems be resolved? What can be done to assure peace in the Middle East? What steps should be taken to eliminate racial prejudice in hiring in our country? What should be done to eliminate crime in the United States? Problems of this type defy simple solutions, if indeed they can be resolved at all. Yet it seems clear that little will be gained if we simply turn our backs on reality in the hope that such difficulties will somehow magically disappear.

One of the fundamental tenets of inquiry is that conclusions must be supported by valid evidence. As students learn to respect evidence and come to understand the complex nature of most problems they'll confront in the social studies, they should develop a realistic sense for both the potential and the limitations of inquiry. Rather than viewing all problems as being capable of resolution, students trained in inquiry are much more likely to pursue evidence as far as possible but to suspend judgment and to accept conclusions as being tentative until additional clarifying evidence becomes available. Even then, solutions to problems are considered to be tentative, with the possibility always being that fresh evidence may emerge at some future time that will warrant the modifying of conclusions. In this sense, inquiry never ceases and knowledge never stagnates. In social studies classes where closure at the completion of a unit is highly prized, such tentativeness may initially prove uncomfortable to both the teacher and the students. Nevertheless, a healthy dose of intellectual humility and the recognition that most problems defy simple solutions are essential to sound inquiry.

9. Inquiry can lead to student cynicism and the debunking of our country's heroes.

On the contrary, we feel that the best way to breed cynicism is to withhold facts that raise questions about traditionally cherished beliefs, only to have them emerge at a later date after our students have left the protective environment of the school. No responsible teacher is interested in debunking for the sake of shock effect or sensationalism. However, dealing with human beings in human terms, considering their faults as well as their accomplishments, can serve to illuminate the motives of our leaders, past and present, and can help students to understand their behavior. Failure to analyze in a fair and balanced fashion the shortcomings as well as the achievements of so-called heroes borders on deception and distorts the process of inquiry. Rather than generating cynicism, we feel that inquiry can lead to a more healthy and realistic view of the world and can result in increased sensitivity to human behavior.

Finally—

We launched this statement by writing that we've chosen to view the readers of this book as persons who are either committed to or are willing to attempt inquiry-oriented teaching. If you've already tried your hand at teaching for inquiry in the social studies, you may have found little more than confirmation of your ideas and a bit of comfort in the preceding comments. If your inclination has not been in the direction of inquiry-oriented teaching, we *hope* that our comments have aroused your curiosity about the approach and have served to encourage you to give inquiry a fair trial in your classroom.

In either case, we now come to the heart of the book. The following chapters are a reflection of our conviction that young people should, can, and will learn to think carefully, critically, rationally, reflectively. As a social studies teacher, you occupy a position that provides you with unique opportunities to cultivate in your students the habit of responsible thought. It is our hope that you will find the ideas dealt with in the following pages to be of help in this enterprise. Good inquiring!

M. Eugene Gilliom
The Ohio State University
Columbus, Ohio

Bibliography

Beardsley, Monroe C. *Thinking Straight*. 3d ed. Englewood Cliffs, N.J.: Prentice-Hall, 1966.

Beyer, Barry K. *Inquiry in the Social Studies Classroom: A Strategy for Teaching*. Columbus, Ohio: Merrill, 1971.

Bruner, Jerome H. *The Process of Education*. New York: Vintage Books, 1960.

Burton, William H.; Kimball, Roland B.; and Wing, Richard L. *Education for Effective Thinking*. New York: Appleton-Century-Crofts, 1960.

Dewey, John. *How We Think*. Boston: Heath, 1910.

Ehman, Lee; Mehlinger, Howard; and Patrick, John. *Toward Effective Instruction in Secondary Social Studies*. Boston: Houghton Mifflin, 1974.

Fair, Jean, and Shaftel, Fannie, eds. *Effective Thinking in the Social Studies.* Thirty-seventh Yearbook of the National Council for the Social Studies. Washington, D.C.: The Council, 1967.

Fenton, Edwin. *Teaching the New Social Studies in Secondary Schools: An Inductive Approach*. New York: Holt, Rinehart & Winston, 1966.

Fraenkel, Jack R. *Helping Students Think and Value*. Englewood Cliffs, N.J.: Prentice-Hall, 1973.

Goldmark, Bernice. *Social Studies: A Method of Inquiry.* Belmont, Calif.: Wadsworth, 1968.

Hullfish, H. Gordon, and Smith, Philip G. *Reflective Thinking: The Method of Education*. New York: Dodd, Mead, 1961.

Hunt, Maurice P., and Metcalf, Lawrence E. *Teaching High School Social Studies*. 2d ed. New York: Harper & Row, 1968.

Jewett, Robert E. "The Problems Approach and the Senior High School." In *Problem-Centered Social Studies Instruction: Approaches to Reflective Teaching*. Curriculum Series No. 14 of the National Council for the Social Studies. Washington, D.C.: The Council, 1971.

Mallan, John T., and Hersh, Richard. *No G.O.D.S. in the Classroom: Inquiry Into Inquiry.* Philadelphia: Saunders, 1972.

———.*No G.O.D.S. in the Classroom: Inquiry and Secondary Social Studies.* Philadelphia: Saunders, 1972.

Massialas, Byron G., and Cox, C. Benjamin. *Inquiry in Social Studies.* New York: McGraw-Hill, 1966.

Newmann, Fred M., and Oliver, Donald W. *Clarifying Public Controversy: An Approach to Teaching Social Studies.* Boston: Little, Brown, 1970.

Oliver, Donald W., and Shaver, James P. *Teaching Public Issues in the High School*. Boston: Houghton Mifflin, 1966.

Phillips, Richard C. *Teaching for Thinking in High School Social Studies*. Reading, Mass.: Addison-Wesley, 1974.

Raths, Louis E.; Jonas, Arthur; Rothstein, Arnold; and Wasserman, Selma. *Teaching for Thinking: Theory and Application*. Columbus, Ohio: Merrill, 1967.

Robinson, James H. *The Mind in the Making*. New York: Harper & Row, 1921.
Scheffler, Israel. *The Anatomy of Inquiry*. New York: Knopf, 1963.
Taba, Hilda. *Curriculum Development: Theory and Practice*. New York: Harcourt, Brace & World, 1962.

Case studies increasingly are being used by social studies teachers as a means for initiating inquiry by bringing problems and issues of the "real world" into the classroom. A typical case focuses on a human dilemma, presenting the students with conflicting points of view or interpretations of an event, a decision, or a situation. The students are challenged to examine the case, consider alternative ways of resolving the conflict, and justify their conclusions. Although case studies focus on a limited portion of human experience, they may be thought of as scraps of reality from which our perceptions of the world are distilled. They can effectively provide a glimpse into human nature and human relationships, and can serve as a means for personalizing the social studies.

The purpose of this chapter is to identify and illustrate the many forms which case studies can assume, to provide practical suggestions for designing case studies, and to offer tips for using case studies effectively in the inquiry-oriented social studies classroom.

Chapter 1

Case studies

Case studies have been used successfully for years in schools of business, law and medicine as a means of bringing reality closer to the classroom, but only recently have they been given more than casual attention by social studies teachers. In the case-study approach students are confronted with accounts of lifelike situations, which involve problems or dilemmas of concern to them that grow out of the content of the social studies. Although most cases are written, they can be presented orally or visually; written cases can be supplemented by such devices as slides, films, transparencies, and recordings. Cases can be hypothetical or based on fact and can be as long and complex or as simple and brief as the situation demands. For example, one case might in several paragraphs describe a middle-aged father's despair when he discovers that his teenage son is hooked on heroin. Another might in great detail and with supporting documents present a famous court case involving the right to legal counsel. In either instance the student is presented with a slice of life, which he is asked to mull over, dissect, and make sense of. Although cases are particularly useful when dealing with contemporary problems, they can also be used effectively when studying history and any of the social sciences.

The case-study approach is based upon the assumptions that social studies instruction should revolve around an interaction of ideas and that students should cultivate the habit of independent thought. The use of case studies alone obviously will not guarantee the achievement of these goals, but through an analysis of cases, students can in dramatic and personal fashion be provided with the raw materials out of which conceptualization can take place and decisions on important issues can be made.

One of the outstanding virtues of the case-study approach is that it is well suited to taking students out of the role of passive observers and making them active participants in the process of learning. The approach may be described as being essentially democratic, as opposed to the "telling" method, which often tends to be dictatorial and patriarchal. When analyzing case studies, all members of the class, teacher *and* students, possess essentially the same basic information regarding the situation under scrutiny. If the discussion of the case is properly handled, it should bring out opinions of the students as well as those of the teacher. In such a discussion, students no longer are limited to dealing simply with an elder in a master-student relationship; rather, they are encouraged to interact with a large number of equals whose ideas must be heard to the end and whose criticisms must be evaluated.

The use of cases does not at all rule out a rigorous study of social studies content. Rather, it encourages students to view content in a more positive and realistic light than is normally the case. Instead of being regarded as a collection of isolated details to be memorized and regurgitated for the benefit of the teacher on examination day, concepts, facts, and ideas are dug into, hashed over, assimilated, and used as they are needed for dealing with the problem at hand.

Using case studies in the inquiry-oriented classroom

The case-study approach is particularly appropriate for the development of inquiry skills. In a typical case students are confronted with a problem situation, which they are required to analyze and come to grips with. The challenge is theirs: to delimit the problem and define it in manageable terms; to examine and classify available information that bears upon the problem; to suggest possible solutions, testing and elaborating on those that seem most valid; to verify conclusions; and, finally, to extend the solution, considering the implications of their findings for understanding similar problems.

As students analyze the tangle of circumstances and facts surrounding the case, they face the challenge of cultivating *their own* ideas and testing them against those developed by others. With practice, they soon begin to throw ideas and facts into fresh combinations in an effort to formulate appropriate solutions for the problem at hand. In time, they will become increasingly sensitive to the limitations of the facts provided in the case and will recognize the need for further data before valid conclusions can be reached. When a student asks, "What additional information is needed to make a sound decision in this case and how can I get it?" an important stage has been reached in his development as an inquirer.

Successful use of case studies, as with other techniques designed to stimulate inquiry, to a great extent depends upon a climate of openness in the classroom. A free interchange of ideas is necessary, and this will occur only if intellectual autonomy is demonstrated in practice as well as valued in theory. If students are expected to interact honestly and openly regarding significant and touchy issues, they must *know* that opinions of all shades are welcome and that their ideas will receive a fair hearing and analysis. They must be inclined to suspend judgment until all available facts are in, and even then to view "truth" as being tentative. They must be willing to tackle all questions in a spirit of objective inquiry and to accept the responsibility for their own decisions. You, the teacher, inevitably must accept the bulk of responsibility for creating a climate in which inquiry can occur—a classroom in which the students are disposed to raise questions and search for answers, as opposed to chorusing "accepted" responses to someone else's questions.

Drawing on the many forms case studies may assume, you can construct them to serve specific purposes at various stages of inquiry. For example, cases can be designed to initiate inquiry by providing essential background information, posing key problems, raising issues, focusing on key concepts, and arousing student interest by serving as a link between the world of the student and the unit to be pursued. They can be used effectively in the middle stages of the study by providing data needed to resolve questions under consideration and to test hypotheses. Finally, cases can be useful in the culminating stages of inquiry when used to "stretch" the thinking of the students by having them apply their newly won understandings to a fresh set of problems or circumstances.

The social studies comprise almost countless problems, issues, and areas of value conflict that touch the lives of secondary students and can appropriately be inquired into through the use of case studies. Provocative cases can be developed, for example, to point up conflicts in the areas of race relations, ecology, civil liberties, sex, freedom of the press, academic freedom, and politics. Chapter 2 provides numerous opportunities for using case studies as vehicles for inquiring into value conflict.

In a society in which violence has increasingly been turned to in recent years as a means for resolving differences of opinion, it can be argued convincingly that adolescents today desperately need to sharpen their inquiry skills through recognizing and dealing with issues of personal and public concern. It would appear that such sharpening will take place only as students are encouraged to subject their own beliefs to constant reanalysis and to deal rationally with the many issues facing members of our society today. The social studies classroom can be an arena within which this pursuit can be carried out, and the case study should prove to be one helpful tool for social studies teachers who commit themselves to this kind of teaching.

Types of case studies

Case studies can take many forms and can be designed to deal with a broad range of concepts from history and the social sciences and to focus on an unlimited variety of human problems and concerns. Sources of materials for creating cases are everywhere—newspapers, magazines, novels, biographies, speeches, eyewitness accounts, committee hearings, statistical reports, charts and graphs, textbooks, diaries, letters, commission reports, transcripts of trials, and so forth. Depending upon the nature and source of the information provided and the style in which they are constructed, cases can be divided into nine basic types: court cases, open-ended episodes, interpretive essays, cases based on documents, memoirs, eyewitness accounts, vignettes, chronicles, and narratives.* Following is a brief consideration of each of the types, accompanied by illustrative examples and recommendations for possible usage.

Court cases

Court cases are based upon legal decisions made in the courts and are especially effective when studying issues related to such topics as the protection of civil rights, the role of the police in society, responsibilities of the individual under the law, and the changing nature of the Constitution. The cases from which to choose for investigation are almost limitless, with the choice depending upon the purpose of the study. If you plan to deal with issues related to the nature of legal evidence and the protection of citizens against illegal entry into a private home, for example, the *Rochin* case described here could be used effectively.

> *The stomach pump incident*
>
> On the morning of July 1, 1949, three Los Angeles deputy sheriffs arrived at the home of Antonio Rochin following a tip that Rochin was pushing narcotics. The outside door to the two-story house was open, so they entered, went upstairs, and forced open the door to Rochin's bedroom.
>
> When they entered, the deputies found Mrs. Rochin in bed, and Rochin sitting on the bed beside her. When Rochin realized what was happening, he grabbed two capsules from the nightstand beside the bed and quickly put them into his mouth. The deputies physically attempted to prevent Rochin from swallowing the capsules, and when this failed, they tried to make him cough them up.
>
> Rochin was immediately handcuffed and rushed to a hospital, where, following the instructions of one of the deputies, a doctor administered a stomach pump. After the tube was forced down his throat and a vomit-inducing chemical was pumped into his stomach, Rochin vomited up two capsules containing morphine. The capsules were considered to be sufficient evidence to convict Rochin of possession of narcotics, and he was sentenced to prison. Rochin's lawyers appealed the case to the Supreme Court.†

A number of significant issues can be surfaced by the students in their reading of the *Rochin* case: Should evidence that is seized by the police operating without a warrant be considered admissible in court? Should recourse against the police be open to Rochin, since they seem to have broken the law while in the process of arresting him for lawbreaking? Should the police have the right to subject a suspect to a stomach pump against his will?

---

*This scheme for categorizing case studies is an adaptation of an approach recommended by Donald Oliver and Fred M. Newmann in *Social Education* 31 (February, 1967): pp. 108–13.

†*Rochin v. California*, 342 U.S. 165 (1952).

After such issues have been brought out, the class can turn to a consideration of the merits and disadvantages on each side of the questions raised. Through such an analysis, they should begin to recognize that our lives are constantly complicated by the necessity of resolving conflicts between two or more goods rather than simply making choices between good and evil. As students attempt to resolve the issues implicit in this case, for example, they should discover the tenuous balance existing in a society that attempts to protect the rights of individual citizens and preserve the sanctity of the private home while at the same time assuring protection of the society itself from illicit drug traffic.

Once the students have suggested various ways in which the issues could be resolved, they can address themselves to the ethical, legal, and practical implications of accepting each of the resolutions recommended. It would be helpful then to test their insights against those of Mr. Justice Frankfurter, who delivered the following opinion when the case was appealed to the Supreme Court:

> We are compelled to conclude that the proceedings by which this conviction was obtained do more than offend some fastidious squeamishness or private sentimentalism about combatting crime too energetically. This is conduct that shocks the conscience. Illegally breaking into the privacy of the petitioner, the struggle to open his mouth and remove what was there, the forcible extraction of his stomach's contents—this course of proceeding by agents of government to obtain evidence is bound to offend even hardened sensibilities. They are methods too close to the rack and the screw to permit of constitutional differentiation.
>
> . . . it would be . . . [a denial] of the responsibility which the course of constitutional history has cast upon this Court to hold that in order to convict a man the police cannot extract by force what is in his mind but can extract what is in his stomach. . . .
>
> On the facts of this case the conviction of the petitioner has been obtained by methods that offend the Due Process Clause.
>
> *Reversed.* . . .

As a final exercise designed to extend the students' comprehension of the issues and principles involved in the *Rochin* case, they can be asked to analyze and respond to the following similar cases:

1. In 1953 a panel truck crashed into another car and three people were killed, the driver of the truck surviving. The police found an almost empty bottle of whiskey in the truck and smelled whiskey on the driver's breath. While he was unconscious, a sampling of his blood was drawn off and tested. On the basis of the test, which indicated a heavy alcohol content, he was convicted of manslaughter. In light of the *Rochin* decision, was the evidence illegally obtained? Explain.
2. A man confessed to a murder after having been questioned by police for thirteen hours. There was some evidence that the confession was obtained by force and trickery, although there seems little doubt that the man was guilty. Should the

confession be excluded on the ground of forced self-incrimination? Was violation of due process sufficient ground for permitting an obvious lawbreaker to go free? Why or why not?

3. A man on trial for murder in California refused to take the witness stand. He was afraid his previous criminal convictions would be disclosed to the jury if he was forced to answer questions. He was convicted, after the prosecuting attorney told the jury that his failure to take the stand to deny evidence offered against him was in itself evidence of guilt. He appealed to the Supreme Court in 1947 on the ground that his rights under the Fifth Amendment had been violated. How would you have decided had you been on the Court?
4. A bootlegger was convicted in the state of Washington in the 1920s on the basis of evidence obtained through wiretapping. Wiretapping itself was illegal in the state of Washington. Did the admission of wiretap evidence at the trial compel the accused to be "a witness against himself"? Did the wire tapping constitute illegal "search and seizure"? Should such evidence always be excluded from the courts?*

Open-ended episodes

Case studies of this type include unfinished stories that the reader is asked to complete. These are especially useful in assessing the students' feelings and perceptions regarding a problem or issue to be studied and in bringing to light value conflicts among class members. It is highly probable that having students finish the episode in the manner they see fit will bring out a wide variety of conflicting viewpoints and recommended courses of action. When this occurs, the stage is set for discussing the students' frames of reference and perceptions of the case, and for considering the implications of accepting the various suggested endings.

Let us assume that in a sociology course or in a course dealing with current American problems you are preparing a series of lessons on drug abuse. You want to extend the study beyond a clinical analysis of the effects of drugs to touch on a number of basic related issues. You might, for example, decide to confront the students with questions relating to peer influence and loyalty as well as those touching on the legal and moral aspects involved in the sale and use of drugs. The following open-ended episode includes a number of provocative issues.

To tell or not to tell

Gary and Susan had been neighbors and the best of friends since their early days in elementary school. Through the years they had dated occasionally, but their relationship remained that of best friends rather than growing into a seri-

* Bernard Feder. *The Process of American Government: Cases and Problems* (New York: Noble and Noble, Publishers, Inc., 1972), pp. 571–72.

ous romance. Gary was considered a loner by most of his acquaintances at school, and when something bothered him it was Susan in whom he confided and from whom he sought advice.

In the spring of their senior year in high school, Susan became aware that Gary was stopping by less frequently; and she heard rumors that he was experimenting rather heavily with drugs. When they occasionally met, Gary never mentioned drugs to Susan; and she decided not to pry—partly because she feared risking her friendship with him and partly because she feared the rumors would be confirmed.

The spring and summer passed, and in the autumn Susan began her freshman year at a small college in another section of the state. Gary enrolled at a local university, and they did not see one another until the Thanksgiving vacation that autumn.

One evening during vacation, as Gary and Susan chatted about their first months at college, Gary rather casually mentioned that he had tried a variety of drugs and had found that a quick and simple way of picking up much needed cash was to make drugs available to students in the local junior high schools. To Susan's astonishment he described in detail the drugs he was pushing, the meeting places where transactions took place, and the prices he was able to demand.

Her worst fears confirmed, Susan was in a quandary. Gary clearly was violating the law and possibly was jeopardizing his health and his future. Susan appreciated Gary's confiding in her, but she was concerned not only for the welfare of her long-time friend but for those junior high school students who were buying drugs from him. What should she do? Ignore the situation? Try to talk out her feelings and fears with Gary? Go to the police? After a great deal of worry and soul searching, Susan finally decided to . . .

To complete the statement ". . . Susan finally decided to . . . ," the students will need to resolve a number of questions. Their investigation will probably begin with problems of clarification and definition, and lead to higher-level questions dealing with motives and recommended courses of action. The questioning sequence could approximate the following:

With what kinds of drugs had Gary experimented? What kinds of drugs had he sold to the junior high school students?

In what psychological and physical ways are persons affected if they take the kinds of drugs Gary has been selling? What bearing, if any, should this information have on Susan's decision?

While deciding on her course of action, what conflicts will Susan face? Possibilities include the conflict between Susan's loyalty to Gary and her desire to act for the good of society; the conflict between pressure from Susan's peers not to report Gary and her desire to protect junior high school students from something she considers undesirable; the conflict between Susan's upholding what she might consider to be an unjust law and her recognition that Gary is involved in illegal and possibly dangerous activity; and the conflict between Susan's desire to help Gary and her fear that such efforts could result in his being arrested and sentenced to a term in jail.

Once questions such as these have been brought to light and considered from all possible angles, students can be asked to suggest ways to resolve Susan's dilemma and to consider the legal, moral, and social implications of their final recommendations. (See chapter 2, "Inquiry into Values," on values clarification.) Because of the conflicting values involved, it is unlikely that the students will emerge from such a discussion with neat and unanimously agreed upon solutions. Rather, their opinions regarding Susan's dilemma predictably will represent a range of convictions as diverse as the makeup of the class itself. So it is in life. What can be expected as a result of the study is that students will better recognize the interrelationships of the many complexities involved in a case of this type, and that they will better comprehend the processes by which one comes to grips with troublesome legal and moral issues.

Interpretive essays

Interpretive essays include items that have been written for the purpose of purveying the author's interpretation of a matter of concern. They usually take the form of monographs, editorials, or articles. Case studies in this category can be especially helpful in familiarizing students with techniques commonly used in attempting to influence thinking, such as leading questions, faulty analogies, non sequiturs, and hasty generalizations. They are also helpful in teaching students to recognize the influence of an individual's frame of reference in his interpretation of events. The following selection, "Space and senselessness," is an example of an interpretive essay that can be used effectively to introduce a study of foreign policy.

Space and senselessness

Two American physicists recently attended a meeting in Moscow on space science and technology. They returned full of apprehension over the extent to which a spirit of arrogance and hostility toward the United States was reflected in Soviet policy.

The featured speaker at the conference banquet was the Soviet Minister of Military Aviation. Despite the presence of the American guests, the Soviet official called for a full program of anti-ballistic missile development by the U.S.S.R. He said Soviet intelligence had incontrovertible proof that the United States was well advanced with a maximum ABM missile program and that the Soviet Union was thus forced to speed up and enlarge its own ABM installations. In an icy, matter-of-fact manner, he proceeded to assert that Soviet planners were going to seize and maintain superiority over the United States—not just in anti-ballistic missiles but in the use of space stations and devices that could deliver a succession of nuclear bombs on a string of American targets.

The Soviet Minister ignored the forthcoming arms control talks between the U.S.A. and the U.S.S.R. He said nothing about the need for effective agreements between the two countries that could give security to both countries by forestalling a new and dangerous upward spiral in the world arms race. It almost seemed as though the Soviet Minister welcomed American ABM activity as giving Soviet military planners a good reason for enlarging their own power.

It was a chilling, grim experience for the Americans, all the more since the dinner chairman had earlier declared that a basic purpose of the meeting was to promote a cooperative spirit among nations in the quest for world peace. Other speakers had addressed themselves to this theme, declaring that the exploration of outer space should redound to the credit of all mankind, and that considerable emphasis should be given to common efforts in space by the U.S.S.R. and the U.S.A. This stated purpose, however, was completely shattered by the remarks of the Soviet military official.

The Americans came away heartsick. Before arriving in Moscow they had expressed strong convictions about the need for arms control talks between the U.S. and the U.S.S.R., for they recognized that an intensification of the arms race carried with it no security for anyone, only greater danger of war. But the kind of militaristic nonsense they had just heard reduced almost to the vanishing point the chances for a mutual and rational effort to slow down and reverse the world arms race. Nor were the Americans reassured the following day when several Soviet scientists sought them out to say they were sorry about what had happened at the dinner. The Americans said they were grateful to their Soviet colleagues but that they could not ignore or minimize the significance of the Soviet official's address, for they knew it would have been impossible for him to have said what he did unless it reflected current Soviet policy.

Fitting into the mood of the Soviet Minister's talk was an item in the Moscow press saying the Supreme Soviet Council had just decreed that, in the event of a landing on the moon or any other extraterrestrial bodies by Soviet spaceships, the only flag to be left behind would be the Soviet flag. The clear meaning was that the U.N. flag, with its world symbolism, was not to be planted on the moon.

What deeply troubled the Americans was not just the Soviet Minister's ABM speech or the anti-U.N.-flag news item, but the frightening implications of these events and what they portended for the chances of peace.*

After reading the selection, the students can be asked to analyze the events described and, basing their opinions upon their analysis, state what they feel the essay implies about Soviet foreign policy. The sequence of questioning could be something like this:

What is your interpretation of the events described in the article?

What evidence can you find in the article to support your interpretation?

From your analysis of this article, describe the attitudes of the Soviet representatives toward the American physicists. How do you account for the Soviets' holding these attitudes?

From your analysis of this article, how would you characterize the Soviets' attitude toward arms control? International diplomacy? Foreign policy? Militarism? World peace? Space exploration?

---

*Norman Cousins, *Saturday Review*, July 12, 1969 © by Norman Cousins and the *Saturday Review*.

> If these characteristics are accurate, what type of Soviet foreign policy would seem logically to evolve? Do you approve of this kind of foreign policy? Why or why not?

When their opinions are based upon their analysis of the essay and their preconceived ideas of Russian behavior, students almost invariably characterize Soviet foreign policy as being hostile and suspicious toward the United States and as being grounded in military power and the threat of force. After the initial analysis, they can be asked to read the second portion of the case.

> Now, there is just one thing wrong with all the foregoing. The conference took place not in Moscow but in Denver, Colorado. It was not the Soviet Minister of Military Aviation who was the main dinner speaker but the Secretary of the U.S. Air Force. The news item about the flag pertained to U.S. congressional declarations. The visitors were not American scientists but Soviet scientists. Apart from the transposition of the words U.S.A. and U.S.S.R. the facts are as stated above. The implications with respect to peace are the same. The human race is in jeopardy whenever power, insensitivity, and ignorance are joined together, whatever the national banner.*

The students' analysis of policies that they had been led to believe were those of the Soviet Union can now be tested by applying their observations to American policies. Now that the roles of the U.S.S.R. and the United States have been reversed, do the students still contend that the nation described in the essay pursues a foreign policy based on threats and armed might? If they feel that the description of American policy *is* accurate, they can be asked to support this contention with evidence and examples. If they feel that the essay *does not* fairly describe American policy, they can be asked to account for their original interpretation of the essay and to consider the degree to which their preconception of Russian policy influenced their thinking. It is at this point, of course, that the students can most effectively consider the impact of their frames of reference on their perception of events. Finally, the students can be asked to respond to and evaluate the author's final statement that "the human race is in jeopardy whenever power, insensitivity, and ignorance are joined together, whatever the national banner."

Cases based on documents

Case studies in this category are developed around documents of different types, including speeches, diaries, letters, research reports, surveys, contracts, laws, and testimonies. As with cases of other types, those based on documents can serve a variety of purposes—as a means of introducing a problem or an issue, as a vehicle for providing needed data, or as a tool for

---

*Norman Cousins, *Saturday Review*, July 12, 1969.

summarizing a unit of study. The use of documents of a personal nature, such as diaries or letters, can add a human dimension to the social studies, and can serve to focus on man's struggle for survival and human dignity. The following letter, for example, written in 1944 by a German soldier who was entrapped with the remnants of the German army during the Russian encirclement of Stalingrad, provides a touching glimpse into the thoughts and feelings of a single man caught up in a horrible conflict not of his doing.

> *Letter from Stalingrad*
>
> . . . You are my witness that I never wanted to go along with it, because I was afraid of the East, in fact of war in general. I have never been a soldier, only a man in uniform. What do I get out of it? What do the others get out of it, those who went along and were not afraid? Yes, what are we getting out of it? We, who are playing the walk-on parts in this madness incarnate? What good does a hero's death do us? I have played death on the stage dozens of times, but I was only playing, and you sat out front in plush seats, and thought my acting authentic and true. It is terrible to realize how little the acting had to do with real death.
>
> You were supposed to die heroically, inspiringly, movingly, from inner conviction and for a great cause. But what is death in reality here? Here they croak, starve to death, freeze to death—it's nothing but a biological fact like eating and drinking. They drop like flies; nobody cares and nobody buries them. Without arms or legs and without eyes, with bellies torn open, they lie around everywhere. One should make a movie of it; it would make "the most beautiful death in the world" impossible once and for all. It is a death fit for beasts; later they will ennoble it on granite friezes showing "dying warriors" with their heads or arms in bandages.
>
> Poems, novels, and hymns will be written and sung. And in the churches they will say masses. I'll have no part of it, because I have no desire to rot in a mass grave. I have written the same thing to Professor H——. You and he will hear from me again. Don't be surprised if it takes a while, because I have decided to take my fate into my own hands.*

Because of its very personal nature, this case is especially promising as a springboard for investigating the realities of war and the value conflicts a citizen encounters when he faces decisions regarding his possible participation in war. With these purposes in mind, one might launch a study of the case by having the students read the letter and identify the feelings expressed by the letter writer—fear, bitterness, fatalism, anger, resolution, pessimism, frustration, and so forth. They can then be asked to write a characterization

---

*Franz Schneider and Charles Gullans, trans., *Last Letters from Stalingrad* (New York: Morrow, 1962), pp. 46–47. Reprinted by permission of William Morrow & Co., Inc. ©1961 by The Hudson Review, Inc.

of the man, pooling their observations of his feelings and describing their perceptions of the situation in which he is caught.

Attempting to assume the frame of reference of the letter writer and drawing on information provided in the document, the students can next be asked to identify what they think would be the writer's feelings about patriotism. In an attempt to clarify the *students'* perception of patriotism, they might at this point be asked a number of questions: What do *you* consider an acceptable definition of patriotism? Does this definition agree or disagree with that which you attributed to the letter writer? If so, why? If not, why not? On what assumptions regarding the role of government and the role of a citizen did you base your definition? Once definitions and basic assumptions have been clarified, one can move on to consider the implications of accepting a particular point of view about patriotism. This stage of the study obviously would require that students go beyond their reactions to the letter and begin to seek additional data relevant to the questions at hand. Several fundamental and important issues should emerge: On what basis should an individual decide whether to support actively or to oppose his country's foreign policy in time of war? If he decides to oppose it, how should he express his opposition? If he decides to support it, how should he express his support? What should be the government's policy toward individuals who actively oppose official policy that supports the waging of war? Should the same policies exist in time of peace?

Memoirs

The memoir is a narrative based upon personal experiences and memories. Episodes are presented in the first person and reflect the opinions and attitudes of the writer.

Case studies in the memoir category can add a personal, human touch to the study of significant events, and are particularly useful in launching a study of incidents involving conflicting values and decision making. Let us assume, for example, that as a part of a study of World War II and the postwar arms race, you decide to focus on conflicts involved in the decision to drop the atomic bomb on Hiroshima and Nagasaki. To introduce the study, students can be given the following firsthand account by Dr. Michihiko Hachiya of the explosion of the atomic bomb over Hiroshima.

> *The agony of Hiroshima*
>
> August 6, 1945. The hour was early; the morning still, warm, and beautiful. Shimmering leaves, reflecting sunlight from a cloudless sky, made a pleasant contrast with shadows in my garden as I gazed absently through wide-flung doors opening to the south.
>
> Clad in drawers and undershirt, I was sprawled on the living room floor exhausted because I had just spent a sleepless night on duty as an air warden in my hospital.

Suddenly a strong flash of light startled me—and then another. So well does one recall little things that I remember vividly how a stone lantern in the garden became brilliantly lit, and I debated whether this light was caused by a magnesium flare or sparks from a passing trolley.

Garden shadows disappeared. The view where a moment before all had been so bright and sunny was now dark and hazy. Through swirling dust I could barely discern a wooden column that had supported one corner of my house. It was leaning crazily and the roof sagged dangerously.

Moving instinctively, I tried to escape, but rubble and fallen timbers barred the way. By picking my way cautiously I managed to reach . . . my garden. A profound weakness overcame me, so I stopped to regain my strength . . .

What had happened?

All over the right side of my body I was cut and bleeding. A large splinter was protruding from a mangled wound in my thigh, and something warm trickled into my mouth. My cheek was torn . . . .

Where was my wife?

Suddenly thoroughly alarmed, I began to yell for her: "Yaeko-san! Yaeko-san! Where are you?"

Blood began to spurt. Had my carotid artery been cut? Would I bleed to death? Frightened and irrational, I called out again. "It's a five-hundred-ton bomb! Yaeko-san, where are you? A five-hundred-ton bomb has fallen!"

Yaeko-san, pale and frightened, her clothes torn and bloodstained, emerged from the ruins of our house holding her elbow . . . .

"We'll be all right," I exclaimed. "Only let's get out of here as fast as we can."

She nodded, and I motioned for her to follow me. . . .

We stood in the street, uncertain and afraid, until a house across from us began to sway and then . . . fell almost at our feet. Our own house began to sway, and in a minute it too collapsed in a cloud of dust. Other buildings caved in or toppled. Fires sprang up and whipped by a vicious wind began to spread.

It finally dawned on us that we could not stay there in the street, so we turned our steps toward the hospital . . . .

We started out, but after twenty or thirty steps I had to stop. My breath became short, my heart pounded, and my legs gave way under me. An overpowering thirst seized me, and I begged Yaeko-san to find me some water. But there was no water to be found. After a little my strength somewhat returned and we were able to go on . . . .

Our progress was interminably slow, until finally my legs refused to carry me farther. I told my wife, who was almost as badly hurt as I, to go on alone. This she objected to, but there was no choice. She had to go ahead and try to find someone to come back for me.

Yaeko-san looked into my face for a moment, and then, without saying a word, turned away and began running toward the hospital. Once she looked back and waved . . . .

Could I go on?

I tried. It was all a nightmare—my wounds, the darkness, the road ahead. My movements were ever so slow; only my mind was running at top speed.

In time I came to an open space where the houses had been removed to make a fire lane. Through the dim light I could make out ahead of me the hazy outlines of the Communications Bureau's big concrete building, and beyond it the hospital. My spirits rose because I knew that now someone would find me; and if I should die, at least my body would be found.

I paused to rest. Gradually things around me came into focus. There were the shadowy forms of people, some of whom looked like walking ghosts . . . .

All who could were moving in the direction of the hospital. I joined in the dismal parade when my strength was somewhat recovered, and at last reached the gates of the Communications Bureau.

Familiar surroundings, familiar faces. There was Mr. Iguchi and Mr. Yoshihiro and my old friend Mr. Sera, the head of the business office. They hastened to give me a hand, their expressions of pleasure changing to alarm when they saw that I was hurt. I was too happy to see them to share their concern . . . .

Later I learned that the hospital was so overrun that the Communications Bureau had to be used as an emergency hospital . . . .

My private nurse, Miss Kado, . . . set about examining my wounds without speaking a word. No one spoke. I asked for a shirt and pajamas. They got them for me, but still no one spoke. Why was everyone so quiet?

Miss Kado finished the examination, and in a moment it felt as if my chest was on fire. She had begun to paint my wounds with iodine and no amount of entreaty would make her stop. With no alternative but to endure the iodine, I tried to divert myself by looking out the window.

The hospital lay directly opposite with part of the roof and the third-floor sunroom in plain view, and as I looked up I witnessed a sight which made me forget my smarting wounds. Smoke was pouring out the sunroom windows. The hospital was afire!

"Fire!" I shouted. "Fire! Fire! The hospital is on fire!"

The sky became bright, as flames from the hospital mounted. Soon the Bureau was threatened and Mr. Sera gave the order to evacuate. My stretcher was moved into a rear garden and placed beneath an old cherry tree. Other patients limped into the garden or were carried until soon the entire area became so crowded that only the very ill had room to lie down. No one talked, and the ominous silence was relieved only by a subdued rustle among so many people, restless, in pain, anxious and afraid, waiting for something else to happen . . . .

The heat finally became too intense to endure, and we were left no choice but to abandon the garden. Those who could fled; those who could not perished. Had it not been for my devoted friends, I would have died, but again they came to the rescue and carried my stretcher to the main gate on the other side of the Bureau.

Here a small group of people were already clustered, and here I found my wife. Dr. Sasada and Miss Kado joined us.

Fires sprang up on every side as violent winds fanned flames from one building to another. Soon we were surrounded. The ground we held in front of the Communications Bureau became an oasis in a desert of fire. As the flames came closer the heat became more intense, and if someone in our group had not had the presence of mind to drench us with water from a fire hose, I doubt if anyone could have survived.

> Hot as it was, I began to shiver. The drenching was too much. My heart pounded; things began to whirl until all before me blurred . . . .
>
> I murmured weakly, "I am done."
>
> The sound of voices reached my ears as though from a great distance and finally became louder as if close at hand. I opened my eyes; Dr. Sasada was feeling my pulse. What had happened? Miss Kado gave me an injection. My strength gradually returned. I must have fainted . . . .
>
> My next memory is of an open area. The fires must have receded. I was alive. My friends had somehow managed to rescue me again.
>
> A head popped out of an air-raid dugout, and I heard the unmistakable voice of old Mrs. Saeki: "Cheer-up, Doctor! Everything will be all right. The north side is burned out. We have nothing further to fear from the fire."
>
> Hiroshima was no longer a city, but a burned-over prairie. To the east and to the west everything was flattened. The distant mountains seemed nearer than I could ever remember. The hills of Ushita and the woods of Nigitsu loomed out of the haze and smoke like the nose and eyes on a face. How small Hiroshima was with its houses gone.*

After reading the memoir, the students can be asked to identify and record their reactions. How did they feel? Fearful? Angry? Sad? Ill? Pitying? Revengeful? How do they account for their reactions? If they had been American or Japanese soldiers at the time, how would they have felt at the news of the bombing?

Once the students' feelings regarding the case have been brought out, the stage is set for dealing with the basic issue inherent in the situation: Should the United States have dropped the atomic bomb on Hiroshima and Nagasaki? Obviously, a simple yes or no answer will not suffice. Evidence must be gathered regarding the destruction and aftereffects of the bombings, pre-Hiroshima casualties suffered by both the Allies and the Japanese, the estimated ability of the Japanese to prolong the war, and possible alternatives to dropping the bomb. As the students attempt to resolve the basic issue, a number of underlying conflicts and related problems will probably emerge: Can killing ever be justified? Should certain weapons—poison gas, the use of bacteria, nuclear bombs—be outlawed? Should a nation be expected to inform an enemy in time of war when it is planning a particularly destructive act? Should the use of *any* available weapons be ruled out by a nation if it is facing defeat by an enemy? What means should be considered "acceptable" by a nation in its attempt to protect the lives of its own citizens? What is the distinction between a moral and an immoral act?

After the students have studied the evidence and have worked through the basic issues, it would be well for them to reread "The Agony of Hiroshima" and to deal again with the feelings they recorded earlier. Do they feel differently about the memoir now? If so, how? If changes have occurred, how can

---

*Michihiko Hachiya, *Hiroshima Diary: The Journal of a Japanese Physician, August 6 – September 30, 1945*, trans. Warner Wells (Chapel Hill: University of North Carolina Press, 1955), pp. 1–8.

they be accounted for? What bearing should one's feelings have on the decisions he makes? Considering all of the evidence gathered and the feelings expressed, do they now feel that the United States' decision to use the atomic bomb was justified? What are the implications of their decision for dealing with similar moral dilemmas?

A study such as this will not result in unanimity of opinion among students when it is complete. This is to be expected. Such an exercise can, however, help students to recognize the extreme complexity of significant issues and can serve to caution them against dealing with human problems in simple yes or no terms.

Eyewitness accounts

Eyewitness accounts include descriptions of events as observed by a particular writer. They differ from the memoir in that the writer has viewed the events "from the wings" rather than having personally participated in them. As with memoirs, eyewitness accounts can be especially effective in adding a personal, human touch to learning in the social studies, and can be effective tools for launching inquiry. Sherwood Anderson's description of the Ford automobile assembly-line operation in 1930 is a good example of an eyewitness account. Even Anderson's staccato prose reflects the tedious labor and the pressures confronting the workers.

> *Assembly line*
>
> It is a big assembly plant in a city of the Northwest. They assemble there the Bogel car. It is a car that sells in large numbers and at a low price. The parts are made in one great central plant and shipped to the places where they are to be assembled. There is little or no manufacturing done in the assembling plant itself. The parts come in. These great companies have learned to use the railroad cars for storage.
>
> At the central plant everything is done on schedule. As soon as the parts are made they go into railroad cars. They are on their way to the assembling plants scattered all over the United States and they arrive on schedule.
>
> The assembling plant assembles cars for a certain territory. A careful survey has been made. This territory can afford to buy so and so many cars per day.
>
> "But suppose the people do not want the cars?"
>
> "What has that to do with it?"
>
> People, American people, no longer buy cars. They do not buy newspapers, books, foods, pictures, clothes. Things are sold to people now. If a territory can take so and so many Bogel cars, find men who can make them take the cars. That is the way things are done now.
>
> In the assembling plant everyone works "on the belt." This is a big steel conveyor, a kind of moving sidewalk, waist-high. It is a great river running down through the plant. Various tributary streams come into the main stream, the main belt. They bring tires, they bring headlights, horns, bumpers for cars. They flow into the main stream. The main stream has its source at the freight cars,

where the parts are unloaded, and it flows out to the other end of the factory and into other freight cars.

The finished automobiles go into the freight cars at the delivery end of the belt. The assembly plant is a place of peculiar tension. You feel it when you go in. It never lets up. Men here work always on tension. There is no let-up to the tension. If you can't stand it get out.

It is the belt. The belt is boss. It moves always forward. Now the chassis goes on the belt. A hoist lifts it up and places it just so. There is a man at each corner. The chassis is deposited on the belt and it begins to move. Not too rapidly. There are things to be done.

How nicely everything is calculated. Scientific men have done this. They have watched men work. They have stood looking, watch in hand. There is care taken about everything. Look up. Lift up thine eyes. Hoists are bringing engines, bodies, wheels, fenders. These come out of side streams flowing into the main stream. They move at a pace very nicely calculated. They will arrive at the main stream at just a certain place at just a certain time.

In this shop there is no question of wages to be wrangled about. The men work but eight hours a day and are well paid. They are, almost without exception, young, strong men. It is, however, possible that eight hours a day in this place may be much longer than twelve or even sixteen hours in the old carelessly run plants.

They can get better pay here than at any other shop in town. Although I am a man wanting a good many minor comforts in life, I could live well enough on the wages made by the workers in this place. Sixty cents an hour to begin and then, after a probation period of sixty days, if I can stand the pace, seventy cents or more.

To stand the pace is the real test. Special skill is not required. It is all perfectly timed, perfectly calculated. If you are a body upholsterer, so many tacks driven per second. Not too many. If a man hurries too much too many tacks drop on the floor. If a man gets too hurried he is not efficient. Let an expert take a month, two months, to find out just how many tacks the average good man can drive per second.

There must be a certain standard maintained in the finished product. Remember that. It must pass inspection after inspection.

Do not crowd too hard.

Crowd all you can.

Keep crowding.

There are fifteen, twenty, thirty, perhaps fifty such assembling plants, all over the country, each serving its own section. Wires pass back and forth daily. The central office—from which all the parts come—at Jointville is the nerve center. Wires come in and go out of Jointville. In so and so many hours Williamsburg, with so and so many men, produced so and so many cars.*

---

*Sherwood Anderson, *Nation*, May 28, 1930.

Although "Assembly line" was published in 1930 as a revealing commentary on working conditions in factories at that time, it can be used in initiating a study of mass production and its effects on the individual in today's technological society. An analysis of the case, for example, can focus on alienation in modern society, the labor movement, or the problems created by cybernetics, with the choice being that of the teacher and his or her particular group of students.

Vignettes

The vignette is a brief word picture that provides a glimpse of a limited piece of human experience. No attempt is made to develop a plot or to develop characters fully. Material in this category focuses on an individual in a very specific set of circumstances and, if carefully chosen, can present to the student a dramatic and potent taste of the human dimension of social problems. Consider the following selection from Upton Sinclair's *The Jungle*:

> *The Jungle*
>
> There was another interesting set of statistics that a person might have gathered in Packingtown—those of the various afflictions of the workers. When Jurgis had first inspected the packing plants with Szeduilas, he had marveled while he listened to the tales of all the things that were made out of the carcasses of animals, and of all the lesser industries that were maintained there; now he found that each one of those lesser industries was a separate little inferno, in its own way as horrible as the killingbeds, the source and fountain of them all. The workers in each of them had their own peculiar diseases. And the wandering visitor might be skeptical about all the swindles, but he could not be skeptical about these, for the worker bore the evidence of them about on his own person—generally he had only to hold out his hand.
>
> There were the men in the pickle rooms, for instance, where old Antanas had gotten his death; scarcely a one of these that had not some spot of horror on his person. Let a man so much as scrape his fingers pushing a truck in the pickle rooms, and he might have a sore that would put him out of the world; all the joints in his fingers might be eaten by the acid, one by one. Of the butchers and the floorsmen, the beef boxers and trimmers, and all those who used knives, you could scarcely find a person who had the use of his thumb; time and time again the base of it had been slashed, till it was a mere lump of flesh against which the man pressed the knife to hold it. The hands of these men would be criss-crossed with cuts, until you could no longer pretend to count them or to trace them. They would have no nails, they had worn them off pulling hides; their knuckles were swollen so that their fingers spread out like a fan. There were men who worked in the cooking rooms, in the midst of steam and sickening odors, by artificial light; in these rooms the germs of tuberculosis might live for two years, but the supply was renewed every hour. There were those who worked in the chilling rooms, and whose special disease was rheumatism; the time limit that a man could work in the chilling rooms was said to be five years. There were the wool pluckers, whose hands went to pieces even sooner than the hands

> of the pickle men; for the pelts of the sheep had to be painted with acid to loosen the wool, and then the pluckers had to pull out this wool with their bare hands, till the acid had eaten their fingers off. There were those who made the tins for the canned meat, and their hands, too, were a maze of cuts, and each cut represented a chance for blood poisoning.
>
> Some worked at the stamping machines, and it was very seldom that one could work long there at the pace that was set, and not give out and forget himself, and have a part of his hand chopped off. There were the "hoisters," as they were called, whose task it was to press the lever which lifted dead cattle off the floor. They ran along upon a rafter, peering down through the damp and the steam, and as old Durham's architects had not built the killing room for the convenience of the hoisters, at every few feet they would have to stoop under a beam, say four feet above the one they ran on, which got them into the habit of stooping so that in a few years, they would be walking like chimpanzees. Worst of any, however, were the fertilizer men, and those who served in the cooking rooms. These people could not be shown to the visitors—for the odor of a fertilizer man would scare an ordinary visitor for a hundred yards, and in some of which there were open vats near the level of the floor, their peculiar trouble was that they fell into the vats; and when they were fished out, there was never enough of them left to be worth exhibiting—sometimes they would be overlooked for days, till all but the bones of them had gone out to the world as Durham's Pure Leaf Lard.*

This particular case is useful in studying the plight of immigrants to the United States in the early twentieth century and in introducing the topic of reform movements. By developing a "feel" for the almost unbelievable working conditions faced by many immigrants at that time, students should come to understand better the efforts of the muckrakers and the stimuli underlying the movement to organize labor.

One method of launching a study of this case is to consider the frame of reference of the author, attempting to trace his motives for writing the book. What, for example, was it in Upton Sinclair's background that led him to write *The Jungle*? Was the book an accurate account of existing conditions? Upon what evidence did he base his descriptions? How did various people react to the book when it was published (1905)? What was Sinclair's purpose in writing the book? Once questions such as these have been grappled with, the students will be ready to move on to a more thorough analysis of the case itself.

One line of inquiry can be launched by having the students consider the motives and responsibilities of the stockyard owners. This in turn can lead to an analysis of business ethics and the clash between the desire to earn a profit in industry and the choice of creating a quality product and providing

---

*Upton Sinclair, *The Jungle* (New York: World Literature, 1905), pp. 100–102.

fairly for the welfare of the workers. After pursuing this analysis, the students can be asked to identify what they believe are sound principles of business ethics and to describe what course of action might have been open to Jurgis to improve his lot. They can then discover what in fact happened to Jurgis by reading further into *The Jungle*, and, in an attempt to test their observations and recommendations, can search out similar instances in the history of American labor. The students' insights can be stretched even further by having them study selected industries and labor organizations as they exist today and account for any changes in working conditions and labor-management relations that have occurred since the days of *The Jungle.*

Chronicles

The chronicle is a historical record written as an objective presentation in chronological order. It describes an event or series of events that have occurred in the past, and is especially useful for dealing with the phenomenon of cause and effect. The following account of Gandhi's 1932 fast is an example of the chronicle type of case study.

> *Gandhi's "tussle with God"*
>
> At 11:30 a.m. he had his last meal of lemon juice and honey with hot water. The fateful hour approached. The little group prepared themselves for the ordeal by singing a beautiful song. . . .The jail bell at last struck twelve and with its last stroke was finally sealed a decision as fixed as the polestar and as irrevocable as fate. Gandhi's "tussle with God" had commenced.
>
> Great anxiety was felt when Gandhi commenced his fast whether he would be able to stand the physical strain of it for any length of time. For one thing, he was not the same man as he was when he undertook his twenty-one days' fast at Delhi in 1924. He was eight years older now, which means a great deal to one who is already over sixty. Moreover, it was one thing to fast at Dilkash, near the Ridge, a free man, under the loving custodianship of a Charlie Andrews and the expert care of doctors . . . who knew his constitution and personal habits intimately, and quite another thing to fast in a segregated special yard in the Yeravda Prison under the surveillance of the jail authorities, who perhaps knew how to deal with a recalcitrant prisoner refusing to take food, but certainly had no experience of long fasts or of fasting men of Gandhi's type. In fairness to them it must be admitted that so far as personal solicitude for Gandhi was concerned they, from the very highest, left nothing to be desired. But they were handicapped by the red-tapism of jail regulations.
>
> On the morning of the twenty-first he was removed to a special segregated yard. There, under the thick shade of a low mango tree, on a white iron cot on which [were] spread a jail mattress and a jail bedsheet, he remained for the greater part of the day. His two companions . . . were there with him. Around the cot were placed a number of chairs for visitors. Near the cot, on one side, was a stool on which was to be found a . . . collection of odds and ends: books, papers, writing material, bottles of water, soda-bicarb, and salt. From time to time he would pour out some water from one of the bottles, in

which he would dissolve soda and salt and sip it slowly according to need and inclination . . . .

Gandhi was as buoyant and cheerful as ever, and outwardly hardly betrayed any signs of a man who is racing against time and is being rushed with every second toward the abyss of the beyond. But to a close observer it did not take long to discover how fully conscious he was of the grim reality facing him. During his Delhi fast, for instance, one could not help being struck by the way in which he economized his strength. He had reduced it to a science. But now he simply did not mind. It was a limited fast then. He knew the period that he had to pull through. The present fast was going to be a "fast unto death." If he survived it, it would not be so much because of the efficacy of the medical measures that might be adopted but because God willed it. It was predominantly a spiritual wrestle in which the physical factor played only a secondary part. Although the jail authorities had allowed him to have his own nurses, one could notice that he was extremely reluctant to avail himself of their services. What mattered a few more pangs or less of physical suffering to a man who was thirsting only for the grace abounding of the Almighty, and who in any case would soon be beyond all pain? Nor could Gandhi forget even for a moment that he was still a prisoner and that whatever facilities he was allowed were by way of a privilege. And everybody who has come in close touch with Gandhi knows how disinclined temperamentally he is to avail himself of any special privileges of this kind . . . . During his Delhi fast, he used to take water with scientific precision hourly. On the present occasion he did it only in a haphazard way. The physical exertion, as also the strain caused by speaking, induced nausea at an early stage. As the fast proceeded and the body tissue burned away, his whole frame was racked by excruciating aches—those terrible aches which at Delhi had to be alleviated by frequent massage and shampoo and a variety of other means . . . .

Warning signals were not, however, lacking to remind all concerned that there was a limit beyond which flesh and blood could not go. The physical exhaustion grew with every hour that passed. The voice grew feebler. [It was] only when, now and then in the course of animated discussions, his eyes shone and the face lit up that one felt the presence of an indomitable will that had remained unaffected in spite of the ravages on the body . . . .

On the twenty-fourth, Dr. Gilder and Dr. Patel of Bombay, after examining Gandhi, in consultation with the jail doctors, opined that the margin of safety would soon be passed if unnecessary interviews and the strain of negotiations that were being carried on with him were not stopped . . . .

On the twenty-sixth the prognosis became alarming . . . .

The morning and evening prayer appointments were kept as punctiliously as ever, Gandhi always sitting up in his bed for prayer. . . .From early in the morning, as soon as the jail opened, an endless round of interviews, meetings with friends and visitors, and consultations with the members of the conference that was deliberating outside would commence and continue—with a brief lull at noon, when he would have a bath . . . and steal a brief nap—till late in the night sometimes. To this was added the pressure of attending to his daily mailbag. Letters, telegrams, messages containing all sorts of suggestion,

> . . . and even personal requests came pouring in in increasing volume till they threatened to swamp Gandhi's little secretariat in the Yeravda Prison.*

When studying this case, students can be asked initially to describe the impact of Gandhi's action by analyzing British and Indian responses to the fast and by searching out possible relationships among the phenomena. This analysis can be followed by the students' considering what the status of the Indian independence movement would have been in 1946 had Gandhi *not* conducted his fast. A study such as this, of course, requires digging into additional data on the period so that students will understand better the complexities surrounding Gandhi's actions. As religious, political, economic and social dimensions of the fast come into focus, students can be expected to recognize that such an event must be viewed as a part of a total complex of related circumstances and happenings.

The concept of multiple causation can be developed further by having students investigate and place in proper perspective any of the numerous events in history that commonly suffer from oversimplified "single-cause" analysis—slavery caused the American Civil War; Lincoln freed the slaves; the sinking of the *Lusitania* caused the United States to enter World War I; the Chesapeake Affair caused the War of 1812; Herbert Hoover caused the Great Depression; the assassination of Archduke Ferdinand caused World War I.

Narratives

The narrative describes a connected succession of events involving either real or fictitious persons caught up in human concerns or conflicts. A plot is usually detectable, although it is not necessarily fully developed. The narrative is particulary helpful in introducing the study of a historical period by providing helpful background information and by inviting students' emotional involvement in the situation described.

"The Case of George Watkins (1773)" is of the narrative type, describing one man's dilemma as he faced the decision of supporting either the Loyalists or the Sons of Liberty immediately prior to the American Revolution.

> *The case of George Watkins (1773)*
>
> George Watkins was not smiling as he strode through the door of the White Horse Inn near Boston Harbor. He was worrying about what had been going on in the Colonies. Only a few months earlier, Boston's "Indians" had held their "Tea Party" nearby. He wondered how the radicals, who claimed to be fighting for freedom, could feel they had a right to destroy private property.
>
> One careful look at George Watkins told you a lot about the man. He was tall, erect, and broadshouldered. He wore carefully tailored trousers and a

*Pyarelal, "The Epic Fast," in *The Gandhi Reader: A Source Book of His Life and Writings,* Homer A. Jack, ed. (Bloomington: Indiana University Press, 1956), pp. 282-286.

waistcoat. His shoes were slightly worn but carefully polished. Here was a man of taste and character who had known wealth.

George took a table in the room reserved for the more prosperous, well-educated people. He ordered a mug of ale from the barmaid.

"And the English," he thought to himself, "do they respect private property?" He was bitter about the English. Ten years before, early in 1763, George had put almost all his money into land west of the Allegheny Mountains. He had expected to sell the land later at a good profit. Then the English announced the Proclamation of 1763, forbidding any Englishmen to settle west of the Alleghenies. The land he bought was, for all practical purposes, taken away from him. He could not sell it. It didn't seem that the English government respected the right to property any more than the radicals.

As Watkins sat in deep thought, Dr. Soame Johnson came to his table. Watkins and Johnson had been friends for many years, but of late they argued more and more over the English treatment of the colonies.

"I've been thinking, Soame," said Watkins, "our people in England just don't seem to understand our problems. I'm not sure they want to understand them. We seem to have lost our voices. I wonder if this Sam Adams might not have something when he speaks up about independence."

Dr. Johnson looked startled. "There are few of us who don't think King George needs a lesson in how to run his colonies. But I certainly cannot go along with fire-breathers like Hancock and Adams. We should do what we must, calmly and legally."

"But England doesn't even seem to want to meet us halfway," said Watkins. "And fellows like Adams and Hancock are in this thing so deep now, they've either got to have a fight or lose their shirts. They look to be in fighting trim, too."

Dr. Johnson's voice rose: "We both know Hancock is a convicted smuggler who'll cut his country's throat just to save himself from jail! If this fuss ends, John will have to pay 100,000 pounds to England for the smuggling he's done. Do we want a war just so a man can get away with breaking the law?"

"But Hancock was only forced to smuggle because England was worrying more about herself than about us," said Watkins. "And Hancock is too good a businessman and shipper to foot the bill for England's trouble."

Johnson's face flushed. "George, are you defending a common criminal? Hancock was found guilty and fined. You don't deny that?"

"No."

"And if you're willing to defend a criminal, why not defend Sam Adams, too? You and I both know Sam Adams wants to fight England and turn this country into a slaughterhouse because he hates kings and noblemen. No matter what's offered him now, he'll never be satisfied. Look at the kind of man he is. He was at the bottom of his class at Harvard. His father was poor. Because of that he hates everyone who isn't poor—and that includes you, George. He can't make money or keep it so he argues that everyone who can must be dishonest. He was made tax collector of Boston and lost his job because he was behind in his accounts. Now he hates the government that ousted him. Sam Adams is powerful in the colonies because he tells the dissatisfied, the lazy, the idle that they're the only honest people. I tell you we can't have war, no matter what, because if men like Adams start running the show there won't be a decent businessman or doctor or lawyer or any man of property left at all in America. And the country will be governed by riffraff out of the gutters."

Dr. Johnson puffed with the effort of his speech.

Watkins replied very slowly, "You know, Soame, I can't help but agree with much of what you say. But are you sure you're painting the whole picture? The English have not governed us very well. And I am not sure that they can govern well. Just yesterday I received a letter from Joshua Tuttle, who is in England right now. He is convinced that the English government is corrupt. Enormous salaries, pensions, bribes, quarrels, padded accounts, illegal contracts, and illegal jobs—all using up the tax money. Maybe England is more of a stone around our necks than a protector of our rights."

Johnson rose to his feet, leaned forward, and pounded on the table.

"Open your eyes! Do you know what Sam Adams and his gutter crowd are doing? They have mobbed and beaten ministers, lawyers, and doctors who have done nothing more than express their opinions. Yes, the finest men we've got have been thrown out of every town in the colony. Those rebels say they are fighting for freedom. Yet they do not permit anyone the freedom to disagree with them.

"And what are you going to do, Watkins? Join those guttersnipes and rabblerousers? I say, let's stand up for our rights and be counted—as good Englishmen—to protect our rights to property and liberty."

Johnson got up and stamped out of the room. A wry smile came over Watkins' face. He thought of Johnson's last statement—"protect . . . property and liberty." England's Proclamation had taken almost all his property.

His musing was broken by loud voices coming from the barroom, where the common people drank and talked. He caught several words, "smuggling . . . Stamp Act . . . stupid Englishmen." Watkins arose and walked over to the doorway. A tall, dark sailor was speaking in loud tones. And Dr. Johnson, interrupted in his flight, stood bristling at the sailor's words.

"So what are these laws supposed to do, these Trade and Navigation Acts? They're supposed to strangle our trade and make us servants of our royal master, His Majesty George the Third. Has George ever been to America? Has he ever worked aboard a trading ship? He calls it smuggling when honest merchants and self-respecting sailors try to make a living. I say it's not American smuggling that's the cause of this trouble, it's English tyranny."

Dr. Johnson snorted back at him. "I don't care what's at the heart of this trouble—call it tyranny if you will—but smuggling is law-breaking, and that's not good no matter who does it. You seamen and your masters have taken the law into your own hands too long. Right now the English laws are our laws, and most of us are Englishmen. If you'll break the laws of your government when that government is England, who's to say you'll obey them if we set up a government of our own? Or do you want no government, so you won't have to pay any taxes or obey any laws at all?"

The tall sailor banged his glass on the bar, straightened up to full height, and glared down at Johnson: "The difference is, my fine fat fellow, that American shippers are willing to pay American taxes to pay for things that help America.

But American shippers ain't goin' to stuff the bellies of a bunch of English lords."

Johnson's face reddened. He stormed for the door.

The sailor shouted after him, "Why don't you go back to your king, then, and kiss his boots and pay him tribute? Because that's the law. I say law is what men say is fair and just and right for all the people, not what some king dreams up three thousand miles away."

There was a shout of approval from the little crowd at the bar. But several men who had kept silent throughout the argument quickly left the inn.

Watkins turned from the doorway and returned to his table. He was puzzled and worried. He knew the need for a fair and reasonable government in this new world—a government which understood the temper and desires of a new brand of freedom. But he wondered how such a government could be born out of the contempt for law displayed by men like the sailor.

Was Sam Adams like this tipsy sailor? He had to find out. The next time Sam Adams spoke, he would go to listen.

Meeting at Lincoln. George Watkins tasted the crisp fall evening air as he rode to Lincoln. He felt a tingle of excitement. Tonight he would finally see and hear Sam Adams.

When he dismounted from his horse, he could see that there was already a crowd in front of the meetinghouse, talking, laughing, grumbling, arguing. Rawboned farmers had come from all corners of Lincoln, Concord, Lexington, and adjoining towns to hear the great Sam Adams.

The babble suddenly quieted. Watkins looked back down the dirt road as he hitched his horse. He knew it must be Sam Adams coming. So here was the man the poor loved and cheered, and Watkins both feared and admired.

Sam Adams climbed down from his horse, tied it, and threaded his way through the groups of men in front of the meetinghouse. He mounted the steps, turned, and raised his hands. Dead silence fell over the crowd.

"Friends and fellow countrymen," he began. "We have been subjected to greater tyranny and injustice than any people has ever endured. The crops which we have raised with much sweat and toil are taxed without our consent. Our ships can no longer trade. The rights and privileges which we have always had are denied us. Our people are murdered by the King's soldiers . . ."

Adams went on, talked of his favorite organization, the Sons of Liberty, and how it was linked to similar groups by Committees of Correspondence.

As he continued speaking, denouncing the king and demanding "the rights of free men," wave after wave of excitement swept over the crowd. It reached a fever pitch, then almost a frenzy. George Watkins felt the excitement despite himself. Yet, as the farmers shouted and cheered and drew closer to the speaker, Watkins and others like him drew farther toward the outskirts of the crowd.

Suddenly a voice rose against Adams. The crowd stirred angrily. But Adams carefully stopped. "No, my fellow countrymen," he said softly, "let this gentleman speak."

The dissident turned out to be James Cartwright, a widely known Lincoln minister. He mounted the meetinghouse steps and shouted, "My fellow Englishmen, my fellow townsmen, this man Adams who stands before you and seizes your reason, as if by witchcraft, is a godless traitor. Worthy people of high character have warned me against him. He is preaching treason. Friends, have you forgotten that without England our fathers could never have settled this land? You shout against British soldiers but your memories are short. Ten years ago you cheered these same soldiers when they saved your wives and children from bloodthirsty Indians. You speak against the laws of England. But if it were not for England we would all be slaves of an irresponsible French King. May God protect our beloved England that has struggled so long to protect the lives and property of all her countrymen."

The crowd had been confused. Then a murmur of protest grew into a roar. Deacon Cartwright's words were drowned in a sea of angry voices.

Sam Adams rose again to the highest step of the meetinghouse. His clear, slow voice cut through the tumult. "Here is a defender of tyranny, an enemy of the Sons of Liberty right in our midst. Need I speak more of the dangers that stalk our homes and firesides!"

The crowd jostled Cartwright and spit on him as he went down the steps. Someone pushed him to the ground. He scrambled to his feet and dashed blindly into a tree on the outskirts of the crowd. The crowd laughed. A voice shouted, "Let's get him, boys. Let's show him what happens to kinglovers." The crowd began to move after him.

George Watkins suddenly found his voice in the confusion. "No," Watkins shouted as loud as he could. "Let him go. Let's hear Sam Adams out. He has something more important to say."

The crowd began to mill back toward the meetinghouse steps. Sam Adams went on.

What, Watkins wondered to himself, had possessed him to enter the brawl, to join this mad crowd? Had he really wanted to save the deacon? Or was he really interested in more of what Sam Adams had to say? If the time came to fight, if war came with England, would he be running with Deacon Cartwright, or fighting beside Sam Adams?*

The Watkins case is an example of one type of vehicle that can be used to illustrate conflicting values—in this instance, regarding the role of government and the rights of the governed. When discussed in class, it can help students to clarify their own values regarding the question, "Who should govern?" Oliver and Newmann recommend that each student check on Table 1.1 those statements that represent the values he or she holds of "good" government. The student can then be asked to compare the set of values checked with those chosen by fellow students and to try to account for any differences

---

*Donald Oliver and Fred M. Newmann, *The American Revolution,* pp. 9–13. Special permission granted by THE AMERICAN REVOLUTION, published by Xerox Education Publications, © Xerox Corp., 1967. This case is fictional, but authentically represents conditions of the time. It is a good example of the cases that appear in the Harvard Social Studies Project Public Issues Series.

Table 1.1
Beliefs about "good" government

(√)		A	B
	1 It would be wrong to change the system of government we have inherited. It has the benefits of long experience.		
	2 A leader is not finally responsible to the people, but only to God, from whom he receives authority.		
	3 Fair decisions can be made only by impartial leaders who have no special interest whatsoever at stake. Only these people should be allowed to govern.		
	4 Leaders should not bow to the prejudiced interests of the people, but should be guided by a sense of law. Legal rights and the general welfare should be their only guidelines.		
	5 Each man should have a say in determining his own fate. Thus the government should be run by representatives chosen by a majority of the people.		
	6 A country belongs to those men who own property in it, and they should govern.		
	7 Power should be separated and divided among several ruling groups. Centralized power often brings tragic mistakes.		
	8 The power to govern should be given to the most capable people, to those who have demonstrated intelligence and skill. The average man does not have enough skill to govern his fellowman.		
	9 Life is naturally a struggle. Those strong enough to seize power earn the right to govern.		
	10 Time, money, and effort are saved when a small, unified group runs the government. It is inefficient and wasteful to split power among groups who will bicker and delay decisions.		

that might exist. It is then recommended that the students classify each of the statements on the table by entering the appropriate letter for each of the following classifications in column A:

A. Competence and "know-how"
B. Tradition or familiar customs

C. Religion, belief in a Supreme Being
D. Law, the written and spoken rules of the society
E. Separated power
F. Strength—"might makes right"
G. Property ownership
H. Impartiality
I. Majority rule
J. Efficiency

After reviewing the case and searching out the different values held by George Watkins, Dr. Soame Johnson, and Samuel Adams, each student should then mark the initial of each man in column B of the table next to the value statements he or she thinks Watkins, Johnson, or Adams would support. The challenge is to account for any differences that may appear and to consider the implications of holding a particular set of values. Finally, students can be asked to return to the original lists of values they identified as being their own, to reconsider them in light of the discussion of the Watkins case, and to discover the implications of their holding the values they now espouse.

The students' analysis of the Watkins case and the comparison of their perceptions of the value conflicts involved can enhance their understanding of many of the basic issues involved in the conflict between the colonists and the British, and in a broader sense can help them more clearly comprehend the nature of values and value conflicts. It is hoped that through such a study they will also come to recognize some of the adequacies and inadequacies of their own values about government and will increasingly sense the importance of grounding values in evidence.

Designing case studies

Although excellent case studies dealing with a wide variety of subjects are now published commercially, with a bit of time you can design your own. In fact, teacher-constructed cases have one clear advantage over those available on the market in that they can be written in response to the idiosyncrasies, interests, and reading levels of the particular students for whom they are intended. Although no commonly agreed upon set of rules exists for designing case studies, it might be helpful to consider the processes through which one commonly moves when developing them.

Step one—identify objectives

Like any learning activity, a case study should be viewed as only one part of a comprehensive teaching strategy, and should be designed with specific objectives clearly in mind. Before developing a case, consider, for example: What is it that you want the students to learn as a result of studying this case? What issues do you want them to confront? What concepts do you hope to focus on? What mood do you hope to create? What inquiry skills do you want your students to sharpen? Any consideration of objectives should grow out of the goals established for your course, and should reflect your sensitivity to the backgrounds and sophistication of your students. Once you have decided what it is you hope to accomplish by using a case study, you are ready to develop the case itself.

Step two—select the case materials

Potential sources of cases are unlimited, as indicated earlier in this chapter, and can range from newspaper accounts to diaries and from novels to government documents. Your challenge is to come up with a case that promises to meet your objectives by engaging your students in lively inquiry.

A general rule in designing effective cases is to provide enough information to involve the students in the case at hand, but not so much detail that issues or key concepts become unnecessarily clouded or lost in a barrage of unrelated trivia. On the other hand, it is occasionally useful to build into the case a limited amount of diversionary material to provide the students with practice in sorting the irrelevant from the significant data when solving a problem. Cases should be close enough to the students' experience so that they can identify with persons involved in the situations described, and they should be realistic enough to be believable. During the course of a school year it is advisable to make use of several different types of cases, not only for the sake of interest and variety, but for the purpose of having students work with and analyze various forms of data. All case materials, of course, should be chosen or written with consideration for the backgrounds, reading levels, and interests of the students involved.

If suitable materials for development of a case are unavailable, you might effectively write your own. Let us assume, for example, that you are teaching a twelfth-grade sociology class and have decided to study the phenomenon of peer influence on an individual's choice among competing values. The students might first be asked to respond to a questionnaire establishing the degree to which they seem to value such characteristics as social participation, group loyalty, individual achievement, responsibility, respectability, thrift, self-reliance, good manners, and honesty. After the results have been accumulated and analyzed, you could write a case study designed to "stretch" the students' commitment to the values that seemed to have been indicated in the survey and to point out contradictions that probably will emerge. For example, chances are that such a survey will indicate that most class members value honesty and are opposed to cheating. At the same time, it is predictable that they are under severe pressure to conform to group norms that might be in conflict with these beliefs. What should a student do, for example, if he or she espouses a personal commitment to honesty, but is placed under severe pressure by friends and by the necessity of passing a course to participate in group cheating? The following open-ended episode can be useful in focusing on the problem.

To cheat or not to cheat

Jerry Higgins is nearing the end of his senior year in high school and is looking forward to the possibility of attending college during the coming autumn. College expenses being what they are today, it is vital that he receive the academic scholarship for which he has applied. In order to qualify for the financial aid, Jerry must earn grades of no less than B in each subject he is carrying so as not to drop below the required average. Everything has gone well in each of his courses except trigonometry. Although he has worked diligently at the course, the pieces just have not fit together for him. He has spent many hours on the homework assignments and has met individually with the teacher, Mr. Biggs, on several occasions. Still he finds that he is on the verge of receiving a grade of C or even a D in the course. Jerry has been told by Mr. Biggs that his final grade will depend upon his performance on the final examination. Jerry would like to think that Mr. Biggs would see the importance of his receiving the scholarship, would realize that he has attempted to master the subject, and would award him with a B for his effort even if he does poorly on the final. Such is not the case, however. Mr. Biggs is a rather remote man who values scholarship, and he grades on an absolute curve. *Nothing* could convince him to change a grade for any reason.

The evening before the final Jerry surrounds himself with his class notes and the textbook, but soon realizes that cramming will be futile. There is no way that he can do well enough in the examination to assure his receiving the B he needs. Just as despair begins to settle in, the telephone rings. Tom Smith, Jerry's best friend, is calling to ask him to join the crowd at the local pizza hangout. Why not? Further study would be futile. He decides to join the gang.

Jerry arrives at the pizza parlor, settles into a booth and begins to talk with Tom about tomorrow's trigonometry final. To Jerry's surprise, Tom casually informs him that his worries are over. With that, he pulls out a copy of the examination Mr. Biggs is planning to give tomorrow. The copy of the examination had accidentally been dropped on the floor of the mimeograph room at school, and Tom claims to have found it merely by chance. Several of Jerry's friends who are also scheduled to take the final crowd around the booth and frantically begin to read the examination and to jot down notes on scraps of paper.

A barrage of feelings descend upon Jerry at once. A feeling of hope—an answer to his problem has suddenly emerged. A feeling of relief—the scholarship may not be out of reach after all and his parents will be enormously pleased if he does well on the examination. A feeling of uneasiness—using the copy of the examination would be cheating. Or would it, considering the effort he has already put into the course? A feeling of fear—what if he used the examination and were caught? What if his friends used the examination and he were questioned about it? A feeling of anger—if Mr. Biggs had *really* done a good job of teaching and if he were *really* interested in students it wouldn't be necessary for Jerry to even consider using the test. A feeling of frustration . . . what should he do?

> As Jerry hesitates to look at the examination, his friends begin to chide him and to assure him that "Old Man Biggs" will never know the difference. In fact, Jerry senses that his reluctance to read the examination is viewed by his buddies as being suspicious and threatening. After all, if Jerry doesn't take advantage of the opportunity and does poorly on the final, wouldn't he be tempted to tell Mr. Biggs what had happened in order to salvage his own grade? Finally, Jerry decides to . . .

Although this case was written for use in senior high school, it could easily be rewritten to focus on similar conflicts at the junior high school level. The case in that instance might look something like this:

> Jerry Higgins is an eighth-grade student and is looking forward to buying a new mini bike. He has saved as much money as possible during the past year by delivering newspapers and doing odd jobs around the house. Jerry's parents have told him that they will give him permission to buy the bike and will provide him with the additional money he needs *if* he receives all grades of no less than B on his final report card. Everything has gone well in each of his courses except mathematics. He has worked hard in the course, but he just can't seem to do well. He has tried to keep up with the homework assignments and has even talked with the teacher, Mr. Biggs, about the trouble he is having. However, unless Jerry does very well on the last test of the year, it seems certain that he will get a C or maybe even a D in the course. Jerry has thought about telling Mr. Biggs of the importance of the grade to him and about his hoping to get the mini bike, but he is certain that *nothing* could convince Mr. Biggs to raise his grade unless he does well on the final test.
>
> On the evening before the big test Jerry begins to review his mathematics, but soon realizes that he has fallen so far behind that he cannot possibly do well enough to get the grade he needs. Just as he puts the math book aside, the telephone rings. It is Jerry's best friend, Tom Smith, who invites him over to shoot baskets in the back yard. When Jerry arrives, he finds Tom and several of his other friends gathered around and reading something. It is a copy of Mr. Biggs' mathematics test, which Tom had found on the floor of the mimeograph room at school.
>
> Jerry has mixed feelings. A feeling of hope—an answer to his problem had been found. A feeling of relief—his parents would be very happy if he were to receive a good grade in math and he would be able to get the mini bike. A feeling of uneasiness—using the test would be cheating. Or would it? He has already worked hard in the course, and perhaps he deserves a better grade than Mr. Biggs would probably give him. A feeling of fear—what if he used the test and were caught? What if his friends used the test and he were questioned about it? A feeling of anger—if Mr. Biggs had *really* done his job right, and if he were *really* interested in his students, it would be unnecessary for Jerry to think about using the test. A feeling of frustration—what should he do?
>
> As Jerry hesitates to look at the test, his friends begin to tease him and tell him, "Old Man Biggs will never know the difference." Perhaps they are right. After all, if Jerry doesn't look out for himself, who will? A good grade in math and the mini bike seem to be at stake. Finally, Jerry decides to . . .

Step three—develop a discussion strategy

After the case has been constructed, it is a good idea to sketch out a series of questions to be used when analyzing the case with your students. The kinds of questions posed will be dictated in large part by the objectives you have for using the case. They should be stated in such a way as to help the students clarify their perceptions of the case and should serve as guides for analysis rather than as terminals of thought. The discussion should be conducted in such a way as to focus on the several conflicts that are described, and questions should encourage a variety of levels of response.

In developing a discussion strategy, it is helpful to plan a total—albeit tentative and flexible—sequence of questions designed to move the students through a step-by-step analysis of the case. Such a sequence can be thought of in five stages: (1) questions that require students to *clarify* and *define* what they have observed; (2) questions that require an *explanation* of the events described; (3) questions that require *evaluation* and *judgment* of the issues under consideration; (4) questions that require students to deal with the *implications* of their decisions regarding the case; and (5) questions that require an *application* of the students' findings in a new setting. Applying this type of questioning strategy to "To Cheat or Not To Cheat," a discussion might proceed something like this:

Clarification and Definition
- What happened in this case? What did you observe? Notice? Find? See?
- What are the major conflicts involved in the case?

Explanation
- Why did Jerry react as he did? Why did he feel hopeful? Relieved? Uneasy? Fearful? Angry? Frustrated?
- Why did Jerry's buddies seem suspicious and threatening?

Evaluation and Judgment
- What are the various ways in which the conflicts could be dealt with?
- What criteria would you apply in deciding on the best course of action?
- Basing your response on these criteria, what would you do if you were Jerry?

Implications
- What are the implications of your recommended choice of action regarding: Jerry's performance on the test and the grade he will receive? His relationship with Mr. Biggs? The choices he might make in future similar situations?
- What are the implications of your choice of action regarding *your* values?
- Judging from the action you are recommending, what is your definition of cheating? Honesty? Friendship?
- How does your decision square with your responses on the value survey?
- If contradictions exist, how do you account for them? How will you deal with them?
- What are the implications of your holding contradictory beliefs?
- What does our analysis of the case seem to imply about the effect of peer influence on an individual's choice among competing values?

Application

Considering what you have decided regarding Jerry Higgins' dilemma, what course of action would you take in the following case? Here it would be a good idea to provide the students with a similar but different case study, perhaps using a different format, and pointing up the same kinds of conflicts faced by Jerry Higgins.

In the final stages of discussion, studies can be presented to the class, indicating that teenagers commonly profess one set of beliefs while at the same time acting on another. The case can be reconsidered in light of these findings, and the discussion can be broadened to deal with the general phenomenon of peer influence on an individual's choice among competing values.

Your classes can be organized in a variety of ways for discussing the case. One approach is to have the students read and analyze the case and to respond to a general discussion, identifying the issues and attempting as a total group to resolve them. Another is to break the class into small groups and to respond to the case at that level, sharing group reactions and analyses in a general discussion later. A third approach is to use the case as the basis for role-playing episodes, which can then be subjected to analysis by the class. If, for example, in the discussion of the case the class suggests that Jerry's best move would be to confide in his parents regarding the matter, a role-playing episode could be set up, having one student assume Jerry's role and two other students the roles of his father and mother. Or an episode could be organized involving Jerry and Tom, Jerry and his friends, or Jerry and Mr. Biggs. Such spontaneous confrontations will add drama and unpredicted dimensions to the discussion and can help to bring out student feelings about the dilemma.

The teacher's role in analyzing case studies

As with other approaches designed to encourage inquiry, the students themselves should assume an active role in analyzing the problems and issues with which they are confronted. The analysis should focus on *their* ideas, insights, and potential solutions. You should neither totally withdraw from the discussion nor dominate it. Rather, you will best serve your students as an orchestrator of the discussion—a person who poses key questions, encourages clarification, assures that everyone receives a fair hearing, provides pertinent data, and keeps the discussion moving in the direction of ultimate resolution. If your students have had few opportunities to participate in discussions, you may initially find it necessary to assume a more active and dominant role in dealing with the case. As your class gains experience through participating in discussions, however, you should be able to take on a more passive role, shifting more and more responsibility to the students. In any instance, successful analysis of case studies will depend largely upon your ability to create a classroom atmosphere conducive to a free interchange of ideas and opinions.

Obviously, the case study approach is not the ultimate technique for initiating inquiry in the social studies. As with any teaching technique, it can suffer from overexposure and should be used judiciously. However, if you view your teaching role as that of a catalyst who challenges the students to explore and test fresh alternatives to problems at hand, and if you are seeking a means of injecting a much-needed note of realism and vitality into the study of social studies, case studies may serve you very well.

Bibliography

Ang, H. S. "Case Method in Teaching Marketing." *Improving College and University Teaching* 22 (Summer 1974): 190–91.

Beckman, M. D. "Evaluating the Case Method." *Education Forum* 36 (May 1972): 489–97.

Brennan, William J., Jr. "Teaching the Constitution." *New York State Education* 54 (November 1966): 11–13.

Connally, Gerald E. "One Family's Hunger in the United States." *Social Education* 38 (November/December 1974): 662–63.

Desmond, Kathleen. "The Urban Poor in Northeast Brazil." *Social Education* 38 (November/December 1974): 661–62.

Dunwiddie, William E. "Using Case Studies in Social Studies Classes." *Social Education* 31 (May 1967): 397–400.

Elenko, William. "The Case for a More Creative Case Study." *The Journal of Business Education* 42 (February 1967): 201–202.

Feder, Bernard. "Case Studies: A Flexible Approach to Knowledge Building." *Social Studies* 64 (April 1973): 171–78.

Fitzsimmons, Frank P. "The Case Method of Teaching." *School and Society* 78 (1953): 102–105.

Gilliom, M. Eugene. "The Case Method: Adapted for Social Studies." *The Clearing House* 42 (December 1967): 217-21.

Gullahorn, John T. "Teaching by the Case Method." *School Review* 67 (1959): 448–60.

Hall, Susan J. "The Sahel: The 'Shore' of Disaster." *Social Education* 38 (November/December 1974): 659–61.

Hoover, Kenneth H., and Hoover, Helen M. "The Case Approach to Teaching." *The High School Journal* 51 (April 1968): 318–24.

Hunt, Pearson. "The Case Method of Instruction." *Harvard Educational Review* 21 (1951): 175–92.

Jones, R. F. "The Case Study Method." *Journal of Chemistry Education* 52 (July 1975): 460–61.

King, David C. "Using Case Studies To Teach About Global Issues." *Social Education* 38 (November/December 1974): 657–58.

McAdoo, J., and Nelson, P. "Teaching Speech Communication Via the Case Method." *Today's Speech* 23 (Summer 1975): 29–32.

McLaughlin, W. D. "Labor Unions and the Case Method of Study." *Social Studies* 60 (December 1969): 329–32.

McNair, Malcom P., ed. *The Case Method at the Harvard Business School.* New York: McGraw-Hill, 1954.

Morosky, Robert L. "The Case Method Approach in Teaching History." *The Social Studies* 57 (October 1966): 199–204.

Newmann, Fred M., and Oliver, Donald W. "Case Study Approaches in Social Studies." *Social Education* 31 (February 1967): 108–13.

O'Neil, R. M. and O'Neil, K. E. "Using Tort Cases in the Classroom." *Social Education* 32 (March 1968): 261–72.

Oliver, Donald, and Newmann, Fred M. *The American Revolution.* Columbus, Ohio: American Education Publications, 1967.

Parker, Donald, and Econopouly, Nicholas. "Teaching Civil Liberties by the Case Method." *Social Education* 25 (October 1961): 283–84.

Sanbonnmatsu, J. L. "Jenny and Ken: A Teacher Developed Case Study in Human Relations." *Speech Teacher* 23 (November 1974): 320–24.

Shaver, James P., and Larkins, A. Guy. "Case Method and the Study of International Affairs." In *National Council for the Social Studies Yearbook* 38 (1968): 215–36.

Starr, Isador. "Teaching the Bill of Rights." *Social Education* 23 (1959): 373–78.

Villanueva, A. B. "Dialog On the Case Method." *Improving College and University Teaching* 22 (Summer 1974): 159–60.

It is virtually impossible to deal very deeply with the social studies without touching on the values people hold and the conflicts that emerge from competing values. Because inquiry by its very nature focuses on problems and issues, social studies teachers who take an inquiry approach will eventually find it necessary to deal with value questions in the classroom. This chapter develops the position that values have both cognitive and affective components, and it presents a broad selection of practical techniques for helping students to recognize and to resolve value conflicts.

Chapter 2

Inquiry into values

A value is an idea—a concept—of what someone thinks is important in life. When a person values something, he or she regards it as being worthwhile, that is, of worth—worth having, worth doing, or worth trying to obtain. The social studies, by their very nature, contain much information about values.

The more we can find out about what people value, the better, for in so doing we learn a lot about the kinds of decisions they are likely to make, the leaders they will follow, the policies they will endorse, and the things on which they are likely to spend time, money, and energy. Indeed, it is virtually essential to inquire into values if we are to learn and understand very much about a people—about their society, their culture, art, ideas, history, economics, or government.

Another reason for social studies teachers to help students learn about and investigate values lies in the nature of values themselves. Values are not only ideas about worth, but also powerful emotional commitments. People care deeply about the things that they value.

If one accepts the definition of values as both emotional commitments and ideas about worth, it follows logically that teachers interested in values inquiry need to plan for both the emotional growth of students and the development of their intellectual abilities. Indeed, it can be argued that intellectual and emotional development are interdependent—very much of one cannot take place without the other. As Beck writes: "Often we try to help a child understand a particular aspect of ethical theory; for example, we try to help him understand the need for reciprocal relationships (as in promise-keeping and formation of contracts); and we find that we fail, because there is a lack of sensitivity, a lack of concern, a lack of emotional development—a lack of *noncognitive* development which prevents him from having this cognitive insight. On the other hand, there are cases where we try to help a person become more sensitive to other people and their needs and more disposed to help them, and the [problem] is his lack of understanding of the place of concern for others in a person's life."* Teachers who wish to help students inquire into values, therefore, will need some procedures that they can use to help students both think and feel. The purpose of this chapter is to suggest what some of these procedures might be.

Values as standards

Values serve (though often implicitly) as standards by which we determine if a particular object, person, idea, event, or action is good or bad, desirable or undesirable, beautiful or ugly, worthwhile or not worthwhile, or someplace in between. "That's a striking painting; the people in it look like they are alive." "That music is exciting. It turns me on." "Mary is a tremendous person; always so kind and thoughtful." "I like novels in which the characters seem like real people!" What values would you say these statements reflect?

We also set standards to achieve or acquire other values we consider important. These are often called *instrumental values* or *means*. Thus a pianist may practice three hours every day without fail because such practice will enable him or her to play the piano very well. Practice in this instance is an instrumental value.

The most important standards that we have are the ones by which we judge conduct—by which we determine what kinds of actions are proper and worthwhile and what are not. These standards are our *moral values*. They are guides to what is right and just. Thus a person may argue that it is not right to kill another person because human life is sacred.

Value indicators

A person's words, as set down in printed speeches, letters, proclamations, editorials, articles, or other forms of written communication, can provide us with clues about what he values. Statements that indicate what an individual or group thinks *should be*, whether it happens to be the case at present or not, are especially revealing. "Sam, you shouldn't make so much noise in the halls." "Alice, you should buy that dress." "Women should be completely equal to men." "All people should be able to move freely from one nation to another." Written or spoken statements like these, which suggest what *ought to be* or what *should be* done, are called *value judgments*.

People's *actions* also can give us clues as to what they value. Try noticing what a person does with his or her spare time without being coaxed or

---

*Clive Beck, "The Development of Moral Judgment," in James A. Phillips, Jr., ed., *Developing Value Constructs in Schooling: Inquiry into Process and Product* (Worthington, Ohio: Ohio Association for Supervision and Curriculum Development, 1972), p. 44.

threatened. Suppose, for example, that someone spends most of her free time tutoring young children who are having trouble learning to read. She spends a lot of time looking for suitable books and other materials that the children can use, finding quiet places to work with them, designing some special materials, and, of course, working with the children themselves. If the person is not required to do this and is not being paid for doing this, we would be inclined to believe that she considers tutoring to be an important and worthwhile thing to do.

Take a look at the behaviors listed below. What do you think these people value that causes them to behave in these ways?

- John runs to school because he is late.
- Mr. Jones refuses to sell his home to anyone who is not white.
- Phyllis Allen, a lawyer, frequently defends people without charging them a fee if she feels that their rights under the U.S. Constitution are being violated.
- Robert Thomas continually writes letters to his city councilman, gets hundreds of signatures on a petition, and appears in person at city council meetings to appeal for pollution controls to be placed on the amount of waste that industrial plants may discharge into the air.
- Hopi Indian children never try to win at games.
- Many American soldiers who kill their enemies in wartime are given medals; in peacetime, they are imprisoned and sometimes executed.

Both a person's words and actions, therefore, may constitute evidence of what he or she values, though actions are usually a better indication of what is valued than are words alone. We cannot be absolutely certain about values, of course, since the person may be trying to deceive or confuse us, and thus, the more evidence we have, the more accurate a picture we are likely to obtain of what is valued. The reasons people give for their values also reveal quite a bit about them.

Reasons for valuing

The reasons we give for valuing things (a particular type of person, an object, a certain way of behaving) can tell others quite a bit about us. Certain foods, modes of dress, or types of music may be valued because we find them pleasing to our senses. We feel good when we eat and drink, hear, or wear such things; often we will go to a considerable amount of time or trouble to obtain or be near them. Vintage wines, diamond rings, land at the seashore, or government contracts may be valued because they are worth (or may become worth) a large amount of money. Certain kinds of tools, appliances, or materials may be valued because they work better than others. Certain states of affairs or living conditions may be valued by some because under these conditions they may live in ways that they find desirable. Some things may even be valued for no other reason than because people who value these things have been told they are worth valuing—that they are "important" or "worthwhile." Finally, certain ways of acting toward other human beings may be valued because of deeply felt beliefs, based on experience and reflection, that these ways of acting are right and just.

Degrees of value

Values differ considerably in the amount of importance that people attach to them. Some values, such as liking chocolate rather than vanilla ice cream, or rock rather than country and western music, are essentially personal preferences. We are not likely to argue that other people must also value such things, though we usually find ourselves rather pleased if they do.

There are other values, however, that many people consider to be far more important than personal preferences, and they will often argue that other people should also hold them. World peace is such a value for many people; human dignity another; equal opportunity a third. It is argued that these values are essential to the maintenance of life in general, and to the quality of life in particular. Many other values, such as honesty, cleanliness, tact, or bravery, fall somewhere in between these extremes.* Most of us are not likely to argue that these values are essential to the survival of the species. Yet we do view them as being more important than personal preferences. And a value that is essentially a personal preference at one time may over time, or in certain contexts, take on the status of a more basic, fundamental value (ecology—developing and maintaining a clean and healthy environment—is an example).

Value conflict

As people grow up and develop, and experience more of the world and what it has to offer, they often find that some of the values that they have acquired conflict. For example, consider the hypothetical (but representative) case of Robert Smith. As long as he could remember, Robert has heard his parents emphasize the values of honesty and loyalty. A "good" person is one who always tells the truth and stands by his friends. One of his friends, however, has copied from Robert's paper during a history examination without Robert's realizing it at the time. Now the teacher has asked both Robert and his friend to explain the fact that their papers are identical, even to having the same crossed-out words. Robert knows his friend copied from his paper, and wants to be loyal to him; yet he also wants to tell the truth, since he knows his teacher and his parents will be disappointed in him if he doesn't. What should he do?

---

*James P. Shaver and William Strong, *Facing Value Decisions: Rationale-Building for Teachers* (Belmont, Calif.: Wadsworth, 1976).

Value conflicts may be not only intrapersonal, within oneself, as the above example suggests, but also interpersonal or between individuals. The values of one person may be so different from those of another that the two individuals may find themselves strongly disagreeing with each other. Arguments for and against capital punishment are a case in point. One argument advanced by those who argue for the death penalty is that it will serve as a deterrent to future murderers. Those who argue against it often state that taking an additional life will not replace the one that is gone. Conflicts in values are often brought out when people make different value judgments.

Studying values in social studies classrooms

With these distinctions in mind, let us now consider some procedures that a teacher interested in values inquiry can use in the classroom. In particular, we shall consider some procedures and strategies designed to help students do the following:

- clarify their own values
- identify the values of others
- compare and contrast values
- analyze value judgments
- discuss moral dilemmas
- engage in role playing
- empathize with others placed in difficult situations
- participate in discussions about values

Clarifying personal values

One of the most widely used approaches to values inquiry found in the schools today is the values clarification approach espoused by Raths, Harmin, and Simon in their book, *Values and Teaching*.* Raths and his colleagues concern themselves with what they call the *process* of valuing. They see values as being based on three processes: choosing, prizing, and acting. They suggest a variety of activities and techniques that teachers can use to engage students in one or more of these processes. Here are some examples:†

The clarifying response is a way of responding to student statements to get them to reflect on what they have chosen, what they prize, or on what sorts of

*Louis E. Raths, Merrill Harmin, and Sidney B. Simon, *Values and Teaching* (Columbus: Merrill, 1966).

†For additional and different examples of value clarification activities, see Sidney B. Simon, Leland W. Howe, and Howard Kirschenbaum, *Values Clarification: A Handbook of Practical Strategies for Teachers and Students* (New York: Hart, 1972); Leland W. Howe and Mary Martha Howe, *Personalizing Education: Values Clarification and Beyond* (New York: Hart, 1975); and J. Doyle Casteel and Robert J. Stahl, *Value Clarification in the Classroom* (Pacific Palisades, Calif.: Goodyear, 1975).

things they are doing in life. Here is an example of a teacher-student exchange in which the teacher makes use of a clarifying response:

Teacher: You say, Glenn, that you are a liberal in political matters?

Glenn: Yes, I am.

Teacher: Where did your ideas come from?

Glenn: Well, my parents, I guess, mostly.

Teacher: Are you familiar with other positions?

Glenn: Well, sort of.

Teacher: I see, Glenn. Now, class, getting back to the homework for today. . . . (returning to the general lesson.)*

The primary purpose behind clarifying responses is to get students to look more closely at their behavior and ideas, thereby "clarifying" for themselves what they really value. Moralizing is deliberately avoided.

The *value sheet* is a thought-provoking story, statement, or set of questions that contains value implications for students to reflect on and write or talk about. Consider the following:

A bar tab

Yesterday, John Watson was sentenced to five years in prison. Watson, an employee of a local convenience store, was found guilty of having stolen $7.00 from the cash register.

This evening a group of civic-minded citizens are eating dinner together in a private dining room of the local country club. Among those present at dinner is Judge Harkness, the judge who sentenced Watson.

During the course of polite conversation, the Watson trial is mentioned. One of the diners compliments Harkness for his courage in "using the letter of the law to protect the entire community of Milltown."

A second speaker, not to be outdone, complimented Harkness for his wise and humane act. He proceeded to praise Harkness for "keeping young blacks in line, thus protecting a satisfied black community from any illusion that a dissatisfied minority could bend the law in order to change their circumstances."

A slightly tipsy diner announced, with some difficulty, "You have shaped another future leader of our country and have thus helped to shape the destiny of America."

Caught up in the spirit of the occasion, the president of a local industry arose and announced that he would offer Watson a job upon his release from prison. "I want to show the world just how tolerant, concerned, and humane the citizens of Milltown are," he explained. For this announcement, he received a standing ovation from his fellow diners.

---

*Raths, *et al.*, *Values and Teaching*, pp. 54–55.

The conversation passed on to other topics and John Watson was quickly forgotten. Two hours later, as diners were preparing to leave, the manager of the country club appeared at the doorway.

The manager said, "Forgive me for disturbing you, gentlemen, but we still have a bar check for $7.00 that has not yet been paid."

Before the manager could continue, one of those in the party said, "Forget it, Harry. What's $7.00?" In response to this, those in the dining party laughed and applauded. As for the manager, he smiled his agreement and left.

Discussion starters

1. Who is John Watson?
2. Given this reading, what does it mean to enforce the *letter* and ignore the *spirit* of the law?
3. Suppose that this reading is an example of what it means to be tolerant. In what sense could it be argued that tolerance is bad?
4. What should happen to John Watson? To Judge Harkness? To the diners?*

Rank ordering asks students to differentiate among possible alternatives in terms of relative goodness and badness, and to examine and clarify their preferences in terms of priorities. Consider this activity:

Justice in a pinch

At one point or another, all of us have had to decide whether or not we were justified in "breaking" a rule or "bending" the law. Imagine that you have an opportunity to help determine what should occur in the following situation.

> Ocala, Florida—Police here report they have apprehended two men who allegedly chased a calf down a back country road and ran it down with their car.
>
> Officers said that Bob Smith, 52, and his brother-in-law, James Jens, 34, were arrested as they prepared to butcher the calf on a table in Smith's garage.
>
> Smith, an unemployed father of eight, said, "I knew what I done wrong, but I can't afford to buy meat at these prices, and my family's got to eat."
>
> Smith and Jens were arrested and placed in jail.

A controversy erupts as to what should happen to Smith and Jens. Different persons in the community believe that different actions should be taken in order to serve the cause of justice. Seven possible actions are listed below:

Suppose you are helping to decide what will happen to Smith and Jens. Rank order the possible policies from the one that you believe is best for this situation to the one that you believe is worst for it. To do so, place a "1" by the most preferable action, a "2" by the second most preferable action, and so on until you have placed a "7" by the least preferable action.

---

*From J. Doyle Casteel and Robert J. Stahl, *Value Clarification in the Classroom: A Primer* (Pacific Palisades, Calif.: Goodyear, 1975), p. 20. Copyright © 1975 by Goodyear Publishing Company. Reprinted by permission.

——Smith and Jens should be ticketed for reckless driving and charged with killing a fur-bearing animal without a license.
——Smith and Jens should be ordered to pay the owner of the calf the market value of the animal.
——Smith and Jens should be sent to prison.
——Smith and Jens should not be punished because the high cost of beef prompted their action.
——The court should dismiss the case since Smith and Jens aren't "real" criminals like murderers, rapists, and thieves.
——Smith should be congratulated for trying to provide for the needs of his family.
——Smith and Jens should be punished, but the judge should take into consideration that Smith is unemployed and has a family.*

The public interview is an activity in which student volunteers are publicly interviewed about some of their beliefs, feelings, and actions. Simon, Howe, and Kirschenbaum describe the procedures involved:

> The teacher asks for volunteers who would like to be interviewed publicly about some of their beliefs, feelings, and actions. The volunteers sit at the teacher's desk or in a chair in front of the room, and the teacher moves to the back of the room and asks the questions from there.
>
> The first few times, the teacher reviews the ground rules. The teacher may ask the student any question about any aspect of his life and values. If the student answers the question, he must answer honestly. However, the student has the option of passing if he does not wish to answer one or more of the questions which the teacher poses. The student can end the interview at any time by simply saying, "Thank you for the interview." In addition, he may, at the completion of the interview, ask the teacher any of the same questions that were put to him.†

Here is an example of a public interview as described by Raths:

Teacher: All right, Paul, you be the first. Others may have a chance another time. Take my seat, Paul. I'll sit in the back. How do you feel, Paul?

Paul: (In the teacher's chair) O.K., I guess.

Teacher: Do you recall what you say if you would rather not answer a particular question? (Making certain the safeguards are understood)

Paul: I pass.

Teacher: And if you want to end the interview before time runs out?

Paul: I say, "Thank you for your questions."

---

*Casteel and Stahl, *Value Clarification*, p. 90.

†Simon, Howe, and Kirschenbaum, *Values Clarification*, pp. 139–40.

Teacher: Fine, Paul, now on what topic would you like to be interviewed?

Paul: My sister.

Teacher: Would you care to tell us something about your sister, Paul?

Paul: Not especially. Except that we hate each other. I want to be interviewed, asked questions, rather than just to say something.

Teacher: O.K., Paul. What do you hate about your sister?

Paul: Well, she is two years younger than I am, and she always is in the way. Like she argues about what TV program to watch, and she hangs around me when I'm playing, and she . . . she is just a nuisance.

Teacher: Are there sometimes when you *like* having her around?

Paul: No, absolutely not. (Laughter.)

Teacher: How do you define hate? What do you mean by that word?

Paul: Terrible. Like I want to murder her. She should go away.

Teacher: What's the difference between hate and dislike?

Paul: One is stronger. Hate is stronger.

Teacher: What is the difference between hating someone and hating things that the person does?

Paul: Hmmm. I just thought of a time when I didn't hate my sister. Once we were walking along and someone said how nice we looked together, we were younger and were walking hand in hand. It was a good feeling. But, I don't know, if you hate enough things a person does I guess you end up hating the person. Is that right?

Teacher: What do you think?

Paul: I don't know.

Teacher: Paul, what are you going to do about the situation between you and your sister? Apparently you don't like things the way they are.

Paul: What can I do? I know what I'd *like* to do . . . (Laughter.)

Teacher: Well, one thing you can do is keep away from her. Another is to try to work things out so that there is less argument and conflict between you. What other alternatives are there?

Paul: I don't know. I don't know. But thank you for your questions. Can I go now?

Teacher: Certainly, Paul, that's the rule. Whenever you want. Thank you . . .*

Values voting involves a teacher reading aloud one by one questions that begin with the words, "How many of you . . . ?" For example, "How many

*Raths *et al., Values and Teaching*, pp. 143–44.

of you like to go on long walks or hikes?" After each question is read, the students take a position by a show of hands. Those in the affirmative raise their hands; those in the negative point their thumbs down, while those who are undecided fold their arms. Those who want to pass do nothing. Discussion is tabled until after the teacher has completed the entire list.

The sorts of questions asked range from the innocuous to the provocative. Here is a sample voting list that has been designed for use with secondary students:

How many of you:

1. think teenagers should be allowed to choose their own clothes?
2. will raise your children more strictly than you were raised?
3. watch TV more than three hours per day?
4. think the most qualified person usually wins in school elections?
5. think there are times when cheating is justified?
6. could tell someone they have bad breath?
7. think going steady is important in order to achieve social success?
8. regularly attend religious services and enjoy it?*

Value continuums ask students to indicate where they stand on a particular issue or topic by marking their positions on a line that extends from one extreme to its opposite. Students may later share the reasons for their positions with the rest of the class if they wish, or they may pass. Here are some examples:

1. What should the U.S. attitude be on involvement with other countries?

Help every country even if not asked to do so	• • • • •	Help no country—complete isolation

2. How far would you go to be popular with your group?

Do anything, including risking safety	• • • • •	Do nothing at all

3. What are your newspaper habits?

Never look at one, not even comics or sports pages	• • • • •	Read every word, from comics to editorials

4. How patriotic are you?

Griping Gary: My country's not so hot	• • • • •	Stars and Stripes Sam: My country's never wrong†

Values clarification activities offer many possibilities that teachers can use to help students think about their own values. The clarifying response, in

*Simon *et al.*, *Values Clarification*, p. 39.

†Selected from Simon *et al.*, pp. 119–26.

particular, has much to recommend it. It is accepting of student ideas, nonthreatening, and encourages students to think about alternatives. Values clarification activities are less useful, however, when it comes to helping students identify and compare the values of others, analyze value judgments, or resolve value conflicts.

Identifying the values of others

The 1976 Yearbook of the National Council for the Social Studies describes several sets of questioning strategies that teachers can use to promote value analysis in their classrooms. One of these strategies, designed to help students make reasoned inferences about the values of other people, will be presented in this section, and a second strategy, designed to help them compare and contrast the values they have identified, will be presented next.* Both strategies involve presenting students with a *value incident* (a statement, argument, description, or illustration in which an individual does or says something that indicates or implies what he or she thinks is important) and then asking the class to make reasoned inferences about the values they see reflected in the incident. Charts are used to record student responses for later analysis.

Value incidents can be found among many different kinds of data, such as stories, cartoons, songs, advertisements, editorials, newspaper columns, court rulings, and comic strips. For example, here are three possibilities to consider. Notice their diversity, plus the fact that all three illustrate, imply, or pose the recommendation of something.

> We are a government and a people under law. It is not merely *government* that must live under law. Each of us must live under law. Just as our form of life depends upon the government's subordination to law under the Constitution, so it also depends upon the individual's subservience to the laws duly prescribed. Both of these are essential.
>
> Just as we expect the government to be bound by all laws, so each individual is bound by all of the laws under the Constitution. He cannot pick and choose. He cannot substitute his own judgment or passion, however noble, for the rules of law. Thoreau was an inspiring figure and a great writer; but his essay should not be read as a handbook on political science. A citizen cannot demand of his government or of other people obedience to the law, and at the same time claim a right in himself to break it by lawless conduct, free of punishment or penalty.†

* * *

---

*Adapted from Carl Ubbelohde and Jack R. Fraenkel, eds., *Values of the American Heritage: Challenges, Case Studies and Teaching Strategies,* 46th Yearbook of the National Council for the Social Studies (Washington, D.C.: The Council, 1976). Reprinted by permission of The National Council for the Social Studies.

†Abe Fortas, *Concerning Dissent and Civil Disobedience* (New York: Meridian Books, New American Library Inc., 1969), p. 55.

Reprinted by permission of Field Newspaper Syndicate.

* * *

> *Strength in 77 Seconds*
>
> That's all it takes to help build powerful muscles, and a trim body.
>
> No strenuous exercises . . . no elaborate gym equipment . . . no lengthy, tedious work-outs. You don't need time, space, or energy to multiply your strength . . . to broaden your shoulders . . . to increase your lung capacity . . . to trim your waistline . . . to develop vigor. Now the same method of Isometric Isotonic Contraction that trained the German Olympic Team and other world-famous athletes can help YOU build a powerful physique. Yes, even if you are 30, 50 years old or more. Unlike ordinary isometric contraction devices, the TENSOLATOR combines both Isometric and Isotonic benefits in a series of quick 7-second exercises that you do once a day in your own room—less than 2 minutes in all! Muscles grow stronger, shoulders broaden, chest expands, waist tapers down—and you feel like a new man. Fast? We guarantee impressive results in 10 days or your money back without question. Send for the big brochure that shows step-by-step illustration of the Tensolator Method.*

The key characteristic that all value incidents have in common is that they represent instances in which an individual indicates in some way what he or she considers important. This is a crucial characteristic, for students cannot be expected to identify the values of someone if the incident to which they are exposed does not show that individual doing or saying something that reflects his or her values.

After the value incident has been read (looked at, listened to, etc.), the teacher (or another student) asks the class several questions, in a predetermined sequence, about the incident, thereby encouraging them to analyze the incident in terms of the values they think it reflects. The questioner's task is to:

- ask for facts;
- ask for inferences about reasons why the facts occurred;
- ask for inferences about what the individual values;
- ask for specific evidence to support the inferences.

Here is one set of questions organized along these lines:

1. What is this (story, editorial, cartoon, etc.) about? What is happening in this incident?
2. What do you think are his or her reasons for saying or doing this?
3. What values do these reasons suggest to you as being important to this individual? Why?

---

*THOYLO Corporation, New York, N.Y.

Figure 2.1. A values information chart

What happened? FACTS	Why do you think it happened? REASONS	What does this suggest the individual(s) involved considers important? VALUES

Students should be encouraged to suggest as many different possibilities as they can in response to questions 2 and 3. As they seek to answer the questions, it is often helpful to prepare a *values information chart* on the blackboard (or in student notebooks) as shown in Figure 2.1.

Once the chart contains a sizable amount of information (the more the better), the class can be asked to *focus* on the third column of the chart and then discuss the questions that follow:

4. Why do you suppose people consider ________ (choose a particular value from the third column) important?
5. Would you endorse such a value yourself?

Each of these questions is asked for a particular purpose. Question 1 asks students to identify the acts and/or words of an individual in a particular situation in which values come into play. Questions 2 and 3 ask the class to make inferences as to the reasons for, and values underlying, this behavior. (Notice that there are "correct" answers to question 1 but not to questions 2 and 3. The teacher should take great pains to encourage any and all responses to these questions.) Question 4 then encourages students to think about why people value what they do.

A special remark needs to be made about question 5. This is not a question to be debated. It is a question calling for a show of personal commitment on the part of the student. The teacher should accept all student responses here, no matter what they might be. Any or all students also have the right to answer or not to answer this question.

Comparing and contrasting values

The assumption underlying the previous set of questions is that teachers can use them to help students make reasoned inferences about what other people value. Asking students to look for indications of value in a particular instance is helpful in alerting them to the fact that actions and words are value indicators. A single incident, however, is a very shaky foundation upon which to base an inference about another person's values. We can be mistaken, for the individual(s) involved may be trying to confuse or mislead us.

They may be acting under duress or unusual stress. They may be acting a certain way out of fear or ignorance. The idea of consistency of actions over time is therefore an important concept for students to understand and think about. It is of help in encouraging this to ask students to follow a given individual's (for example, a public official's) words and actions (as reported in the press and other media) over time. What contradictions do the students notice? In what way(s) would they modify their original conclusions? And why? What *specific evidence* caused them to modify previous conclusions? A focus on evidence for any conclusion is crucial, since it helps students to see that conclusions vary in terms of how warranted they are. Attention to the amount of evidence available that supports or refutes a conclusion, therefore, should be continual.

Figure 2.2 presents a skeleton of a chart that can be used to compare an individual's statements and actions over time, along with differing conclusions that students make about the individual's values. Along the top are entered the things to be compared (that is, different sayings or actions of the same individual at different times). Down the left-hand side are the questions to be asked.

Figure 2.2 is designed to help students investigate how the same person's words and actions hold up over time. Teachers can also help students to consider what *different* people do or say in the same situation by asking a set of predetermined questions in a given order. In this case, the questioner:

Figure 2.2. Comparing and contrasting the values of the same individual in different situations

Questions	First action or saying	Second action or saying	Third action or saying	Etc.
What happened? (Facts)				
Why did it happen? (Reasons)				
What does the person (s) or group (s) consider important? (Values)				

- asks for facts (that is, what did an individual do or say in a particular situation?)
- asks for reasons (why did he or she do this?)
- asks for inferences about what the individual values.
- asks for specific evidence that supports the inference.

This information can be charted or recorded on a retrieval chart, kept individually by students in their notebooks, or kept jointly on a bulletin or blackboard. Students are then asked these same questions about another individual who is involved in the same situation (or a similar situation at another time), and the information obtained is recorded on the same chart. When this additional information has been obtained, the questioner:

- asks for differences among the two (three, etc.) instances as far as actions or words go.
- asks for similarities among the two (three, etc.).
- asks for conclusions about people's values in this kind (or kinds) of situation.

Consider this example: A teacher is administering an examination and is called out of the room momentarily. Three girls all behave differently. One asks another girl for the answer to a problem on the exam; the second girl refuses to give the answer; the third girl then shows the first girl her paper. Using the sequence suggested earlier, Figure 2.3 presents a series of questions that could be asked to help students identify and then compare and contrast possible values implied in this incident.

As before, question 1 asks students to tell what the different individuals in the situation said and/or did. Questions 2 and 3 ask students to make inferences as to the reasons for, and values underlying, this behavior. Question 4 asks students to try to connect the facts, reasons, and values in some way. Questions 5 and 6 ask for observed differences and similarities in the behavior of the individuals, while question 7 asks for tentative conclusions that might explain why people act in certain ways in various situations.

Analyzing value judgments*

As mentioned earlier, statements that suggest what ought to be or should be done are called value judgments. Students frequently come across or are presented with such statements, both in and out of their classrooms. It seems

*Part of this section has been adapted from Jack R. Fraenkel, "Strategies for Developing Values," *Today's Education*, November–December 1973, pp. 49–53. Reprinted by permission of *Today's Education*, Journal of the National Education Association.

Figure 2.3. Comparing and contrasting values of different individuals in the same situation

Questions	Girl 1	Girl 2	Girl 3
1. What happened?			
2. Why did this happen?			
3. What do you think this girl values?			
4. What makes you think she values this?			
5. What differences do you notice in what the girls did?			
6. What similarities do you notice in what the girls did?			
7. Why do you think people act the way they do in these situations?			

only logical to suggest that helping them to analyze and to assess value judgments will be to their benefit, since such judgments are usually made for a reason. Seeking out and assessing these reasons can help students determine whether the judgment is one with which they would concur.

Value judgments usually will take one of two forms. Some are assertions about the worth or quality of something (for instance, "John F. Kennedy was a great man"). Others are statements that indicate that some person or group should follow a given course of action (for example, "The United States should cease giving any aid whatsoever to dictatorships"). Let us call the first type *definitional value claims* and the second type *propositional value claims*. How can we help students deal with each type?

Many value disputes arise because people have different meanings in mind for the value terms that they use. In the statement, "John F. Kennedy was a great man," the term *great* must be defined. Such a word, being an abstraction, is very difficult to define precisely. However, the teacher needs to encourage and help students to make the attempt.

A student might translate "great" into terms that are more easily understood (for instance, "famous," "renowned the world over"). She might point to examples of persons she considers great, indicating the characteristics or attributes they possess that make them great. The more characteristics the student can name, the better, because it then becomes easier to determine the degree to which a given individual deserves the label in question. Thus, greatness might be attributed to a person who (1) holds a high (this term also would have to be defined) office; (2) is recognized for high achievement in his or her field; (3) has contributed to the betterment of mankind. According to this definition, a person would have to meet all three criteria to be considered great.

However, when a student defines a term, it is quite possible that other students will disagree with the definition. When that happens, the teacher has two alternatives to pursue. One possibility is to ask the class to consult a dictionary. The second possibility is for the discussants to agree among themselves that the term means such-and-such in this instance (though not necessarily beyond this instance) so that discussion may proceed. If students are unable to agree on a stipulation, the class will have no recourse but to "agree to disagree" for the time being and to continue the search for meanings upon which they can concur.

If students are to assess *propositional* value claims intelligently, they must not only be clear about the value terms involved, but also must consider what might happen if the claim were to become reality. Suppose, for example, that during a class discussion on international politics, a student claims that the armaments possessed by nation-states should be limited to small-scale weapons. Other students disagree, arguing that those nations capable of manufacturing and/or otherwise obtaining heavier armaments are entitled to build as large and powerful a store of armaments as they wish. Helping students to understand the specifics of the claims and to come to some defensible conclusions of their own requires that a teacher engage them in several operations. The key term in the claim must be defined, and the consequences that might result from both proposals must be identified and evaluated.

First comes the problem of defining the value term. There are two things the teacher might do. He can ask the student for examples of what is meant by a "small-scale" weapon. It is often helpful here for the teacher to suggest examples to help the students clarify for themselves and the class what is meant: Does the term include anything larger than a machine gun? What about weapons-carrying vehicles, like tanks? How about submarines? Aircraft carriers? Bombers? Hand grenades? Small-scale nuclear rockets? Or the teacher can also ask students for the defining characteristics of a small-scale weapon (can any weapon that drops bombs be considered "small-scale"?).

When the meaning of the value term is clear, at least for the purposes of the discussion at hand, the matter of consequences needs to be investigated. What is likely to happen if such a policy as that being advocated is followed? Are there any examples of nations disarming to this extent in the past? If so, what happened to them? These are factual-type questions and require students to do some research to see what they can find out. Historical records, documents, photographs, eyewitness accounts, newspaper reports, diaries, journals—all are grist for the mill. As much relevant and documented information as possible needs to be collected.

All data offered as evidence to support or refute the likelihood of a consequence occurring must then be checked for relevance and accuracy. We determine the relevance of data by checking to see if they refer to the particular consequence being considered. We check the accuracy of data by determining whether or not what is presented or referred to is correct—i.e., is not in error, fake, or revised in some way.

When students are unable to find historical parallels, the teacher must encourage the class to *think out* what *might* happen. In our previous example, will the countries that disarm benefit in some way? If so, how? What about those countries that do not disarm—won't they be able and likely to take advantage of the others? Who would see to it that such disarmament actually took place? What kinds of expenses would be involved? What might be the repercussions of such disarmament on people in the future? Students will most likely predict consequences depending on their previous inclination toward the policy advocated. Usually, however, they will be unaware of some possible consequences, and it is the teacher's responsibility to present additional examples that illustrate the consequences of accepting a given policy.

Notice that obtaining as much relevant and documented information as possible is extremely important. Students cannot make intelligent predictions about consequences if they have no data with which to work.

Moral reasoning

As was mentioned earlier, it is a fact of life that values conflict. Conflict between values results when a person must choose between two or more desired alternatives. Individuals often are unable to act or act unwisely when faced with such choices, choosing a particular alternative without comparing its advantages and disadvantages with others available. Again, it seems only logical to argue that helping students to choose more wisely from among valued alternatives is a worthwhile goal for teachers to pursue. One way to go about this is to help students become aware of the fact that alternatives exist, and to evaluate the consequences of each choice. How might this be done?

Recently a number of educators have been arguing for the development of "moral" reasoning—that is, reasoning about moral issues—in social studies classrooms. The essence of their approach lies in engaging students in the discussion of *moral dilemmas* and then exposing them to different justifications for various actions given by other students or the teacher.

A moral dilemma is a situation in which an individual is faced with a choice between two or more desired courses of action, both (or all) of which are possible and feasible under the circumstances, but neither of which can be followed without producing some sort of physical or mental conflict or stress. An example might be a police officer faced with the choice of allowing a soapbox speaker to continue speaking to an increasingly angry and threatening crowd (thereby possibly permitting someone to get hurt physically), or of ordering the speaker to stop and thus possibly infringing on his constitutional rights. Moral dilemmas can be found in a variety of different sources, including newspaper and magazine articles, comic strips, advertisements, and editorials.

The leading contemporary advocate for the development of moral reasoning is Professor Lawrence Kohlberg of Harvard University. Much of his work has its roots in the thinking of John Dewey, and especially the stage theorizing of Jean Piaget. Kohlberg has specifically incorporated several Piagetian concepts into his own work—particularly the ideas of stage sequence and of conflict, dissonance, and imbalance. Using hypothetical ethical dilemmas (e.g., Should a doctor "mercy kill" a fatally ill patient who is requesting death because of pain?), Kohlberg interviewed children and adults in the United States, Turkey, Taiwan, Mexico, and Malaysia, and classified their responses into six groups in terms of the *types of reasons* they gave for their decisions. In all of the cultures that he studied, he identified three levels of moral development—the preconventional, the conventional, and the postconventional. Each of these levels has two stages within it, for a total of six stages of moral reasoning (see Table 2.1).

Preconventional children, though often well-behaved in a stereotyped sense and responsive to cultural labels of what is good or bad, act either because of the consequences involved (punishment, reward, exchange of favors) or because of the physical powers of authority figures (parents, teachers, etc.).

Children at the conventional level tend toward conformity. Living up to the expectations and maintaining the rules or laws of one's family, group, or nation is viewed as good in its own right. Concern is shown for not only conforming to but also for supporting and justifying the social order. According to Kohlberg, most adult Americans are to be found at this level.

At the third level, the postconventional, individuals tend to think in terms of autonomous moral principles rooted in the concept of justice that they conceive of as having universal applicability. Such principles are viewed as being distinct from the authority of the individuals or groups who hold them, or from a person's affiliation with those individuals or groups. The single soldier who refused orders to participate in the massacre at the Vietnamese village of My Lai in 1968 was identified as being at this level.

The stage of moral reasoning that a particular child has achieved is determined by having judges evaluate the child's responses to a hypothetical moral dilemma. These stories are philosophical in nature, and involve questions of responsibility, motive, or intention.

Table 2.1
*Kohlberg's stages of moral development**

Preconventional level

Stage 1: Punishment-and-obedience orientation. The physical consequences of an act determine whether it is good or bad, regardless of the meaning or value of these consequences to an individual. Avoidance of punishment and unquestioning obedience to superiors are valued in their own right.

Stage 2: Instrumental relativist orientation. What satisfies one's own and occasionally others' needs is good. "You scratch my back and I'll scratch yours" is a prevailing attitude of individuals at this stage.

Conventional level

Stage 3: Interpersonal concordance or "good boy-nice girl" orientation. What pleases or helps others and is approved by them is good. There is much conformity to stereotypical notions of what is "natural" or "nice" or majority behavior. Behavior is frequently judged by intention ("she means well").

Stage 4: "Law-and-order" orientation. Maintaining the social order, showing respect for authority, and doing one's duty is good. One earns respect by obeying fixed rules, laws, and authority.

Postconventional level

Stage 5: Social contract legalistic orientation. Values agreed upon by the society, including individual rights and rules for consensus, determine what is right. There is an emphasis upon rules of *procedure* for reaching consensus. The emphasis is on "the legal point of view," but with stress on the possibility of *changing* law in terms of rational considerations or social usefulness, rather than freezing it in terms of "law and order" as at stage 4. Aside from what is constitutionally and democratically agreed upon, what is right or wrong is a matter of personal values.

Stage 6: Universal ethical-principle orientation. What is right is a matter of conscience in accord with self-chosen principles, viewed as logical, consistent, and universal. These principles are abstract and ethical (e.g., the Golden Rule), as opposed to the concrete moral rules (e.g., the Ten Commandments) of stage 4. These universal principles in essence are the principles of justice, of the reciprocity and equality of human rights, and of respect for the dignity of human beings as individual persons.

---

*Adapted from Lawrence Kohlberg, "Moral Education in the Schools: A Developmental View," *School Review*, Spring 1966, p. 7. Published by The University of Chicago Press.

Remember that the stages of moral reasoning are not differentiated by the nature of the decision itself but rather on the basis of the *reasons* given for the decision. Here is an example:

> In Europe, a woman was near death from cancer. One drug might save her, a form of radium that a druggist in the same town had recently discovered. The druggist was charging $2,000, ten times what the drug cost him to make. The sick woman's husband, Heinz, went to everyone he knew to borrow the money, but he could only get together about half of what it cost. He told the druggist that his wife was dying and asked him to sell it cheaper or let him pay later. But the druggist said, "no." The husband got desperate and broke into the man's store to steal the drug for his wife. Should the husband have done that? Why?*

Like Piaget, Kohlberg argues that progression through these stages is sequential and invariant, and also that not all people reach the highest stages. He estimates, in fact, that less than 20 percent of adult Americans reason at the postconventional level. Furthermore, he believes that the six stages are universal, holding true in all cultures, and that each stage represents a *higher* level of reasoning than the one immediately preceding it. He came to this conclusion by observing that no subjects found to be at stages 1 through 4 had gone through stages 5 or 6, while those individuals at stages 5 or 6 had gone through stages 1 through 4. Though individuals do not skip stages, they may move through them either quickly or slowly and may be found half in and half out of a particular stage at any given time. As individuals progress through the stages, they become increasingly able to take in and synthesize more and different information than they could at earlier stages, and become more able to organize this information into an integrated and systematized framework. Moral thought, then, is viewed as operating in the same manner as any other kind of thought.

What implications does Kohlberg's theory have for values education? The most significant implication, perhaps, lies in Kohlberg's argument that progression through the stages is a *natural* development, one that teachers can further by presenting students with moral dilemmas like the one involving Heinz and his wife, and then discussing what the character(s) involved should do. The teacher must insure, however, that students are exposed to the arguments of individuals who are reasoning *one* stage *above* their own level. Kohlberg suggests that children and adolescents *prefer* the highest level of moral reasoning that they can understand; that they are able to comprehend all stages lower than their own, as well as one stage, and even, on occasion, two stages higher than their own. They tend to reject the arguments of individuals reasoning at lower stages, finding them simplistic and

---

*L. Kohlberg, "Stage and Sequence: The Cognitive-Developmental Approach to Socialization," in D. Goslin, ed., *Handbook of Socialization Theory and Research* (Chicago: Rand McNally, 1969).

in some cases naive, but they usually cannot understand the arguments of those who are reasoning more than one stage above their own. Students with extensive peer-group participation (i.e., discussion of moral dilemmas) were found to advance more quickly through the stages than students without such participation.*

Galbraith and Jones have developed a model lesson plan, as well as a list of "probe questions," that teachers can use to engage students in the discussion of moral dilemmas. The plan is of interest in that it provides *alternative* dilemmas to use in case the original dilemma fails to generate discussion. They argue that "although alternative dilemmas involve the same story, the same characters, and the same moral issues, they change the situation described in the original problem in an effort to promote disagreement about what the main character should do." The following is an example of such alternative dilemmas and probe questions, together with the original dilemma they are designed to accompany.

Helga's dilemma

Helga and Rachel had grown up together. They were best friends despite the fact that Helga's family was Christian and Rachel's was Jewish. For many years, this religious difference didn't seem to matter much in Germany, but after Hitler seized power, the situation changed. Hitler required Jews to wear armbands with the Star of David on them. He began to encourage his followers to destroy the property of Jewish people and to beat them on the street. Finally, he began to arrest Jews and deport them. Rumors went around the city that many Jews were being killed. Hiding Jews for whom the Gestapo (Hitler's secret police) was looking was a serious crime and violated a law of the German government.

One night Helga heard a knock at the door. When she opened it, she found Rachel on the step huddled in a dark coat. Quickly Rachel stepped inside. She had been to a meeting, she said, and when she returned home, she had found Gestapo members all around her house. Her parents and brothers had already been taken away. Knowing her fate if the Gestapo caught her, Rachel ran to her old friend's house.

Now what should Helga do? If she turned Rachel away, the Gestapo would eventually find her. Helga knew that most of the Jews who were sent away had been killed, and she didn't want her best friend to share that fate. But hiding the Jews broke the law. Helga would risk her own security and that of her family if she tried to hide Rachel. But she had a tiny room behind the chimney on the third floor where Rachel might be safe.

Question: Should Helga hide Rachel?

Alternative dilemmas. If the class agrees that Helga SHOULD hide Rachel, one of the following alternative dilemmas can be used to provoke disagreement.

---

*Kohlberg, "Moral Education in the Schools," p. 17.

A. Suppose Helga had only met Rachel once and did not know her well. What should she do in that case?
B. Suppose Helga's father and mother heard what was happening at the door and told her not to let Rachel in the house. In that case what should she do?

If the class agrees that Helga SHOULD NOT hide Rachel, one of the following alternative dilemmas can be used to provoke disagreement.

A. Suppose that several of Helga's friends were also hiding Jews from the Gestapo. What should Helga do in that case?
B. Suppose Helga heard the Gestapo coming and knew that Rachel would be shot on sight within a few minutes if she did not hide her. What should she do in that case?

Probe questions

1. What is the most important thing that one friend owes to another? Why?
2. Should a person ever risk the welfare of relatives for the welfare of friends? Why?
3. Should a person ever risk his or her own life for someone else? Why?
4. Is a person ever justified to hide someone who is fleeing from the authorities?
5. From Rachel's point of view, what should Helga do?
6. From the point of view of Helga's father, what should Helga do?*

The questions that Galbraith and Jones propose should encourage students to analyze alternatives. However, such queries do not explore the consequences of these alternatives. Some additional questions are needed. Here are a few examples:

- What might happen to a person if he or she does this (that is, pursue these alternatives)?
- What might happen to those not immediately involved? To future generations?
- Would these consequences be desirable?

Teachers should also ensure that students are provided with a variety of dilemmas, particularly ones that are not too simple, so that they will become more aware of the many different kinds of problems that exist in the world. For example, should the United States support an oil-rich nation from which it could receive considerable supplies of oil if that nation is a dictatorship? The important thing is to provide as much breadth as possible in the types of dilemmas to which students are exposed. This is particularly important in the senior high school grades, where students can be presented with dilemmas

---

*Ronald E. Galbraith and Thomas M. Jones, "Teaching Strategies for Moral Dilemmas: An Application of Kohlberg's Theory of Moral Development to the Social Studies Classroom," *Social Education*, January 1975, pp. 18–19. Reprinted with permission of the National Council for Social Studies, Ronald E. Galbraith, and Dr. Thomas M. Jones.

involving larger and larger groups of people, including governments and international agencies.*

Building empathy by role-playing

As was mentioned at the start of this chapter, values are not just ideas, but also emotional commitments. They contain a strong "feelings" element. If students are to be helped not only to think about and reflect on values but also to *understand* why other people often have values different from theirs, they must be helped to empathize with others who live in situations and cultures different from their own. How can this be done?

An excellent device to help students get started in exploring feelings in the classroom is role-playing. Role-playing requires students to act out the roles of imaginary or real individuals placed in various situations. Moral dilemmas offer many opportunities for role-playing. As described by Shaftel and Shaftel, role-playing involves the following steps:

1. Warm-up (teacher introduction and the presentation of the dilemmas to be acted out). The dilemma (in printed, visual, oral, or audio form) is presented to the class up to the moment that a decision must be made. The teacher (or questioner) then asks the class: "What do you think (the key character) should (or might) do?"
2. Selecting the role-players (choosing the students to portray the various roles in the dilemma). Students who have identified with various characters in the dilemmas should be encouraged to assume their roles, or if necessary, volunteers should be requested to play them. Shaftel and Shaftel also suggest that students who have been nominated for roles by others should not be assigned such roles, since the reasons behind the nomination may be punitive, or the suggested student may not see himself or herself in such a role.
3. Preparing the rest of the class to be observers. To help other students zero in on the role-playing, they can be assigned to different observer tasks. They can be asked to judge how realistic the role-playing is, and especially to think about how the various role-playing individuals feel as the role-playing progresses.
4. Setting the stage. This involves giving the role-players some time to plan briefly what they will do and how they will do it. The teacher should also check to insure that the necessary materials or props (usually very simple ones, such as a desk, chair, a few scattered objects, etc.) are available.
5. The enactment. Students then act out the roles they have chosen. As Shaftel and Shaftel point out, role-players should be reminded that they are not being evaluated on the basis of their acting ability. The central purpose of role-playing is to help students gain some insights into the feelings and values of other people.
6. Discussion and evaluation. This is a sort of debriefing stage, where teacher and class discuss what happened, how realistic the role-playing was, and how likely it is that the consequences as depicted would actually occur.

---

*For some further ideas on this, see Jack R. Fraenkel, "The Kohlberg Bandwagon: Some Reservations," *Social Education*, April 1976.

7. Further enactments. This stage provides an opportunity for the role-players to reenact the dilemma, or for it to be replayed using different students in the roles.
8. Further discussion. Once again, the role-playing should be debriefed, with the class discussing the new enactment, changes made in the outcome of the dilemma, how realistic this was, etc.
9. Generalizing. At this point, the teacher asks the class to draw some conclusions about what they observed and felt, and then to discuss their conclusions. Some sort of wrap-up question, such as "Why do you think people placed in situations like this act the way they do?" could be asked.*

Another way to generate a discussion of feelings in the classroom is to use a questioning strategy somewhat similar to the one suggested earlier for identifying values. Students are again presented with a value incident that could be role-played, but in this case the questions they are asked are a bit different:

1. What did you do (Where did you go, What happened to you, etc)?
2. How did you feel?
3. Did anybody else feel this way?
4. After listening to the experiences, what can you say about people and how they feel in situations like this?

Question 1 asks students to describe the situation in which they were involved and what they did. Question 2 asks them to relate their feelings—their emotional *reactions* to what they experienced. Question 3 allows other students to realize (it is hoped) that many people may feel things quite differently, but also that many people frequently *feel quite similarly to the way they do*. Question 4 then asks students to draw conclusions about people's feelings.

The assumption underlying these activities and questions is that by forming and comparing inferences about their own and others' feelings in certain instances, students will become more aware of the *similarities* in feelings that different people possess in various situations, and thus be more able to understand how people feel and act.

A word of caution about feelings. It is important that a teacher do his or her best, when it comes to discussions of feelings, not to indicate approval or disapproval of those feelings that he or she personally endorses or does not endorse. Reactions concerning a student's own experiences in the world are uniquely personal and private and should be respected as such, provided that they do not impose on someone else.

---

*Fannie R. Shaftel and George Shaftel, *Role-Playing for Social Values: Decision-making in the Social Studies* (Englewood Cliffs, N.J.: Prentice-Hall, 1967), pp. 76, 79, 84. © by Prentice-Hall, Inc., 1967.

The teacher's role in value discussions

Teachers should think seriously about how they interact with students during the course of a value (or any other) discussion. Put-downs, disapproval of a student's ideas, not encouraging the shy or hesitant ones to express themselves, failure to prevent monopolization of the discussion by a few students, not accepting responses with which the teacher personally disagrees—all these (as well as many other) techniques are almost guaranteed to discourage students from making and discussing inferences about values. One of the tragedies of schooling for many students is that they come to perceive learning as the giving of answers that they feel have been approved by teachers, parents, or authorities in general. As a result, they habitually say what they feel is "expected" of them rather than trying to think through answers for themselves.

If teachers wish to encourage students to participate in discussions about values, they must be fully aware of what they *say* and what they *do* as they interact with their students. Here are some suggestions:

Accept all statements that students offer, no matter how silly or unusual they may seem when first presented. This does not mean that you must *agree* with what a student says, only that you should not reject it out of hand. Such acceptance can be expressed by responding in a somewhat noncommittal manner, for example, by saying "I see," or "I understand," or simply "Okay."

Do not require students to talk if they do not want to. The following example illustrates a teacher's willingness to respect a student's desire not to comment on a particular issue.

Teacher: We've been talking the last few days about the issue of morality in government and in particular the question of what a government official should do when his principles come into conflict with what he perceives to be his responsibility to his constituents. Sue, you said yesterday that you felt this same dilemma was one that many military officers had to face when their principles came into conflict with their responsibilities as officers. Can you give us an example to help us understand your reasoning here?

Sue: Well, I mean, like for example a good officer is supposed to follow orders. But what if he feels that an order he's been given is a bad order—I mean, you know, it will really hurt a lot of people if he carries it out. He has got a real tough decision to make.

Teacher: What do you think an officer should do if he finds himself in that kind of situation?

Sue: I guess I think he has to stand by his principles.

Roger: I don't agree. Orders are orders, and it's a soldier's duty to obey them.

Teacher: Always?

Roger: Yeah, otherwise an army can't survive.

Teacher: Let's get some other ideas here, too. Phil, what's your opinion on all this?

Phil: I don't think I have one right now.

Teacher: Okay. But if you get an idea or two later on, don't hesitate to let us know.

When a student is having trouble getting his thoughts out, it is sometimes helpful to restate what he has expressed without indicating approval or disapproval of his ideas, as in the following illustration:

Donna: When I graduated from eighth grade—uh—my family moved to a new place, er, town—uh—in the summer, and I had to start—uh, begin high school there. I didn't know any of the kids, and I didn't—uh, feel very easy when school started.

Teacher: You felt kind of uncomfortable?

Donna: I sure did. It was pretty painful.

Teacher: I can understand why you'd feel that way.

Let students know that you want them to offer their ideas by telling them so. This is how one teacher indicated to his class that he wanted to hear what his students thought:

Racquel: I don't know much about this anyway.

Teacher: I'd really like to hear what you think, Racquel.

Racquel: Well, it doesn't seem fair to me that only seniors should get to go into the inner courtyard to eat their lunch. This school is supposed to be for everybody, isn't it? All students should get to use the inner courtyard and it shouldn't be a special privilege for you to have just because you're a senior.

Teacher: If I understand you, you're saying that it isn't fair for seniors to have the inner courtyard reserved for them as some sort of special privilege.

Racquel: Yes, I am.

Teacher: I see.

Take care not to impose your views on students. If discussions are to prosper, the teacher must encourage consideration and reflection on all ideas that are offered, including his or her own. A helpful procedure here is to prepare on the blackboard or in some other highly visible spot a three-column chart such as the one shown in Figure 2.4. Students can be encouraged to locate and write in the appropriate columns facts that provide evidence to support or refute particular ideas.

Don't hesitate to introduce ideas contrary to those expressed by students to bring out other aspects of an issue. Make sure, however, that students

Figure 2.4

Statements	Evidence to support	Evidence to refute

realize that you are not implying that these are necessarily *the* best ideas or demanding that they accept these ideas. The introduction of contradictory ideas is perfectly justified as a technique to promote discussion and to help students expand their awareness of people's feelings about a values issue. Insisting that students accept your ideas is not only unjust, but also contradicts the reflective examination of various ideas. Here is an example of how one teacher tried to encourage students to consider an idea rather than dismissing it without thinking about it:

Teacher: You have all suggested various things that you think might contribute to decreasing the likelihood of nuclear war in the future. One thing that nobody has mentioned is the possibility that the United States should begin the process by destroying all of its nuclear weapons over a five-year period and then inviting all the other nuclear powers to follow suit.

Student 1: Are you kidding? The Russians would have a fantastic weapons and power edge on us.

Student 2: Are you really in favor of that?

Teacher: I am not saying that I am either in favor of or opposed to the idea. I am simply suggesting that it might be an idea worth looking at. There are some pretty intelligent people in the United States and other countries that favor the United States taking the initiative in this regard, and if we really want to understand as much about this topic as we can, it might be a good idea to understand the reasons why they think this way.

Don't agree or disagree with a particular student when he offers an idea that agrees or disagrees with one of your own. Try instead to encourage other students to offer their views on what has been said. Here is an illustration:

Sid: You'll have to admit, Mrs. Adams [the teacher], that no army in the world could survive if the soldiers in it could decide any time they wanted to as to which orders they were going to obey and which ones they weren't.

Mrs. Adams: Perhaps. Let's see what other people think about this, Sid. What do some of the rest of you think about Sid's point—could an army survive if obedience were not required?

These suggestions can help to establish a supportive classroom climate. The essential point being made is that it is helpful to act and talk in such a way as to encourage rather than discourage students from offering their opinions in class if value inquiry is to prosper.

Summary

This chapter has concentrated on suggesting some ideas and procedures that can be used to explore values in social studies classrooms. At the heart of these ideas and procedures is the notion that values inquiry requires students to take an active part in the analysis of the various issues and dilemmas with which they are confronted. For values inquiry to be successful, it is the students—not the teacher—who must do the inquiring—make the inferences about values, analyze the value judgments, and weigh the alternatives and consequences involved in value dilemmas. The teacher's role is to pose questions, to assist in the collection of relevant information, to provide some value incidents and dilemmas for discussion, to ask for supporting and refuting evidence for positions students take, and to encourage all students to participate in the discussions.

Inquiry into values is not all there is to social studies teaching, or even to inquiry. But it is a very important part of each. My hope is that the ideas and procedures presented in this chapter will encourage you to engage your students in such inquiry soon.

Bibliography

Barr, Robert D., ed. *Values and Youth.* Washington, D.C.: National Council for the Social Studies, 1971.

Beck, Clive. "The Development of Moral Judgment." In *Developing Value Constructs in Schooling: Inquiry into Process and Product,* edited by James A. Phillips, Jr. Worthington, Ohio: Ohio Association for Supervision and Curriculum Development, 1972.

Casteel, J. Doyle, and Stahl, Robert J. *Value Clarification in the Classroom: A Primer.* Pacific Palisades, Calif.: Goodyear, 1975.

Ennis, Robert H. *Logic in Teaching*. Englewood Cliffs, N.J.: Prentice-Hall, 1969.

Fraenkel, Jack R. *Helping Students Think and Value: Strategies for Teaching the Social Studies.* Englewood Cliffs, N.J.: Prentice-Hall, 1973.

———. "The Kohlberg Bandwagon: Some Reservations." *Social Education,* April 1976.

———. "Strategies for Developing Values." *Today's Education,* November–December 1973, pp. 49–53.

Galbraith, Ronald E., and Jones, Thomas M. "Teaching Strategies for Moral Dilemmas: An Application of Kohlberg's Theory of Moral Development to the Social Studies Classroom." *Social Education,* January 1975, pp. 18–19.

Hall, Robert T., and Davis, John U. *Moral Education in Theory and Practice.* Buffalo, N.Y.: Prometheus Books, 1975.

Howe, Leland W., and Howe, Mary Martha. *Personalizing Education: Values Clarification and Beyond.* New York: Hart, 1975.

Hunt, Maurice P., and Metcalf, Lawrence E. *Teaching High School Social Studies.* New York: Harper & Row, 1968.

Kirschenbaum, Howard, and Simon, Sidney B. *Readings in Values Clarification.* Minneapolis: Winston, 1973.

Kohlberg, Lawrence. "Moral Education in the Schools: A Developmental View." *School Review,* Spring 1966, p. 7.

———. "Stage and Sequence: The Cognitive-Developmental Approach to Socialization." In *Handbook of Socialization Theory and Research*, edited by D. Goslin. Chicago: Rand McNally, 1969.

Metcalf, Lawrence E., ed. *Values Education: Rationale, Strategies, and Procedures,* 41st Yearbook of the National Council for the Social Studies. Washington, D.C.: The Council, 1971.

Meyer, John, *et al.*, eds. *Values Education: Theory/Practice/Problems/Prospects*. Waterloo, Canada: Wilfrid Laurie Press, 1975.

Nelson, Jack N. *Introduction to Value Inquiry*. Rochelle Park, N.J.: Hayden, 1974.

Newman, Fred M., with Oliver, Donald W. *Clarifying Public Controversy*. Boston: Little, Brown, 1970.

Oliver, Donald W., and Shaver, James P. *Teaching Public Issues in the High School*. Boston: Houghton Mifflin, 1966.

Raths, Louis E., *et al., Values and Teaching*. Columbus: Merrill, 1966.

Ruggierio, Vincent Ryan. *The Moral Imperative*. Port Washington, N.Y.: Alfred, 1973.

Scriven, Michael. *Student Values as Educational Objectives*. Boulder, Colo.: Social Science Education Consortium, 1966.

Shaftel, Fannie R., and Shaftel, George. *Role-Playing for Social Values: Decision-Making in the Social Studies*. Englewood Cliffs, N.J.: Prentice-Hall, 1967.

Shaver, James P., and Strong, William. *Facing Value Decisions: Rationale Building for Teachers.* Belmont, Calif.: Wadsworth, 1976.

Simon, Sidney B., *et al. Values Clarification: A Handbook of Practical Strategies for Teachers and Students.* New York: Hart, 1972.

Superka, Douglas P., *et al., Values Education: Approaches and Materials*. Boulder, Colo.: Social Science Education Consortium, 1975.

Ubbelohde, Carl, and Fraenkel, Jack R., eds. *Values of the American Heritage: Challenges, Case Studies and Teaching Strategies,* 46th Yearbook of the National Council for the Social Studies. Washington, D.C.: NCSS, 1976.

Since the early 1960s, simulations increasingly have drawn attention as potentially powerful teaching tools for use in the social studies. Although countless thousands of American youngsters have participated in simulations, to characterize current trends in the field is a bit like trying to grasp one's reflection in a pool of water—we know it's there because we see it, but upon attempting to grasp it we find it elusive and difficult to capture. In a sense, simulations, like Topsy, have simply "growed," and they are now available in virtually every subject included under the social studies umbrella. Simulations have been widely accepted by social studies teachers who want to bring a bit of the outside world into the classroom and who wish to involve their students in inquiry.

This chapter considers simulations as tools for sparking and sustaining inquiry. It deals with the problem of definitions, offers tips to teachers who wish to design simulations of their own, and surveys simulations that have been produced commercially.

Chapter 3

Simulations

Simulations have become increasingly recognized as powerful teaching tools, especially in the social studies. Students may be able to gain insights into current and historical problems within the field of social studies through acting out such situations as these:

- In a sociology class in a suburban Chicago high school, a group of "have-nots" vents its frustration and bitterness at being relegated to inescapable lower-class status.
- In a government class in Atlanta, a young campaign manager eagerly presents the case for his presidential candidate to skeptical voters in an attempt to enlist their support and campaign contributions.
- In an economics class in Los Angeles, groups of pseudoindustrialists huddle over maps and stacks of data, deciding where it would be most desirable and profitable to locate a new factory they are establishing.
- In a social studies class in Oregon, a young couple is "married," and faces the challenge of negotiating the hazards of wedded life.
- In a history class in New York City, a priest-king in ancient Mesopotamia is faced with solving problems of expanding population, irrigation, and foreign trade.
- In a geography class in Wichita, a group of Kansas farmers attempts to solve economic problems facing them in the year 1888.

All of these students have one thing in common. They are participating in simulations—an approach to teaching the social studies that tries to approximate real-life conditions in the classroom. It requires students to assume roles as diverse as those of ghetto residents and seal hunters, and to grapple with problems ranging from choosing a career to formulating a foreign policy. In recent years the market has been virtually flooded with simulations. Today, more than 700 of them are being produced commercially for use in every discipline in the social studies and at all grade levels. And the list continues to expand rapidly. In addition, thousands of teachers are using simulations of their own design. Considering that the approach was virtually unknown in elementary and secondary schools until well into the 1960s, the growth we are now witnessing is astounding. Seldom, it seems, has a teaching technique captured the imagination of social studies teachers in such swift fashion.*

Terminology

Before considering reasons why simulations have gained widespread popularity among social studies teachers, it would be well to deal with the knotty problem of terminology. If one thing is certain in the simulations field, it is that confusion exists regarding the definition of terms. This problem is a result in part of the relative newness of the approach, but is compounded by the wide variety of ways in which the simulations are used. In the literature, such terms as simulation, role playing, social simulations, educational games, and simulation games are used commonly, and in many cases interchangeably. These five basic terms, used throughout this chapter, will be defined in this section, and the chief characteristics of each type of simulation will be considered. Distinctions among types of simulations are at best often blurred, however, and in categorizing them one commonly must deal in shades of gray.

Simulation

A simulation is essentially an operating model of a physical or social process that is abstracted from reality and simplified for purposes of study and analysis. *Physical processes* involve only nonhuman interactions. Human beings may be affected by the processes, respond to them, or try to change them, but the processes themselves are essentially physical in nature.

---

*Although simulations have grown popular in American education during the last decade, origins of the technique can be traced back thousands of years. One early relative of modern simulations, for example, is the Chinese war game "Wei-hai" (meaning encirclement) which originated about 3000 B.C., and is the forerunner of the popular Japanese game "Go." Another early predecessor is Chaturanga, an ancient Indian game also involving principles of war, which is claimed to be the precursor of our modern version of chess.

Since the early 1800s, military experts have used simulations for the training of officers and for the study of military tactics. In the 1950s nonmilitary educational simulations were developed in the fields of business and management, and in the early 1960s professional educators began to recognize the potential of the approach for elementary and secondary schools. The work and publications of such influential persons as Clark Abt, Harold Guetzkow, James Coleman, and Sarane Boocock spearheaded the movement, which has resulted in the widespread interest in simulations today.

Simulating conditions of weightlessness encountered by astronauts when they enter outer space is an example of modeling a physical process. *Social processes*, on the other hand, are those that deal with human interactions. They may involve the manipulation of physical components—money, natural resources, property, etc.—but the processes themselves are essentially social and interpersonal in nature. Simulating the decision making involved in passing a bill through Congress is an example of modeling a social process.

Although simulating physical processes is appropriate in some of the social studies (for example, simulating the silting action in stream beds through the use of a model in a geography course), it is the social processes with which the social studies and this chapter are primarily concerned. Examples of social processes for which simulations could be designed for use in the social studies could include:

The creating of strategies designed to win a political campaign.
The struggle of blacks attempting to escape the urban ghetto.
The resolving of conflicts among nations caught in a dispute over territorial rights.
The decision making of consumers faced with economic dilemmas.
The resolving of misunderstandings among people of widely differing cultures.
The making of decisions in a representative democracy.
The reconstructing of an ancient culture through an analysis of artifacts.
The resolving of problems faced by citizens of a hypothetical country as they attempt to establish an effective form of government.
The resolving of problems and conflicts related to ecological imbalance.
The interactions of factions involved in a political revolution.
The handling of economic decisions in planning a family budget.
The striving of national leaders to achieve economic and political stability.
The resolving of stress situations growing out of racial tension.
The forming and implementing of strategies designed to strengthen a national position in the international economic community.
The resolving of problems of land use in an urban setting.
The resolving of problems related to the conflict between federalism and state rights.
The functioning of various elements in an economic system.

Simulations cannot be and should not pretend to be total reality. Rather, they are operating models—miniaturized representations of the significant factors of the social process being studied. They are reality simplified, much like road maps, which identify basic features of a terrain but delete the irrelevant. They can range in complexity from a model of the interaction of community members deciding where to locate a new park to a model of the governments of hypothetical nations working through diplomatic channels to avert war.

Nearly all simulations used in the secondary school are of the *all-human* variety, in which the process being studied is modeled by the participants interacting with one another. Roles usually are assigned, objectives are stated, and the sequence of action is determined by rules. An increasing number of *human-machine* simulations, however, are being developed for use with the computer. In this type of simulation students respond to a carefully developed computer program and proceed at their own pace and depth. One advantage of computerized simulations is that they can help to individualize instruction. We can anticipate an increase in their use in the secondary classroom as computers become more accessible, technical know-how continues to develop, and programmed simulations become increasingly available. Since the vast majority of simulations used in the secondary school today are of the all-human variety, however, in this chapter we shall concentrate solely on that type. (See chapter 6 for further discussion of computer-based instruction.)

Role playing

Role playing is a key feature of most simulations, as students usually assume and act out their versions of hypothetical or real-life characters who function in the social process being studied. Role playing itself, however, is merely a technique used to present particular complexities and relationships of the process and is not synonymous with simulation. Role-playing activities, as they are commonly used in the classroom, tend to be more spontaneous and less tightly structured than simulations. They rarely are designed to deal with more than a single phenomenon. When students in class act out their versions of political candidates delivering speeches, for example, they are role playing. They are not, however, modeling a social process in which interaction among people is clearly identifiable and in which scores of interrelated decisions and actions are called for.

Social simulations

Social simulations are operating models of social processes in which the participants seek to achieve goals. Students are usually assigned roles through the use of profiles that provide background data for the roles being assumed, such as sex, age, income, social class, and political convictions. Acting the roles, they respond to problems defined in an introductory scenario that sets the stage for the simulation. The roles may be imaginary, or they may be based upon historical figures, depending upon the purpose of the exercise. In either case, social simulations focus on social interaction and decision making, and they often involve conflict of interest. Students usually develop and carry out strategies for accomplishing specific goals, and in this limited sense they may compete with other groups or individuals. Social simulations are distinguished from *simulation games* and *educational games*, however, in that there normally are no winners. Rather, cooperative action, negotiation, compromise, and bargaining usually are encouraged.

An example of a social simulation has been developed by Mr. Cliff Allen, a social studies teacher at Parkrose (Oregon) Senior High School. In his contemporary living course, Mr. Allen introduces his students to the realities of married life by compressing ten years of married life into a nine-week simulation. Students are paired, a mock wedding ceremony is staged, and the young married "couples" confront the challenges of finding a place to live, getting a job, developing a family budget, and dealing with unanticipated crises that commonly plague and often destroy marriages. The result has been that students have come to view marriage in a much more realistic and down-to-earth fashion.*

Educational games

Educational games are based upon contrived competition carried on under the constraint of rules; at the end there are winners and losers. These games deal in a limited way with social phenomena, but they do not present the student with valid operating models of the real world. Educational games often require the use of game boards on which the action is plotted as players compete with one another. An example of such a board game is Monopoly. Winners in educational games are usually determined by a combination of cleverness in playing the game and the element of chance. This is not to suggest that games of this type should not be used by the social studies teacher, for many of them are very effective for teaching useful skills and concepts. Some of the best educational games have grown out of the Nova Academic Games Project, including WFF 'N Proof (The Game of Modern Logic), WFF (The Beginner's Game of Logic), ON-SETS (The Game of Set Theory), and the Propaganda Game. Games such as these capitalize on what seems to be man's natural desire to compete, and motivation among students participating in them typically is very high. Educational games *do* have a place in the social studies classroom, but they should not be confused with simulations.

Simulation games

Simulation games incorporate dimensions of both the social simulation and the educational game. They are operating models of social processes that normally use role playing and that have a competitive gaming dimension. The nature of competition in simulation games, however, differs from that in

---

*Linda Bird Francke with Mary Alice Kellogg, "Conjugal Prep," *Newsweek*, June 2, 1975, pp. 64–65.

educational games. Competition in educational games is "manufactured"—created essentially for its own purpose. In simulation games competition is an important part of the social process being modeled. Its inclusion in the simulation is required if participants are to understand the nature of the competition and the forces underlying it, and if they are to comprehend fully the process being studied. Winners and losers normally emerge in simulation games, but their successes or failures usually reflect the interaction of the social forces being simulated. Teachers have found the competitive nature of simulation games to be a key factor in motivating students, and the majority of simulations designed for the secondary school fall into this category.

In the remainder of this chapter we will limit our concern to all-human social simulations and simulation games. The term simulation will be used in a broad sense when discussing general developments in the field. Distinctions based upon the definitions developed in this section will be made when appropriate.

Examples of simulations

SUNSHINE and STARPOWER, the two simulations presented in part here, will serve as examples of social simulations and simulation games. They also illustrate contrasting formats and styles of simulation construction. SUNSHINE is a rather complex social simulation that takes from four to six weeks of class time to complete. STARPOWER is a relatively simple simulation game that requires only about three hours of class time. Each presents a model of a social process involving the interaction of human beings, and each involves role playing. The roles in SUNSHINE are more fully developed and clearly defined, while those in STARPOWER are left open to broader personal interpretation. A primary difference between the two simulations is the degree to which they involve competition. In SUNSHINE, competition is played down, and winning or losing is not heavily emphasized. In STARPOWER, competition is vital to the functioning of the model, and gains are normally made at the expense of other participants.

A social simulation—SUNSHINE

SUNSHINE* simulates current racial problems in a typical American city. It is an inexpensive, carefully designed, and well-organized exercise, usable at all levels of the secondary school with groups of twenty to thirty-six students. It is appropriate for American history, urban affairs, black studies, or contem-

*The description of and quotations from SUNSHINE are used by permission of INTERACT Company.

porary problems courses. Although participants in one sense compete with one another by trying to improve their standing in the community, there are no clearly defined winners and losers. Rather, the focus is on compromise, the successful resolution of issues, and improving the welfare of the total community. SUNSHINE, therefore, is a good example of a social simulation. Its stated purpose is as follows:

> SUNSHINE simulates a typical American community of 50,000 moving toward and through two racial crises which many American cities have experienced or are facing. Because students are "reborn" as black or white citizens at the beginning of the simulation and because of what happens to them in their simulated community, they become concerned about the racial issues boiling around them in the classroom. Suddenly sensing somewhat how blacks and whites feel when confronting one another in public meetings over some racially tense situation, they find they must commit themselves to act. The students learn facts and concepts concerning the history of the American Negro, but the simulation fails if that is all they do. For the simulation succeeds only if the students feel compelled to use these facts and concepts to develop public and private action to help resolve the most crucial domestic issue of our time.

Participants in the simulation assume roles of community members who live in the six neighborhoods of SUNSHINE, ranging from a minority-populated, low-income section called Dead End to the white and prosperous Mt. Olympus (Fig. 3.1). During the course of the exercise the participants, while facing and attempting to resolve a variety of community-based conflicts, attempt to improve their personal status and self-image as well as the living conditions in SUNSHINE. At the beginning of the simulation, students are given a guide that introduces the exercise and provides background regarding the community of SUNSHINE.

Incorporated: 1925

Location: In your state

Population and ethnic breakdown:

31,450	Whites
13,850	Blacks
4,700	Others—Spanish-Mexican Americans: Oriental Americans; Native American Indians
50,000	Citizens

Economy: Key industries are auto assembly, fertilizer, and electronics parts and assembly. Unemployment is now 5.7% overall, yet 8.4% among Chicanos and Orientals and 11.6% among Negroes.

Housing Patterns: As population increased during and after World War II, most whites moved from Dead End and East End into the suburbs south of Happiness

Figure 3.1

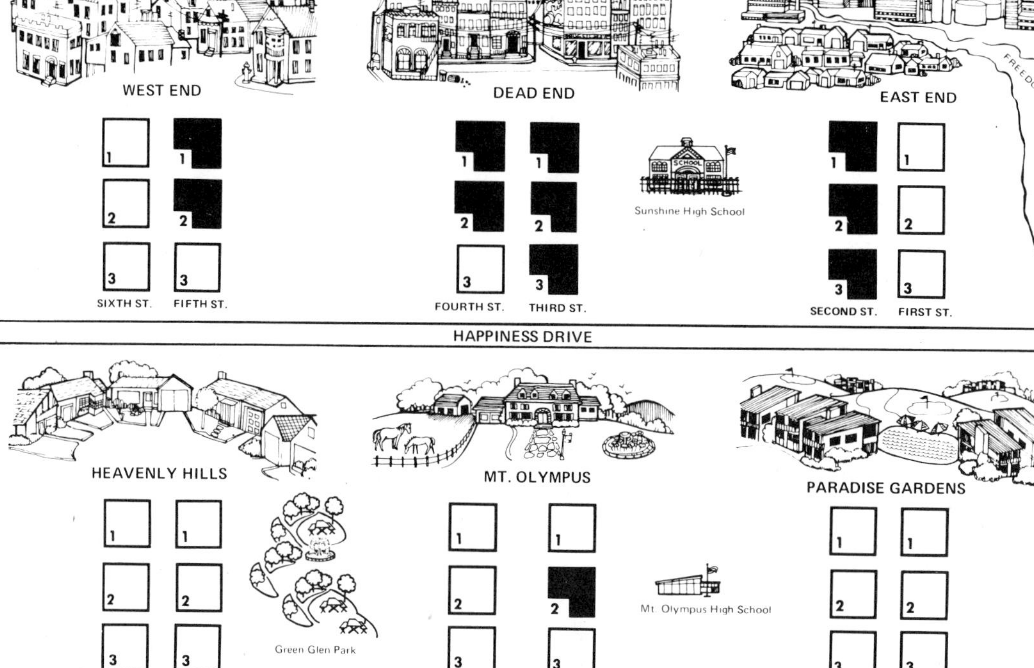

Drive. Blacks and other minority groups moved into the two vacated neighborhoods. Consequently, the neighborhoods now have the following characteristics:

—Dead End and East End—tenements, rental housing, homes under $15,000 (50 to 90% Black)

—West End—Old, individually designed homes under $25,000 (30 to 40% Black)

—Paradise Gardens and Heavenly Hills—housing development and condominium homes from $25,000 to $50,000 (95 to 100% White)

—Mount Olympus—individually designed homes $50,000 to $125,000 (95 to 100% White)

Churches: Presumably segregated by religious preference, the churches are actually segregated by housing patterns, ethnic background, and income.

Schools: Although schools are not segregated by law, education is basically segregated because of school attendance boundaries, jobs and income, and housing patterns. Thus, only a handful of Sunshine's Caucasian youth south of Happiness Drive attend schools with Negro children. The high school attendance boundary, drawn in 1953 along Happiness Drive, necessitates bussing students from West End to Sunshine High School. The two high schools of about 2,000 students each have equal staff and facilities, but widely different ethnic populations:

—Sunshine High School
63% (1260 students) Blacks
20% (400 students) Chicanos and Orientals
17% (340 students) Whites
—Mt. Olympus High School
91% (1820 students) Whites
7% (140 students) Chicanos and Orientals
2% (40 students) Blacks

For several reasons the Sunshine Unified School District is not an "impoverished school district." First, the community has adequate industry and many fine homes, both of which mean considerable property taxes for schools; second, the state provides state taxes for its schools; finally, the federal government, as a result of the federal-aid-to-education acts, has made available through the State Department of Education federal funds for compensatory education programs—if the school districts apply for such funds. But as of the present, Sunshine's white school board has steadfastly refused to seek federal funds due to its opposition to "Socialism and federal control."

Riots: Although no riots or wide-spread demonstrations have yet hit Sunshine, on the night of Martin Luther King's assassination in 1968, Negroes threw Molotov cocktails against "Victory Arch" on the Mt. Olympus High School campus and vicious fighting broke out between Blacks and Whites. Faint traces of the burned scar still tarnish the stone arch at the entrance to the campus, and many citizens remember the humiliating coverage given the event in photographs in *Life* magazine.

Teachers working in various settings can restructure the social, physical, and economic makeup of SUNSHINE to make it more appropriate for study by their particular students. The character of the community should be reflected by a map similar to Figure 3.1, which is provided to each participant. Students' identity tags provide the following kinds of information:

Community Identity: Heavenly Hills

ADDRESS: 1 Golden Avenue

AGE: 29

ETHNIC BACKGROUND: White

OCCUPATION: Bricklayer

INCOME: $650 per month

EDUCATION: 12th Grade

GENERAL DESCRIPTION: You have four children, two cars, and a nice home whose yard you keep immaculate. You have no objection to black neighbors as long as they work as hard as you. You support gradual integration of the White Gradualists.

SUNSHINE's Teacher's Guide provides the following overview of the simulation:

> After taking Racial Attitudes Test 1 (if this option is used), students start SUNSHINE by being "reborn" when they pull identity tags indicating ethnic group, skin color, education, job, income, neighborhood and political pressure group affiliation. This "rebirth," performed in front of all their classmates, is followed by their desks becoming "homes" in the six neighborhoods of various ethnic and socio-economic make-up that will simulate Sunshine city and its suburbs.
>
> Following this initial organization, students are introduced to how self-image concepts motivate behavior and to how slavery can produce certain self-images. Then the skill activities of how to gather and organize information are introduced and practiced. These activities are followed by a general sweep of black American history, each lesson emphasizing one important element of that history which has contributed to contemporary black and white Americans' images of themselves. Integrated with this "research" phase are pressure cards describing some happening in the community which affects the images of various citizens in various ways. Eventually, these pressures cause factions to arise in SUNSHINE over two major racial crisis situations: equal educational opportunity and control of crime and the conditions causing it.
>
> The concluding phase of the simulation is designed so that students may use newly acquired knowledge in planning presentations containing their solutions for an educational crisis situation and a crime crisis situation. Student-citizens form pressure groups and factions, nominate and work to elect their candidates for the school board and city council, and plan and give presentations designed to win their elected officials' favor. In short, students are given the opportunity to learn the democratic process by actually participating in it—not listening to some adult describe how good or bad it is.
>
> Finally, the simulation ends with the administration of a post racial attitudes test (if the pre-test was given), an essay test evaluating the simulation as a learning experience, and debriefing sessions. (A general knowledge test of various elements of black history was also given earlier.) These evaluation devices, taken together, measure how much traditional learning this simulation has produced. But perhaps the most important aspect of SUNSHINE is that students, given the opportunity to "walk a mile in another man's shoes," may learn to be more tolerant of that man's problems and may even learn to work with "that man" to help solve their mutual problem: acquiring satisfactory self-images in a democratic society.

The following observations were made by a teacher who used SUNSHINE with his eighth and ninth graders, and who wrote with great enthusiasm of the excitement generated in the classroom when his students became involved in SUNSHINE. He bears testimony to the effectiveness of the exercise, and offers clues as to why many social studies teachers have embraced simulations enthusiastically.

> There are numerous examples of student involvement [that] could be cited, but perhaps one will suffice as being representative. One incident involved the resi-

dents of the ghetto and a confrontation with their "slumlord." The ghetto dwellers were being bitten and frightened by rats in their homes. Immediately, the residents of the ghetto formed a community action group that sent representatives into the community to seek help on how to handle their problem. The group's first interview was with a local lawyer. The lawyer could not give them enough information, but referred them to the local housing authority. From there they were referred to eight other agencies, the last of which referred them to a lawyer. The lesson learned by the students was a beautiful example of the total despair of the poor in dealing with the governmental agencies and red tape.*

A simulation game—STARPOWER

STARPOWER† is a highly effective simulation game in which a three-level society is created through an unequal apportionment of wealth and power. The exercise involves trading and bargaining, and the winners of the competition are those three participants who accumulate the most points (wealth) by the end of the session. It is appropriate for either junior or senior high school, and it is particularly helpful for initiating inquiry and for dealing with such concepts as justice, power, and equality. In the director's instructions, STARPOWER is introduced as follows:

> This is a game in which a low mobility, three-tiered society is built through the distribution of wealth in the form of chips. At first glance, it looks something like a poker game without cards; the players trade and bargain for chips, each hoping to gain as many points as he can. After a round of trading, the groups will be given labels—those with the most points will be called squares; those with the least, triangles; and those in between, circles. After a bonus round which can lead to some shuffling of positions, and a second trading-round for which the game director has secretly "stacked the deck" in favor of the squares, the squares are clearly in a position of dominance.
>
> In simulated fashion, the trading has created a society of haves and have-nots. In subsequent rounds, a triangle or a circle can acquire enough wealth to replace a member of a higher group, but the mobility rate will not be high.
>
> At this point, the squares are given the power to make the rules of the game—and almost invariably they will make rules that secure or enhance their position of power. The other two groups, of course, will consider these rules unfair, even labeling them as dictatorial, fascist or racist. When the frustration reaches a certain level, the game usually ends in some form of revolt against the

---

*Don Hogan, McMinnville, Oregon, in Katherine Chapman and Jack E. Cousins, *Simulation/Games in Social Studies: A Report* (Boulder, Colo.: Social Science Education Consortium, 1974), p. 12. The students were mixed eighth and ninth graders, and the course was an elective social studies course called "Sunshine."

†The description of STARPOWER is used by permission of Western Behavioral Sciences Institute.

> rules and the rule-makers. In a game setting which protects against undue abrasion of personal feelings, the group will experience on the one hand an exercise of total power, and on the other, the helplessness of those who feel the system working unfairly against them.
>
> As with all simulations, the de-briefing or discussion session following the game is as vital as the game itself. Game requires a minimum of 18 players, 30 is optimum and 35 the maximum.*

STARPOWER is based upon the assumption that participants in a highly competitive situation will do everything possible to increase their wealth and to consolidate their power even at the expense of their peers. In a fashion pregnant with implications, this is exactly what normally happens during the simulation game. As participants become disenfranchised and frozen into the "lower classes," their frustrations and defiant reactions begin to emerge. Once the conflict among classes has been created, the moment is ripe for exploring issues related to the distribution of wealth, the relationship between the social system and individuals' behavior, and relations among members of different races, social classes, and various interest groups.

When asked to explain what he had learned by participating in STARPOWER, one twelfth-grade student responded:

> The game of STARPOWER is about capitalism—material wealth determines social position, chances for success, in addition to future breaks and governing power. We begin by discovering that random distribution of wealth doesn't mean equal distribution of wealth, nor does the free market tend to equalize wealth distribution. On the contrary, if anything, we find that it concentrates the wealth. From then on, the plot thickens, the rich get richer, the poor get comparatively poorer. Competition gets strong, selfish traits show up, people get frustrated with the game and skip class. (But you can hardly skip life!)†

Thus far we have dealt with the problem of terminology as related to simulations, and have provided examples of social simulations and simulation games. In the following section we shall consider reasons why simulations have gained widespread popularity among social studies teachers.

Why all the excitement about simulations?

Advocates of simulations speak of them with almost boundless enthusiasm. The professional literature brims with claims testifying to the effectiveness of

---

*R. Garry Shirts, Starpower (Del Mar, Calif.: Simile II, 1970), p. 1.

†Student of Thomas Kiljik, Minneapolis, Minnesota, grade 12, in Katherine Chapman and Jack E. Cousins, *Simulation/Games in Social Studies: A Report* (Boulder, Colo.: Social Science Education Consortium, 1974), p. 19.

the approach. Teachers who have used simulations consistently rank them among their most effective and stimulating teaching techniques. Why? What is it about simulations which has led to such widespread acceptance among teachers?

Among the values commonly claimed for simulations are that they:

. . . *are highly motivating*. By their very nature, simulations involve students actively in the learning process. They are taken out of the passive role commonly assigned them and are thrust into activities which command their attention and interest. Students usually respond to this challenge with enthusiasm. It is not totally clear what it is about simulations that is so appealing—excitement, novelty, suspense, competition, drama. Suffice it to say, however, that most students enjoy them and prefer them to most conventional classroom activities.

. . . help to *develop a sense of efficacy*. The school experience for many students is almost totally passive in nature. They are told, directed, required, drilled, tested, and graded. All too often they have little opportunity to exert positive, observable influence within their environment—to make things happen. It is no wonder that students commonly suffer a sense of powerlessness—a feeling that they have little control over their lives. Simulations alone cannot solve this problem, of course. They do invite student action, however, in such forms as negotiating, bargaining, planning, debating, and making decisions. In simulations students move from the role of passive recipients of other persons' decisions to that of causers of events.

. . . *encourage empathy*. The role-playing component of most simulations requires that students step into the shoes of others—that they assume new identities, frames of reference, and life-styles. As they confront problems they may never have encountered and frustrations they probably have never known as a part of their own life-styles, they begin to develop sensitivity for the feelings and aspirations of others.

. . . *foster the learning of content*. Simulations can help to bring clarity to abstract concepts by providing students with concrete examples and first-person experiences. Facts assume fresh meaning and importance as they are used to resolve problems and to make decisions. In simulations, content tends to be viewed in an integrated fashion, since the process being simulated is seldom limited to firm disciplinary boundaries.

. . . *teach group processes*. In nearly all simulations students interact with others to carry out their roles or to achieve their goals. Interaction may take many forms—caucusing, bargaining, debating, persuading, or consulting. A more open, natural classroom atmosphere usually results, and students are inclined to communicate more freely both with one another and with the teacher.

. . . *bring reality to the classroom*. One complaint about the social studies often voiced by students is that topics they study are divorced from the world in which they are living. Simulations alone cannot bridge this gap to reality, but they can help by bringing a taste of the outside world into the classroom. Historical events become more meaningful, political processes more understandable, and human nature more comprehensible as participants deal with simulated conditions and dilemmas with which they are faced.

. . . *develop inquiry skills*. Simulations are particularly well suited to involving students in inquiry. Rarely do simulations lead to predetermined, "right" answers to the problems they pose. Rather, participants become actively involved in decision making: stating problems, analyzing data, allocating resources, considering alternative strategies, and contemplating the consequences of their choices.

. . . *foster learning at diverse levels*. Through the judicious creation and assignment of roles, and the modification of objectives and rules, simulations can be geared for use with students with varying degrees of abilities and interests. Gifted students can participate at a level appropriate to them without having a detrimental effect on slower students, who can take part actively and constructively at their own pace. Many educators feel that the peer teaching that can result from such interaction is one of the greatest attributes of simulations.

In spite of the claims made for simulations and the enthusiasm with which they have been embraced by teachers, it is clear that they do not represent a solution to all of our instructional problems in the social studies. Critics point to the possibility that simulations can present an oversimplified view of reality, thus providing students with misinformation and misconceptions; that success in many simulations depends upon shrewdness and cleverness, thereby encouraging questionable values; that simulations are too time-consuming; and that simulations can diminish teachers' control over their classes. Those educators who are proponents of simulations feel that such problems can be minimized if simulations are carefully constructed and properly conducted.

It is sobering to realize that research measuring the effectiveness of simulations as teaching tools has been largely inconclusive. Findings seem to confirm that students are motivated by simulations and that they enjoy participating in them. There is little evidence, however, that simulations are more effective than other instructional approaches in teaching for critical thinking, attitude change, or the learning and retention of factual knowledge.* Considering the paucity of research, it appears that enthusiasm for simulations is generated more by "feel" and intuition than by hard evidence. Alice Kaplan Gordon pinpointed the dilemma by suggesting that "educators

---

*Cleo H. Cherryholmes, "Some Current Research on Effectiveness of Educational Simulations: Implications for Alternative Strategies," *American Behavioral Scientist* 10 (1966): pp. 4–8.

are in the ironic situation of having found an answer without knowing the question."*

In light of the lack of conclusive research in the field, it seems advisable to weigh the potential of simulations somewhat cautiously. Yet, perhaps research techniques have not yet been devised to measure accurately the true impact of the approach. Perhaps the claims made for simulations *are* valid. If they are—even if only some of them are—it appears that we have at our disposal a highly promising and exciting teaching tool, clearly worth giving a fair trial in the classroom. Let us turn our attention, then, to the designing and using of simulations.

Designing your own simulations

Hundreds of excellent simulations are currently being produced commercially, as indicated by the directory at the end of this chapter. There is no reason, however, why you cannot design effective simulations of your own. In fact, some experts in the field feel that designers of simulations learn significantly more about the processes being dealt with than do those who simply participate in them. This suggests the intriguing idea that the writing of simulations should involve not only teachers, but students as well. Although creating simulations is a time-consuming and demanding task, the home-grown varieties are advantageous in that they can be designed with specific local problems and circumstances in mind and can draw on the teacher's and the students' unique backgrounds and interests. As with any creative enterprise, writing simulations does not always follow a smooth, clearly defined progression; however, the following twelve basic steps can be identified:

Step one —Select the process to be focused on and the objectives to be achieved.
Step two —Analyze the components of the process to be simulated.
Step three —Determine the span of time to be covered by the simulation, its setting in time, and its geographic location.
Step four —Identify roles to be assumed.
Step five —Identify participants' objectives.
Step six —Identify participants' resources.
Step seven —Identify the sequence of action and the nature of interaction among the participants.
Step eight —Determine rules by which the simulation will operate.
Step nine —Establish scoring procedures and criteria for success.
Step ten —Determine the final form for presentation.

---

*Alice Kaplan Gordon, *Games for Growth* (Palo Alto, Calif.: Science Research Associates, 1970), p. 150.

Step eleven —Plan for debriefing.
Step twelve —Provide for a trial run and make needed changes.

In this section, each of the twelve basic steps will be considered separately. The RAILROAD GAME,* an example of a relatively simple simulation game, will be analyzed in step-by-step fashion to illustrate the application of the design procedures.

Step one—Select the process to be focused on and the objectives to be achieved. In the initial stage of planning, careful attention should be given to concepts and understandings to be learned, skills to be practiced, and values to be dealt with. The processes with which the social studies are concerned are primarily social, as opposed to those that are physical. Processes chosen for study should be selected with an eye toward the age, interests, abilities, and needs of the students involved, and should fit logically within the framework of the course.

> *Example*: The RAILROAD GAME was designed as a part of a unit entitled *The Railroad Era*, which deals with the development of the rail system in the United States in the 1860s and 1870s. The express purpose of the simulation game, according to its authors, is "to help students understand pressures of business competition and the various ways competitors can respond to a monopolistic buyer." It is anticipated that participants will increase their understanding of the competitive process involved in the expansion of the railroads, and will develop a broadened grasp of such concepts as public interest, cost, price, profit, and monopoly. In addition, issues relating to the right of the government to intervene in the affairs of business and the role of the government in protecting the welfare of the public are introduced.

Step two—Analyze the components of the process to be simulated. The process chosen for study should be capable of being abstracted and replicated with reasonable reliability, and sufficient data should be available to assure a sound investigation. The various components of the process should be identified and their interrelationships analyzed. Consider, for example: Who are the persons involved? What is the relative importance of their roles? Under what pressures are they functioning? What influences do they have on other people? What expertise do they bring to the attempt to resolve the issues at hand? What resources are available? On what bases are decisions normally made in cases such as this one? What are the underlying financial, political, and social forces at work?

---

*Description of and quotations from the RAILROAD GAME are reprinted with special permission granted by THE RAILROAD ERA, published by Xerox Education publications, © Xerox Corp., 1967.

Figure 3.2. Interrelationships in the RAILROAD GAME

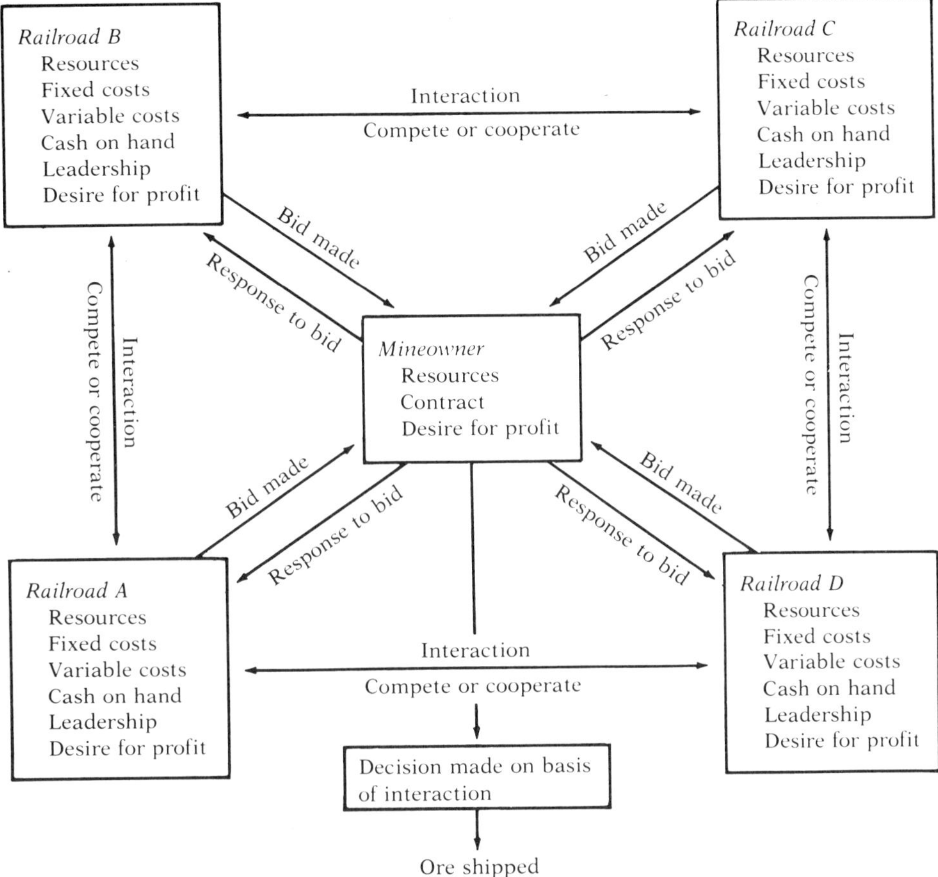

Bear in mind that the simulation is a *simplification* of reality, and cannot be a full duplication of real life. It should focus only on the essential conflicts and relationships of the process being simulated. To clutter the simulation with unneeded data would detract from the primary purpose of the exercise.

When identifying the components of the process and the various ways in which they interrelate, it is often helpful to sketch a model as shown in Figure 3.2.

> *Example*: The model of the competitive process upon which the RAILROAD GAME was developed involves economic relationships among a mineowner and four groups of railroad managers in Oretown. The mineowner is under contract with the millowner twenty miles away in Steeltown to deliver a minimum of twenty trainloads of iron ore each week. Each of the railroads is faced with

bidding for and winning the mineowner's business in an attempt to remain solvent and to earn a profit. The interrelationships involved in this process can be expressed by the paradigm in Figure 3.2. The model does not indicate *how* the various components of the simulation game will interact. It does imply, however, that interaction will occur in response to the competitive desire for profit. Obviously, the model is an abstraction that includes only those aspects of reality considered significant for purposes of the simulation game. It is the task of the designer in the succeeding steps to define further the interrelationships within the model and to assure reasonable validity through his structuring of the simulation game itself.

Step three—Determine the span of time to be covered by the simulation, its setting in time, and its geographic location. Decisions regarding such variables are dictated largely by the nature of the process being simulated. Some simulations are designed to represent a portion of a day, while others represent a span of time extending over many years. A simulation of the resolving of an issue growing out of a conflict in values among a group of adolescents, for example, might be limited to a time span of an hour or less. On the other hand, in a simulation of the development of long-range land-use patterns in an urban community, the span of time would necessarily be greater.

Likewise, decisions as to the setting in time and geographic location are dictated by the nature and purpose of the simulation. In some instances it may suffice merely to identify the time and place in general terms such as "England in the late eighteenth century" or "the capital of the hypothetical nation Zerbia in the year 2001." In other instances, when specific historical events are being simulated or when particular geographic, social, political, or economic processes are being studied, specificity becomes important. Precise time and place specifications, for example, would be made for a simulation of the meeting of the Constitutional Convention in Philadelphia in July 1776 or for a meeting of community, police, and government leaders in Los Angeles following the Watts riots in the summer of 1965.

"Overplanning" should be avoided at this stage. Whereas it is necessary to provide adequate parameters for the simulation, only essential elements should be focused on.

Example: The setting for the RAILROAD GAME is established simply as the United States sometime in the 1870s. Although this description may appear to be vague, since the focus of the simulation game is on business problems of that period rather than on specific conflicts involving particular railroads, the description is perfectly adequate. The time span covered is a period of seven days.

Step four—Identify roles to be assumed. This is a vital step in the planning of a simulation, and care taken here can help greatly to assure the validity and success of the exercise. Two basic tasks are involved: (1) the identification of the roles played by individuals or groups of people in the real world process being simulated, and (2) the defining and casting of roles in a way that assures the active meaningful participation of each student. Bear in mind that the nature and quality of the action in a simulation will be a reflection of the roles that have been identified and the manner in which they have been defined. Realism and believability are important. It is largely from the interaction of the roles that the desired problems and conflicts emerge; therefore, it is advisable when defining them to build in the personality characteristics, commitments, and values that assure the interaction required by the model.

Naturally, the number and nature of roles in a simulation will be predetermined to a great extent by the process being dealt with. In a simulation of a school board in the process of negotiating a contract with local teachers, for example, the following kinds of roles could realistically be included: school board members, administrators, teachers, representatives of teachers' organizations, parents, local politicians, persons from the media, and representatives of various pressure groups. Although many roles must be assumed by individual students, it is often possible to expand the number of participants by building group roles into the exercise. Examples of such roles could be: members of a Parent-Teachers Organization, groups of students, and members of pressure groups.

Example: The RAILROAD GAME can effectively be used by a class of from twelve to thirty-five students. The teacher assumes the role of the mineowner who is required to ship a minimum of twenty trainloads of iron ore per week from the mines in Oretown to the refineries in Steeltown. One student fills the role of clerk, while the remainder of the class divides into four groups to assume the management of Railroads A, B, C, and D.

Step five—Identify participants' objectives. Most simulations are developed around issues and problems involving a conflict of interests. It is important, therefore, that the participants clearly understand their objectives. Depending on the process being simulated, success may take many forms—the amassing of wealth, the election of a candidate, the accumulation of power, the prevention of war, the resolution of an issue, the marketing of a product, the passage of a bill, and so forth.

The very nature of simulation games dictates that competition be built into them. The objective is to win, and success is determined by winners' being recognized. Success in social simulations, however, might be achieved by all participants when, for example, an issue has been jointly resolved or a political platform has been unanimously agreed upon. In either format, a clear statement of objectives is required.

Example: In the RAILROAD GAME the primary objective of the mineowner is to maximize his profit by fulfilling his contract with the mills in Steeltown (twenty trainloads of ore to the mills each week) at the lowest possible cost to him. The mineowner makes a profit of about $500, minus transportation costs,

Figure 3.3. Resources in the RAILROAD GAME

Railroad 'A' Budget

Engines and Rolling Stock:
2 trains, each having 1 steam engine and 10 freight cars

Cash on Hand: $200

Fixed Costs:

	Cost per Day
Maintenance and replacement of capital equipment	$ 9.00
Interest on bonds	16.00
Principal on bonds	15.00
Common Stock dividends	10.00
Total Fixed Costs	$50.00

Variable Costs: (Paid when trains run.)

Crew wages (5 men at $2 a day each), per train	$10.00
Fuel and supplies, per train	10.00
Total Variable Costs	$20.00

Break-Even Chart: (Minimum charges needed to cover costs.)

Number of trains used:	ONE	TWO
Fixed Costs:	$50.00	$50.00
Variable Costs:	20.00	40.00
Total Costs:	$70.00	$90.00
Break-Even Point:	$70.00	$45.00

Railroad 'B' Budget

Engines and Rolling Stock:
2 trains, each having 1 steam engine and 10 freight cars

Cash on Hand: $200

Fixed Costs:

	Cost per Day
Maintenance and replacement of capital equipment	$ 9.00
Interest on bonds	16.00
Principal on bonds	15.00
Common Stock dividends	10.00
Total Fixed Costs	$50.00

Variable Costs: (Paid when trains run.)

Crew wages (5 men at $2 a day each), per train	$10.00
Fuel and supplies, per train	10.00
Total Variable Costs	$20.00

Break-Even Chart: (Minimum charges needed to cover costs.)

Number of trains used:	ONE	TWO
Fixed Costs:	$50.00	$50.00
Variable Costs:	20.00	40.00
Total Costs:	$70.00	$90.00
Break-Even Point:	$70.00	$45.00

---

for each trainload of ore shipped. The objective of each group of railroad managers is to earn a profit by contracting with the mineowner at the highest possible price to ship his ore to Steeltown. The winner among the railroad managers is the one who has earned the greatest profit by the completion of the simulation.

Step six—Identify participants' resources. Resources may range from tangible assets such as raw materials, land, or money to intangible assets such as political power, a formal education, or social status. The kind and amount of resources should approximate reasonably those that play a significant role in the functioning of the real world process. If the simulation is to be valid, there must be a logical relationship between the use or misuse of resources and the resulting consequences to the participants. Decisions must be made regarding the specific form resources will assume (points, dollars, acres, votes, etc.), as well as the manner in which they will be distributed among the participants. The nature and amount of resources assigned should, of

Railroad 'C' Budget

Engines and Rolling Stock:
3 trains, each having 1 steam engine and 10 freight cars

Cash on Hand: $240

Fixed Costs:

	Cost per Day
Maintenance and replacement of capital equipment	$12.00
Interest on bonds	15.00
Principal on bonds	13.00
Common Stock dividends	20.00
Total Fixed Costs	$60.00

Variable Costs: (Paid when trains run.)

Crew wages (5 men at $2 a day each), per train	$10.00
Fuel and supplies, per train	10.00
Total Variable Costs	$20.00

Break-Even Chart: (Minimum charges needed to cover costs.)

Number of trains:	ONE	TWO	THREE
Fixed Costs:	$60.00	$ 60.00	$ 60.00
Variable Costs:	20.00	40.00	60.00
Total Costs:	$80.00	$100.00	$120.00
Break-Even Point:	$80.00	$ 50.00	$ 40.00

Railroad 'D' Budget

Engines and Rolling Stock:
3 trains, each having 1 steam engine and 10 freight cars

Cash on Hand: $240

Fixed Costs:

	Cost per Day
Maintenance and replacement of capital equipment	$ 12.00
Interest on bonds	15.00
Principal on bonds	13.00
Common Stock dividends	20.00
Total Fixed Costs	$ 60.00

Variable Costs: (Paid when trains run.)

Crew wages (5 men at $2 a day each), per train	$ 10.00
Fuel and supplies, per train	10.00
Total Variable Costs	$ 20.00

Break-Even Chart: (Minimum charges needed to cover costs.)

Number of trains:	ONE	TWO	THREE
Fixed Costs:	$60.00	$ 60.00	$ 60.00
Variable Costs:	20.00	40.00	60.00
Total Costs:	$80.00	$100.00	$120.00
Break-Even Point:	$80.00	$ 50.00	$ 40.00

---

course, be consistent with the objectives and roles of the persons or groups being represented in the simulation.

> *Example*: The mineowner in the RAILROAD GAME has as his primary asset mines that can produce a maximum of five trainloads of ore per day. Significant to the strategy of the simulation game, he also possesses sufficient wagons for sending ore independently to Steeltown in case he cannot come to terms with any of the railroads. This method is crude, however, and the mineowner neither makes nor loses money when wagons are used.

The resources of each railroad are indicated by the budgets in Figure 3.3.

Step seven—Identify the sequence of action and the nature of interaction among the participants. It is essential to plot the flow of action in the simulation to assure that the sequence of activities is structured realistically and that the desired interaction will occur in logical order. Some simulations are more tightly structured than others, of course, depending upon the purposes of the teacher, the format used, and the nature of the process being simulated. Simulation games, for example, normally are highly structured, and the sequence of events is clearly predetermined by the rules. On the other hand, a social simulation of a political convention would likely be much less tightly organized, and would probably incorporate a healthy dosage of spontaneity. A useful technique at this stage is to trace step by step on paper the anticipated action and all potential reactions. Mapping out the sequence in this manner provides a visual overview of the simulation and helps in eliminating unnecessary "dead spots" during which participants are inactive and in checking the validity of the simulation.

Although it is impossible to pattern the sequence of activity in a simulation exactly after the real world model, it is well to approximate the original as closely as possible. This is particularly true when the sequence itself is an important component of the process. An example might be the series of events and decisions involved in passing a bill through Congress to its ultimate culmination as a law.

Example: The sequence of action in the RAILROAD GAME is described below.

A. Mineowner posts the number of trains of ore he would like to ship on the first day. He may ship only part of the number posted if he feels the bids are too high.

B. Mineowner goes separately to each of the four railroads once to bargain with them in an attempt to get the lowest bid for carrying the ore. The final price offered by each railroad must be written down on a slip of paper.

C. Mineowner may return to any or all of the four railroads to give them information, accurate or inaccurate, about the bids submitted by other railroads. The mineowner may do this in an effort to get even better prices. Each railroad may submit revised bids in writing if the managers think it desirable to do so.

D. Mineowner announces which railroad gets how much business and pays the railroad or railroads the amount of money due to each. He does *not* announce how much money changes hands or what the winning bid was. At this point, the mineowner's clerk tallies the cost, income, and cash balance of each railroad on the tally sheet provided.

E. Each railroad has two kinds of expenses, fixed costs and variable costs, listed on its expense sheet. Fixed costs include such items as maintenance of equipment, interest on bonds, principal on bonds, and stock dividends. Variable costs include crew wages, fuel, water, and supplies. These costs depend on how many trains a railroad uses. Thus they are payable only if a railroad gets some business in a day. Each railroad must subtract all costs from its cash accounts at the end of each round.

F. If at any point a railroad cannot make a required payment, it is considered to be bankrupt and is eliminated from the game.

G. After each round, one representative from each railroad may meet with representatives from other railroads to discuss the prices they will bid for the next round, and other matters of competition. Each railroad sends a representative only if it wishes to do so.

H. Return to step A and begin the next round.

Step eight—Determine rules by which the simulation will operate. When designing the operating rules for a simulation, it is essential to bear in mind the interaction you are hoping to achieve among participants. With that focus in mind, constraints on the participants can be drawn up that will maximize the chances of the interaction's occurring and will minimize the chances that the exercise will veer into irrelevant tangents. When possible and practical, the rules should approximate limitations that exist in the real world process.

It would be practically impossible to identify and regulate all alternative actions. Logical constraints operating in the process being simulated can be identified, however, and they can usually be incorporated into the exercise. For example, in a simulation involving Quakers, violence should not be built in as a realistic option for that group. Similarly, other groups may be limited by other realities—lack of political power, shortage of natural resources, climate, lack of wealth, age limitations, size of population, and so forth. Once such realities and constraints have been discovered, the rules should be written to reflect as accurately as possible their importance in the functioning of the process in the real world.

In constructing the rules, it is helpful to run through each of the roles mentally, envisioning the decisions and choices of action open to each participant, and looking for possible loopholes, contradictions, and areas of confusion. When weaknesses in the rules have been identified, troublesome sections should be rewritten until a workable set of restraints emerges. In the final version, the rules should be stated in simple, straightforward language, and they should be as few in number as possible.

During this stage of planning it is well to decide how conflicts among participants will be dealt with and how appeals to justice will be handled. The teacher or a student, for example, may be established as the ultimate source of authority, ruling on appeals as they arise. When appropriate a chance factor can be built into the simulation through the use of dice, chance cards, or a spinner. A spinner such as the one in Figure 3.4, for example, can be easily constructed out of scraps of plastic, wood, or cardboard at little or no expense.

> *Example*: The following rules for the RAILROAD GAME not only serve to govern the participants, but also set the stage for the action that will follow.
>
> Four Railroads run between Oretown and Steeltown. The four independent lines compete for the business of carrying ore from the mines in Oretown to the mills in Steeltown.
>
> The class divides into four groups. These groups take the parts of the managers of the four railroads. The competitive "game" the groups will play is divided into rounds. Each round represents one business day.
>
> [*Editor's Note*: Rules make easier reading after the game begins. Don't try to memorize all the rules at the start. Skim the rules first for general understanding. Then refer back to the rules as play goes on. Play the game, don't talk about it at great length before starting.]

Figure 3.4. Spinner

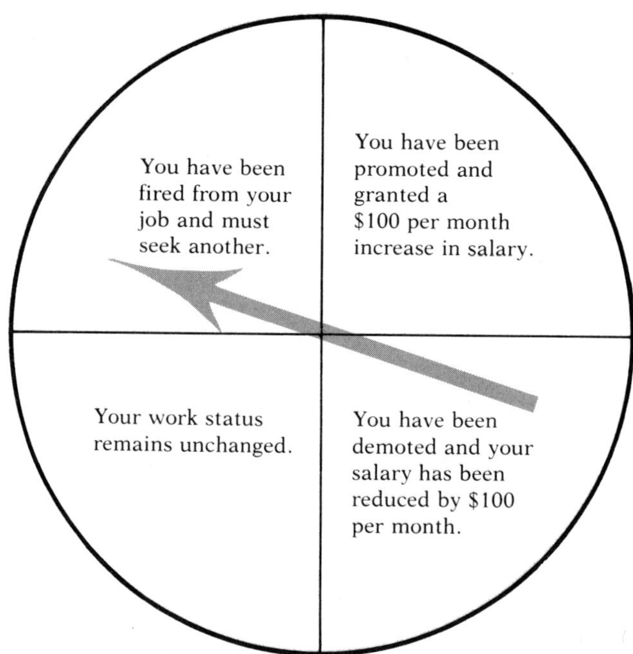

The railroads bid each day (round) for that day's business. The mineowner (teacher) each day awards the job of carrying all or part of the output of the mine to whichever railroad or railroads he wishes. Presumably, business goes to the railroad or railroads that bid the lowest. The winner of the game is the railroad that makes the most money.

All trains consist of one engine and ten ore cars. Railroad A has two available trains. Railroad B has two available trains. Railroad C has three available trains. Railroad D has three available trains. No engine can pull more than ten cars; no money can be saved by using fewer than ten cars.

Each railroad has a break-even point, determined by the fixed costs and variable costs it must pay from its income. The railroads have already cut these costs as far as they can. These costs are shown on the separate expense tables given to each railroad by the teacher. At the start of the competition, each railroad keeps its business information secret from the other railroads.

Each railroad must submit a bid for the day's business. The bid should, ideally, be high enough on each day's shipment to meet costs and make a profit, yet low enough to get the contract for the shipment if possible. A railroad's bid may vary according to the number of trains the mineowner will use.

The mineowner has a contract with the millowner in Steeltown. The round trip run by train takes a full day. The contract says that the mine must ship a minimum of 20 trainloads to the mill each week (seven rounds). The most the mine can produce is five trainloads of ore a day.

In other words, the mineowners must send at least 20 trainloads a week, but cannot send more than 35 trainloads a week.

The mineowner, if he cannot come to terms at all with any railroad, can send ore to Steeltown in wagons he owns. But this method is crude. The mine neither makes profit nor loses money by using wagons—but the mineowner wants to make a profit.

For the mineowner

Your mining business obviously has an advantageous position in relation to the four competing railroads.

Your firm makes a profit of about $500, minus transportation costs, for each trainload of ore.

The railroads are disadvantaged by their competitive situation. They have cut their costs as far as possible. If necessary, you can continue operating at the break-even point with wagon deliveries much longer than they can endure. The pressures of the railroads' competition against each other, however, should make it unlikely that you would have to use wagons for any long period.

In spite of your advantages, you should take every opportunity to maximize your profit by driving the cost of transportation down to the railroads' break-even point, or even below it if you can bargain hard enough. (One exception: You want the railroad competition to continue because you benefit from it. What might happen to you if one railroad were to achieve a monopoly? Thus you may decide at some point to award business to a railroad that is not the low bidder but appears to be on the verge of failing.)

Step nine—Establish scoring procedures and criteria for success. Success in a simulation should be determined by the degree to which the participants have achieved their objectives. Success can assume many forms, ranging from the prevention of war to the delivery of votes for a political candidate. Due to the competitive nature of simulation games, they invariably include means for determining winners and losers. This usually is done through scoring procedures that reflect the success or failure of each participant or group of participants. When simulation games involve a rather simple objective such as accumulating money, scoring is a fairly uncomplicated process. When different participants have different objectives, however, the process is more complicated. In those instances it is well to devise a method of conversion by which achievements are evaluated comparatively and are translated into a point system.

Since there are no winners and losers in social simulations, other means must be developed for evaluating the participants' actions. The most promising approach seems to be a post simulation analysis in which participants openly discuss the degree to which individuals and group objectives were achieved and jointly evaluate the quality of decision making and actions taken during the simulation.

Example: Since the basic objective of all of the participants in the RAILROAD GAME is to earn a profit, the winners are those who at the completion of the

Table 3.1
Tally sheet A

Mineowner	Round	1	2	3	4	5	6
Number of Trainloads	Posted						
	Sent						
	Required to Meet Contract						
Contract Awarded	Winning Bid						
	Company Awarded Bid						

Tally sheet B

Railroads	Round	1	2	3	4	5	6
	Cash on Hand	200					
	+ Day's Income						
Railroad "A"	Total Cash						
2 Trains	− Fixed Costs	50	50	50	50	50	50
	− Variable Costs: $20/Train						
	Total Costs						
	New Cash Balance						

exercise have accumulated the most cash. Tally sheets such as those in Table 3.1 are provided with the simulation game to facilitate record keeping. Tally sheet A can be copied onto a chalkboard so that the entire class can be apprised of overall developments as they occur. Each railroad is provided with a record-keeping form similar to Tally Sheet B.

Step ten—Determine the final form for presentation. Throughout the planning of a simulation you probably will have in mind a rough idea of the form the exercise ultimately will assume. At this stage of planning, however, the simulation begins to assume a polished form, and final questions must be resolved regarding the format to be used. One basic decision, of course, is whether the purposes of the exercise will best be served by a social simulation or a simulation game, and whether it should be of the all-human or human-machine variety. The nature of the process being simulated bears heavily on the decision. Generally speaking, processes involving a great deal of interaction among people but which do not have a competitive dimension are best suited to the social simulation. When the process being modeled involves interaction of a heavily competitive nature, the simulation game tends to be more appropriate.

Instructions for participants should now be completed, role descriptions refined, and final decisions made regarding required space, time, and equipment. Decisions must also be made regarding the manner in which the exercise will be initiated. Most simulations are introduced to the participants through the use of a scenario—a description which provides background for the problems to be studied and sets the stage for the action that is to follow. The scenario need not be elaborate and should include *only* information needed to assure a common understanding among the participants and to launch the activity effectively.

> *Example*: Since the RAILROAD GAME presents an operating model of a social process in which competition plays a significant role, it can be categorized as a simulation game. Participants need relatively little information other than the railroad budgets and the tally sheets prior to starting the activity. In fact, they are advised in the student guide merely to skim the rules prior to playing the game and not to talk about it at great length before starting. The scenario for the RAILROAD GAME is rather simple and to the point—" 'Railroad competition was bitter in the 1870s. Could you have met its tough demands? This "game" —simulating a real-life business problem—puts you on your mettle in meeting the challenges that faced railroad managers.' "

Step eleven—Plan for debriefing. A postsimulation debriefing is vital to the success of the approach. The purpose of the debriefing is to summarize and analyze the experience and to discover the implications it holds for dealing with the real world. Questions raised in the debriefing should be closely related to the objectives established for the exercise. Although it is impossible to predict ahead of time the exact focus the analysis will assume, during the planning it is well to give some thought to the type of follow-up experiences that would seem most appropriate.

Normally the debriefing assumes the form of a discussion in which several things occur: participants summarize and analyze their perceptions of what occurred during the exercise; strategies and decisions are reviewed and evaluated; interactions among participants are reconstructed and analyzed; motivations are analyzed; and the uses of resources are evaluated. Occasionally case studies are used in the debriefing to "stretch" the students' newly found insights and to have them apply in a new setting the knowledge they have gained from participating in the simulation.

At some point during the debriefing, students should compare the simulated process with that of the real world. Similarities and differences should be identified, and if significant distortions have occurred, they should be discussed and accounted for. Finally, the students should evaluate the simulation exercise itself and recommend changes that make the approach more effective.

> *Example*: Although the following suggestions for debriefing that appear in the teacher's guide to the RAILROAD GAME are rather limited, they do provide some focus for the follow-up discussion: "In discussing the game after playing it, the teacher can raise at least two issues: competition and possible responses to it; and the legitimacy and enforcement of contracts. If the students had become involved in the game, and if they responded strongly to one team's breaking the pool or the mineowner's breaking a contract, it may, in fact, be best to start with the specific issue of cheating and the breaking of promises. It has been found that students can objectively discuss what they have learned only after this issue is resolved."

Step twelve—Provide for a trial run and make needed changes. It is advisable to postpone writing the final version of the simulation until after it has been subjected to at least one trial run in the classroom. After the run-through, the students themselves can analyze the experience and provide invaluable feedback regarding the effectiveness and validity of the simulation. Necessary changes can then be made in the sequence of action, role descriptions, the allocation of sources, rules, etc. Difficulties confronted in administrating the simulation should also be noted, and suggestions for dealing with them should be written up and made available to other teachers who may use the technique. Of course, simulations, like any other teaching method, should be subject to constant review and revision.

Using simulations in the classroom

Setting the stage

Before introducing a simulation, make certain that students have adequate background for studying the process to be simulated. It may be advisable to assign and discuss background readings and to involve students in preliminary research. If at all possible, the simulation should "emerge" logically and naturally from the lead-up study so that students view it in accurate perspective.

The simulation is normally introduced a day or so before the exercise is launched. Rules, the scenario, background data, and role profiles should be issued to the students so that they can study them before the simulation begins. Keep in mind that the simulation is to be used by a specific group of students in a specific setting, and that the experience should be geared to their capabilities and interests. Don't hesitate to adjust the rules when appropriate, or alter the exercise to make it more relevant and meaningful.

At the beginning of the first session of the simulation several minutes are usually devoted to a final briefing in which rules are reviewed, roles are clarified, and the sequence of action is explained. One tendency to be avoided is overintroduction. Rules in simulations, as in most games, are much more difficult to comprehend prior to their being used; therefore, it is advisable to get into the exercise as quickly as possible with the assumption that the rules will clarify as the simulation proceeds. After making any needed physical arrangements (locations to represent geographical areas, etc.), and after quickly dealing with any unanswered questions, the simulation is ready to begin.

Supervising the simulation

Effective supervision of a simulation demands that you be thoroughly familiar with its rules and procedures. It is advisable to run through the simulation several times in your mind prior to conducting it "live," and to try to anticipate questions and conflicts that might arise when students participate. It is almost impossible to foresee *all* potential problems, however, and at some points during the exercise you must rely on your creativity and imagination when dealing with unexpected situations. If you have the purposes of the simulation thoroughly in mind and are familiar with the various dimensions of the social process being studied, you should be able to react to unexpected questions quickly and effectively without distorting the exercise.

Time keeping, record keeping, and scoring chores occasionally must be handled during the simulation, and you must decide ahead of time how these will be managed. Although on occasion you may choose to fill such roles yourself, they can usually be handled effectively by students.

In some simulations you may assume an assigned role and participate in the exercise along with your students. Depending upon the nature of the role, such involvement can be effective; however, you should be careful not to dominate the simulation to the point where you inhibit the actions and decisions of the students. Normally, you will operate most effectively by circulating about the room, observing negotiations, responding to questions, providing advice when it is needed, and generally orchestrating the exercise.

Conducting the debriefing

Experts in the field generally agree that the most significant learning payoff of a simulation usually comes with the debriefing. During this stage of the exercise the students reflect upon the total experience, analyzing their own actions and those of their peers, and attempting to comprehend what happened and why it occurred. The debriefing provides the students the opportunity to clarify and expand upon the process that has been studied and to consider the implications of their findings.

Ron Stadsklev suggests that fruitful procedures for debriefing can be based upon the "EIAG" (E-experience, I-identify, A-analyze, G-generalize) experimental learning model. Accordingly, he recommends the following steps for consideration:

1. EXPERIENCE—This comes before debriefing, of course, but there are questions for the teacher: Why did you choose the game experience for this class for this

particular learning? Are you doing your own thing? Teaching decision-making? Simulating a life experience through a simulation game? Helping students cope with their environment? Trying to achieve a specific learning objective?

2. IDENTIFY—Specifically, what are you trying to do in the debriefing process? Look for the facts? Explain the symbolism in the game? Surface feelings and reactions? Generate data? (Questions for students which can be used in this step: What do you think this represents in real life? What made you feel good or bad during the game? What did you feel was the most significant thing that happened? What are the factors that explain your low score (or high score)? How did you feel when . . . ? What did you say when . . . ? What did he do when you . . . ?)
3. ANALYZE—What are you, the teacher, asking the students to analyze? Outcomes from the game? Cause and effect relationships? Alternative decisions and strategies? (Questions which can be used to stimulate student analysis: What problems did you face and how did you attempt to meet them? How were you affected by this event? What relationships do you see in these data? Why did events, actions, or strategies result in . . . ? Why did these feelings or attitudes develop?)
4. GENERALIZE—What are you, the teacher, hoping the students have learned? Check back with the goals or objectives you listed in No. 1. These steps for the student are useful in the generalizing process:
   a. Review specific roles, events, and interaction in the game experience that led to a conclusion. Specificity is necessary.
   b. Compare that conclusion to what the student thinks real life is.
   c. Search for "real life" data that support or disprove the conclusion (or conclusions).*

Although you will usually assume a more dominant role in the debriefing than you did during the simulation, bear in mind that your primary task is to aid the students in analyzing and appraising their own actions and decisions—not to insist that they now come up with heretofore elusive "right" answers.

Evaluation of student growth resulting from participating in a simulation is another important follow-up activity. Helpful suggestions for evaluating in this area are provided in chapter 7, pp. 276–325.

The role of the teacher in using simulations

To a great extent, the degree to which a simulation proves to be an effective teaching-learning tool will be a reflection of your attitude regarding the experience and the manner in which you perceive and carry out your role. If you view the simulation as little more than a break from the textbook and consider it to be simply a version of entertainment, it is predictable that your

*Ron Stadsklev, "A Basic Model for Debriefing," *Simulation/Gaming/News* 1 (1973); p. 6.

students will respond in kind. On the other hand, if you use the simulation to extend beyond the textbook and to involve students in the dynamics of problem solving and decision making, chances are they will respond positively and enthusiastically. By the same token, if you assume the role of purveyor of truth and defender of absolute quiet and order in the classroom, the simulation will probably have little chance of succeeding. Not that simulations should be accompanied by total chaos and confusion—no responsible teacher wants that. However, since simulations almost always require a great deal of interaction among students, the noise level of classes using them will naturally be a bit higher than usual—a small price to pay for students' becoming caught up in the business of learning. This does not imply that you abandon your responsibility as the instructional leader. Rather it suggests that when using simulations you move off center stage and assume a role in which you encourage questioning and support experimentation. To do this effectively, it is essential that you create an atmosphere within which the students feel free to share ideas, to debate, and to move about both physically and intellectually.

In underscoring the importance of the role of the teacher who uses educational games (simulations), Alice Kaplan Gordon makes the following suggestions:

> The key is willpower.
>
> 1. Resist the temptation to correct minor errors.
> 2. Resist the temptation to offer a better strategy that the student does not perceive.
> 3. Resist the temptation to test or review, in minute detail, students' understanding of the rules or roles of the game.
> 4. Resist the temptation to correct any elaboration or alteration of the rules of the game.
> 5. Resist the temptation to keep perfect order. The noise level produced by thirty students talking at the same time need not exceed human tolerance.
> 6. Resist the temptation to stymie any points that seem to be irrelevant to the discussion. They often prove to be relevant; at worst, they will be brief digressions.
> 7. Resist the temptation to constrain the moderate physical movement a game may require.
> 8. Resist the temptation to answer students' questions about the game with that's not in the rules.
> 9. Resist the temptation to avoid admitting lack of knowledge about a point of the games' operation, or an aspect of the process under study.
> 10. Resist the temptation to consider a game a less serious form of education than a textbook.*

*From *Games for Growth* by Alice Kaplan Gordon. © Science Research Associates, Inc. Reprinted by permission of the publisher.

Words of caution

If you decide to use simulations in your teaching, you should go into them with your eyes open. Whereas they clearly appear to be powerful teaching tools, they also have their limitations.

The time factor

Simulations demand a commitment of time that obviously could be used for other learning activities. Classroom time is needed for such matters as introducing the simulation; organizing the class into groups; filling out forms; distributing such materials as maps, chance cards, budgets, spinners, and dice; assigning roles; and, of course, conducting the simulation and leading the debriefing. In addition, before launching the simulation you will need to devote time outside the classroom to digesting the rules of the exercise and to conducting at least one dry run.

Not all simulations are elaborate and extensive, of course, and many can be completed in two or three class periods. Yet, properly conducted, simulations are time-demanding activites. You should recognize and weigh this factor when considering whether you will use them.

The cost factor

Many simulations can be bought quite reasonably, often for less than $10.00 per kit. The price of many others, however, would strain the average school's social studies budget, ranging from $50 to $300. Furthermore, although simulations can be used time after time with different groups of students, they eventually do wear out. In the meantime, pieces are sometimes lost and must be replaced, and consumable forms such as budget sheets must be replenished.

The financial status of your social studies department may rule out your using expensive simulations. The same purposes often can be accomplished, however, with a more modest version, or you might consider designing your own. In the long run, the cost factor should be considered in light of the potential of simulations as teaching tools.

The management factor

At first glance, simulating often appears to be a rather messy business. Typically, students talk and move about, often arguing, debating, and creating a din that sometimes spills into the hall. The classroom commonly appears to be in disarray. Students' desks are awry, and the area surrounding the teacher's desk is no longer considered sacred territory. To the untrained eye such activity may be viewed as irresponsible and disruptive. To the trained eye, it may be seen as productive, student-oriented learning at its best. Not that simulations lead to chaos. They don't—or shouldn't. Yet, intensive student involvement often results in a higher level of noise than more traditional activities.

When planning a simulation, if you sense that it will "turn your students on," it is well to prepare the administrators and neighboring teachers for the activity, and to assure them ahead of time that you will remain firmly in control of your classes.

Logistical problems also must be attended to. It may be necessary to make arrangements to meet in the school cafeteria or in another classroom conducive to simulation activities. Furniture may need to be arranged, appropriate forms duplicated, and visual displays organized. If the simulation is a particularly complicated one, you may have to rely on the help of a fellow teacher to conduct it. If this is the case, you'll need time to review the rules with that teacher and to clarify the responsibilities you both will assume.

In short, the successful management of a simulation requires careful planning and attention to detail. Is it worth the bother? That is a decision only you can make for yourself. It is our judgment that it is.

Summary

The state of the art of simulation clearly appears to be a healthy one. Upon reading the writings produced by serious thinkers in the field, one is convinced of the potential of the approach and of the likelihood that a body of sound supporting theory will continue to develop. The near-frantic pace at which simulations have been produced recently will predictably decrease. As the approach loses some of its novelty, simulations probably will be accepted as simply one of many effective teaching techniques available to the social studies teacher. It seems clear that simulations are here to stay, and teachers seeking a method to enliven their instruction would do well to pay them heed.

In this chapter we have attempted to deal with the problem of terminology in the simulation field, have suggested reasons for the widespread enthusiasm for the approach, and have considered procedures for designing simulations and using them in teaching. It has been our intent to develop a broader understanding of simulations, and through that understanding to lead to their more enlightened use. Discrimination in selecting simulations is essential. To use a simulation casually simply because it happens to be on the social studies shelf is to prostitute the approach. Simulations should be used judiciously, and should be selected with an eye toward the interests, abilities, and backgrounds of the students involved.

The following section includes descriptions of a wide variety of simulations appropriate for every subject in secondary social studies.

Sources and descriptions of selected simulations

The fifty-one simulations briefly described following provide a mere sampling of those currently available for use in the social studies. The simulations were selected because of their demonstrated popularity and because they are broadly representative in terms of subject matter, sophistication, complexity, format, and cost. The copyright date can be found in parentheses following the title of the simulation. Information regarding subject, grade level, number of participants, and time required is approximate, and is subject to interpretation depending on local circumstances. The cost of each item is listed as of summer 1975. Due to the continuing inflationary trend, however, changes in prices can be expected, and it would be wise to check current prices with the publisher before ordering. Addresses of the sources are listed at the end of this section.

CAMPAIGN (1970)

Subject: Civics, government
Grade level: Junior high, senior high
Number of participants: 16–40
Time required: 10–15 hours
Cost: $142.50
Source: Instructional Simulations, Inc.

Deals with the nomination and election of state legislators within a two-party system. Participants plan strategies designed to produce a winning political campaign. Dimensions of the political process that are focused on include precinct workers, pressure groups, nominating conventions, political platforms, speech making, vote switching, and news coverage.

CLUG (Community Land Use Game) (1972)

Subject: Economics, urban development
Grade level: Senior high
Number of participants: 3–30
Time required: 3–20 hours
Cost: $5.50 per participant
Source: Free Press

Designed to teach principles of urban and regional economics. Participants, assuming the roles of private entrepreneurs, are faced with making decisions regarding property assessments, tax rates, land use, employment, prices, and trade agreements.

CONFLICT (1974)

Subject: International relations, government
Grade level: Senior high
Number of participants: 24–42
Time required: 6 hours
Cost: $50.00 (A do-it-yourself kit is available for $7.50)
Source: Simile II

Designed to stimulate participants to consider various alternatives for achieving world order. The simulation is set in the future, and students, representing various nations, attempt to resolve a conflict resulting from the violation of a disarmament agreement.

CONSUMER (1969)

Subject:	Economics, consumer education
Grade level:	Junior high, senior high
Number of participants:	11–34
Time required:	2–6 hours
Cost:	$30.00
Source:	Bobbs-Merrill Company

Simulates an economic setting in which goods are offered for sale for cash or credit. Participants assume the roles of consumers, credit agents, or salesmen. Decisions must be made regarding credit, interest rates, the value of products, contracts, collateral, and repossession.

CRISIS (1966)

Subject:	International relations
Grade level:	Junior high, senior high
Number of participants:	18–36
Time required:	2–6 hours
Cost:	$25.00 for a 25-student kit; $50.00 for a 35-student kit
Source:	Simile II

Simulates an international crisis among six nations faced with resolving an explosive incident in a strategic mining area. Each nation is challenged to secure control of the mine's resources while avoiding armed conflict. Through debate, the building of alliances, written communications, and the formation of policies, participants develop a greater sensitivity to the complexities of international relations.

CULTURE CONTACT (1969)

Subject:	Anthropology, sociology
Grade level:	Junior high, senior high
Number of participants:	20–30
Time required:	2–4 hours
Cost:	$36.50
Source:	Games Central

Highlights misunderstandings that can occur when peoples of two widely differing cultures come into contact. Participants assume various roles within the two cultures and attempt to achieve their goals while facing intercultural barriers such as language, different forms of government, and conflicting values.

DANGEROUS PARALLEL (1969)

Subject:	International relations, government
Grade level:	Senior high
Number of participants:	18–36

Time required: 5 hours
Cost: $60.00
Source: Scott, Foresman and Company

Simulates events at the outbreak of the Korean War. Participants assume ministerial roles in six imaginary nations and attempt to resolve a conflict between two neighboring small nations. The exercise focuses on the relationships between international decision making and the consequences that are a result of those decisions.

DEMOCRACY (1969)

Subject: Government
Grade level: Junior high, senior high
Number of participants: 6–11
Time required: 2–4 hours
Cost: $8.00
Source: Bobbs-Merrill Company

Illustrates the decision-making process in a representative democracy. The total simulation is composed of eight games, which develop from simple to complex. Participants, assuming at various times the roles of citizens and legislators, learn through this simulation to recognize the necessity of negotiation and compromise in government.

DESTINY (1969)

Subject: History
Grade level: Junior high, senior high
Number of participants: 25–40
Time required: 15–30 hours
Cost: $12.00
Source: INTERACT

Involves the interaction among six factions involved in the Cuban crisis of 1898: Spanish diplomats, the Cubans, newspapermen, businessmen, imperialists, and anti-imperialists. Participants assume the position of assigned factions and attempt to influence presidential decisions regarding the crisis.

DIG (1969)

Subject: Anthropology, history
Grade level: Junior high, senior high
Number of participants: 14–36
Time required: 15–30 hours
Cost: $12.00
Source: INTERACT

Requires that participants working in teams assume the roles of archeologists excavating and analyzing artifacts created by hypothetical civilizations. The exercise stresses the interrelationship of economics, government, family structure, language, religion, and recreation.

DIRTY WATER (1970)

Subject: Ecology
Grade level: Junior high, senior high
Number of participants: 2–10
Time required: 1–3 hours
Cost: $10.00
Source: Damon Educational Division

Focuses on problems related to ecological balance and water pollution. Participants assume the role of water pollution control officials who are responsible for stocking a lake. The challenge is to avoid polluting the lake by avoiding overpopulation, managing finances efficiently, and avoiding possible upstream contamination. (Board game.)

DISUNIA (1968)

Subject: American history, government
Grade level: Junior high, senior high
Number of participants: 20–35
Time required: 20–30 hours
Cost: $12.00
Source: INTERACT

Approximates problems faced by Americans during the Revolutionary period, 1731–1789. Participants assume the roles of representatives of seven states on a new planet in 2087. Problems to be dealt with are concerned with the achievement of economic and political stability and military security.

DIVISION (1968)

Subject: History
Grade level: Senior high
Number of participants: 18–36
Time required: 20–30 hours
Cost: $12.00
Source: INTERACT

Deals with problems confronting the United States in the 1850s. Participants study issues that divided the country at that time, focusing on the election of 1860. Electoral bargaining, multiple causation, and the complexities of political compromise are at the heart of the simulation.

ECOLOGY (1970)

Subject: Ecology and history
Grade level: Junior high
Number of participants: 2–4
Time required: 1–3 hours
Cost: $10.00 (deluxe); $7.00 (smaller version)
Source: Damon Educational Division

Illustrates the relationship between man's activities and his natural environment. Participants attempt to achieve a workable balance among population, technology, and the natural environment. Four stages of man's development are focused on: hunting, agricultural, industrial, and environmental. (Board game.)

ECONOMIC SYSTEM (1969)

Subject:	Economics (contemporary economic problems)
Grade level:	Junior high, senior high
Number of participants:	7–15
Time required:	2–6 hours
Cost:	$25.00
Source:	Bobbs-Merrill Company

Simulates a competitive economic system, and focuses on the interrelationship among various elements in the system—mineowners, manufacturers, workers, and farmers. Participants assume roles and simulate the production, marketing, and consumption of goods while attempting to operate profitably and maintain a high standard of living.

EMPIRE, GAME OF (1970)

Subject:	American history (colonial period, international trade)
Grade level:	Junior high, senior high
Number of participants:	15–36
Time required:	4–5 hours
Cost:	$76.00
Source:	Denoyer-Geppert Company

Demonstrates the economic circumstances faced by the American colonists as a part of the British Empire in 1745. Participants assume the roles of London merchants, New England merchants, European merchants, Colonial farmers, Southern planters, and British West Indian planters. The objective is to trade one's own products advantageously so as to obtain needed products not manufactured or grown locally.

FARMING, THE GAME OF (1969)

Subject:	Geography, history
Grade level:	Senior high
Number of participants:	10–30
Time required:	4–6 hours
Cost:	$29.95 (manual may be purchased for $1.20)
Source:	The Macmillan Company, School Division

Exposes participants to factors that influenced decisions made by farmers in western Kansas during three different periods, beginning in 1888. Decisions must be made regarding production and investment.

FLIP (1970)

Subject:	Economics (consumer education, marketing)
Grade level:	Junior high, senior high
Number of participants:	1–40
Time required:	3–5 hours

Cost:	$47.50
Source:	Instructional Simulations Incorporated

Deals with budgeting, life-style, credit management, payment schedules, investment programs, purchase options, and income management. Participants encounter realistic economic problems.

GENERATION GAP (1969)

Subject:	Sociology (human relations)
Grade level:	Junior high, senior high
Number of participants:	4–6
Time required:	1–3 hours
Cost:	$15.00
Source:	Bobbs-Merrill Company

Simulates the interaction between a parent and an adolescent son or daughter as they face conflicts that commonly arise between parents and teenagers. A basic purpose is to develop better understanding and appreciation for the complexities involved in resolving conflicts within a family.

GHETTO (1969)

Subject:	Sociology, economics (contemporary, urban problems)
Grade level:	Junior high, senior high
Number of participants:	10–20
Time required:	5–7 hours
Cost:	$24.00
Source:	Bobbs-Merrill Company

Designed primarily to introduce students of middle and higher socioeconomic groups to problems and pressures encountered by the urban poor. Participants assume roles of fictional persons and allocate their time among several alternatives: work, play, school, hustling (crime), passing time, and neighborhood improvement. Participants should come to understand how neighborhood conditions affect them personally and how they might be improved.

GRAND STRATEGY (1970)

Subject:	History, government (international relations)
Grade level:	Senior high
Number of participants:	10–30
Time required:	1–2 hours
Cost:	$31.50
Source:	Games Central

Explores the political, diplomatic, and military exchange among ten western countries during World War I. Participants are organized into nation teams that attempt to achieve their political goals with a minimum of economic and military cost.

HERSTORY (1972)

Subject:	Social studies, sociology, marriage and the family, women's studies

Grade level:	Junior high, senior high
Number of participants:	20–40
Time required:	25–35 hours
Cost:	$12.00
Source:	INTERACT

Focuses on sexual roles and varying life-styles in American society. Male and female participants are paired by chance and simulate marital experiences, including performing domestic tasks, working professionally, getting divorced, and occasionally remarrying. Participants are encouraged to reexamine the assumptions they make about sexual roles, and to reflect on their own goals and expectations.

HUMANUS (1973)

Subject:	Future studies, human relations, psychology, sociology
Grade level:	Junior high, senior high
Number of participants:	5–7
Time required:	2–5 hours
Cost:	$10.00
Source:	Simile II

Simulates problems faced by members of a "survival cell," the only known survivors of a worldwide catastrophe. The objective of the group is to insure continued human existence through their link with the outside world, a "survival computer" called Humanus. Crucial decisions must be made that require participants to explore their assumptions about the nature of people, the nature of society, relationships among people, and the process of change.

IMPACT (1969)

Subject:	Community action
Grade level:	Junior high, high school
Number of participants:	20–40
Time required:	15–25 hours
Cost:	$162.50
Source:	Instructional Simulations, Inc.

Demonstrates the roles of power, social status, and prestige in decision making in a community. Participants assume roles of community members who are confronted with a wide variety of problems they are required to resolve.

INNER-CITY PLANNING (1971)

Subject:	Political science, sociology, contemporary urban problems
Grade level:	Senior high
Number of participants:	12–40
Time required:	6–8 hours
Cost:	$16.80
Source:	The Macmillan Company, School Division

Develops students' insights into the complexities of modern urban planning. Participants assume roles of special-interest groups in an urban renewal area, including planning authority, public housing agency, community representatives, businessmen, and educators. In the simulation the special-interest groups attempt to influence the city planning authority in its decisions.

INTER-NATION SIMULATION KIT (1966)

Subject:	Contemporary problems, international relations, political science, world history
Grade level:	Senior high
Number of participants:	14–as many as desired
Time required:	10–30 hours
Cost:	$1.50 per participant; $68.00 for instructor's kit
Source:	Science Research Associates, Inc.

Simulates relations among nations and international organizations. Participants are assigned to nations and are provided with information regarding their nation's wealth, form of government, defense position, population, and basic resources. Relying on this information, participants plan their goals and strategies and deal with crises that arise during the simulation.

JURY GAME (1974)

Subject:	Government
Grade level:	Junior high, senior high
Number of participants:	25–35
Time required:	3–5 hours
Cost:	$15.00
Source:	Zenger Publications

Introduces participants to the American jury system by simulating the jury selection process. Participants assume roles of jurors, attorneys, judges, defendants, plaintiffs, court reporters, and observers. Materials are included for conducting mock trials based on two civil cases and two criminal cases.

LIFE CAREER (1969)

Subject:	Human relations, career education
Grade level:	Junior high, senior high
Number of participants:	2–30
Time required:	9–10 hours
Cost:	$35.00
Source:	Bobbs-Merrill Company

Simulates problems faced by a fictitious person over a fifteen-year period as he allots his time and plans his activities in the areas of education, job training, family life, work, and leisure time. Participants plan the life of the fictitious person involved, and periodically reap the consequences of their decisions in the form of satisfaction points.

LIFE SKILLS: FEMALE IMAGES (1972)

Subject:	Social studies, women's studies
Grade level:	High school
Number of participants:	4–8

Time required: 2–5 hours
Cost: $27.50
Source: Instructional Simulations, Inc.

Focuses on issues of primary concern to mature female students. Participants are faced with a series of tasks that require that they define terms and consider perceptions of themselves within a framework of potential identities. Each of these units is developed around a five-step instructional strategy: concept presentation, evocation, objective or subjective inquiry, application, and evaluation.

LOCATION OF THE METFAB COMPANY (1969)

Subject: Geography, economics
Grade level: Senior high
Number of participants: 15+
Time required: 5–8 hours
Cost: $98.70 (as part of the unit, "Manufacturing and Agriculture")
Source: The Macmillan Company, School Division

Develops the idea that the location of manufacturing is an outgrowth of a complex of related decisions. Participants decide on the location of a new branch for the company, considering such factors as the availability of raw materials, skilled labor, potential markets, shipping costs, and pollution level in cities.

MAHOPA (1972)

Subject: American history, anthropology, contemporary problems, minority studies
Grade level: Junior high
Number of participants: 20–40
Time required: 15–20 hours
Cost: $12.00
Source: INTERACT

Helps participants to gain an understanding of the history, culture, and values of the American Indian. Students are introduced to many aspects of Indian life through readings, discussions, role playing, independent research, activities, and projects.

MARKET GAME (1967)

Subject: Economics (supply and demand)
Grade level: Junior high, senior high
Number of participants: 20–50
Time required: 2–4 hours
Cost: $2.00
Source: Joint Council on Economic Education

Demonstrates the functioning of supply and demand in a competitive market. Using wheat as a commodity, participants negotiate and trade at the best prices available.

NO DAM ACTION (1974)

Subject:	Civics, government, sociology, ecology
Grade level:	Upper junior high, senior high
Number of participants:	20–40
Time required:	8–25 hours
Cost:	$117.50
Source:	Instructional Simulations, Inc.

Involves participants with realistic environmental issues. Focusing on a water management controversy, students role play individuals who must make decisions regarding a proposed project. Attention is given to the relationships among the biosystem, geosystem, and ecosystem.

NAPOLI (1965)

Subject:	Government
Grade level:	Junior high, senior high
Number of participants:	16–40
Time required:	2–5 hours
Cost:	$35.00 for 25 participants; $50.00 for 35 participants
Source:	Simile II

Simulates the functioning of a legislature, as representatives strive to be reelected by working for the passage or defeat of eleven bills brought before the house. Each member of the legislature represents one of two political parties and one of eight geographical regions. Participants become familiar with such activities as speech writing, logrolling, and negotiating during the process of the simulation.

PANIC (1968)

Subject:	American history, economics
Grade level:	Junior high, senior high
Number of participants:	20–40
Time required:	20–35 hours
Cost:	$12.00
Source:	INTERACT

Simulates economic conditions in the United States during the period 1920-1940. Participants assume the roles of various economic pressure groups as a mock Congress attempts to resolve the economic crises.

PARTY CENTRAL (1974)

Subject:	History, government, sociology
Grade level:	High school
Number of participants:	23–30
Time required:	10–15 hours
Cost:	$47.50
Source:	Instructional Simulations, Inc.

Focuses on events which led to the fall of the Weimar Republic in Germany in 1933. Participants assume roles as members of the German Reichstag and reenact the German political situation between 1925 and 1933. Political, economic, and social issues are debated, as students attempt to gain control of the government for one of six political parties.

POLICE PATROL (1973)

Subject:	Civics, government
Grade level:	Junior high, senior high
Number of participants:	20–35
Time required:	1–9 hours
Cost:	$12.50
Source:	Simile II

Develops in the participants an understanding of the role of police and authority in the United States. Role-playing incidents are based upon realistic situations faced by members of typical police forces. Students examine their attitudes toward the police, and compare themselves with other students sampled in a nationwide survey.

POLLUTION: NEGOTIATING A CLEAN ENVIRONMENT (1970)

Subject:	Sociology, ecology
Grade level:	Junior high, senior high
Number of participants:	4–32
Time required:	1–3 hours
Cost:	$22.50
Source:	Simulations Systems

Deals with problems related to the development of a cleaner environment. Participants assume roles in one of four groups functioning in society—business and industry, citizens, conservationists, and state government. Each group negotiates to work out an acceptable balance between its desire to improve the quality of environment and its achievement of personal and collective goals.

PORTSVILLE (1969)

Subject:	Geography, urban growth
Grade level:	Junior high, senior high
Number of participants:	4–24
Time required:	8–12 hours
Cost:	$319.55 (As part of the unit, "Geography of Cities")
Source:	The Macmillan Company, School Division

Involves participants in determining where a city should be located and where industries, commercial enterprises, housing, and other urban features should be placed. The growth of Portsville is studied during three different historical periods, and, given geographical features on a game board, participants construct their versions of the city with sets of colored plastic blocks representing various economic functions.

POWER (1972)

Subject:	Multidisciplinary
Grade level:	High school

Number of participants: 9–35
Time required: 2–5 hours for each of four simulations
Cost: $13.98
Source: Scott, Foresman and Company

Helps students to understand how authority figures can manipulate a communications network in maintaining power. Four alternative scenarios based on an international crisis, a national political struggle, an urban conflict, and a corporate battle are used to illustrate the concept of power. In each of the settings, participants are divided into four groups: communicators, bankers, media representatives, and observers. By assuming these roles, it is anticipated that the students will become more familiar with individual and group behavior, and that they will better understand motivation and the process of decision making.

RADICALS VS. TORIES (1972)

Subject: American history
Grade level: Junior high, senior high
Number of participants: 24–100
Time required: 3–4 hours
Cost: $10.00
Source: History Simulations

Simulates the conflict between those favoring close ties with Great Britain and those favoring independence during the American Revolution. Assuming roles of Radicals, Tories, or Moderates, participants attempt to persuade their peers to join them in voting on the proposal to go to war against Great Britain. The purpose of the simulation is to develop in the students an understanding that the movement for American independence was not unanimous, and that there were convincing arguments both for independence and for conciliation.

ROAD GAME, THE (1974)

Subject: Multidisciplinary
Grade level: Junior high, senior high
Number of participants: 12–32
Time required: 2–4 hours
Cost: $1.50 (Contained in Intercom Booklet No. 75, *Teaching Global Issues Through Simulation*)
Source: Intercom

Focuses on such group processes as competition, teamwork, communication, and conflict resolution. Four teams interact by drawing roads from one area of a large map to another. Conflicts are resolved, first through bargaining or direct action and later through a judicial procedure.

SIMPOLIS (1974)

Subject: Civics, community and social problems
Grade level: Senior high
Number of participants: 23–50
Time required: 3–6 hours

Cost: $36.50
Source: Games Central

Deals with seven urban problem areas, including education, housing, civil rights, poverty, crime, and pollution. Through the use of role-playing techniques, participants establish priorities for treating the problems and propose reasonable solutions without alienating other groups of citizens.

SIMOC—SIMULATED SOCIETY (1969)

Subject: Political science, sociology, economics
Grade level: Senior high
Number of participants: 20–40
Time required: 5–6 hours
Cost: $4.95 per participant
Source: Free Press

Simulates a society within which participants assume roles of citizens. Stress conditions are created so that students must reevaluate the nature of the simulated society and examine the processes of social conflict and social control. Primary objectives of the exercise are to gain popularity, wealth, or power, and successfully to establish and maintain social order.

SITTE (1969)

Subject: Urban problems, community development
Grade level: Junior high, senior high
Number of participants: 20–40
Time required: 3–4 hours
Cost: $35.00 for 25 participants, $50.00 for 35 participants
Source: Simile II

Simulates the functioning of a municipal government. Participants assume roles in one of five interest groups labeled Business, Disenfranchised, Government, Ad Hoc Committee for Parks and Trees, and Taxpayers Association. Additional roles are those of the director-messenger, the analyst, and the mass media. The challenge to the students is to produce changes in an imaginary city by influencing decisions regarding city planning and government.

SMOG (1970)

Subject: Urban systems, ecology
Grade level: Junior high, senior high
Number of participants: 2–4
Time required: 2–4 hours
Cost: $11.00
Source: Damon Educational Division

Places participants in the roles of elected officials who are responsible for controlling the quality of air in their town. The purpose of the exercise is to give the student practice in decision making, and to acquaint him with problems related to air pollution and city management. (Board game.)

STARPOWER (1970)

Subject:	Political science, sociology
Grade level:	Junior high, senior high
Number of participants:	18–40
Time required:	2–3 hours
Cost:	Sample set, $3.00; Classroom set for 25, $35.00
Source:	Simile II

Involves participants in the operation of a low-mobility, three-level society based upon the distribution of wealth in the form of chips. Designed so that a breakdown develops in communication, trade, and societal order as discriminated members of the society react to an imbalanced distribution of wealth and power.

SUNSHINE (1972)

Subject:	American history, contemporary problems, urban problems
Grade level:	Junior high, senior high
Number of participants:	20–36
Time required:	20–30 hours
Cost:	$12.00
Source:	INTERACT

Simulates current racial problems in the hypothetical American city of Sunshine. Participants assume roles of community members who live in six neighborhoods ranging from a minority-populated, low-income section called Dead End to the white and prosperous Mount Olympus. Participants attempt to improve their personal status and self-image as well as the living conditions in the community while facing and attempting to resolve a variety of community-based conflicts.

SYSTEM I (1969)

Subject:	Cross-discipline—classification of information
Grade level:	Junior high, senior high
Number of participants:	Individually; groups of 2 to 4
Time required:	Flexible
Cost:	$14.50
Source:	Instructional Simulations, Inc.

Familiarizes participants with the methodology of information classification. Using subject matter selected by the teacher, students employ classification matrixes while translating principles of analysis into action.

THEY SHOOT MARBLES, DON'T THEY? (1974)

Subject:	Government, psychology, sociology, urban studies
Grade level:	Junior high, senior high
Number of participants:	8–50
Time required:	3–8 hours

Cost: $40.00
Source: Urbex Affiliates, Inc.

Challenges the participants to design and control a society. Marbles are used as the medium of exchange and may represent money, power, mobility, status, skill, employment—whatever the students perceive as being important to them. A police force regulates play as participants carry out such activities as developing a government structure, establishing courts and welfare systems, purchasing land, and developing real estate.

TRACTS (1969)

Subject: Interdisciplinary—geography, political science, sociology, urban studies
Grade level: Junior high, senior high
Number of participants: 8–48
Time required: 5–7 hours
Cost: $47.50
Source: Instructional Simulations, Inc.

Simulates problems of land use in the city. Participants assume roles as members of interest groups competing for influence in an urban land development project. Interest groups include private land developers, public housing authorities, industry, and a city planning commission. The exercise illustrates the arguments and actions of various sectors of the community when land cannot serve equally the interests of all parties without compromise and negotiation.

TRIANGLE TRADE (1969)

Subject: American history, economics
Grade level: Junior high, senior high
Number of participants: 15–44
Time required: 3–4 hours
Cost: $16.00
Source: Simulation Systems

Introduces participants to the economic structure of the New England colonies and the mercantile system of Great Britain during the seventeenth century. Students assume roles of major historical parties involved in the triangular trade route, and, through bargaining and trading, come to recognize the conflicts, deficiencies, and economic implications that existed within the system.

Names and addresses of distributors and publishers of simulations

Academic Games Associates, Inc., 430 East Thirty-third Street, Baltimore, MD 21218
American Education Publications, 55 High Street, Middletown, CT 06457
American Universities Field Staff, 3 Lebanon Street, Hanover, NH 03755
Amidon, Paul S. and Associates, Inc., 5408 Chicago Avenue South, Minneapolis, MN 55417

Avalon Hill Company, 4517 Hartford Road, Baltimore, MD 21214
Baldicer Games, Box 1176, Richmond, VA 23209
Benefic Press, 10300 West Roosevelt Road, Westchester, IL 60153
Board of Cooperative Educational Services, 845 Fox Meadow Road, Yorktown Hts., NY 10598
Bobbs-Merrill Company, 4300 West 62nd Street, Indianapolis, IN 46268
Cardinal Printers, Inc., Wesleyan University, Middletown, CT 06457
Center for International Studies, University of Missouri-St. Louis, St. Louis, MO 63121
Changing Times Education Service, 1729 H Street, N.W., Washington, DC 20006
Classroom Dynamics, 231 O'Connor Drive, San Jose, CA 95128
Communications Workers of America, Education Department, 1925 K Street, N.W., Washington, DC 20006
Cuna Mutual Insurance Society, P.O. Box 391, Madison, WI 53701
Damon Educational Division, 80 Wilson Way, Westwood, MA 02090
Denoyer-Geppert Company, 5235 Ravenswood Avenue, Chicago, IL 60640
Didactic Systems, Inc., P.O. Box 500, Westbury, NY 11590
Division of Educational Research Services, University of Alberta, Edmonton, Alberta, Canada
Dynasty International, Inc., 815 Park Avenue, New York, NY 10021
Edu-Game, P.O. Box 1144, Sun Valley, CA 91352
Education Development Center, 15 Mifflin Place, Cambridge, MA 02138
Educational Games Company, Box 363, Peekskill, NY 10021
Educational Methods, Inc., 20 E. Huron, Chicago, IL 60611
Entelek, Inc., 42 Pleasant Street, Newburyport, MA 01950
Envirometrics, Inc., Suite 900, 1100 17th Street, N.W., Washington, DC 20036
Environmental Simulation Laboratory, 109 E. Madison, Ann Arbor, MI 48104
Federal Reserve Bank of Minneapolis, Director of Public Information, Minneapolis, MN 55440
Free Press, Department F, Riverside, NJ 08075
Games Central, 55 Wheeler Street, Cambridge, MA 02138
Games Research, Inc., 48 Wareham Street, Boston, MA 02118
Harwell Associates, Inc., Box 95, Convent Station, NJ 07961
Herder and Herder, 232 Madison Avenue, New York, NY 10021
History Simulations, D.N. Dal Porto, P.O. Box 2775, Santa Clara, CA 95051
Holt, Rinehart & Winston, Inc., Media Department D-1, Box 3670, Grand Central Station, New York, NY 10017
Houghton Mifflin Company, 666 Miami Circle, N.E., Atlanta, GA 30324
HRW Associates, P.O. Box 2634, Anaheim, CA 92804
Institute of Applied Art, Ltd., 10042 109 Street, Edmonton, Alberta, Canada
Instructional Simulations, Inc., 2147 University Avenue, St. Paul, MN 55114

INTERACT, P.O. Box 262, Lakeside, CA 92040
International Learning Corporation, 245 SW 32nd Street, Ft. Lauderdale, FL 33301
Richard D. Irwin, Inc., 1818 Ridge Road, Homewood, IL 60430
Joint Council on Economic Education, 1212 Avenue of the Americas, New York, NY 10036
John Knox Press, 341 Ponce de Leon Avenue, N.E., Atlanta, GA 30308
Law in American Society Foundation, 33 North LaSalle Street, Suite 1700, Chicago, IL 60602
Learning Games Associates, 2253 Medford Road, Ann Arbor, MI 48104
Lincoln Filene Center, Tufts University, Medford, MA 02155
Lockheed Missiles and Space Company, P.O. Box 504, Building 534, Sunnyvale, CA 94088
The Macmillan Company, School Division, 866 Third Avenue, New York, NY 10022
Media Innovators Exchange, P.O. Box 4485, Anaheim, CA 92803
Mental Health Research Institute, University of Michigan, Ann Arbor, MI 48104
National Academic Games Project, P.O. Box 214, Newhall, CA 91322
National Council for Geographic Education, 115 North Marion Street, Oak Park, IL 60301
Ohio Council on Economic Education, College of Business Administration, Ohio University, Athens, OH 45701
Olcott Forward, Inc., 234 N. Central Avenue, Hartsdale, NY 10530
Oxfam-American, Inc., 509-1028 Connecticut Avenue, N.W., Washington, DC 20036
Pact, 163 Madison, Detroit, MI 48226
Prentice-Hall, Inc., Englewood Cliffs, NJ 07631
Proctor and Gamble Co., P.O. Box 599, Cincinnati, OH 45201
Psychology Today Games, 1330 Camino Del Mar, Del Mar, CA 92014
Random House, 201 East 50th Street, New York, NY 10022
Reader's Digest Services, Inc., Education Division, Pleasantville, NY 10570
Reese, Jay, 3235 West 17th Avenue, Eugene, OR 97402
Research and Development Center in Educational Simulation, College of Education, University of Georgia, Athens, GA 30601
Rowland, Jasper M., 1545 Harmony Road, Akron, OH 44313
Science Research Associates, Inc., 259 East Erie Street, Chicago, IL 60611
Scott, Foresman and Company, 1900 East Lake Avenue, Glenview, IL 60025
Seabury Press, 815 2nd Avenue, New York, NY 10017
Short, Ronald W., 1005 Banbury Drive, Spokane, WA 99218
Simile II, 218 12th Street, P.O. Box 910, Del Mar, CA 92014
Simulation Systems, Black Butte Ranch, OR 97759
Sinauer Associates, Inc., 20 Second Street, Stamford, CT 06905
Social Education Magazine, National Council for the Social Studies, 1201 16th Street, N.W., Washington, DC 20036

Social Studies School Service, 10000 Culver Blvd., Culver City, CA 90230
Stem, P.O. Box 393, Provo, UT 84601
Unitarian Universalist Association, 25 Beacon Street, Boston, MA 02108
Urbandyne, 5659 S. Woodlawn Avenue, Chicago, IL 60637
Urbex Affiliates, Inc., P.O. Box 2198, Ann Arbor, MI 48106
Warmac, P.O. Box 953, North Platte, NE 69101
Wff 'N Proof, Box 71-OE, New Haven, CT 06501
World Affairs Council of Philadelphia, John Wanamakers Store, 13th and Market St., Philadelphia, PA 19017
Xerox Education Sciences, Xerox Education Group, 600 Madison Avenue, New York, NY 10022

Guides to simulations

Belch, Jean. *Contemporary Games, Volume II, Bibliography*. Detroit: Gale, 1974.

Johnson, Edward R. *Simulation and Gaming in Business and Economics in the 1960's: A Bibliography*. Iowa City: College of Business Administration, The University of Iowa, 1969.

Klietsch, Ronald G.; Wiegman, Fred B.; and Powell, Jim R., Jr. *Directory of Educational Simulations, Learning Games, and Didactic Units*. St. Paul, Minn.: Instruction Simulations, 1969.

Social Science Education Consortium. *Social Studies Curriculum Materials Data Book*, 2 vol. Boulder, Colo.: The Consortium, 1975.

Stadsklev, Ron. *Handbook of Simulation Gaming in Social Education (Part II: Directory)*. University, Ala.: Institute of Higher Education Research and Services, 1975.

Twelker, Paul A. *Instructional Simulation Systems: An Annotated Bibliography*. Corvallis, Ore.: Continuing Education Publications, 1969.

Werner, Roland, and Werner, Joan. *Bibliography of Simulations: Social Systems and Education*. LaJolla, Calif.: Western Behavioral Sciences Institute, 1969.

Zuckerman, David W., and Horn, Robert E. *The Guide to Simulations/Games for Education and Training*. Lexington, Mass.: Information Resources, 1973.

Professional Organizations

American Council on Educational Simulation and Gaming. Paul A. Twelker, President. P.O. Box 5131, Industrial Station, 453 No. Snelling Avenue, St. Paul, MN 55104.

American Educational Research Association: Special Interest Group: Simulation Systems. John R. Dettre, SIG Secretary-Treasurer. University of Kentucky, Lexington, KY 40506.

The National Gaming Council. Environmetrics, 1100 17th St., N.W., Washington, DC 20036.

Journals and newsletters

Behavioral Simulation Newsletter. Behavioral Simulation and Gaming Group, Political Science Department, Peoples Avenue Complex, Building D, Rensselaer Polytechnic Institute, Troy, NY 12181 (no charge).

Instructional Simulation Newsletter. Simulation Systems Program, Teaching Research Division, Oregon State System of Higher Education, Monmouth, OR 97361 (three issues annually, no charge).

ISI Learning Letter. Instructional Simulations, Inc., 2147 University Avenue, St. Paul, MN 55104 (five issues annually, $1.00).

Occasional Newsletter About Uses of Simulations and Games for Education and Training. Project SIMILE, Western Behavioral Sciences Institute, 1150 Silverado Road, LaJolla, CA 92037 (three issues annually, $5.00).

People's Computer Company. P.O. Box 310, Menlo Park, CA 94025 (five issues annually, $4.00).

Political and Social Simulation Newsletter. Haverford College, Haverford, PA 19041 (monthly issues, $6.00).

SAGA Journal. Simulation and Gaming Association, 4833 Greentree Road, Lebanon, OH 45036 (four issues annually, $5.00).

Simulation and Games: An International Journal of Theory, Design and Research. Sage Publications, 275 South Beverly Drive, Beverly Hills, CA 90212 (four issues annually, $18.00).

Simulation/Gaming. Box 3039, University Station, Moscow, ID 83843 (six issues annually, $6.00).

Simulation in the Service of Society Newsletter. Box 994, LaJolla, CA 92038 (twelve issues annually, $9.00).

Simulation Journal. Box 2228, LaJolla, CA 92038 (sent to members of Society for Computer Simulation—membership is $25.00 per year. Library subscription is $38.00 per year).

Simulation Sharing Services Newsletter. 221 Wiley Street, Morgantown, WV 26505 (ten issues annually, $5.00).

Bibliography

Abt Associates, Inc. *Game Learning and Disadvantaged Groups*. Cambridge, Mass.: Abt, 1965.

Abt, Clark C. "Education is Child's Play." In *Inventing Education for the Future*, edited by Werner A. Hirsch. San Francisco: Chandler, 1967, pp. 123–55.

———. "Games for Learning." In *Simulation Games in Learning*, edited by Sarane S. Boocock and E. O. Schild. Beverly Hills, Calif.: Sage Publications, 1968, pp. 65–83.

———. "Games Pupils Play—Why Education Games Win Converts." *Nation's Schools* 80 (1967): 92–93.

———. *Serious Games*. New York: Viking, 1970.

———. *Simulation and the Group*. Paper read at conference sponsored by the Commission of Educational Media of the Association for Supervision and Curriculum Development, NEA, Boston. Cambridge, Mass.: Abt, October 1968.

Adams, Denis M. *Simulation Games: An Approach to Learning*. Worthington, Ohio: Jones, 1973.

Allen, Robert W. "The Fourth 'R'," *California Journal of Educational Research* 16 (1965): 75–79.

———. *A Study Conducted at the Burbank Unified School, Burbank, California*. Burbank Unified School District, 1964.

Attig, J. C. "Use of Games as a Teaching Technique," *Social Studies* 58 (1967): 25–29.

Barton, Richard F. *A Primer on Simulation and Gaming*. Englewood Cliffs, N.J.: Prentice-Hall, 1970.

Beck, Isabel. *Simulation: Designs for Involvement*. Los Angeles: Southwest Regional Laboratory, May 1968.

Belch, Jean. *Contemporary Games. Vol. I.* Detroit: Gale, 1973.

Bogdanoff, E., *et al. Simulation: An Introduction to a New Technology*. Santa Monica, Calif.: System Development Corporation, March 1960.

Boocock, Sarane. "An Experimental Study of the Learning Effects of Two Games with Simulated Environments." *American Behavioral Scientist* 10 (1966): 8–18.

———. "Games Change What Goes On in the Classroom." *Nation's Schools* 80 (1967): 94–95.

Boocock, Sarane S., and Schild, E. O. eds. *Simulation Games in Learning.* Beverly Hills, Calif.: Sage Publications, 1968.

Boocock, Sarane S.; Schild, E. O.; and Stoll, Clarice. *Simulation and Control Beliefs*. Baltimore: Johns Hopkins, November 1967.

Boocock, Sarane S., *et al*. *Simulation Games Program: Annual Report*. Baltimore: Johns Hopkins, May 1968.

Brodbelt, Samuel. "Simulation in the Social Studies: An Overview." *Social Education* 33 (1969): 176–78.

Bronstein, Russel H., and Maidment, Robert. *Simulation Games: Design and Implementation*. Columbus: Merrill, 1973.

Carlson, Elliot. "Games in the Classroom." *Saturday Review* 50 (1967): 62–65, 82–83.

Chapin, June R. "Simulation Games." *Social Education* 33 (1969): 798–800.

Chapman, Katherine. *Guidelines for Using a Social Simulation/Game*. Boulder, Col.: ERIC Clearinghouse for Social Studies/Social Science Education and Social Science Education Consortium, Inc., 1973.

Chapman, Katherine, and Cousins, Jack E. *Simulation/Games in Social Studies: A Report*. Boulder, Colo: ERIC Clearinghouse for Social Studies/

Social Science Education and Social Science Education Consortium, 1974.

Chapman, Katherine; Davis, James E.; and Meier, Andrea. *Simulation/Games in Social Studies: What Do We Know?* Boulder, Colo.: ERIC Clearinghouse for Social Studies/Social Science Education and Social Science Education Consortium, 1974.

Chartier, Myron R. "Learning Effect—An Experimental Study of a Simulated Game and Instrumental Discussion." *Simulation and Games* 3 (1972): 203–18.

———. "The Ten Commandments for Game Facilitators." *Simulation/Gaming/News* 11 (March 1974): 8–9.

Cherryholmes, Cleo H. "Some Current Research on Effectiveness of Educational Simulations: Implications for Alternative Strategies." *American Behavioral Scientist* 10 (1966): 4–8.

Chesler, M., and Fox, R. *Role-Playing Methods in the Classroom*. Chicago: Science Research Associates, 1966.

Christine, Charles, and Christine, Dorothy. "Simulation, A Teaching Tool." *The Elementary School Journal* 67 (1967): 396–98.

Coleman, James S. "Academic Games and Learning." In *Proceedings of the 1967 Invitational Conference on Testing Problems*, pp. 67–75. Princeton: Educational Testing Service, 1968.

———. *The Adolescent Society*. Glencoe, Ill.: Free Press, 1961.

———. "In Defense of Games." *American Behavioral Scientist* 10 (1966):3-4.

———. "Learning Through Games." *National Education Association Journal* 56 (1967): 69–70.

Davis, O. L., Jr. "Simulation: Looking Toward the Future." Paper presented at conference sponsored by the Commission on Educational Media of the Association for Supervision and Curriculum Development, NEA, Boston. Austin: University of Texas, 1968.

DeKock, Paul. "Simulations and Changes in Racial Attitudes." *Social Education* 33 (1969): 181–83.

Duke, Richard D., and Greenblat, Cathy S. *Gaming, Simulation: Rationale, Design and Applications*. New York: Halstead, 1975.

Edwards, Keith J.; DeVries, David L.; and Snyder, John P. "Games and Teams." *Simulation and Games* 3 (1972): 247–69.

Farran, Dale C. "Games Work with Underachievers." *Scholastic Teacher* 5 (November 1967): 10–11.

Fletcher, Jerry L. "Evaluation of Learning in Two Social Studies Simulation Games." *Simulation and Games* 2 (1971): 259–86.

Francke, Linda Bird, with Kellogg, Mary Alice. "Conjugal Prep." *Newsweek*, June 2, 1975, pp. 64–65.

Gearon, John D. "Simulation and Stimulation—Teaching Politics and Government in High School Social Studies." *Social Education* 32 (1968): 273–78.

Geriach, V. S. "Academic Games and Simulation in Instruction." *Audiovisual Instruction* 12 (1967): 609–10.

Gibbs, G. I. *Handbook of Games and Simulation Exercises*. Beverly Hills: Sage, 1974.

Gilliom, M. Eugene. "Trends in Simulation." *The High School Journal* 58: (1974): 265–72.

Gillispie, Philip H. *Learning Through Simulation Games*. Paramus, N.J.: Paulist Press, 1973.

Glazier, Ray. *How to Design Educational Games*. 5th ed. Cambridge, Mass.: Games Central, 1974.

Gordon, Alice Kaplan. *Games for Growth*. Palo Alto, Calif.: Science Research Associates, Inc., 1970.

Guetzkow, Harold, ed. *Simulation in Social Science*. Englewood Cliffs, N.J.: Prentice-Hall, 1962.

Guss, Carolyn. "Role-playing Simulation in Instruction." *Audiovisual Instruction* 11 (1966): 443–44.

Heinkel, Otto A. "Evaluation of Simulation as a Teaching Device." *Journal of Experimental Education* 38 (1970): 32–36.

Heitzmann, William Ray. *Educational Games and Simulations*. Washington, D.C.: National Education Association, 1974.

———. "The Validity of Social Science Simulations: A Review of Research Findings." *Education* 94 (December 1973): 33–37.

Heitzmann, William Ray, and Staropoli, Charles E., "Social Science Simulations and Attitudinal Change." *Southwestern Journal of Social Education* 3 (Spring–Summer 1974): 11–14.

Heyman, Mark. *Simulation Games for the Classroom*. Bloomington, Ind.: Phi Delta Kappa, 1975.

Inbar, Michael, and Stoll, Clarice S., eds. *Simulation Gaming in Social Science*. New York: Free Press, 1972.

Kasperson, Roger E. "Games as Educational Media." *Journal of Geography* 62 (1968): 409–22.

Klietsch, Ronald G., and Dodge, Dorothy. *An Introduction to Learning Games and Instructional Simulations: Curriculum Guidelines.* Newport, Minn.: Instructors Simulations, 1968.

Livingston, Samuel A. "Six Ways to Design a Bad Simulation Game." *Simulation/Gaming/News* 1 (1973): 15.

Livingston, Samuel, and Stoll, Clarice S. *Simulation Games*. New York: Free Press, 1973.

———. *Simulation Games: An Introduction for the Social Studies Teacher*. New York: Collier Macmillan, 1973.

Marfuggi, Joseph, and Pearson, Craig. *Creating and Using Learning Games*. Palo Alto, Calif.: Learning Magazine, 1975.

Maxon, Robert C. "Simulation: A Method that Can Make a Difference." *The High School Journal* 57 (December 1973): 107–11.

Mulially, Genevieve. "Games in the Classroom." *Montana Education* 44 (February, 1968): 40–42.

Nesbitt, William A. *Simulation Games for the Classroom*. New York: Crowell, 1971.

Plumpton, Russell A. *Methods of Determining Pupil Readiness for Specific Units of Instruction Through Simulated Environment Media: Final Report.* Bedford Hills, N.Y.: Board of Cooperative Educational Services, 1964.

Raser, John R. *Simulation and Society.* Boston: Allyn & Bacon, 1969.

Robinson, James A. "Simulation and Games." In *The New Media and Education: Their Impact on Society*, edited by P. H. Rossi and B. J. Biddle, Garden City, N.Y.: Doubleday, 1967, pp. 93–135.

Ryan, T. Antoinette. "Use of Simulation to Increase Transfer." *School Review* 76 (1968): 246–52.

Shaftel, Fannie R., and Shaftel, George. *Role-playing for Social Values*. Englewood Cliffs, N.J.: Prentice-Hall, 1967.

Simulation in Perspective: Learning Versus Research Origins. Position Paper #113. St. Paul, Minn.: Instructional Simulations, 1970.

Smith, J. P. "Academic Games in the Classroom." *School and Society* 96 (1968): 184–85.

Social Science Education Consortium, Inc. *Social Studies Curriculum Materials Data Book*. Boulder, Colo.: The Consortium, 1972.

Stadsklev, Ron. "A Basic Model for Debriefing." *Simulation/Gaming/News* 1 (1973): 6.

———. *Handbook of Simulation Gaming in Social Education (Part I: Textbook).* University, Ala.: Institute of Higher Education Research and Services, 1974.

———. *Handbook of Simulation Gaming in Social Education (Part II: Directory).* University, Ala.: Institute of Higher Education Research and Services, 1975.

Tansey, P. J., *et al. Educational Aspects of Simulation*. New York: McGraw-Hill, 1971.

Taylor, John L., and Walford, Rex. *Simulation in the Classroom*. Baltimore: Penguin Books, 1972.

Twelker, Paul A. "Designing Simulation Systems." Paper presented at the American Educational Research Association Convention, Los Angeles, February 1969. Monmouth: Teaching Research, Oregon State System of Higher Education, 1969.

———. "Simulation: What Is It?" Why Is It?" Paper presented at the conference, Simulation: Stimulation for Learning, sponsored by the Commission of Educational Media for the Association for Supervision and Curriculum Development, NEA, San Diego, Calif., April 1968. Monmouth: Teaching Research, Oregon State Stystem of Higher Education, April 1968.

———. "Some Reflections on Instructional Simulation and Gaming." *Simulations and Games* 2 (1972): 145–53.

Twelker, Paul A., and Layden, Ken. *Educational Simulation/Gaming.* Stanford, Calif.: ERIC Clearinghouse on Media and Technology, Stanford University (August 1972).

Wagner, Guy. "What Schools Are Doing: Using Challenging Learning Activities." *Education* 86 (1966): 379–81.

Wentworth, Donald R., and Lewis, Darrell R. "A Review of Research on Instructional Games and Simulations in Social Studies Education." *Social Education* 37 (1973): 431–40.

Wing, Richard L. "Simulation as a Method of Instruction in Science Education." *Science Teacher* 35 (May 1968): 41–42.

When involved with inquiry, students necessarily confront a wide variety of evidence, ranging from case studies to quantitative. Typically, social studies teachers have relied much more heavily on nonmeasurable, descriptive data than on measurable data. With the development of increasingly sophisticated means for gathering and processing information, however, it is important for students to learn to interpret data in a wide variety of forms. The purpose of this chapter is to help teachers to inject quantitative analysis into the social studies. It is richly illustrated with practical, workable examples, and should be particularly helpful to teachers who have had a minimum of training in mathematics.

Chapter 4

The quantitative perspective on inquiry in the social studies

Who are you?. . .

This question momentarily baffles us and requires us to sort out a tremendous amount of information. We must ask ourselves: How can I convey who I am? What should I include and what should I omit to give an appropriate response—one that tells who I am without being either too secretive or too embarrassingly explicit?

The chances are that in the course of responding to this question, most people will make some reference to the various groups to which they belong. Many will refer to their ages and to important events during the course of their lives. Many will automatically indicate the size of their families or will give some evidence of their socioeconomic backgrounds by indicating their levels of education or their occupations, where they live, or other indicators of their life-styles and values.

Consider the following three personal statements taken from responses of members of a high school faculty to the question: "Who are you?"

1. I am Jane Smith.* I am married and have three children. I teach eleventh-grade English at Lodestone High School. I am a graduate of Indiana University, where I majored in American literature and education. I met my husband Jim while I was in college and married him a week after we both graduated from college. We now live in a four-bedroom split-level house about three miles from Lodestone High and seven miles from the downtown area where my husband has his law office.
2. My name is Mark Healy. I see myself as a member of several important social groups. I am black, young, college-educated, and a social studies teacher at Lodestone High School, an upper-middle-class school in a suburban development. I am not married now and may not marry because I believe that marriage is an artificial social and legal convention. I grew up in a poor neighborhood in Chicago located about eight miles south of the Loop. My mother still lives in the old neighborhood, but my father, who was a postal worker, died three years ago.

---

*All proper names given are fictitious.

I attended several colleges and universities before I finally graduated from college last year at the age of 29, thanks to the Vietnam war and the GI Bill.

3. I am Karen Sears. To answer your question, I would have to say that I don't really know exactly who I am. I know that I like a number of things, including teaching math here at Lodestone High School, classical music, golf and bowling, collecting antiques, and traveling. I am 24 years old and grew up in Oregon. I have been engaged twice, but am still not married. I have decided to postpone marriage until I feel that I have accomplished a few things of significance on my own. I am an active member of the local chapter of the National Organization for Women (NOW) and have worked for the passage of the Equal Rights Amendment. Several years ago, when my parents were divorced, I found myself drifting spiritually and emotionally. I found strength in a recommitment to God and to my childhood religion. I am still searching for the "real" me, but suspect that I will never find her.

As each of these individuals give us personal information, or *data*, we are able to place each of them in a certain category. Without discounting the uniqueness of each person, we can understand each of them better because we can classify them according to the various social groups to which they belong. We expect them to hold certain values and outlooks as a result of their identifications with these groups. Unconsciously, when we assess individuals in this manner, we are *quantifying* them, viewing them in the context of the larger *aggregates*, or collections, to which they belong. We also find ourselves *drawing inferences* about each person, guessing what each is like on the basis of the data we have been given. Among the *indicators*, or references to common measurable attributes, given were: age, sex, race, marital status, level of education, occupation, class background, level of religious commitment, number of children, and number of group or organizational affiliations.

If we were to ask all members of a high school faculty to answer the question, "Who are you?" we would have a sort of map of their collective backgrounds, social and political outlooks, and tastes. If we were interested in knowing where every member of the faculty stood with regard to a particular issue, or if we specifically wanted information about a selected group of indicators, such as marital status, age, or level of education, we could put together a questionnaire that included questions relative to our interests. The result would be a more carefully controlled map of the faculty's response pattern.

All of us are familiar with questionnaires. Most of us have completed several during the course of our lives, along with college, graduate school, credit card, and job applications, which tend to ask for certain standardized data. As we fill out these various forms, we are supplying information about ourselves that will allow the questioner to group us according to the attributes that we share with others. Thus the total response to any given questionnaire or application form can be quantified. Most of us, then, already are acquainted with the quantitative perspective as it is used to describe aspects of human reality. Furthermore, we are familiar with various types of statistics and are able to read them, repeat them, and question their significance.

Purpose of this chapter

The primary purpose of this chapter is to introduce teachers to forms of quantitative thinking that will help them to extend their inquiry teaching skills. We hope to describe several terms and procedures commonly used in social science research and to help teachers become aware of some sources of quantitative information. Finally, we suggest several teaching strategies that make use of quantitative information to promote inquiry within the secondary social studies classroom, and we give examples of data analysis techniques and procedures for using them.

It is our hope that this chapter will provide some guidelines that will help teachers assist students to:

- develop an awareness of numerical expressions.
- develop the ability to define aspects of human behavior in quantitative terms.
- feel comfortable with quantification at the same time that they develop a healthy skepticism for many numerical expressions.
- critically evaluate (1) simple statistical expressions, (2) the results of surveys and polls, (3) the results of some small-group experimental research.
- develop the ability to read and understand several different types of visual data displays, such as pie graphs, bar graphs, line graphs, Lorenz curves, contingency tables, crisscross diagrams, and scatterplot diagrams.
- develop the ability to read other tables of quantitative data and to draw inferences from them.
- develop the ability to locate, organize, and display quantitative data in some of the forms listed above as a way of approaching the process of inquiry problem solving.

One warning is in order, however. This chapter will *not* be an introduction to various forms of statistical analysis. Many people assume that quantification implies complex statistical procedures. This is not the case. It is not mathematics that is critical to quantification techniques. It is, rather, the capacity to attack a problem systematically and with precision, to think in a logical fashion, to seek out information from a variety of sources, to combine this evidence in meaningful ways, and to extract meaning from the total process of inquiry that we hope to emphasize. These are the essential skills of inquiry, no matter what form of data gathering and analysis is employed.

Much quantitative analysis can be achieved solely through the ability to read and interpret visual representations of information or through the ability to manipulate and arrange data in a visual form. The exercises suggested in this chapter involve quantification that uses simple mathematical processes accessible to all high school students. Furthermore, the sources of quantitative information that will be mentioned here are not exotic, and they should not be difficult to locate.

This chapter is organized into six major sections: (1) The introduction, which includes a statement of the purposes of this chapter and a consideration of the role of quantification in history; (2) "Quantitative Data," which includes the definition and sources of quantitative information; (3) "Inquiry Learning Using Quantitative Data"; (4) "The Process of Inquiry Teaching Using Quantitative Data"; (5) "Examples of Data Analysis Techniques"; and (6) "Summary and Conclusions."

Anticipating some teacher concerns about using quantitative information

Many teachers who are otherwise open-minded and innovative hesitate to use quantitative methods in their teaching. We feel that this is because they share certain common concerns about quantification, which seem to focus around four areas.

New terminology The skills and outlooks discussed in this chapter have been adapted from recent advances in social science research by scholars in the forefront of their respective fields. As is true for all advances of this kind, new terms and phrases have emerged. Many of these are taken directly from the physical sciences and mathematics. In fact, the vocabulary of the problem solver in the physical sciences has already found its way into the writings of social studies scholars and classroom practitioners. Words such as *concept, evidence, measurement, hypothesis, theory, data, empiricism, test,* and *data processing* are commonly used in teaching methods textbooks. Terms that have been used in this chapter should not be unfamiliar to most social studies teachers.

Numbers and number manipulation Many may feel anxiety when confronted with numbers and the task of manipulating them. As has been mentioned, however, much quantitative analysis requires little or no numerical manipulation. The most sophisticated procedures that you would ever be called upon to employ demand no mathematical skills that you did not already possess before entering high school. Much quantitative analysis can be achieved solely through visual representation of the data, without resorting to any manipulation of numbers beyond that necessary to arrange your information to convey some meaning.

Need for specialized study Often quantitative methods are viewed as too time-consuming to learn. However, the techniques suggested in this chapter should convince teachers that opportunities to make use of quantitative information are readily available and easy to introduce into the classroom without requiring extensive further study.

Elimination of the human element This concern is common to people at all levels of the educational spectrum who have not been trained in quantitative techniques. It has been intensified, moreover, by the errors of early practitioners, who viewed the techniques as ends in themselves and who failed to recognize the utility of combining these methods with traditional procedures.

There is some evidence that different aptitudes and types of thinking are required for science and mathematics from those required for the more "verbal" fields of English or history. Educational researchers are currently at work preparing new forms of IQ tests that will provide a more complex and comprehensive definition of intelligence than can be obtained from conventional IQ tests. Once these new instruments are developed, the "split" between persons with numerical abilities and persons with verbal abilities may be confirmed. These different thinking abilities may account for the self-imposed divisions between people who prefer science and mathematics and people who prefer to study art, history, or the social sciences.

This process of self-selection and grouping has several unfortunate effects, however. As humanities-centered individuals move further away from intellectual interaction with individuals in the fields of mathematics and science, they may begin to assume that all scientific and mathematical operations exist in opposition to the "human" concerns of social science and history. They may begin to equate all numerical expressions with the nonhuman world of computers, robots, calculators, and various other nightmare visions of 1984 and beyond.

To avoid some of these feelings about numbers, it is important to emphasize that even though a person uses quantitative methods during the process of inquiry, that person is still dealing with human problems and using evidence and techniques of analysis created by human beings. The errors in this type of research, the gaps in the sources of data, and the way that quantitative information is used and misused highlight the fact that the human element, far from being missing, is all too present!

The techniques that we suggest in this chapter involve "beginning at the beginning" with students, helping them first to develop quantitative awareness and then slowly to acquire the more demanding skills and outlooks that quantification implies. Although the chapter contains several ideas of a "cookbook" variety, which could be incorporated into a class without too much prior planning or thought, we sincerely hope that this chapter will be used also to help students acquire new habits of inquiry. We hope that the teacher will think in terms of a yearlong commitment to developing quantitative awareness, rather than in terms of one or two quick experiments with the teaching techniques suggested.

Quantification and history

Since the major part of the social studies curriculum involves the study of history, let us begin by considering the relationship of quantification to the study of history.

Many assume that there is no place for quantitative data in history and that the use of quantitative analysis defeats the purpose of history as a humanistic, artistic form. We do not deny that some forms of written history exist by themselves as works of art and as inspirations to the human spirit. Furthermore, we recognize that the historical theories put forward by several historians, both today and in the past, are not only persuasive and shrewdly framed, but likely to be confirmed by rigorous forms of analysis. We can understand, too, that many would prefer reading a work of history to reading a monograph illustrated with tables and graphs in addition to references to a number of baffling mathematical formulas. However, we *do* deny that the process of studying history differs substantially from the process of inquiry learning.

There are a number of similarities between the two processes. Both seek to obtain information to answer a specific question or to help resolve a perplexity of some kind. Both require care and precision during the process of data gathering. Both require that persons be explicit about the sources of information they have relied upon. Quantitative data gathering, however, requires three adjustments in the more familiar method of historical research: (1) a problem or question must be phrased differently from one used in historical inquiry; (2) a different form of data must be collected (quantitative rather than qualitative); and (3) a different way of organizing and displaying the data gathered must be employed (tables and graphs, rather than words). Otherwise, the process is the same. It is adherence to this process that unifies, rather than separates, the various fields of the social studies. The process of inquiry underpins the interdisciplinary perspective that we see as a healthy antidote to the overspecialization and compartmentalization of individuals and their disciplines today.

For example, a historian who encounters a typical inquiry problem, such as "What was life like in the South prior to the Civil War?" will think of aspects of life, such as quality of housing, dress and diet, cultural orientation, political outlook, aspects of social interaction within a slaveowning society. Typical data might include written accounts by Southerners in the form of letters, diaries, novels, or poems; records of interviews with prominent Southerners, runaway slaves, or former slaves; journalistic reports of those who visited the South: and comparisons written and offered by ex-Southerners or by those who were able to spend time in the South prior to the Civil War. A historian can also make use of sketches and paintings of Southern scenes and political cartoons, slogans, speeches, voting patterns, and other sources of information about the region. Once these data have been gathered, the historian transforms them into a word portrait that serves as an answer to the original problem posed.

There are some cautions to be observed. As historians themselves are at pains to point out, this portrait of the Old South would only represent *one person's* answer to the question, "What was life like in the South prior to the Civil War?" This person might have filtered out some key information that would have altered the portrait drawn, perhaps because it conflicted with other information gathered or with the researcher's own prejudices or points of view. Furthermore, in reporting the results of research, the historian does not always take the time to note which sources were the most influential. Often historians are unable to realize that one source was more influential than another or that one historical point of view dominated the analysis. This is why some works of history must be read with an understanding of the context and outlooks of the historian who wrote them. Finally, there is always the possibility that data gathered in this manner will be only partial. Even when the list of sources cited is lengthy, it is always possible that one or two crucial sources were unavailable or overlooked.

When we read history, we are not always in a position to examine critically the type and nature of the sources used. If the historical period is an unfamiliar one or one that has been previously unexplored, we usually must take the conclusions offered by the historian seriously, until we have the time to read another point of view or to become more familiar with the specific time period under consideration. Historians themselves acknowledge these difficulties with data gathering and reporting. They strive to the best of their abilities to be objective. However, there is always the possibility that their work will be uncritically received and accepted as factual without being subjected to critical examination.

Quantitative data gathering, because it proceeds on a more explicit basis, invites critical examination and makes such examination much easier to conduct. The quantitative historian (or *cliometrician*) would proceed somewhat differently from more traditional historians in an effort to answer the question: "What was life like in the South prior to the Civil War?" First, he or she would also try to narrow the field down to such factors as quality of housing, diet, or dress. However, rather than looking for verbal or visual information, the quantitative historian would seek to develop *measures* that would serve as *descriptors* of these aspects of life. Such measures would have to be available through some source (market records, population data, plantation records, railroad hauling records, and so on); and, hopefully, these same measures would be available for other regions and countries so that the historian could compare conditions in the South with similar conditions elsewhere at that time.

The next step in this process would be to *define operationally* each aspect to be studied, which involves guessing which indicators would reveal the description needed. Thus, quality of dress could be determined by number of yards of silk purchased per person or number of shoes sold per person; quality of housing could be determined by reference to local tax records, which might give such information as acreage per farm, number of rooms per house or dwelling, or number of persons per dwelling; and quality of diet could be measured in terms of amount of flour sold per person or per capita consumption of salt, salt pork, or beef. Using these measures of life-style, the quantitative historian could obtain some idea of how the average Southerner lived, with or without reference to how other Americans or Europeans lived at the same time.* When reporting the results of this form of historical research, the quantitative historian relies on both written explanations and the visual display of data. Data displays take advantage of the symbolic shortcuts provided by numerical expression and require readers to study and comprehend them with as much care as they ordinarily use in comprehending the written word.

The quantitative historian cannot avoid being biased. However, because the focus of the research is carefully defined beforehand and the results are displayed and included in the report, it is easier to examine them critically to decide if the research can be accepted as valid. Gaps in research are immediately apparent. The reader can easily judge whether the most appropriate or best measure was applied to define an indicator. The problem of missing or overlooked data remains, but that, too, can be noted by the alert reader and taken into consideration when the historical work is evaluated. Finally, quantitative history has the advantage of all work using objective numerical measures; it can be *replicated* (repeated) by another researcher using the same measures and the same modes of analysis to determine whether the same results will be obtained. The more times a research study is replicated and the same results obtained, the more confident we can be of the results. Historical research is not always possible to replicate, because it is the expression of the synthesis of one person's research and thinking over a period of time. It would be difficult for a conventional historian to replicate his or her own work. It would be even more difficult for another person to follow the path of discovery and attempt to verify the results that were ob-

*A recent study by R. W. Fogel and S. L. Engerman, *Time on the Cross: The Economics of American Negro Slavery* (Boston: Little, Brown, 1974) uses some of the above measures of quality of life to determine how slaves lived prior to the Civil War. Much to their surprise, the authors found that the diet, dress, and housing provided slaves were not only adequate, for the most part, but better than those offered to many Northern white laborers—a claim frequently made by proslave Southerners that has been discounted by antislave historians.

tained through historical analysis. It is relatively easy, however, to duplicate forms of quantitative data gathering—whether in history or in one of the other social science fields.

Quantitative data

What are quantitative data?

Data is another word for *information*. Data involve descriptive statements about objects, conditions, events, people, places, and feelings. *Quantitative data* can be defined as information put into numerical form. We are used to quantitative descriptions of such phenomena as temperature, altitude, or speed, but we are less comfortable with describing aspects of human reality in quantitative terms. This chapter will focus on that special category of quantitative information that describes the social, economic, and, to some extent, the psychological world, in which we live.

It could be said that quantification involves the use of a special "language," the language of numbers, to express concepts and understandings about human reality, as we use written words to symbolize speech or maps to symbolize geographical reality. It may seem strange to symbolize such concepts as wealth, political stability, or travel safety by the use of numbers, but we commonly use these shortcut symbols to describe reality (whether current or past) or to compare one group of people with another or one condition with another. Thus, the wealth of a nation can be symbolized by its Gross National Product (GNP). Political stability can be measured by the number of wars in which a nation engages or by the number of governments that have come into and gone out of office over a period of time. Traffic safety is commonly measured in terms of deaths per 1,000 people per year or total deaths over a weekend or a holiday period as compared with the "normal" number of automobile-related deaths during a "typical" weekend.

Quantification thus involves a new way of thinking as well as a new way of describing reality. A person who wishes to conduct research using quantitative measures must carefully define the concepts or variables with which he is working. If, for example, a person says to us, "Mary is a happy child," we are provided with qualitative information about Mary that most of us would accept at face value, according to our individual concept of "a happy child." The person doing social science research, however, would seek to define the idea of "a happy child" more fully and at the same time more objectively. Such a person would begin by asking what *observable* behavior characterizes a happy child. He or she might then choose several *indicators*, or carefully defined criteria, for happy behavior that could be measured or counted. Such indicators might be number of smiles per hour or number of giggles per hour or number of jokes or funny stories told per hour. Then, armed with these indicators, our researcher would seek to observe Mary at school or at home over a period of several days or weeks to determine how "happy" she, in fact, was.

The researcher might find that Mary was indeed a happy child, exhibiting more than the average or "normal" number of smiles per hour over a significant period of time. Or Mary might exhibit only moderate happiness when compared to her classmates. This situation might cause the researcher to wonder several things: Were the indicators accurate measures of the happiness of children? Was Mary observed during an "off" period? Does the person who said that Mary was a happy child have other ways of defining happiness that were not measured? Is the person who commented on Mary's happiness projecting some feelings onto Mary so that Mary is seen as "happy," even when she is not? The list of questions could continue and result in the researcher's revising the indicators and returning to observe Mary and her classmates or siblings—with similar or different results.

Some people may protest at this point, "What nonsense! I know what happiness is when I see it! I don't need to measure it or define it in quantitative terms!" However, we are all aware that conventional definitions of happiness (and of other concepts) vary significantly from individual to individual. This immediately raises an issue that is familiar to us all: the difficulty of communicating ideas because people do not always "talk the same language." The language of numbers, however, is universal and relatively easy for all to understand. Individuals, social systems, or economic systems are not defined or described in the more conventional qualitative form of words, synonyms, and adjectives, but with reference to one or more indicators in a manner that will allow no room for doubt as to how they have been defined. There is a precision in the language of numbers that is often lacking in verbal communication. It might even be said that when people communicate using quantitative definitions, they are brought closer together because they are able to share the understanding of precise symbolic meanings. Let us emphasize, however, that we are not advocating the elimination of normal qualitative speech and communication. There are many ways to define and describe things, events, people or concepts. Quantitative description is only one way, but one that involves new ways of thinking about and comprehending human reality.

Once aspects of human reality have been described in quantitative terms, they can be compared. A person may wish to compare levels of immigration to the United States decade by decade over the past 150 years, for example. Such a comparison would be across time, and it would typically involve counting the total number of immigrants from a limited number of important countries at 10-year intervals. A researcher who attempts to compare the level of literacy for ten different nations (or cases) can be said to be engaged in comparative analysis across cases. It would also be possible to compare cases across time. A person can also use quantitative information about a group of people to learn more about an individual within the group or about the group as a whole. Several indicators are sometimes used together to define a concept or to find reasons for existence of certain conditions.

To summarize, then, quantitative data represent information expressed in numerical form. When human behavior is quantified, it is expressed in numerical form with reference to one or more indicators of carefully defined criteria of measurable and observable behavior. Quantification involves assigning a numerical definition to an observable aspect of human behavior. Basically, it involves counting such things as how many times people do something; how much time people spend doing something; how much energy, resources, and/or money are spent to accomplish some particular goal; how many people can be placed into a particular category; and how much of something a group or a nation or a group of nations possesses.

Quantification allows the typical or average aspect of human behavior to be defined. Once concepts are translated into the universal language of numbers, they can be compared and manipulated in ways that will help researchers to obtain more and more concrete information about aspects of human behavior. After a person has learned how to quantify human behavior, it becomes a fascinating challenge to choose the indicators needed to help solve a problem or to locate the sources of quantitative information that can be used as indicators.

Sources of quantitative information

> "Whatever exists at all, exists in some amount."
> Edward L. Thorndike, educational researcher (1874–1949).

Quantitative data can be obtained from four broad sources: (1) what people say, (2) measures of how much money is earned, budgeted, and spent, (3) what people do during the course of their everyday lives, and (4) certain specific aspects of human behavior observed under experimental conditions.

What people say Two basic types of sources are included: (1) information obtained from *survey research* (i.e., surveys, interviews, and polls) and (2) information obtained from *content analysis* (i.e., from examining what is written or reported in newspapers or on television or radio).

Survey research implies asking individuals how they feel about a particular issue, how they are likely to vote, whether they have purchased or intend to purchase a particular product, or whether they intend to take a particular action. We have already noted how familiar this form of quantitative data is. The results of surveys are published and broadcast daily. They are available in magazines, newspapers, and research journals. National news broadcasting services hire pollsters to predict how elections will turn out. The sophisticated techniques for sampling now used, coupled with information from voting behavior in past years, make it possible for experts to predict the results of voting when only 2–5 percent of the returns have been counted. Certain polls, because of their proved reliability, have enormous influence. These include the Nielsen ratings of television viewing behavior and Gallup polls rating the popularity of the President or some other public figure.

However, survey research information is often accepted uncritically and cited without careful examination. The key to accurate survey results is the adherence to certain techniques for determining the population from which a sample is to be drawn and to certain sampling techniques. In addition, questions in a survey or poll should be field tested (tested with a small group of people) prior to their use with a large sample to ensure that they are clear and easily understood and that they acquire the information the researcher is seeking.

Central to accurate polling and surveys is the application of random sampling techniques. A *random sample* is a subgroup of a population that reflects as accurately as possible the characteristics of the larger group. Most nationally recognized survey research groups use several techniques to obtain a random sample. If you wished to obtain a random sample of one of your classes, for example, you could proceed as follows. First, assign a letter of the alphabet to each student. Then assign each student a number, beginning with student A and working through the alphabet until each student has received a number. For example, if the class size is 26, Student A will receive the number 1 and Student Z will receive the number 26. Then write the numbers from 1 to 26 on separate pieces of paper. Place them in a container, and shake them around to mix them. You will then be ready to draw a random sample. If you want to sample twenty percent of the class, you draw out five numbers. The students assigned these numbers constitute your sample and represent a statistical cross section of the class.

Obviously, random selection and random assignment techniques used in national surveys and polls are more sophisticated, but their purpose remains that of ensuring that the group surveyed will not be biased according to age, sex, economic background, occupation, or residence. Unless randomization has been employed, the results of any survey or poll should be viewed with skepticism.

Other aspects of survey research should also be examined. How many people were surveyed? A small number can indicate a biased poll. Also note the source of the sample population. If the individuals surveyed were all from the San Francisco area, for example, then the results of that poll cannot be generalized to other cities or regions of the United States. If only one sex is employed in a sample, results cannot be generalized to include the outlooks of both men and women. How were individuals chosen for the poll? Were they interviewed while passing by on the street, or did they respond to a questionnaire that appeared in a newspaper or to a question broadcast over a particular radio or television station? If so, the chances are that the results reflect a biased sample. This is particularly the case with polls that allow individuals to select themselves. Only those holding strong opinions or those who happened to read or view or listen to a particular media would be likely to respond. This form of bias is frequently present in such phenomena as letters to the editor of a newspaper or magazine, letters to legislators, and other letters expressing support of or opposition to a controversial issue. Well-conducted polls and surveys first choose the individuals they plan to include and then make an effort to contact them to ensure against bias. Students should be made aware of these guidelines for the critical evaluation of survey research and should get in the habit of applying them whenever they are presented with the results of such research.

The second type of information is obtained from *content analysis* of what people say. Content analysis involves analyzing either the written or the spoken words of certain selected groups of people. The content of what is said, how much is said, and the force with which something is said are all included in the special category of *content analysis research.* The quantities obtained from this kind of research include the number of times a certain word is used when writing about an issue over a period of time; how much column space (measured in inches or centimeters) is devoted to a particular topic over a period of time or to certain kinds of topics within a total newspaper or television news broadcast; how many times certain "strong" or "weak" words are used when referring to particular topics, nations, or individuals. Content analysis can focus on headlines, the front page of a newspaper, the editorial page, the entire newspaper or magazine; on the content of speeches made by certain individuals or groups of individuals; or on the entire transcript of nightly national news shows broadcast on television.

The value of content analysis is that it allows the researcher to view a person's writing in an objective manner and enables one piece of writing to be compared with another, again in a more objective manner than is usually the case. If a newspaper is accused, for example, of being reactionary, a researcher could define a series of topics or words that are associated with a reactionary outlook. He could then count the number of times such topics or words appear in the newspaper over a period of ten years. This might involve limiting himself to analyzing only those papers that were issued on a Monday, for example; since otherwise the task of analysis would be staggering. The researcher would also need to analyze newspapers known to be reactionary and those known to be liberal if he is to have a standard with which to compare the particular newspaper accused of being reactionary. In this manner, and after considerable work, he could arrive at an objective measure of the "reactionariness" of the newspaper in question.

Content analysis can be conducted in the classroom by asking students to look for the number of times certain words appear on the front page of the local newspaper. This would enable the class to observe the events that tend to "cause" certain words to appear more frequently or to determine if certain types of news are reported on certain days of the week. The school newspaper could also be analyzed to determine how many column inches have been devoted to a particular topic over a period of time.

National data available for content analysis can be found in the *New York Times Index* (a year-by-year compilation of headlines, organized by topic), *Deadline Data* and *Facts on File* (two publications that provide news summaries of world interest), and the privately published indices of local newspapers. Many school, municipal, college, and university libraries have back issues of prominent newspapers on microfilm. Past issues of such popular magazines as *Life, Time*, and *Newsweek* are usually available for analysis, as are special-audience magazines, such as women's magazines or business journals.

The techniques of content analysis can be applied to visual symbols as well, so that photographs or advertisements could be analyzed according to the themes they express, the number of times certain symbols appear in a magazine or newspaper over a period of time, or the use of certain key words in advertisements seeking to enhance audience appeal.

Measures of how much money is earned, budgeted, and spent A second major category of quantitative information is found in the tabulated statistics of how much money individuals, organizations, businesses, or governments earn, budget, and spend over the course of a month, a year, or several years. Also included in this category of information are various price indices that chart how much certain things cost and show how prices for these things change over time. Such measures include the Consumer Price Index, commodity price indices, the Dow-Jones stock averages, interest rates (i.e., the "cost" of borrowing money), prices of various import and export items, and the price per ton of steel, coal, or aluminum. Every level of government has a means of raising revenue and is accountable for how that money is spent. These budgets are readily available for public inspection. Businesses and corporations publish annual accounts of their earnings, expenditures, and profits. In addition, certain groups, both public and private, such as local chambers of commerce or certain national farmers' organizations, collect economic information and total it for purposes of analysis and comparison.

This vast body of information is a form of *aggregate data*, which will be discussed in detail later in this section. Such economic measures are concerned with the performance of the economic system alone or with systems of government. They are only *indirect* measures of human behavior. Although certain types of human behavior appear to be related to the economic system (e.g., birthrates tend to decline during periods of economic recession), measures of an economic variety do not tell us how individuals or groups of individuals are behaving, but rather indicate the direction of monetary flow or economic strength or weakness. Measures of how money is earned, budgeted, and spent can be used to develop research indicators and can provide insights into the causes of certain human behaviors.

These economic measures are available from local and state governments, from the United States federal government, from other nations throughout the world, and from various international trade organizations, along with the United Nations and the organizations that it sponsors. In addition, business and corporate information is available either from newspapers and magazines or directly from the business itself in the form of annual reports.

What people do during the course of their everyday lives This third category of quantitative information is also a very large one and includes information obtained from three sources: *field studies, recorded public acts*, and analysis of *voting* and *roll-call behavior*.

Field studies are a way of obtaining data about human behavior by observing people engaged in their ordinary activities in various typical environments. Thus, a researcher may place a camera in a grocery or department store to record how people react to the display of a new product or may observe the behavior of nursery-school children while they are at play. Field study research is discussed in considerable detail in chapter 5.

A field study typically involves counting how many times certain behavior occurs (frequency) or how many people behave in a certain way when confronted with a problem or a novel situation. This can mean counting the number of cars that use an intersection at various times during the day or noting how many people stop to look at themselves in a public mirror. If it is not possible to observe a group of individuals over a period of time, a researcher can ask people to provide *self-report data* by asking them to record how they allocate their time during the day or how much time they spend in some activity (such as reading). Self-report data pose several problems of accuracy, however. People can forget to keep a faithful record and then hastily fill in missing information according to their memories. Also, there can be a tendency to "edit" such data, making it appear, for example, that a person reads three hours a day, when in fact he may read only twenty minutes a day and watch television for four hours!

Information obtained from field studies presents other problems as well. It is usually impossible to generalize from such studies because they represent a limited sampling of the population. Field studies are usually limited to a relatively small area and group of people. Furthermore, special conditions can alter the results. Observations of traffic flow during the Christmas season, for example, would not yield "typical" data. If these limitations of field studies are kept in mind, however, they can be used as introductory experiences in quantitative research.

An enormous source of raw data about human behavior can be found in *recorded public acts*, the extensive records kept by governments and other organizations of how many people during a year displayed certain behaviors or could be placed in certain categories. This form of data is termed *aggregate* (or totaled) *data* and contains information obtained from census studies, records of births and deaths, marriages and divorces, and total numbers of students who entered elementary school, graduated from high school, and entered or graduated from college, graduate, or professional schools. It also includes statistics relative to occupations, literacy statistics, and health and crime statistics. The United States government and other governments throughout the world collect and tabulate this information in great quantities. Therefore, it is possible to compare levels of literacy or numbers of deaths per 1,000 population cross-nationally. The United Nations also collects this form of data and publishes them for those interested in cross-national research. In addition, local governments and school boards keep tax assessment records, together with records of achievement, reading, and IQ scores for each school within the system, and information about the level of experience of teachers and average salary scales. State governments conduct their own census studies and other research, which yield aggregate data.

Aggregate data are most often used to develop indicators or criteria for defining and then observing human behavior. Thus, a researcher seeking to study the "quality of education" in a single city could choose such indicators of a "good" school as the average Scholastic Aptitude Test scores from the school, the percent of students in each graduating class attending some form of postsecondary school, or the level of education (measured in years spent in school beyond high school) of a faculty. Other indicators might be dollars expended per pupil, number of library books owned, or average teacher salaries according to level of education and experience.

Aggregate data are also used to determine socioeconomic status by combining measures of income, occupational level or rank, total assessed property valuation, and other measures of property ownership, education, and opportunity.

This form of data is not only abundant but is also easily obtained, since most of it is a matter of public record. Local library reference rooms, school libraries, government offices, and business organizations are common sources of aggregate data. A list of some other sources can be found in the bibliography at the end of the chapter.

When using aggregate data, several cautions are in order.

First, there is a problem of *accuracy*. Although data-gathering techniques are fairly sophisticated and computers make it relatively easy to tabulate and analyze these data, there remains the problem of inaccurate reporting: people claiming more dependents than they have, hospitals reporting more cases of a particular illness than were actually diagnosed, or (a common error to the advantage of old-style machine politicians!) governments reporting more voters than acutally are in residence (or alive!) in a voting district. This problem of inaccuracy is magnified when the aggregate data from another nation are used. Data gathering, especially in some of the newly independent nations, is difficult because of the geographical remoteness of some inhabitants and haphazard because there are few people trained to conduct such research.

Second, aggregate data are often not comparable. This occurs because different measures are applied to the same behavior by different data-gathering agencies. One city may deliberately undervalue real estate, for example, while another assesses it according to strict market values. Comparisons of the level of wealth as measured by assessed property valuation would thus be quite risky. Again, cross-national comparisons are especially difficult because of different currency values or different ways of defining such phenomena as literacy, for example.

Third, aggregate data are often incomplete, and important measures for certain years may be unavailable. This is the case with the complete results of the United States federal census for the years 1890 (lost in a fire), 1910, 1920, 1930, 1940, 1950, 1960, and 1970. Although a great deal of federal census information has been published and released to the general public, certain detailed records that list individuals by name, address, occupation, income, and other personal data are not released until seventy years have elapsed to protect individual privacy. Such information would be a gold mine for those seeking to trace family occupational mobility from generation to generation, for example. Efforts are being made to change the law restricting the use of these data, but currently we can expect the release of the 1910 census in 1980; we may have to wait until the year 2000 for the complete socioeconomic report of the Great Depression.

Each class could prepare records of certain indicators for later use, using aggregate data from school records (IQ scores, achievement test scores, grade reports) and from students themselves, in, for example, an attempt to link school achievement to income or IQ scores to socioeconomic level. However, much of this information is generally confidential and some of it is protected from unwarranted use by federal law; therefore, teachers should exercise caution and common sense when obtaining and displaying it. Exact levels of income or assessed valuations of property should be avoided in favor of other indicators of wealth, such as number of cars owned per family, number of rooms per dwelling per family, or information as to whether parents or guardians rent or own their homes. Other possible aggregate measures might include the following:

Personal characteristics of students

Age entered school
Number of siblings
Age of first inoculations for polio, diphtheria, and other diseases
Age when contracted various childhood diseases
Number of books read per year
Number of hours spent watching television per week

Number of cities lived in during lifetime
Number of awards received
Number of clubs or organizations belonged to
Number of arrests or detentions
Grade point average

Socioeconomic characteristics of students

Age of parents at their marriage
Number of years parents married
Number of children
Age of parents at birth of first child
Number of years of education of parents
Square footage of dwelling
Number of bathrooms in dwelling
Number of television sets owned
Number of telephones owned
Number of cars owned
Number of books owned
Number of periodicals subscribed to

Some characteristics of schools
(to be used to compare one school with another)

Number of teachers in school
Number of female teachers in school
Number of male teachers in school
Number of pupils in school per grade
Level of education of teachers
Number of classrooms in school
Cost per pupil of books, supplies, food, or maintenance
Number of nonteaching personnel in school
Amount of federal money in school budget
Average salaries for male teachers
Average salaries for female teachers
Average yearly budget of school

Once students become accustomed to defining variables by using aggregate data measures, they will begin to develop their own indicators and suggest desirable data to acquire.

A final type of quantitative information about observed human behavior involves the special category of public acts that are labeled *voting behavior* or *roll-call behavior*. Although each individual of voting age in our society votes in private, using a secret ballot, the results of that voting are a matter of public record and reveal a great deal about the preferences and values of a particular voting district, state, or region of the United States. Similarly, recorded voting behavior in other nations is of significance with regard to the types of political parties that receive support, the votes for and against key issues that come before the electorate, and the percentage of people eligible to vote who actually *do* vote. All these measures provide information about a nation or group of people that can be used as indicators when undertaking social science research.

Another type of measurable behavior in this category is the record of how elected officials in local, state, and national governments vote on a particular issue, regulation, or law. Such votes can reveal whether legislators do, in fact, serve the people they represent or, as has been charged, their own special interests. These *roll-call votes* can help to reveal natural voting blocs and alliances within political parties or blocs that occur around a particular issue. Roll-call data also help to define local and national values and the values of representatives at the various levels of government more clearly. Roll-call votes in the United Nations General Assembly and certain votes in the UN Security Council reveal power blocs and alliances, however temporary, and can aid analysts in predicting "world opinion" with regard to certain issues. The votes cast in the UN General Assembly also help to reveal the relative strength of certain long-established power blocs, such as those nations allied with the United States or those voting with the USSR. Some nations are "swing" voters, shifting allegiances as their own self-interests or national goals change. These nations are in a position to play a key role in world politics and can be identified with the help of roll-call analysis.

Voting behavior is a matter of public record. Newspapers and magazines record special votes of interest to constituents, as well as some voting done in the United Nations. The *Congressional Record* records voting in the United States Congress and offers the speeches and comments of representatives as well, which could be subjected to content analysis. Similar publications record votes of state legislatures, municipal governments, school boards, and other elected bodies. These are usually available directly from the legislature or are published and sent to public libraries, colleges, and universities. Voting records for the United Nations General Assembly can be obtained from the UN.

Certain specific aspects of human behavior observed under experimental conditions Quantitative information obtained as a result of *experimental research* is sought to test a researcher's hypotheses about the nature of human behavior. Experimental research involves placing people in special environments and observing them closely as they confront special or unique problem situations. A laboratory environment, similar to a simulation, involves a specially constructed aspect of reality that limits an individual's behavioral options. Placing a subject in a laboratory also allows the researcher to alter the environment of his subjects by adjusting the lighting, sound, or heat of the room. The psychological reality of the subjects can also be altered for experimental purposes in such a way that individuals can be made to feel either welcome or threatened, optimistic or pessimistic, passive or aggressive. The results of laboratory experiments that used voluntary as well as assigned subjects can be found in a number of research journals in the fields of psychology, sociology, education, and political science. Sometimes important experiments are cited in classroom textbooks or are noted in newspapers, on television, and in other media sources.

The criteria for evaluating experimental research are quite similar to those used to evaluate other social science research. The process of random selection and random assignment is essential. The size of the group and the population from which it was drawn should be noted. Generally, the more people involved in an experiment, the more reliable are its results. Bias can enter the laboratory quite easily when only limited sample groups are chosen.*

Another group of data obtained under special, but not necessarily experimental, conditions is one that all teachers are familiar with; namely, the whole range of standardized tests that students are subjected to throughout the course of their school careers. These include IQ tests, reading tests, achievement tests, certain state-prepared achievement tests (such as the New York State Regents Exams), SAT, GRE, Law Boards, and other forms of standardized tests. These various instruments are usually administered under controlled conditions that are usually common for all those taking the test on a particular day; for example, they are given at the same time, in the same place; with the same lighting conditions and levels of heat and noise; and in the same general atmosphere of tension and press for achievement. Often, a person is unable to leave such a test without special precautions, and only standardized breaks are allowed. Part of the ability to perform well on these tests involves the ability to master the standardized test environment, as many critics of these instruments have noted.

Standardized tests are scored and students are ranked according to national norms developed for each test. These tests are known to be highly reliable, although they do tend to ask for factual information and require good reading abilities and training in reasoning. Students take a wide variety of such tests before graduating from high school, yet it is interesting to note that many may have no idea how these tests are developed, what they measure, how they are scored, and why a particular school uses them. An excellent introduction to the quantification of human behavior might be a consideration of the construction and meaning of these tests.

The companies that publish, distribute, and score these tests usually provide explanatory booklets that describe the purpose of a test and tell how it is constructed and scored. In addition, the Educational Testing Service,† which prepares the SAT, GRE and law board tests, also publishes several

---

*For an excellent brief introduction to problems of evaluating experimental research, see D. T. Campbell and J. C. Stanley, *Experimental and Quasi-Experimental Designs for Research.* (Chicago: Rand McNally, 1966).

†The address of this organization and those of other companies that publish standardized tests are given in the bibliography to this chapter.

pamphlets that describe the process of testing. The American College Testing (ACT) Service also provides such information for interested teachers. The process of grading student achievement involves quantifying aspects of human behavior, categorizing that behavior, and ranking it from "excellent" (defined as high point performance on tests and papers and rewarded with a grade of "A") to "unsatisfactory" (defined as poor point performance on tests and papers and given the grade of "F"). Although the topic of testing and grading is discussed in detail in another chapter of this book, it is worth noting that teachers make use of a large mass of quantitative data about students, including data obtained under special conditions, to make qualitative judgments about them as students and as people.

In summary, it can be seen that the sources of quantitative information about human behavior are abundant and accessible. Obtaining information from these various sources takes some time, but its potential classroom uses to spark and inform inquiry makes it worthwhile.

It remains the task of the person conducting an inquiry to transform these various sources of information into indicators that can be used to generate and then support or disprove hypotheses about the way people or groups of people or nations behave. In the next section, we will attempt to answer the question: How can this form of information be used to promote the process of inquiry in the social studies classroom?

Inquiry learning using quantitative data

There is an important distinction between inquiry *learning* and inquiry *teaching*. As we see it, the former implies the process of inquiry thinking outlined in the introduction to this book and labeled "the rational process by which one goes about resolving doubt." It involves the following steps: awareness of a problem or perplexity, attempts at resolving the problem by suggesting hypotheses or possible solutions, testing hypotheses or solutions in practice as part of the process of data gathering, deciding whether the information or data gathered warrant a conclusion, and, finally, coming to a conclusion of some kind—a conclusion that, we hope, resolves the original problem or perplexity. Inquiry teaching, on the other hand, involves the many ways that teachers suggest, encourage, plan for, and provoke the process of inquiry learning within their classes. It requires that a person recognize how inquiry learning proceeds at the same time that he or she is prepared to begin or sustain the process. The inquiry teacher who is involved in the process of inquiry must not lose sight of the entire process of learning. This requires an ability to become involved in the process of inquiry learning and at the same time to be able to view it "from the outside," objectively and in totality. This dual perspective, incidentally, is essential not only for good inquiry teaching but also for good teaching in general.

Quantitative information enters the process of inquiry learning either (1) at the beginning, when a datum (what most people erroneously call "a statistic") serves to provoke doubt or perplexity or suggests a new line of thinking, or (2) during the data analysis phase, when information in quantitative form can be brought to bear to support or disprove hypotheses about the relationship between two conditions. This section focuses upon the general uses to which quantitative data might be put in the process of inquiry learning: (1) to describe aspects of the past or present; (2) to verify hypotheses about the present or the past; and (3) to clarify the values of an individual, a group, an organization, or a society.

To describe aspects of the past or present

Quantitative data can be used to describe an individual, group, or nation or to account for the attitudes of individuals within groups. Describing the conditions within a city, area, or region or the conditions and styles of life in the past requires the use of aggregate data measures, content analysis, and the results of surveys and polls.

Quantitative information can also provide the descriptive tools necessary to verify certain assumptions or statements made about the present or the past. Each day a student is likely to encounter statements that embody largely unverified assumptions about all aspects of life. Sometimes such statements are taken from research reports that could be replicated for the purpose of verification; more often, these statements are presented without reference to any research at all. These statements should warn the student to take a skeptical stance and attempt to gather information to see them either verified or disproved. Examples of such statements are: "The United States is a land of equality" or "Slavery was an inefficient system of labor."

Quantifying the factors in each of the above statements can be a complex task. For example, what is a good measure of equality? Does this refer to equality under the law? economic equality? social equality? equality of opportunity? Should this problem seek to determine the existence of equality in the United States alone, or should a comparative perspective be drawn? Considering the next issue, what is the best measure of efficiency? Is it man-hours per job? rate of production? level of productivity? Would measures of these be available for the pre-Civil War era? Should level of efficiency be measured with reference to the North and West alone or with reference to other nonslave economic systems (e.g., Great Britain) or other slaveowning societies (e.g., Brazil)?

The challenge to the student occurs, then, during the process of definition and operationalization of the variables.

To verify hypotheses about the present or the past

Another use for quantitative information is to test the association between two or more conditions. The simplest case is the bivariate situation, where we examine whether the presence or absence of one variable (labeled x) is associated with the presence of another (labeled *y*), or whether an increase in one variable is associated with an increase in another. One such hypothesis is the statement that level of intelligence is associated with race.

Once a person discovers that certain conditions exist or existed, he must seek out the antecedents or causes of those conditions. Also, if certain assumptions prove impossible to verify (e.g., "The United States is a land of equality"), a person might wonder if this had been true in the past (by reference to historical research) and if so, why it is no longer true (which would involve finding the causes of inequality) or, why it has been assumed true (a search for the causes of a myth, which reference to a comparative historical perspective might help to clarify). Causation implies not only that two variables exist together or are associated, but that one (the *dependent variable*) does not exist without the other (the *independent variable*).

Determining causation requires a student to recognize the existence of a condition and then to hypothesize or guess about the possible causes of the circumstance before engaging in data gathering and analysis. For example, students who notice that the birthrates for the United States from 1860 to 1960 appear to rise and fall with some regularity (even though a steady decline in birthrates is apparent) may attempt to guess the cause of these fluctuations. They might hypothesize that periods of economic decline appear to coincide with a drop in the birthrate or that the end of a war coincides with a rise in the birthrate. The next task would be to gather data to verify these hypotheses about causation and display these data on one or on several separate graphs. Quantitative data then can be used to determine if certain factors existed in association with others under observation.

To clarify the values of an individual, a group, an organization, or a society

Whenever a person is asked to identify the "good" or the "desirable," he is engaged in the process of values clarification. This process is described in detail in chapter 2, but it is important to note that quantitative data can assist in values clarification in several ways.

Personal comparisons A common concern of young people is whether or not they are "typical" of their group. Early adolescents, in particular, value conformity. They will dress, talk, and behave in ways that serve to help them belong to a group or clique rather than to stand outside of it. Quantitative information in the form of survey or interview results can help students determine how typical they are of a particular age group. Once the data have been presented and individuals are able to see where they stand relative to others, then a further inquiry into values can continue. If a student appears to conform to his or her age group, the question can be asked, "Are you pleased to discover this?" and, if so, "Why?" Students thus could be brought to consider why conformity is valued. The student who does not appear to conform to the age group, could be asked, "Do you think that this situation is desirable?" Why are nonconformists urged to conform? Should they do so? What value exists in being a nonconformist? These and other questions can help assist young people in determining, first, where they stand on a particular issue; then, why they have chosen to take that stand. Survey research results provide useful feedback that can help initiate the process of values clarification.

Determining desirable behavior Secondary-school-age individuals are faced with a number of significant decisions, which can affect the subsequent courses of their lives. Among these decisions are the following: Should I engage in premarital sex? Should I experiment with drugs? Should I marry? Should I remain in high school? Which career should I follow? Should I attend some form of school beyond high school?

As is well known, the answers to these and other perplexing questions of adolescence are not always arrived at in a rational manner. Unfocused feelings, strong personal desires, and vague life goals cloud the process of rational inquiry. Occasionally, however, quantitative information in the form of statistical trends can provide a sober basis on which to make a decision. A young woman eager to marry upon graduation from high school might reconsider if she were told that the divorce rate among individuals who marry before age twenty is higher than the rate for other age groups or that the rate of infant mortality for children born to women in their late teens and early twenties is higher than it is for children born to slightly older women. Similarly, information about lifetime earning rates for those who complete high school, as compared to those who drop out, might cause a high-schooler planning to drop out to reconsider those plans.

Defining the good All of us have been involved in conversations in which people have casually asserted that one style of life, income level, or place of residence was more desirable than another. When we take time to examine these assertions, we find that they involve various "hidden criteria" that we are not always aware of. Coming to terms with the criteria that people use to define what is "good" is the underlying goal of inquiry into values. Often, these criteria can have a quantitative dimension.

A useful class exercise that will demonstrate various definitions of "the good" (as well as putting to use other aspects of this chapter) is the "naming the best and worst cities" exercise. You could begin by listing the names of the ten or twenty largest American cities. Students then could be asked to rank these cities from "most desirable place to live" to "least desirable place to live." They should determine which criteria of "goodness" should be used. After discussing student lists in class, the instructor introduces an article from the January 1975 issue of *Harper's Magazine* entitled "The Worst American City," by Arthur M. Louis. In this article Louis employs twenty-four characteristics, all of them expressed as quantitative evidence, to rank the nation's fifty largest cities. The instructor can compare the students' value judgments with the findings in the article from *Harper's*. It might be useful, in fact, to distribute either copies of the article or the ranking of the fifty cities that Louis provides.

Determining how values are allocated A final use of quantitative information to assist an inquiry into values would be to determine what an individual, group, organization, or society values. This involves obtaining a form of descriptive information that indicates the relative importance of one activity or goal over another, according to how much time or money is spent pursuing it. Budget information is particularly useful in making such determinations. If several families with the same yearly income are compared, we might discover that one family spends the major portion of its surplus on a new car each year, while another invests heavily in the stock market, and a third prefers to spend its extra resources on travel and other opportunities for self-improvement and enrichment. This information immediately provides us with the data necessary to draw inferences about the values each family holds. Similarly, per capita expenditures on such items as education, health care, defense, or advertising can serve as a basis for defining the values of one nation as compared with those of another. Thus, we can be defined according to our spending habits and the ways we allocate our time and other personal resources.

To summarize, this section has explored three modes of inquiry learning that can make use of quantitative information. In the next section, we will turn our attention to the ways in which teachers can provoke and sustain inquiry by using quantitative data.

The process of inquiry teaching using quantitative data

Inquiry teaching, as opposed to inquiry learning, implies two basic teacher postures in the classroom: the teacher as the person who provokes inquiry and helps students to acquire the skills necessary to engage in it, and the teacher as the person who acts as a resource for students once they begin to formulate their own problems for inquiry and to work through them. This section will suggest ways in which a teacher can first prepare himself or herself to provoke and sustain quantitative inquiry and can then prepare his or her classes to use quantitative information during the process of inquiry.

Five steps teachers should take to prepare for quantitative inquiry

1. Become familiar with sources of quantitative information This will require several afternoons spent in either the school library or a local public library with a good reference room. Review the section in this chapter on the sources of data and ask the librarian to direct you to the sources that are available. If a college or university library is nearby, search out professional writings contained in either journals or monographs about specific methods of data gathering. Take time to read some of the historical and social science research works that use quantification. A selected bibliography of these readings is included at the end of this chapter.

2. Operationalize concepts Practice operationalizing some of the concepts that you commonly use, both in class and in everyday conversation. See if you can begin to define some of these concepts in quantitative terms. An interesting by-product of this sort of personal exercise should be greater precision when using many common concepts during conversation.

3. Begin to develop a file of quantitative material This would include summaries of research reports, poll results, tables, and graphs. As you read through newspapers and magazines, be alert for evidence of data. Clip these items and save them for later class use. If a table or chart appears in a book that you are reading, photocopy it and place it in the same file. Quite soon, you should acquire a number of pieces of information for use at a later time. While you watch television news programs, keep a note pad and pencil handy to jot down quantitative evidence that is mentioned. If you would like further information about a survey cited during a national news program, for example, write directly to the research organization that provided the material. A list of organizational addresses can usually be found in a library reference room.

Some material collected in these ways can be used in exercises designed to build student skepticism about the reporting of research data. Other material, used by itself, can provoke inquiry. Occasionally, two different studies will be reported that use different data and draw conflicting conclusions. These can be used for exercises that seek to verify quantitative information. A great deal of the material collected will probably serve as resources for inquiry.

4. Study available visuals If your school requires a textbook for your course, take time to read through it and note the tables and graphs included. Study each of these to see if they offer information that could be used for inquiry. Many textbook visuals are self-explanatory and matter-of-fact, but others call into question the issues of data sources, distorted presentation of data, and even the problem of inaccurate or incomplete data. These should be brought to the attention of students. In your informal file of quantitative source material you might find information that can be used to supplement the textbook.

5. Resolve to hold fast to a quantitative outlook This implies commitment to an awareness and regular use of quantitative data, making it a part of your personal outlook and approach to problem solving so that it carries over into the classroom.

A teacher who has taken these personal steps to become familiar with quantification is ready to help students acquire the quantitative perspective and the skills needed to practice it during the process of inquiry.

Ten steps designed to help students engage in quantitative inquiry

We feel that there are ten steps a teacher should follow to prepare his or her students to initiate and conduct their own inquiry exercises using quantitative information. We will discuss each of these below. It is important to stress that these steps are only suggestions. Some classes may immediately catch on to the process of quantitative inquiry; others may never fully grasp the process. Teachers should be sensitive to differences in skill and age level. If you feel that your students are not capable of mastering all of the suggested steps, go only as far as they are able to go. It would be better for students to understand and feel comfortable with basic quantification than to have them feel frustrated and uncomfortable with the process of quantitative inquiry learning.

Step 1—Begin by highlighting number awareness. The first step toward building quantification skills is to draw student attention to various quantitative definitions that they often use. For example, sports statistics define the quality of a team or of an individual player. Baseball statistics have been kept for more than half a century, and many young people make a point of memorizing them to follow the fortunes of their favorite teams more fully during a season. In addition, sports odds or ratios are given for important encounters; for example, one team is favored to win over another by a certain number of points or a certain number of bettors favor one team over another. Point out how these statistics represent a quantification of aspects of human behavior.

There are other ways in which we regularly quantify one another. Salary levels, for good or ill, often define the success and competency of individuals. Grade point averages or cumulative test scores in one subject help to distinguish good students from poor ones. Even aspects of beauty or handsomeness are measured qualities (for example, a woman's "vital statistics" or the size of a man's biceps or neck). There are tables of "desirable" weights for certain heights. Popularity in school is often measured by the number of votes a person obtains for a class office or by the number of events a person attends or is asked to attend. All of these substitute observable, measurable qualities for verbal assessments or provide evidence for assertions made about a person. As students begin to realize how often they have recourse to quantification, they will begin to feel comfortable with the process of quantifying human behavior.

Step 2—Help students practice defining characteristics and concepts in quantitative terms. Teaching students how to operationalize certain characteristics and concepts is the next step. This involves drawing their attention to the many words in their vocabulary that are vaguely or only partially defined and asking them to define the words quantitatively. Since you will have practiced this skill yourself prior to introducing it to your students, you should be able to suggest many possibly quantifiable terms. Among these might be "rich," "poor," "old," "young," "well-educated," "happy," "intelligent," "healthy," "peaceful," "violent," "good," and "bad." Many more terms are likely to come up in class; and once students develop this skill, they will be alert for such words. The class might develop a bulletin board that charts the various quantitative definitions given to certain words. The chart can be expanded as new words occur and are defined in this manner. This step should provide a good deal of fun for both teachers and students, since it requires imagination and careful thought to operationalize characteristics and concepts.

Step 3—Help students become familiar with the way quantitative data are displayed. This involves introducing students to the various types of graphs as well as to tables of quantitative information. Students should learn to read and understand such visual displays and, when given the appropriate data, to draw or construct their own.

The instructor, as well as the students, can make extensive use of visual displays for categorizing, comparing, and analyzing a myriad bits of information concerning any quantifiable topic. Visual displays are simple both to construct and to utilize in the classroom and can yield much insight. Using visual displays can stimulate student interest and greater student participation. After students feel comfortable with the process of analyzing visual displays, they can undertake to construct their own.

In the section, "Examples of Data Analysis Techniques," we discuss a number of visual displays both for describing one characteristic and for determining the association between two or more characteristics.

Step 4—Help students to practice drawing inferences and suggesting trends from teacher-supplied data displays. Once students are familiar with the common forms of data displays, they need to practice studying these and drawing meaning from them. The term "eyeballing" is given to this practice of studying a data display. Here is where a review of textbook visuals and a good personal file of quantitative material will prove useful. At this stage the teacher will have to provide selected visual displays. Students should be taught to study a graph or table carefully. They can then list, in short sentence form, the information they are able to obtain from the visual. Next, they can be asked if the visual provides information useful for predicting future trends. As this approach to "reading" visuals becomes habitual, students will have acquired an important analytic tool.

Step 5—Familiarize students with the sources of data and with how different data are obtained. Building on personal familiarity with sources of data, a teacher can bring to class several data-rich resource books for students to look over and evaluate. The teacher could discuss the various forms of data and how they are obtained. This would include noting some sources of inaccuracy in certain data-gathering techniques. Each student could then be responsible for studying and reviewing one data source. The results of these reviews could be kept in a class card file, which would be available for later reference. As new sources are discovered, either by the teacher or by members of the class, they could be reviewed and added to the file. Students should also get into the habit of bringing in data displays, reports of polls or surveys, or the results of research studies that they encounter in their reading. These could be mounted on posters or otherwise filed for future class reference. As students become familiar with the sources of data, some may wish to become "class experts" about one particular kind. Later, this group of students could serve as resources during the process of inquiry.

Step 6—Help students to develop skepticism toward statistics and data displays. It is important that students recognize that not all data are useful and that some statistics are misleading as well as inaccurate.* Visual displays are often deliberately constructed to exaggerate certain trends or to highlight certain information for the purpose of making a point. This is particularly the case with the so-called scientific information provided in advertisements, which represent a virtual gold mine of opportunities to examine the manner in which information obtained from research and polls is manipulated to serve a particular end. Quantitative information may be used to buttress propaganda statements. Sometimes a visual reflects the use of incomplete data. A graph or table that does not indicate the source of the data given should be suspect. From time to time, it is useful to challenge a visual display or data report by replicating the data-gathering procedures to see if similar results are obtained.

Surveys, polls, and research studies should be examined carefully to determine if they were conducted according to proper research procedures. Sample size or the size of the experimental group should be noted. Was randomization employed? Is the study one that can be generalized to all people, or does it provide information about only a limited group of people? Are the conclusions warranted by the data? Often researchers are tempted to overgeneralize from the data they have obtained. Occasionally, they may

---

*For a delightful, yet detailed, discussion of some of these issues, see Darrell Huff and Irving Geis, *How to Lie with Statistics* (New York: Norton, 1954), a classic work that both teachers and students will find highly readable and useful.

claim something, supposedly based on their data, that has nothing to do with the information they have obtained. Adolescents are natural skeptics. Once they have been "clued in" to the fact that a person should examine *every* statistic, *every* visual display, and *every* research study for evidences of missing data or distortion, it is likely that very little quantitative information will go unchallenged in the classroom.

Step 7—Suggest exercises that require students to describe certain conditions, either in the present or in the past, using quantitative information. Once students have mastered the first six steps, they will be in a position to begin the process of data-gathering and analysis. Initially, the impetus for these will rest with the teacher, who must act to propose inquiry exercises and be prepared to assist students as they conduct them.

As has been noted, data gathering for the purpose of description is the most common form of quantification and the one that should be the easiest for students to master. The possible areas of inquiry seem almost unlimited. Quantitative information can be especially useful as a means of describing such aspects of a historical time period as birthrates, average life-span, health, quality of diet, quality of life in general, level of agricultural production, incidence of trade, level of industrial production, level of prosperity, level of violence in a society, allocation of resources, and so on. Similar measures can help to define living conditions; political and economic stability; or the distribution of land, natural resources, wealth, and power in the present day. Other descriptive information is found in voting patterns, surveys, and polls. Teachers will have to choose the area of descriptive inquiry that is most appropriate for the age of their students and the subject being taught.

Step 8—Suggest exercises that require students to gather quantitative information to verify possibly unwarranted statements. The development of student skepticism about data and the reporting of quantitative information naturally leads to this step in the process of acquiring inquiry skills. Textbooks, newspapers, magazines, and other materials that students are likely to encounter are filled with statements expressed as conclusions that might be difficult to verify. For example, students could be presented with the following statement: "In the United States, the poor lead terrible lives." Is this true? Without denying the existence of devastating poverty in the United States, students could develop indicators for what is "poor" (e.g., level of income, quality of housing, quality of diet) and what could be defined as "a terrible life." The data collected to describe the poor in the United States could then be compared with similar data from other societies. This sort of comparison might reveal that the poor in America are as disadvantaged as the poor in other societies. Conversely, it could reveal that the standard of living associated with poverty in American society might be considered comparatively comfortable in others. This exercise should not be undertaken to dismiss the very real problems of poverty in our society, but it could be used as an introduction to the problem of ecology and waste among the industrialized nations.

Another useful exercise would be to present the results of two different studies of the same phenomenon that arrived at different conclusions. For example, several studies have found evidence of harmful effects of marijuana, while others have been able to discount these harmful side effects. The issue of whether or not to legalize the purchase and sale of marijuana is likely to be a recurrent one in several parts of the United States, and reference to these studies could be a useful way of examining it.

Step 9—Suggest exercises that require students to gather and use quantitative information to clarify their values. As has been mentioned previously, quantitative information can help an individual make decisions about what is good or desirable in itself or what would be a good or desirable course of action. Teachers should be alert to quantitative dimensions in the decisions of their students and, from time to time, should pose such problems as inquiry exercises.

Step 10—Suggest exercises that require students to gather quantitative information to determine association. This form of data gathering involves the most difficult problems of analysis. It is here that statistical methods become useful as a means of making subtle discriminations among sets of relevant data. In the next section, we will present several visual tools that can aid in determining association without resort to statistical analysis. Refer to these for suggested exercises.

Among other things, students could determine whether certain factors (such as economic prosperity or decline, level of agricultural production, levels of trade, epidemics, weather conditions, or other quantifiable factors) accounted for or "caused" certain types of political behavior in the past. Students should be aware, however, that direct causation is often difficult to verify without certain statistical tools. As with other research results, students should be cautious about accepting evidence of causation, particularly for events that occurred in the distant past, unless there is overwhelming evidence supporting it.

As a current events exercise, students could suggest various factors that could account for presidential popularity. Such factors as level of employment, wholesale price indices, level of agricultural production, weather conditions, or incidence of disease could be determined on a monthly basis and plotted on graphs to be compared, for example, with the monthly report of presidential popularity made by the Gallup poll. As the year progresses, students should have some visual evidence of the factors that appear to be related to presidential popularity.

Once students have mastered the above ten steps, they will be ready to initiate and conduct their own quantitative inquiry learning. At that point, the teacher shifts from being the primary initiator of inquiry to being a person who encourages and assists student inquiry. This latter role requires that the teacher (1) be on the lookout for a quantitative dimension to problems raised by students and (2) be in a position to suggest productive paths of inquiry, appropriate indicators, useful sources of data, and the best ways to organize and display information obtained. A teacher who has been dedicated enough to the process of quantitative inquiry to have developed the requisite student skills outlined above should have no difficulty making the shift from one role to the other.

Examples of data analysis techniques

Visual displays for descriptive quantitative analysis

As we said earlier, there exist two basic kinds of tasks associated with quantitative analysis and therefore with quantitative inquiry. The intial task focuses upon *description*, which most social scientists term *univariate* or *one-variable analysis*. The second kind of analysis is termed *associational* or *two-variable analysis*, which emphasizes the relationship between two or more concepts. In univariate analysis the student attempts to determine if a specific condition exists at a given moment in time (e.g., if there is an unequal income distribution among United States citizens) or the value of a certain concept at a given moment (e.g., the percentage of the Gross World Product that is possessed by the developed nations of the world). A student might also want to engage in comparative analysis, either across cases or across time, focusing on only one variable.

The social scientist would tell us that univariate analysis is used to describe each variable: its frequency distribution (the number of times each value of a variable appears), its typical or average value, and the degree of similarity or homogeneity among the cases. These three kinds of descriptive functions, as outlined by the social scientist, are simply sophisticated ways of stating what we have just described; that is, that descriptive displays reveal the principal characteristics of some concept, including the distribution of values.

Univariate analysis of quantitative information adopts one of two distinct approaches, either separately or in combination. The first strategy, visual displays, is designed to yield basic information about a concept or variable as parsimoniously as possible without distortion. Visual displays are primarily of a graphic nature; less often, they are in tabular form. Because the aim of this chapter has been to demonstrate the ease with which quantitative analysis can be employed by students and teachers, visual displays, rather than statistical operations, will be emphasized. However, we do include a brief discussion of some statistical techniques that are useful during the process of quantitative inquiry.

Figure 4.1. Federal expenditures, 1967–1970*

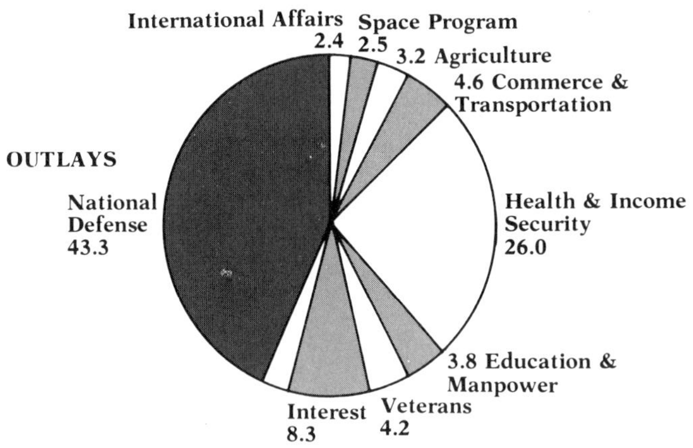

*Values are expressed as percentages. From William Lerner, *Pocket Data Book USA 1971* (Washington, D.C.: U.S. Department of Commerce, 1971), p. 84.

Four types of visual displays can be used to provide descriptive quantitative analysis: pie graphs, bar graphs (histograms), line graphs, and Lorenz curves. In our examples we have ignored most of the nuts-and-bolts issues about the construction of each of these types of displays, preferring instead to focus upon the substantive meaning of each.

Pie graphs Consider the graph shown as Figure 4.1. In the common visual display in this figure, we have compared the federal government's expenditures for a number of major categories. This information could have been presented in a number of other ways as well—as a series of sentences or in tabular form—and similar levels of meaning would have resulted. But the pie graph allows the researcher to display the evidence in such a fashion that a maximum amount of information becomes evident to the reader in the shortest amount of time. Figure 4.1 reveals clearly, for example, that an overwhelming proportion of money is allocated for national defense, and that fully two-thirds of all expenditures are earmarked for defense, health, or income security.

Bar graphs (histograms) A bar graph, or histogram shows the frequency with which certain values of a concept or variable appear in a distribution. This type of display allows us to find the categories of a variable as well as their outer limits quickly. For example, Figure 4.2 reveals the percentage of voter turnout in the 1964 presidential election according to region.

Figure 4.2. Voter turnout in U.S. by region: 1964 (% of voting age participating)*

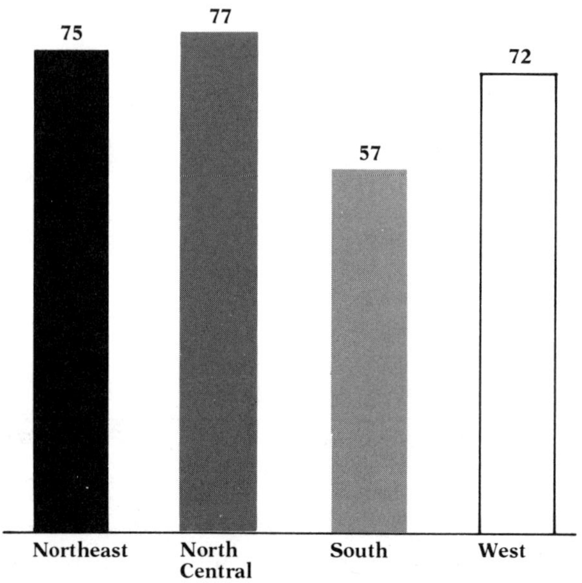

*From Oliver Benson, *Political Science Laboratory* (Columbus: Merrill, 1969), p. 65.

We observe that the United States is divided into four regions—Northeast, North Central, South, and West—and that the South had a significantly lower voter participation than the other three regions. This bar graph represents information at the *nominal* level of analysis; that is, each category—Northeast, North Central, South, and West—represents broad categories with no implied rank order. Bar graphs may also represent *ordinal level* information, where categories are ranked in some fashion, such as elementary school, junior high school, high school, and college, or even *interval level* data, where an endless number of value positions are collapsed (or condensed) into a manageable number of categories.

Figure 4.3 depicts information concerning the increased use of coal by the world's population. This figure allows the student to conceptualize instantly the tremendous consumption of natural resources in just the past 200 years.

Another bar graph describes the distribution of the world's oil (Figure 4.4). This example is really two bar graphs in one, since it represents the amount of oil produced from 1859 to 1970 in selected regions and countries of the world, as well as the known oil reserves for these areas in 1970. We can infer from Figure 4.4 that: (1) the Middle East controls a significant propor-

Figure 4.3. World energy consumption: 1900–2000 A.D.
In millions of metric tons of coal equivalent*

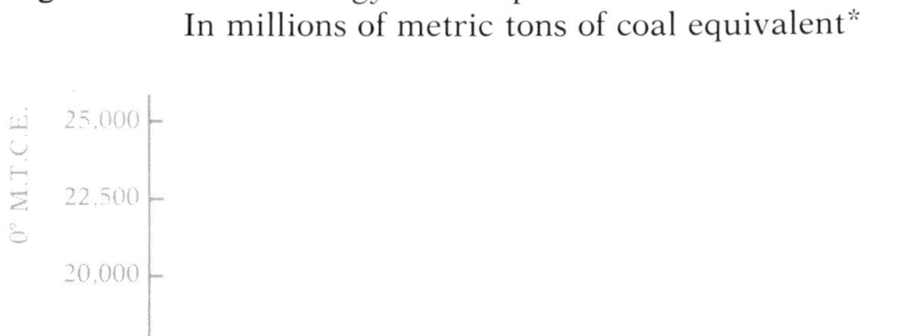
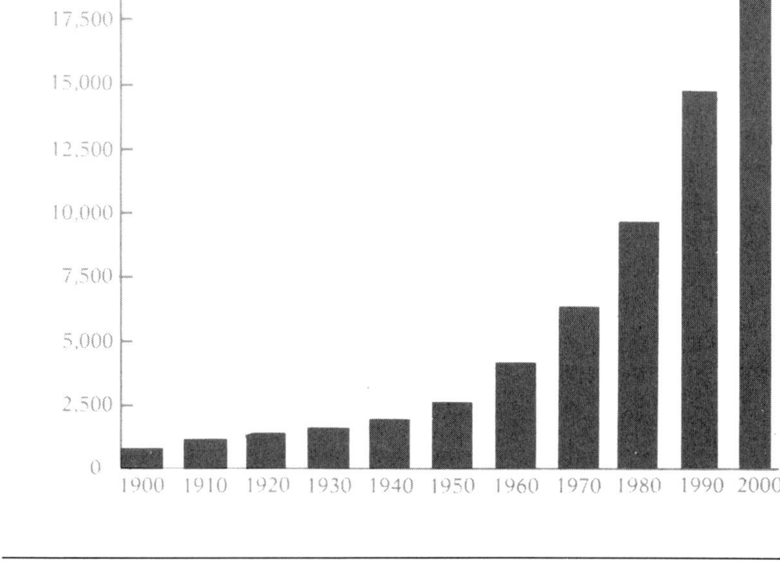

*From "Teaching about Population," *Intercom,* Center for War/Peace Studies, May 1973, p. 46.

tion of known reserves and (2) the Soviet Union is in a better position than the United States in terms of potential future exploitation of this resource.

In each graph the researcher conveyed information about the nature of a distribution. A relatively equal distribution of a variable is designated by bars of approximately equal size, suggesting a lack of homogeneity among the cases. Conversely, if one bar is much larger than the rest, most cases are similar, with the exception of a handful of "deviant" cases.

Line graphs These represent an extremely usable frequency distribution, particularly when comparing a number of moments in time. Here the emphasis is on changes over time, since the cases are years. For example, some researchers have attempted to determine the association between immigration and liberal government policy. Before analyzing this question, of course, we must obtain a descriptive profile over time for each of these variables.

Figure 4.4. Total discovered oil

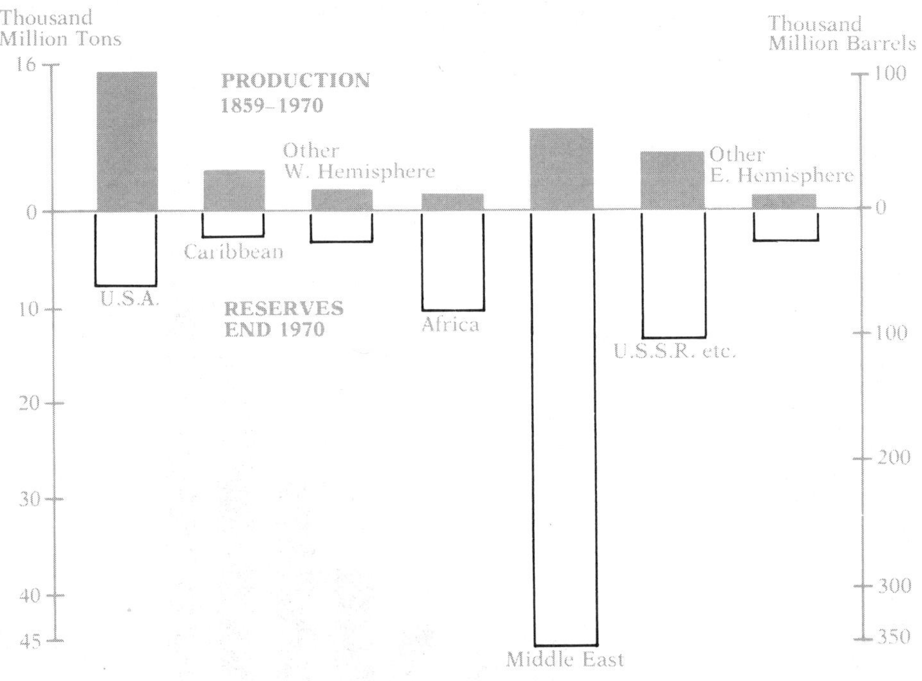

---

*From Richard A. Fredland, *Introducing Developing Areas* (Syracuse, N.Y.: International Relations Programs, 1973), p. 31. By permission of *BP, Statistical Review of the World Oil Industry, 1970,* a publication of British Petroleum Company, Ltd.

Figure 4.5 performs such a function for the level of immigration. As the student can observe, some periods of American history have enjoyed more widely differing immigration rates than others. The next task would be to determine which of these eras were "liberal" ones.

Line graphs can also be used to compare two different concepts for a number of time periods. Consider, for example, Figure 4.6, which compares the level of United States imports and exports for the 1958–1970 time period. Finally, Figure 4.7 compares the rates of various crimes for the forty-year period from 1933 to 1972.

As you can observe, the line graph is particularly suited to changes in the value of a concept over time (i.e., trend analysis). The horizontal axis usually represents years and the vertical axis the levels of the values associated with each year.

Lorenz curves Inequities in the distribution of certain highly valued resources (e.g., wealth, land, health, or education) have been suggested to be at

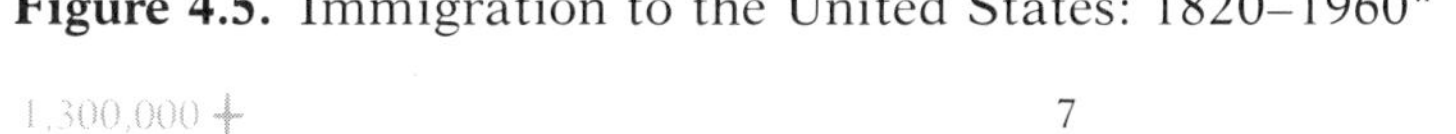

Figure 4.5. Immigration to the United States: 1820–1960*

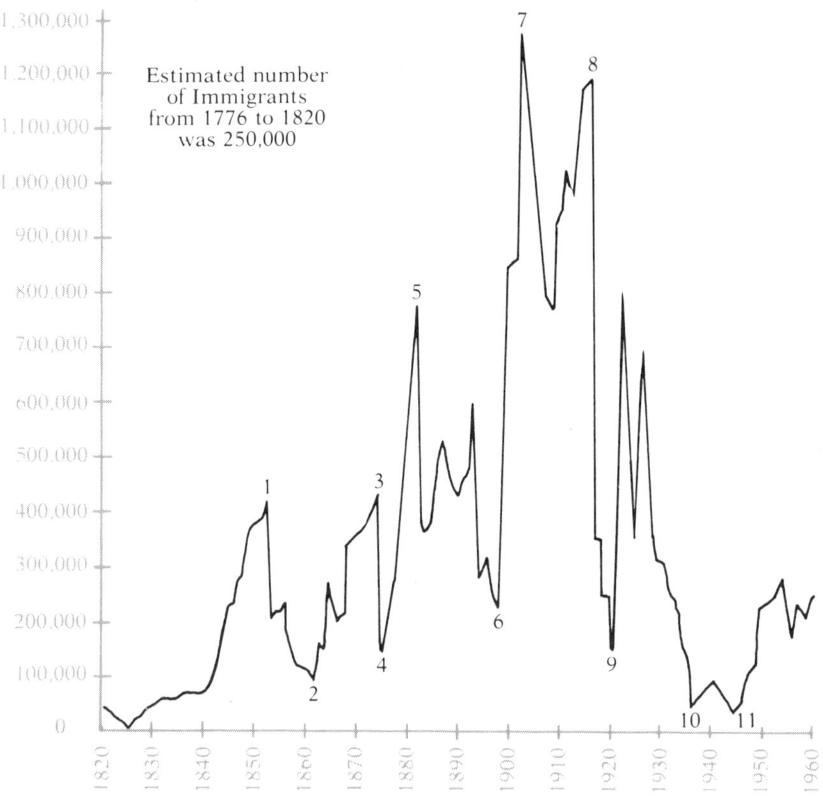

KEY

1—Famine in Ireland; unrest in Germany
2—Depression in U.S.A.
3—Shortage of railroad laborers in settlement of western U.S.A.
4—Depression in U.S.A.
5—Famine in Ireland; militarism in Germany
6—Hard times in U.S.A.
7, 8—Expansion of U.S. industry and demand for unskilled labor
9—World War I
10—Restrictive laws and depression
11—World War II

---

*Reprinted from Sociological Resources for the Social Studies, *Inquiries in Sociology* (Boston: Allyn & Bacon, 1972), p. 183. By permission of the *Philadelphia Inquirer*, William Streckfuss, staff artist.

Figure 4.6 U.S. foreign trade, 1958-1970*

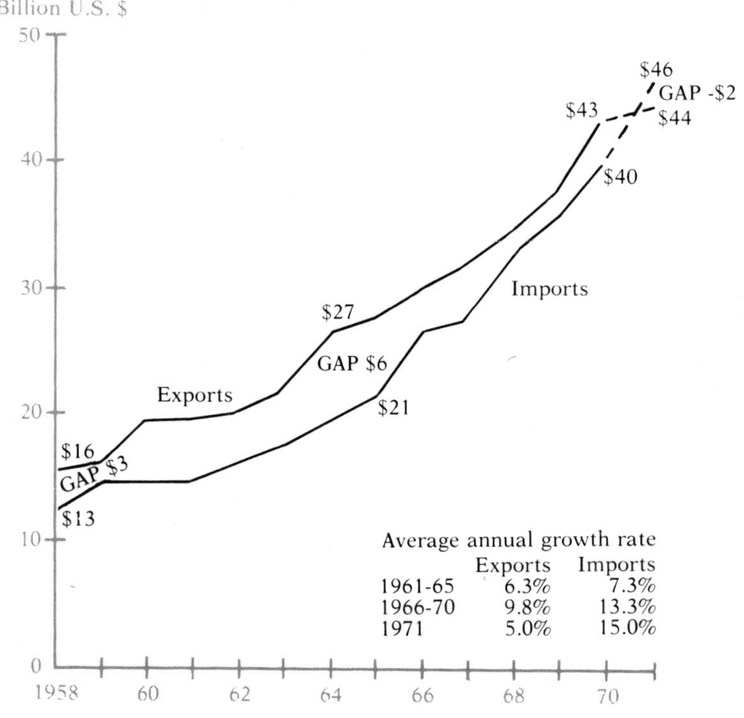

*From *The United States in the Changing World Economy* (Washington, D.C.; U.S. Government Printing Office, 1971), p. 12a.

the root of revolution, both at home and abroad. The Lorenz curve is a graphic line that displays the comparison of one group or nation with another and demonstrates the percentage of some valued good held by each. Thus, a Lorenz curve visually demonstrates *inequalities* of distribution.

Calculating the distribution of world resources enables researchers to rank nations and project future trends. In addition, the information provided by a Lorenz curve, combined with other significant data, can serve as valuable feedback, indicating those nations that are the "haves" and those that are the "have-nots." If domestic and international violence is related to deprivation of valued resources, rational steps could be taken to avoid such violence. This might involve a commitment to economic development on the part of the richer nations or a decision by the less-developed nations to limit the export of certain scarce resources or, at least, to export such resources (such as oil) at higher prices to obtain the capital needed for economic development.

Figure 4.7. Property crime; 1933–1972*

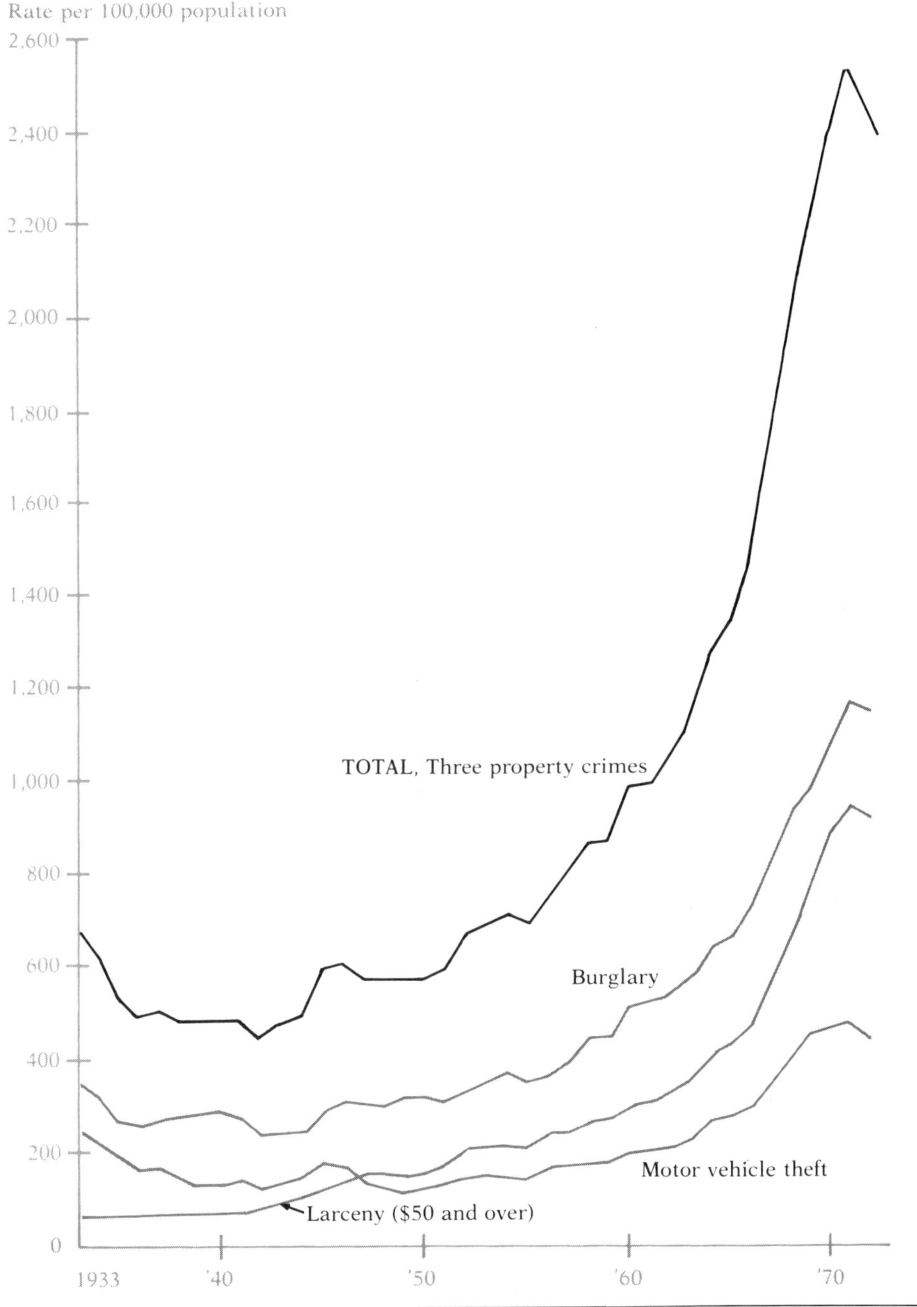

*From *Social Indicators 1973* (Washington, D.C.: U.S. Department of Commerce, 1973), p. 53.

Figure 4.8 represents a hypothetical distribution of the world's wealth among the nations of the world. The horizontal axis (x-axis) represents a proportion of the population; the vertical axis (y-axis) shows the percent of the value. Any point on the Lorenz curve represents the proportion of the population that possesses the corresponding percent of the value shown on the y-axis. In Figure 4.8, for example, 10 percent of the population possesses 70 percent of the world's wealth (point A), 80 percent of the wealth is controlled by 20 percent of the population (point B), and 95 percent of the wealth by 60 percent of the population (point C). Point A is probably the most relevant one, since it reveals quite clearly the unequalness of the distribution. (That is, if 70 percent of the wealth is owned by only 10 percent of the world's population, the remaining 30 percent is controlled by the majority of the population [90 percent].)

If each percent of the population possessed an equal amount of the value (i.e., 20 percent of the people owned 20 percent of the resources, 30 percent owned 30 percent, etc.), perfect equality would exist. This equality is represented in Figure 4.8 by the line of perfect equality, a 45-degree line.

The area between the diagonal line and the Lorenz curve is known as the *area of inequality*; the greater this area, the larger the degree of inequality for the distribution. Compare the two areas in Figure 4.9, each representing extreme degrees of inequality. The one distribution represents a high level of equality; that is, each percent of the population possesses a similar percent of the resource. The line labeled "high inequality," by contrast, shows that valued resources are distributed very unevenly among the population, i.e., a small segment of the population controls a large portion of the value. If the student examines the area of inequality in a given Lorenz curve, he can instantly surmise how unequally the resource or value is distributed among the population.

Figure 4.10 compares the distribution of the production and consumption of total world energy in 1965. As in Figure 4.8, there is a rather large area of inequality for both production and consumption; therefore, we can infer that only a small percent of the world's nations controls a significant proportion of the world's energy.

Figure 4.11 shows an additional use of the Lorenz curve: to compare the distribution of the same resource for different years. The student can see that a more equal distribution of urban population is projected for 1975 than existed in 1959. He can infer this because the curve for 1975 is closer to the line of equality than that for 1959. The student can also say that the distribution of urban population is relatively even among the nations of the world because of the small area between the line of equality and the curve.

Figure 4.12 reveals still another use of the Lorenz curve—comparing distribution of the same resource for the same period of time but among different populations. In this case the student is comparing the distribution of

Figure 4.8. Hypothetical distribution of the world's wealth

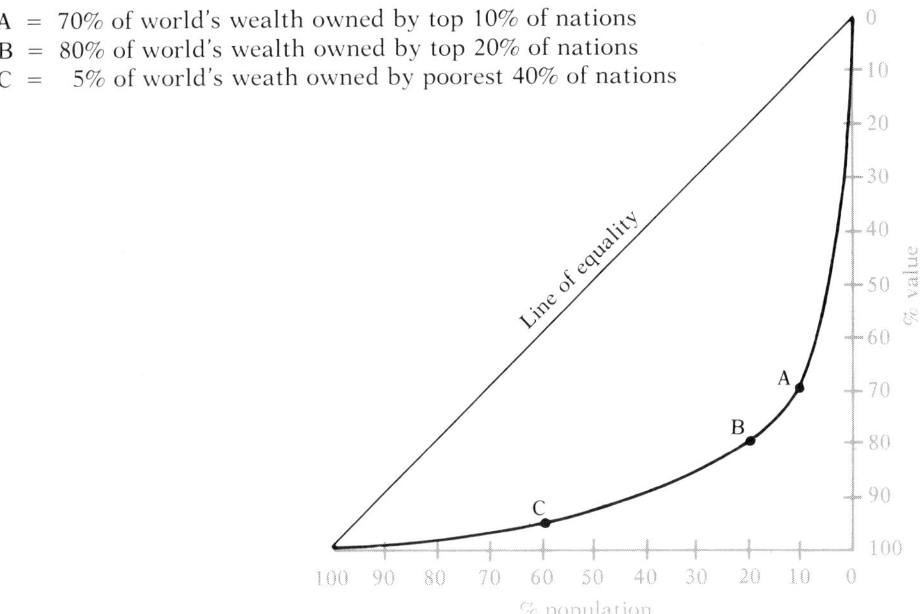

Figure 4.9. High equality and high inequality

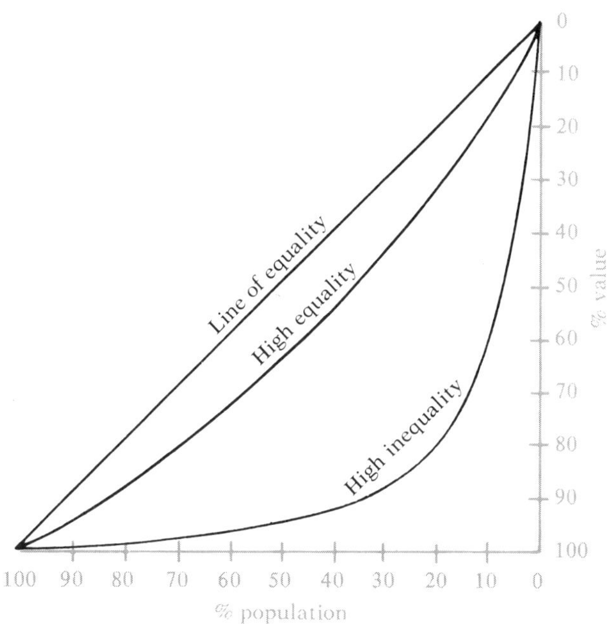

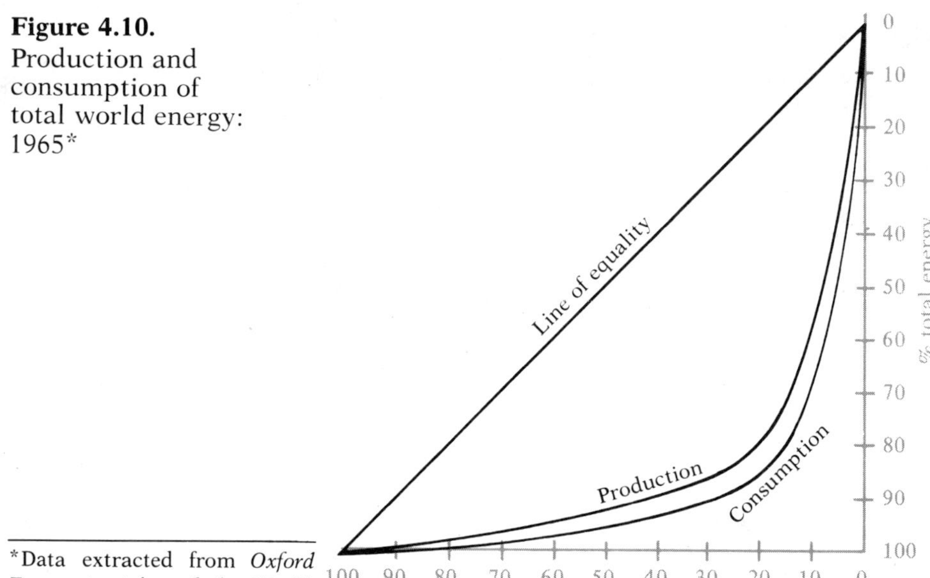

Figure 4.10. Production and consumption of total world energy: 1965*

*Data extracted from *Oxford Economic Atlas of the World, 1972,* p. 41.

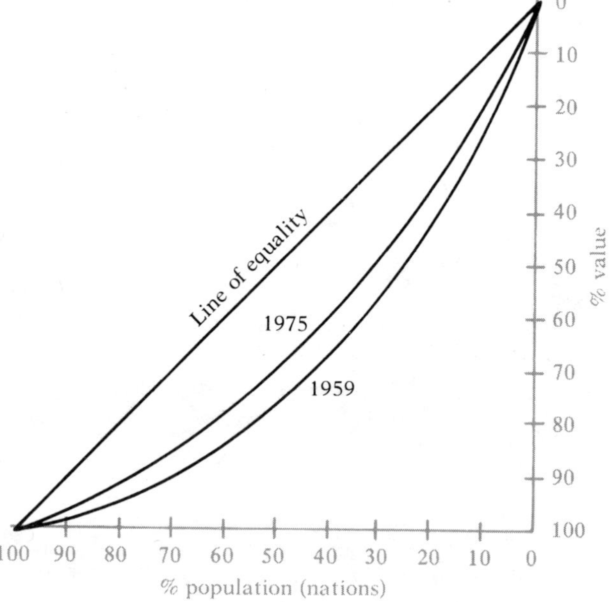

Figure 4.11. World distribution of urban population: 1959 and 1975 (projected)*

*Data extracted from Bruce M. Russett, *World Handbook of Political and Social Indicators* (New Haven, Conn.: Yale University Press, 1964), pp. 342–43.

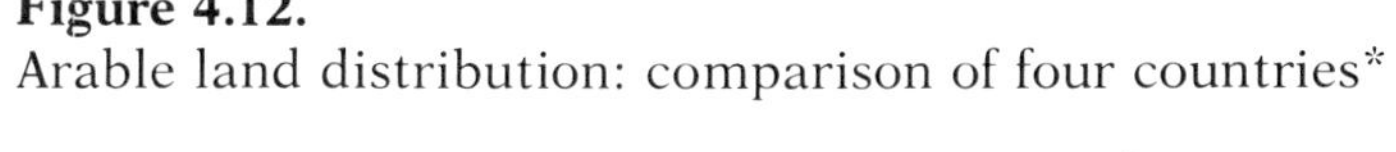

Figure 4.12.
Arable land distribution: comparison of four countries*

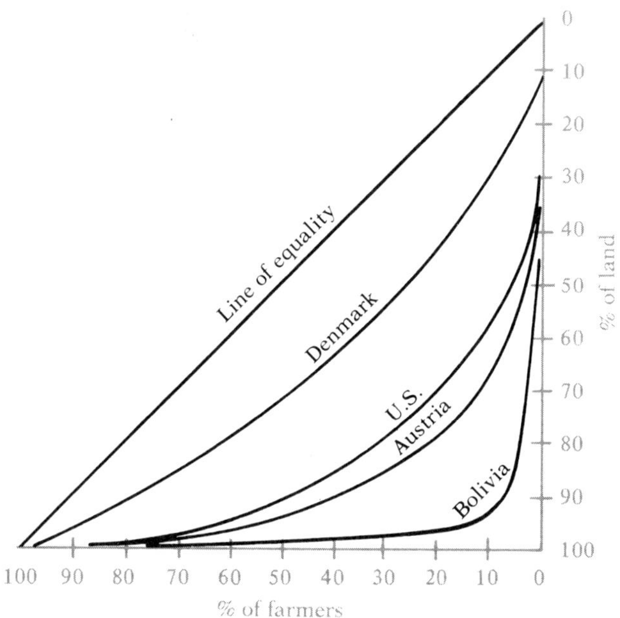

*Adapted from Bruce Russett, *World Handbook of Social and Political Indicators* (New Haven, Conn.: Yale University Press, 1964), p. 237.

arable land in four countries. The four Lorenz curves answer the question: how much land is controlled by the richest farmers? Figure 4.12 reveals that Denmark has the most equal and Bolivia the most unequal distribution among the four countries.

In sum, the Lorenz curve can be used in a variety of ways: (1) examination of one distribution of one population for one moment in time; (2) comparison of two populations for one resource for one moment in time; (3) comparison of two moments in time for one resource for one population; (4) comparison of two resources for one population for one moment in time. The essential point is that the Lorenz curve is easily interpretable and can serve as an occasion for lengthy discussions concerning its implications.

Computing a Lorenz curve once the raw data has been obtained is a relatively simple procedure, which requires six steps.

1. Rank order your cases from the highest to the lowest.
2. Select a sufficient number of percentage points for representing the total number of cases on the x-axis. You will obtain an accurate Lorenz curve

by selecting points that are multiples of 10 (such that you can group them by 10%, 20%, 30%, and so on).

3. Divide the rank-ordered group into categories that represent each percentage. Thus, if you have 100 nations, for example, divide these into 10 groups of 10 each.
4. Determine the proportion of the total resources possessed by each segment. The first 10 percent may possess 42 percent of the resources, the second 10 percent may possess 20 percent of the resources, and so on.
5. Determine the percentage of each resource residing in various proportions of the cases by adding each succeeding segment to the preceding segment. Thus, if 10 percent of the nations possess 42 percent of the resources and the next 10 percent possess 20 percent of the resources, it can be seen that 20 percent of the nations possess 62 percent of the resources, and so on.
6. Determine each pair of values for the x- and y-axes, plot on the graph, and connect the points. The resulting line is the Lorenz curve.

Space does not permit us to work out an example of an actual computation of a real Lorenz curve. However, the tabular information in Table 4.1 demonstrates the final results of such a calculation, which has ranked 100 cases and divided them into 10 groups of 10 each. Columns C and D represent the pairs to be plotted.

Table 4.1
Results of computing information for a Lorenz curve

A Decile of cases	B % of resource for each decile*	C Cumulative % of cases	D Cumulative % of resource
0–10%	42	10	42
11–20%	20	20	62
21–30%	17	30	79
31–40%	10	40	89
41–50%	3	50	92
51–60%	2	60	94
61–70%	2	70	96
71–80%	1.5	80	97.5
81–90%	1.5	90	99
91–100%	1	100	100

*These are hypothetical percentages used only to illustrate the possible distribution across cases.

Often it is not necessary to work through all of these six steps. Sometimes a person can ascertain from a table prepared for analysis that a certain percent of a resource is controlled by the top 10 percent or top 25 percent of the population. A curve can then be constructed by simply plotting this first point and then extending the curve to the end.

Simple forms of statistical analysis

All of the visual displays shown, which were designed for descriptive or univariate analysis—pie graphs, bar graphs, line graphs, and Lorenz curves—represent fairly accurate and efficient ways of ordering information about a concept. There exists another set of descriptive procedures or statistical operations that reveal, in most instances, more precise information about the characteristics of each variable. Students are probably already familiar with one of these, the *mean,* calculated by totaling a number of scores and dividing by the number of cases. (The mean is also called the *average.*) There are several other simple statistical techniques that are useful for descriptive analysis.

One group of simple statistical techniques is called *measures of central tendency,* which yield information about the typical case. Three examples are the *mean*, the *median*, and the *mode*. Specific rules exist for determining which measure is the best one to use in a given situation. Another group is termed *measures of dispersion*, which reveal the extent to which most cases look alike or possess the same value (the level of homogeneity or, conversely, of variability). Three popular statistics in this category are the *range*, the *standard deviation*, and the *coefficient of variability*. Many teachers may already be familiar with these statistical forms as a result of their testing and grading procedures. Since the emphasis of this chapter is upon visual displays, we will do no more than make mention of these terms.*

Visual displays for quantitative associational analysis

We turn now to associational visual displays; that is, displays that reveal the association among two or more characteristics or variables. In this section, we will consider the contingency table, crisscross diagrams, and scatterplot diagrams.

Determining the association among variables is important because it represents a critical step in building theories about human behavior. Our responsibility as teachers is to facilitate the student's ability to comprehend these relationships more easily. The simplest case is the *bivariate situation*,

*For an extensive treatment of these statistics see Philip M. Burgess and James E. Harf, *Theory, Data, and Analysis: A Laboratory Introduction to Comparative and International Politics* (Boston: Allyn & Bacon, forthcoming).

Figure 4.13.
Association between level of satisfaction and degree of political stability*

Political stability	Index of satisfaction: Satisfaction	Frustration	
Stable	20	2	22
Unstable	6	34	40
	26	36	62

*From Burgess and Harf, *Theory, Data, and Analysis.*

Figure 4.14.
Association between religion and party preference*

Party	Religion: Protestant	Catholic and Jew	
Republican	126	99	225
Democrat	71	162	233
	197	261	458

*From Herbert M. Blalock, Jr., *Social Statistics,* 2d ed. (New York: McGraw-Hill, 1972), p. 277.

where we examine whether the presence or absence of x is associated with the presence or absence of y, or whether an increase or decrease in a variable is associated with an increase or decrease in another.

Contingency Tables A *contingency table* serves to display the joint occurrence of variables x and y, and is constructed by cross-clarifying these two variables. By convention, the dependent variable, or *predicted condition,* is shown in the rows; the independent, or *predictor,* variable is given in the columns. Information is usually presented at the nominal level, although the ordinal level is also appropriate.

Figure 4.13 examines the proposition that satisfaction in a nation's population results in political stability for that nation. The index of satisfaction is the independent variable, and political stability is the dependent variable. By examining the cell frequencies, the student can ascertain whether there is or is not a positive association between these two variables. Most of the twenty-six nations that manifested a condition of satisfaction (twenty) had stable political regimes. Conversely, almost all of the thirty-six nations that exhibited frustration (thirty-four) had unstable political systems.

Without employing any statistical routines, therefore, the student can make some judgments about this particualr proposition. The data presented in Figure 4.13 suggest that the proposition is supported by the evidence.

Figure 4.14 examines the proposition that religion (whether Protestant or non-Protestant) is related to party preference (Republican or Democrat). Again, the dependent variable "party" is given in the rows and the indepen-

Figure 4.15.
Size of governmental agencies and level of professionalization*

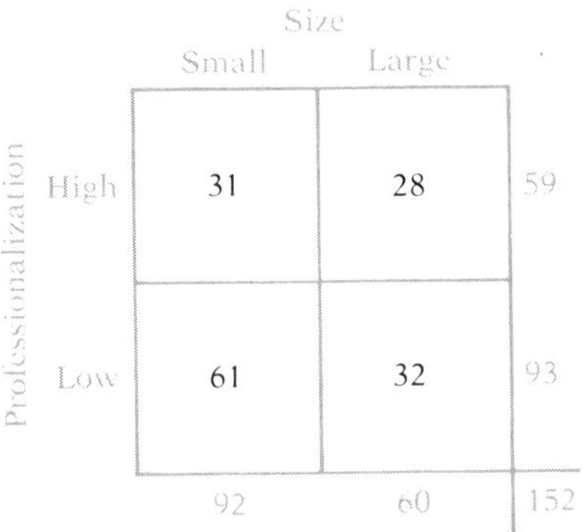

*From *A Basic Course in Statistics with Sociological Applications*, 2d ed., p. 143 by Theodore R. Anderson and Morris Zelditch, Jr. Copyright © 1958, 1968 by Holt, Rinehart and Winston, Inc. Reprinted by permission of Holt, Rinehart and Winston.

dent variable "religion" in the columns. By examining the cell frequencies, the student can observe that of 197 Protestants, 126 are Republicans and 71 Democrats. Of the 261 non-Protestants (Catholics and Jews), 99 are Republicans and 162 are Democrats. Therefore one can conclude, without any statistical operations, that there is a fairly strong relationship between party and religion; that is, Protestants are more likely to be Republicans and Catholics and Jews are more likely to be Democrats.

Figure 4.15 offers a more difficult challenge for interpretation. In this figure the hypothesis is that the size of governmental agencies (the number of agency employees) is related to the level of professionalization (defined as the extent to which members of the operating staff are required to have college degrees). On first glance it is difficult to arrive quickly at a conclusion concerning this hypothesis, since the cell frequencies are relatively similar. However, one can note that one cell (small size and low professionalization) has a frequency of 61, which is larger than the other cell frequencies. Thus the student concludes that there is a small association between these variables. On closer examination of the table, he also can see that large agencies are more likely to have a high level of professionalization than small agencies.

Contingency tables represent the simplest but, nonetheless, an important kind of visual display for demonstrating the association among two or more variables. The student need not be restricted to only two variables but may introduce others that are believed to influence the original two in the theory.

Figure 4.16.
Rank orders for western and southern Europe with regard to diplomats and exports*

*From Burgess and Harf, *Theory, Data, and Analysis.*

Moreover, the student need not construct only two categories for each variable, as in the example. It is critical, however, if the student is to reduce raw information with many values (level of income, for example) to a small number of categories in a contingency table (high and low income), that there be an awareness of the decision rules for establishing the numerical limits of each category.

Crisscross diagrams (comparative rank orders) In the preceding section we used contingency tables to show the relationship between two *nominal* variables. Other kinds of visual associational displays exist for data points measured by ordinal or interval scales. For example, we often use measures that allow us to rank cases along a continuum from "higher" to "lower" or from "more" to "less." These kinds of measures are called *ordinal* scales; they permit us to rank order observations. Even though we do not know the distance (or the intervals) between each case, we do know enough from ordinal-level measures to rank cases along a continuum that represents increasing or decreasing quantitites of a characteristic or attribute of interest. With data that permit us to rank order our cases, we can use a visual analytic display called the *crisscross diagram* to help make some judgments about the strength and direction of the association between the ranks of the two variables being measured.

For example, Figure 4.16 presents the rank orders of Western and Southern European nations for two variables—total number of diplomats sent abroad by a nation and total value of the exports of each nation. The student's purpose is to determine if a nation that ranks high on one list also ranks high on the other. As Figure 4.16 shows, one can acquire a better sense of the association by drawing lines connecting a nation's position on each ranked list, thus creating a crisscross diagram. This procedure allows one to step back and quickly examine all pairs simultaneously. This figure demonstrates that most nations occupy a relatively similar rank on each variable (i.e., nearly all lines approach a horizontal position). There are a few exceptions (Spain, Greece, and Yugoslavia), but such a small number of exceptional cases in a sample of twenty nations does not detract too much from the typical horizontal pattern.

On the other hand, if most of the lines do not approximate a horizontal pattern (i.e., if most nations do not occupy relatively similar rank positions), two possible general conclusions may be drawn. First, if no recognizable pattern to the lines can be discerned, the association between the two variables is probably small. Second, if the lines appear to follow an extreme crisscross path (from the top of one rank to the bottom of the second and vice versa) a strong *negative* association probably exists between the two variables. That is, nations exhibiting high scores on one variable will have low scores on the second one.

Figure 4.17, which displays the rank comparisons of Western and Southern European nations for the two variables "% Communist vote" and "military expenditures as a % of GNP," is an example of the first conclusion. Eyeballing the ranks reveals no discernible pattern of correspondence. It does appear that more lines approach a somewhat vertical rather than horizontal path, which should be interpreted as a negative tendency. But this tendency appears to be slight; therefore, the student might conclude that the association between Communist vote and military expenditures is a very weak one.

An example of the second general conclusion that can be drawn from a crisscross diagram—that a strong negative association exists—is shown in

Figure 4.17.
Rank orders for western and southern Europe with regard to the percentage of Communist vote and military expenditures*

*From Burgess and Harf, *Theory, Data, and Analysis*.

Figure 4.18, depicting the association between freedom of the press and percent of Communist vote for two sample groups, Southern/Eastern European and Southeast Asian nations. As can be observed, extreme cases in each rank are connected with those at the opposite end of the other rank. This clearly discernible extreme crisscross pattern strongly suggests *negative* association between these two variables.

Scatterplots The final associational display of this chapter is the scatterplot, also known as the cross-plot or scattergram. This type of visual rep-

Figure 4.18.
Rank orders for southern/eastern Europe and southeast Asia with regard to freedom of the press and the percent of the Communist vote*

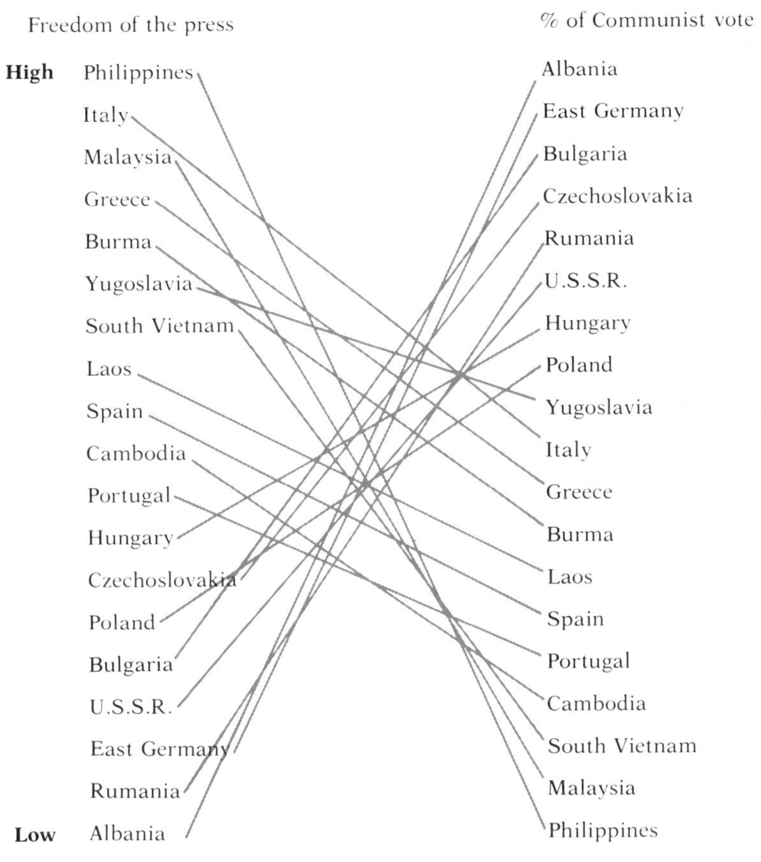

*From Burgess and Harf, *Theory, Data, and Analysis.*

resentation is used primarily for bivariate analysis whose variables are measured at the ordinal (but not rank orders) or interval level. By means of the clustering (or, conversely, the nonclustering) of plotted points on the scatterplot, one can detect the presence or absence of an association between the two variables and also the direction of that association.

Three conventions should be noted in the creation of a scatterplot. First, the independent (or predictor) variable is typically plotted along the horizontal axis (or *abscissa*) and the dependent (or predicted) variable is plotted along the vertical axis (or *ordinate*). Second, the discrete points on each axis

Figure 4.19.
Scatterplot: Government expenditures per capita and university students per total population*
Numbers in scatterplot refer to multiple dots.

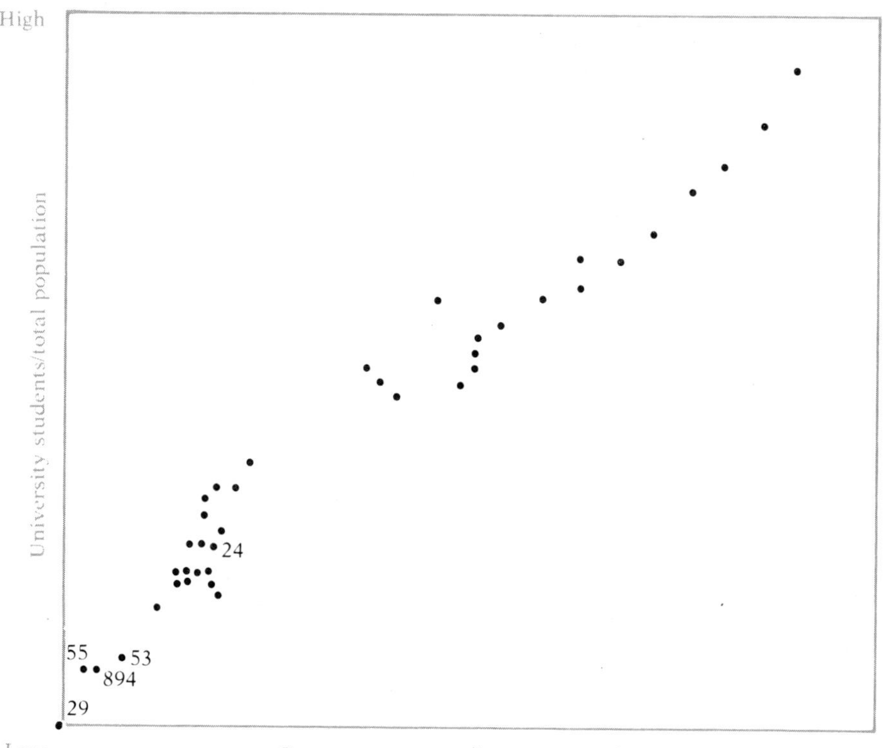

*From James E. Harf's personal data set.

are equidistant. Third, the lowest values of the two variables appear at the intercept of the two axes (called the *origin* or *zero point*).

Figure 4.19 indicates a nearly perfect positive relationship between "government expenditure per capita" and "the number of students in universities as a percentage of the total population." This is certainly not a startling discovery. One would, of course, expect that greater government expenditures per capita would result in the availability of higher education to a larger proportion of the population. In fact, the scatterplot depicts a nearly linear relationship between the two variables; that is, as government expenditure per capita increases by one unit, the number of university students as a percentage of the total population also increases by one unit. One can also ob-

Figure 4.20.
Scatterplot: Number of nations experiencing *coup d' états* and number of people in cities of 25,000/total population*

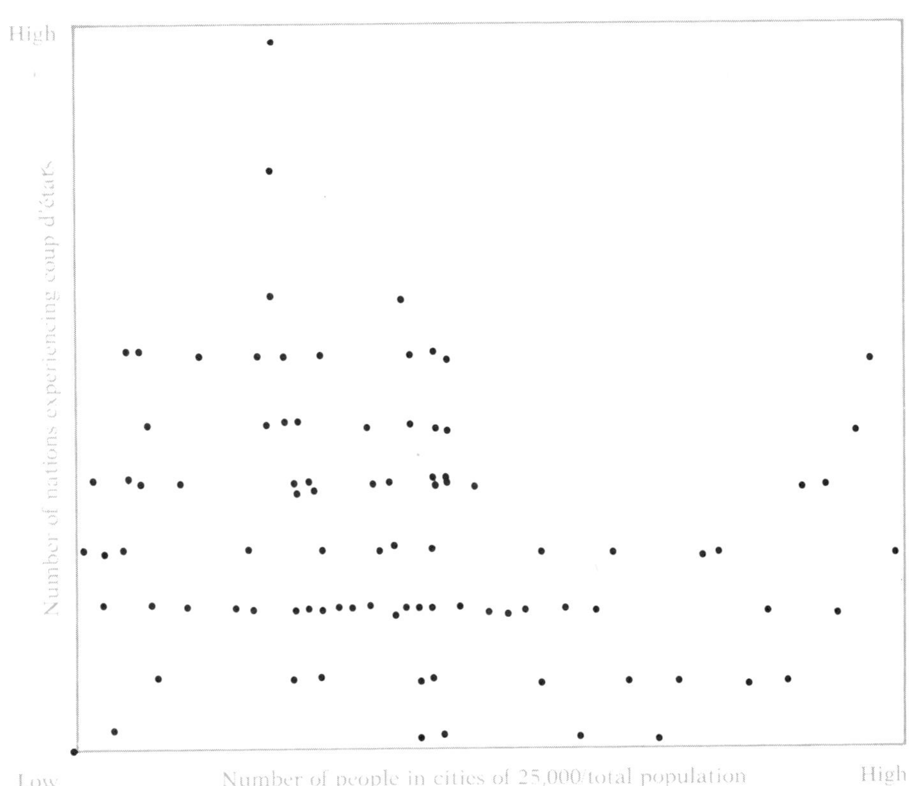

*From James E. Harf's personal data set.

serve that there are few unusual or *deviant* cases; that is, there are very few dots that fall far away from the normal pattern. Whenever a deviant case occurs, the student should examine it carefully, because it may result in a refinement of the theory under investigation.

Figure 4.20 provides an example of almost no relationship between two variables. In this scatterplot the student is examining the relationship between "the number of nations experiencing *coup d'état*" and "the total number of people living in cities of 25,000 or more as a percentage of the total population." Some theorists have suggested that the rural-to-urban migration, which has occurred in most nations of the world, has resulted in the concentration of poor people in the squalor of ghettos and slums in cities.

Figure 4.21.
Scatterplot: Deaths from domestic group violence/million population and GNP/capita*

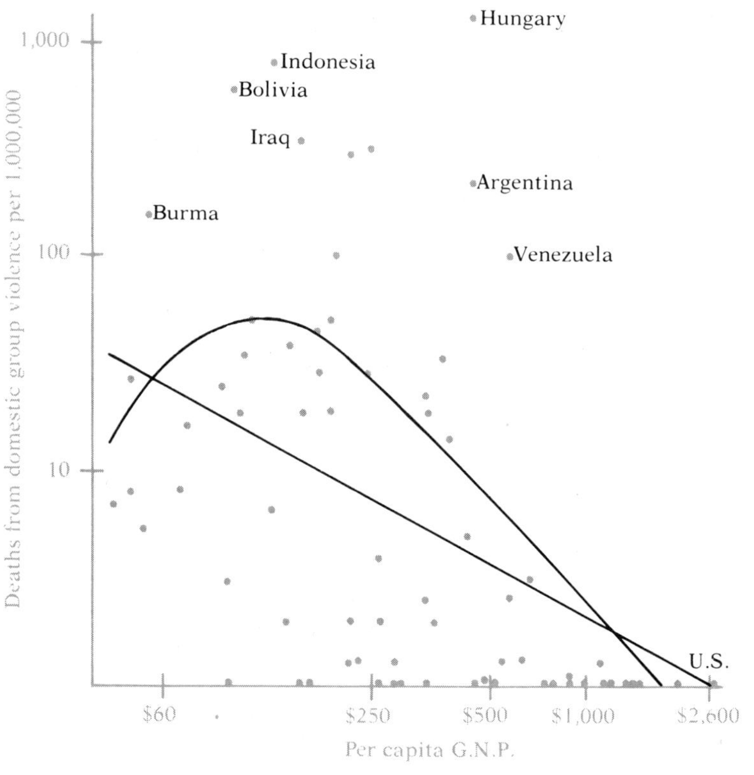

*From Bruce M. Russett, *Trends in World Politics* (London: Macmillan, 1965), p. 137.

This presumably causes great discontent on the part of these people and may lead to outbreaks of violence and even open rebellion. However, Figure 4.20 suggests that this violence or rebellion has not been very successful in overthrowing established governments. It should be emphasized that this scatterplot does not reveal that there is little violence directed against the national government in large cities, but rather that this violence has seldom resulted in the overthrow of the established government. The visual indicator, which reveals very little relationship between these two variables, is the fact that the plotted points are dispersed throughout the scatterplot, rather than clustering in any pattern.

Figure 4.21 reveals a negative relationship. The two plotted variables are "deaths from domestic group violence per 1,000,000 population" and "GNP per capita." The existence of a negative relationship between these two variables means that when GNP per capita is low, there will be many domestic-violence deaths due to the high level of aspirations among the population and a lack of resources on the part of the government to fulfill these aspirations. But as GNP increases and aspirations are fulfilled, the domestic-violence deaths begin to drop. The *curved line* on the scatterplot suggests this latter interpretation. Applying this interpretation to the international system, we would expect much civil strife in the underdeveloped nations of the world. This strife would continue and, perhaps, even increase until economic development attains some acceptable level. However, once this hypothetical level of GNP per capita is reached, economic sources of discontent are diminished; the government is better able to satisfy the demands of the people, simultaneously attaining the capability to coercively control the people.

The scatterplot is not only useful for ascertaining general trends but also allows the student, as we suggested earlier, to discover deviant cases; that is, cases that are far removed from the general pattern. In Figure 4.21, for example, Cuba and Hungary represent extreme cases because of the high distance between their positions on the scatterplot and the general trends as determined by either the straight or curvilinear lines. Deviant case analysis is probably one of the most important uses of scatterplots, since the student is forced to seek out the reasons underlying this different behavior pattern.

The three types of associational displays discussed—contingency tables, crosscross diagrams, and scatterplots—allow the student to examine the general pattern or association between two concepts. In addition, specific cases or clusters of cases that differ from the general pattern can be isolated and the original theory adjusted in light of these findings. There does exist, of course, a variety of statistical procedures accompanying each of these displays that yield precise measures of the association. But, again, these are not necessary for using quantitative evidence to test hypotheses.

Summary and conclusions

This chapter has been an attempt to introduce teachers to the ways in which quantitative information can be used to promote inquiry in the social studies classroom. We have discussed the nature of quantification and the sources of quantitative data. We then reviewed three ways that quantitative data gathering can be used to promote inquiry learning. Finally, we discussed five steps that inquiry teachers can use to prepare themselves to promote quantitative inquiry teaching, as well as ten suggested steps that teachers can follow to prepare their classes to use quantitative data for the purpose of inquiry. A variety of visual displays were included to illustrate the manner in which quantitative information can be used in both descriptive and associational analysis. They were designed to illustrate the fact that information in quantitative form does not require sophisticated mathematical analysis.

We believe that there are several positive benefits to conducting the process of inquiry using quantitative information. It is our feeling that quantitative inquiry:

- helps students acquire good habits of mind, including a respect for logic and reason and the ability to seek systematic solutions to problems.
- helps to build a sense of skepticism in students.
- helps to promote simultaneously a sense of optimism in students, helping them to realize that even if problems cannot be solved, they can at least be analyzed.
- provides the opportunity for students to think in an interdisciplinary manner and in this way engenders a broader outlook.
- provides an opportunity for learning that is open-ended, discussion-oriented, and more in tune with the realities of the so-called knowledge explosion.
- provides students with the opportunity to reflect on their values and the values of their own and other societies, which ultimately leads to greater self-knowledge and awareness.

We recognize that there are also some drawbacks to the use of this facet of inquiry. Among these are:

- The method requires special skills of students that might not be accessible to those who have difficulty reading or doing simple calculations.
- The method requires a new way of viewing social reality that may be unfamiliar and difficult for teachers as well as students to learn.
- The method can yield trivial as well as sophisticated insights.
- There can be a tendency to take the results of inquiry using quantitative data too seriously, overlooking the fact that much of what is known about human behavior is tentative and still part of the overall process of historical and behavioral science research.
- This method of inquiry makes significant demands on teacher time and requires both more planning and more research than other methods of teaching.

In sum, we hope that we have demonstrated both the advantages and disadvantages of this method of inquiry. Further, it is our hope that this chapter will encourage social studies teachers to take the time to familiarize themselves with quantitative information so that they can implement some of the quantitative techniques we have recommended in their day-to-day classroom routines.

Bibliography

Background reading

Alker, Hayward R., Jr. *Mathematics and Politics*. New York: Macmillan, 1965.

Anderson, Theodore R., and Morris Zelditch, Jr. *A Basic Coruse in Statistics with Sociological Application*. 2d ed. New York: Holt, Rinehart and Winston, 1968.

Bauer, Raymond A. *Social Indicators*. Cambridge, Mass.: M.I.T. Press, 1966.

Becker, James M. *An Examination of Objectives, Needs and Priorities in International Education in United States Secondary and Elementary Schools*. New York: Foreign Policy Association, 1969.

Benson, Oliver. *Political Science Laboratory*. Columbus: Merrill, 1969.

Blalock, Herbert M., Jr. *Social Statistics*. 2d ed. New York: McGraw-Hill, 1972.

Bowles, Edmund A., ed. *Computers in Humanistic Research*. Englewood Cliffs, N.J.: Prentice-Hall, 1968.

Burgess, Phillip M., and James E. Harf. *Theory, Data, and Analysis: A Laboratory Introduction to Comparative and International Politics*. Boston: Allyn & Bacon, forthcoming.

Campbell, Donald T., and Julian C. Stanley. *Experimental and Quasi-Experimental Designs for Research*. Chicago: Rand McNally, 1966.

Center for War/Peace Studies. "Teaching About Population." *Intercom,* May 1973.

Charlesworth, James C., ed. *Mathematics and the Social Sciences.* Philadelphia: American Academy of Political & Social Science, 1963.

Corwin, Val R., and Jacob M. Price. *The Dimensions of the Past*. New Haven, Conn.: Yale University Press, 1973.

Downie, N. M., and R. W. Heath. *Basic Statistical Methods.* New York: Harper & Row, 1965.

Dubester, Henry J. *State Censuses*. New York: Burt Franklin, 1969.

Fredland, Richard A. *Introducing Developing Areas: Test Edition, an ISA/NSF Learning Package in International Studies Education*. Syracuse, N.Y.: International Relations Program, 1973.

Gelbaum, Bernard R., and James G. March. *Mathematics for the Social and Behavioral Sciences.* Philadelphia: Saunder, 1969.

Golembiewski, Robert T., William A. Welsh, and William J. Crotty. *A Methodological Primer for Political Scientists*. Chicago: Rand McNally, 1969.

Harf, James E. "Development and Inequality, Notes and Charts." Paper prepared for presentation at the Quad Cities Workshop, May 4, 1973.

Hollingsworth, Thomas H. *Historical Demography*. Ithaca, N.Y.: Cornell University Press, 1969.

Huff, Darrell. *How to Lie with Statistics*. New York: Norton, 1954.

Jenson, Richard, and Charles Dollar. *The Historian's Guide to Statistics*. New York: Holt, Rinehart and Winston, 1971.

Kaplan, Abraham. *The Conduct of Inquiry*. New York: Chandler, 1964.

Kerlinger, Fred N. *Foundations of Behavioral Research*. 2d ed. New York: Holt, Rinehart and Winston, 1973.

Key, V. O., Jr. *A Primer of Statistics for Political Scientists*. New York: Crowell, 1966.

Keyes, Kenneth S., Jr. *How to Develop Your Thinking Ability*. New York: McGraw-Hill, 1963.

Landes, David, and Charles Tilly, eds. *History and Social Science*. Englewood Cliffs, N.J.: Prentice-Hall, 1971.

Lazarsfeld, Paul F., and Morris Rosenberg, eds. *The Language of Social Research*. New York: The Free Press, 1955.

Lerner, William. *Pocket Data Book*, USA 1971. Washington, D.C.: U.S. Department of Commerce, 1971.

Louis, Arthur M. "The Worst American City." *Harper's Magazine*, January 1975, pp. 67–71.

Merritt, Richard L., and Stein, Rokkan, eds. *Comparing Nations: The Use of Quantitative Data in Cross-National Research*. New Haven, Conn.: Yale University Press, 1966.

Messick, David M. *Mathematical Thinking in Behavioral Science*. San Francisco: W. W. Freeman, 1961.

Mueller, John. *Approaches to Measurement in International Relations*. New York: Appleton-Century-Crofts, 1969.

Rowney, Don K., and James Q. Graham. *Quantitative History: Selected Readings in Quantitative Analysis of Historical Data*. Homewood, Ill.: Dorsey Press, 1969.

Ruchlis, Hy. *Clear Thinking*. New York: Harper & Row, 1962.

Russett, Bruce M., *Trends in World Politics*. London: The Macmillan Company, 1965.

———*World Handbook of Social and Political Indicators*. New Haven: Yale University Press, 1964.

Simon, Julian. *Basic Research Methods in Social Science*. New York: Random House, 1969.

Singer, J. David, ed. *Quantitative International Politics: Insights and Evidence*. New York: The Free Press, 1963.

Snyder, Richard C. "Political Education in the Public Schools: The Challenge for Political Science," *Political Science*, 4 Summer 1971.

Social Indicators 1973. Washington, D.C.: U.S. Department of Commerce, 1973.

Sociological Resources for the Social Studies. *Inquiries in Sociology*. Boston: Allyn & Bacon, 1972.

Stelter, Gilbert A. *A Canadian Urban History: A Selected Bibliography*. Social Science Research Publication Series. Sudbury, Ont., Canada: Laurentian University Press, 1972.

Stone, Richard. *Mathematics in the Social Sciences*. Cambridge, Mass.: M.I.T. Press, 1966.

Strasser, Ben B., *et al*. *Teaching Toward Inquiry*. Washington, D.C.: National Education Association, Center for the Study of Instruction, 1971.

Swierenga, Robert. *Quantification in American History*. New York: Atheneum, 1970.

Taylor, C. L. *Aggregate Data Analysis: Political and Social Indicators in Cross-National Research*. The Hague: Mouton, 1968.

"Teaching About Population," *Intercom*, Center for War/Peace Studies (May 1973).

Thouless, Robert. *How to Think Straight*. New York: Simon & Schuster, 1950.

Tufte, Edward R. *The Quantitative Analysis of Social Problems*. Reading, Mass.: Addison-Wesley, 1970.

The United States in the Changing World Economy. Washington, D.C.: U.S. Government Printing Office, 1971.

Woolf, Harry, ed. *Quantification*. Indianapolis: Bobbs-Merrill, 1961.

Selected readings in Quantitative research

Alker, Hayward E., Jr., and Bruce M. Russett. *World Politics in the General Assembly*. New Haven, Conn.: Yale University Press, 1965.

Banks, Arthur S., and Robert B. Textor. *A Cross-Polity Survey*. Cambridge, Mass.: M.I.T. Press, 1963.

Benson, Lee. *The Concept of Jacksonian Democracy: New York as a Test Case*. Princeton, N.J.: Princeton University Press, 1961.

Durkheim, Emile. *Suicide*. New York: The Free Press, 1951.

Fogel, Robert William, and Stanley L. Engerman. *Time on the Cross*. 2 vols. Boston: Little, Brown, 1974.

Gibson, Charles. *Spain in America*. New York: Harper & Row, 1966.

Goldstein, Sidney. *Patterns of Mobility, 1910–1950*. Philadelphia: University of Pennsylvania Press, 1958.

Greven, Philip, Jr. *Four Generations: Population, Land and Family in Colonial Andover, Massachusetts*. Ithaca, N.Y.: Cornell University Press, 1970.

Katz, Michael. *Class, Bureaucracy and the Schools*. New York: Praeger, 1971.

———*The Irony of Early School Reform*. Cambridge: Harvard University Press, 1968.

Knights, Peter R. *The Plain People of Boston, 1830–1860: A Study of City Growth*. New York: Oxford University Press, 1971.

MacLeod, Murdo. *Spanish Central America: A Socio-Economic History, 1520–1720*. Berkeley and Los Angeles: University of California Press, 1972.

Merritt, Richard L., and Donald J. Puchala, eds. *Western European Perspectives on International Affairs: Public Opinion Studies and Evaluations*. New York: Praeger, 1967.

Pryor, Frederick L. *Public Expenditures in Communist and Capitalist Nations.* New York: Irwin, 1968.

Rabb, Theodore. *Enterprise and Empire: Merchant and Gentry Investments in the Expansion of England, 1575–1630.* Cambridge: Harvard University Press, 1967.

Thernstrom, Stephen. *Poverty and Progress: Social Mobility in a Nineteenth Century City*. Cambridge: Harvard University Press, 1964.

Selected sources of quantitative data

(*Note*: The following list of data sources is meant to be *suggestive*, rather than comprehensive. A skilled reference librarian would be able to suggest many additional sources.)

Sources for international data

Europa Yearbook. London: Europa Publications, Ltd. Published annually.

Facts on File: World News Digest. New York: Facts on File, Inc. Published annually.

Food and Agriculture Organization of the United Nations, *Trade Yearbook*. Rome, Italy: The FAO Press. Published annually.

———. *Production Yearbook*. Rome, Italy: The FAO Press. Published annually.

The Hoover Institution on War, Revolution, and Peace. *Foreign Statistical Documents*. Edited by Joyce Ball. Stanford, Calif.: The Institution, 1967.

International Labor Office. *Yearbook of Labour Statistics*. Geneva, Switzerland: ILO Press. Published annually.

International Telecommunications Union. *Report on the Activities of the ITU*. Geneva, Switzerland: The Union. Published annually.

International Union of Official Travel Organizations. *International Travel Statistics*. Geneva, Switzerland: The Union. Published annually.

Keesing's Contemporary Archives, Weekly Record of Important World Events. London: Keesing's Publications Longman Group Ltd. Published weekly.

Lerner, William. *Pocket Data Book*. Washington, D.C.: U.S. Department of Commerce, 1971.

Mitchell, B. R., editor. *European Historical Statistics 1750–1970.* New York: Columbia University Press, 1975.

New York Times Index. New York: New York Times, Inc. Published quarterly.

Ruddle, Kenneth, and Barrows, Kathleen. *Statistical Abstract of Latin America, 1972*. Los Angeles: University of California Latin American Center, 1974.

Russett, Bruce M. *Trends in World Politics*. London: Macmillan, 1965.

———. *World Handbook of Social and Political Indicators*. New Haven: Yale University Press, 1964.

The Statesman's Year-book: Statistical and Historical Annual of the States of the World. New York: St. Martin's Press. Published annually.

Taylor, Charles L., and Hudson, Michael C. *World Handbook of Social and*

Political Indicators. 2nd ed. New Haven: Yale University Press, 1972.
Union of International Associations. *Yearbook of International Associations*. Brussels, Belgium: The Union. Published annually.
United Nations. *Demographic Yearbook*. New York: UN Press. Published annually.
United Nations Department of Economic and Social Affairs. *World Economic Survey*. New York: UN Press, 1974.
United Nations Education, Social, and Cultural Organization. *Statistical Yearbook*. Paris, France: UNESCO Press. Published annually.
———. *World Communications: A 200-Country Survey of Press, Radio, Television and Film*. Paris, France: UNESCO Press, 1975.
United Nations Statistical Office. *Compendium of Housing Statistics*. New York: UN Press, 1971.
———. *Directory of International Statistics*. New York: UN Press, 1975.
———. *The Growth of World Industry 1973 Edition*. New York: UN Press, 1975.
———. *Statistical Yearbook*. New York: UN Press. Published annually.
———. *World Trade Annual*. New York: The UN Press. Published annually.
———. *Yearbook of International Trade Statistics*. New York: UN Press. Published annually.
———. *Yearbook of National Accounts Statistics*. New York: UN Press. Published annually.
United States Department of State, Bureau of Intelligence and Research. *World Strength of the Communist Party Organizations*. Washington, D.C.: Government Printing Office. Published annually.
Wasserman, Paul, and Paskar, Joanne. *Statistics Sources*. 4th ed. Detroit, Mich.: Gale Research Company—The Book Tower, 1974.
World Health Organization. *World Health Statistics*. Geneva, Switzerland: WHO Press. Published annually.

Sources for data about the United States

Most of the quantitative data about the United States of America is collected, tabulated, and published by the U.S. Government. Two excellent basic sources that can help you come to terms with the massive amount of data available are *American Statistics Index: Annual, A Comprehensive Guide and Index to the Statistical Publications of the U.S. Government* (Washington, D.C.: Congressional Information Service. Published annually), and *A Guide to the National Archives of the United States*, available from the General Services Administration, National Archives and Records Service, Washington, DC 20408. Other basic sources follow.

U.S. Department of Commerce, Social and Economic Administration, Bureau of the Census. *Census of Agriculture*. Washington, D.C.: The Bureau, 1969. Issued every 10 years.
———. *Census of Business*. Washington, D.C.: The Bureau, 1972. Issued every 5 years.

———. *Census of Construction Industries*. Washington, D.C.: The Bureau, 1972. Issued every 5 years.
———. *Census of Governments in the United States*. Washington, D.C.: The Bureau, 1972. Issued every 5 years.
———. *Census of Housing by State*. Washington, D.C.: The Bureau, 1970. Issued every 10 years.
———. *Census of Manufacturing*. Washington, D.C.: The Bureau, 1972. Issued every 5 years.
———. *Census of Population and Housing, Employment Profiles of Selected Low Income Areas*. Washington, D.C.: The Bureau, 1970. Issued every 10 years.
———. *Census Tracts for Standard Metropolitan Statistical Areas of the United States* (areas of 50,000 or more population). Washington, D.C.: The Bureau, 1970. Issued every 10 years.
———. *Census of Transportation*. Washington, D.C.: The Bureau, 1972. Issued every 5 years.
———. *Characteristics of the Population by State*. Washington, D.C.: The Bureau, 1970. Issued every 10 years.
———. *Historical Statistics of the United States, Colonial Times to 1970*. Washington, D.C.: The Bureau, 1976.
———. *Special Subject Reports of the Census* (Subjects include education, employment, ethnic groups, fertility, income, low income, migration, occupations, and industry). Washington, D.C.: The Bureau, 1970. Issued every 10 years.
U.S. Department of Health, Education and Welfare, Public Health Service. *Vital and Health Statistics: Data on National Health Resources*. Washington, D.C.: HEW. Issued topically during the course of a year.

Miscellaneous data sources
Association and club membership lists
Business annual reports
Business directories
College class directories
Dictionary of American Biography. New York: Scribner's, 1964.
High school class directories
Probate records
Tax records
Telephone directories
Urban directories compiled by school boards
Who Was Who in America. Chicago: Marquis Who's Who, Inc., 1968. 4 vol.
Who's Who in America. Chicago: Marquis Who's Who, Inc., 1976. Published biannually.

Selected organizations that gather and disseminate quantitative data

American Academy of Political and Social Science, 3937 Chestnut Street, Philadelphia, PA 19104.

American College Testing Program, Box 168, Iowa City, IA 52240.

American Institute of Public Opinion (Gallup poll), 53 Bank Street, Princeton, NJ 08540.

Center for War/Peace Studies, 218 East 18th Street, New York, NY 10003.

Clearinghouse and Laboratory for Census Data (a division of the Center for Research Libraries), 1601 N. Kent Street, Suite 900, Rosslyn, VA 22209.

College Entrance Examination Board, 888 Seventh Avenue, New York, NY 10019.

Consortium for International Studies Education, Center for International Studies, University of Missouri–St. Louis, St. Louis, MO 63121.

Educational Testing Service, Rosedale Road, Princeton, NJ 08540.

European Centre for Population Studies, Pauwenlaan 17, The Hague, Netherlands.

European Coordination Centre for Research and Documentation in the Social Sciences, Grunangergasse 2, Vienna 1010, Austria.

Louis Harris and Associates, Inc. (Harris poll), 1270 Avenue of the Americas, New York, NY 10020.

International Social Science Council, UNESCO, 1 Rue Miollis 75015, Paris, France.

International Union for the Scientific Study of Population, Rue Forguer 5, 4000 Liège, Belgium.

National Opinion Research Center (NORC), 6030 South Ellis Avenue, Chicago, IL 60637.

Population Reference Bureau, Inc., 1755 Massachusetts Avenue, N.W., Washington, D.C. 20036.

Princeton Survey Research Center, 53 Bank Street, Princeton, NJ 08540.

Research Publications, Inc., 12 Lunar Drive, Woodbridge, CT 06525.

Social Science Education Consortium, 855 Broadway, Boulder, CO 80302.

Social Science Research Council, 230 Park Avenue, New York, NY 10017.

University of Michigan, Inter-University Consortium for Political Research, Ann Arbor, MI 48104.

University of Michigan, Survey Research Center, Ann Arbor, MI 48104.

Daniel Yankelovich, Inc., 575 Madison Avenue, New York, NY 10002.

The stuff out of which effective inquiry teaching can be developed is all about us, but often we fail to recognize some of the richest and most promising sources—those that are available in our local communities. This chapter identifies numerous problems and issues at the local level that could become the target of student inquiry, and it presents an extensive collection of resources and leads for the teacher who wants to inject community studies into the social studies curriculum.

Chapter 5

Local community studies

In this chapter we take a close look at the value of incorporating local community studies into social studies curriculums. To provide you with some ideas of what we are trying to do, here is an actual example.

> Crestwood Park—Val Jones, a senior from Crestwood High School, was admitted to Oakville Hospital yesterday afternoon as the result of an accident at the intersection of School Avenue and Duncan Street. Miss Jones was knocked down by an eastbound car driven by Carl Oppenheim of 18 Belvedere Crescent. Her condition is critical.
>
> *(Crestwood Chronicle: Monday, February 17, 1975)*

Several weeks later, a group of Crestwood High School students gathered for an impromptu celebration party. Some of them had undertaken a special survey of traffic entering School Avenue during peak periods to ascertain to what extent the need for traffic lights for the intersection could be justified. Other groups had been analyzing and making reports on other aspects of road safety in the Crestwood community (see Table 5.1). The traffic count group members were especially pleased because they had been able to provide some vital statistics on traffic flows at two particular intersections. The local newspaper editor had been most impressed and planned to use the information in a feature article. Of course, the grand finale for the students was the public statement made earlier that day by Traffic Superintendent Wilson, namely, that traffic lights would be installed at the west junction of School Avenue at the beginning of the next month.

Table 5.1
Summary of traffic count data by Crestwood high school students

	Week 1	Week 2	Week 3	Week 4	Total
Number of cars turning left into School Avenue (West End) Bill (7:30 A.M.–8:15 A.M.)	361	393	283	345	1,382
Number of cars turning right into School Avenue (West End) Anne (7:30 A.M.–8:15 A.M.)	285	243	294	303	1,125
Number of cars turning left into School Avenue (East End) Julie (7:30 A.M.–8:15 A.M.)	183	174	191	165	713
Number of cars turning right into School Avenue (East End) Jack (7:30 A.M.–8:15 A.M.)	203	195	168	194	760
Number of cars turning left into School Avenue (West End) Marcia (4:30 P.M.–5:15 P.M.)	398	340	396	387	1,521
Number of cars turning right into School Avenue (West End) Tim (4:30 P.M.–5:15 P.M.)	304	321	329	313	1,267
Number of cars turning left into School Avenue (East End) Tony (4:30 P.M.–5:15 P.M.)	220	211	234	273	938
Number of cars turning right into School Avenue (East End) Rebecca (4:30 P.M.–5:15 P.M.)	174	183	169	158	684
Total	2,128	2,060	2,064	2,138	8,390

What are local community studies?

Several decades ago, it was fashionable for social studies teachers to imbue students with the goal of becoming responsible citizens within democratic communities. It was assumed by all that there were entities called communities. Supposedly, a community of people was a population aggregate that inhabited a delimitable contiguous territory, shared a historical heritage, possessed a set of basic service institutions, participated in a common mode of life, was conscious of its unity, and was able to act in a corporate way.*

*Edward G. Olsen, *School and Community* 2d ed. (Englewood Cliffs, N.J.: Prentice-Hall, 1954), p. 51.

It is very doubtful whether such a community exists today, if it ever did. Distance is no longer an insurmountable factor, due to superhighways and powerful cars. Furthermore, our way of life, propagated by the media, tends to make us more and more materialistic and individualistic.

Yet students have the opportunity, if desired, of joining and becoming active participants in a wide range of specialized communities. In addition to being members of residential communities, they may be involved in sporting, social, religious, and, in many cases, reluctantly, school communities! These communities may not be closely interrelated spatially or even ideologically. In fact, it is likely that such communities could exhibit many differences, even antipathies, toward one another, like opposing big-city gangs or religious sects.

But the importance to the social studies teacher is that many of these communities are readily available—microcosms of reality for students to observe, to participate in, and to contribute to. In particular, the residential local community is proximate to most students and may contain within it retail, industrial, sporting, social, and religious communities.

Why the interest in local community studies?

Let's be realistic! It is unlikely that local community studies will foster marked student advances in the growth of citizenship responsibilities, the growth of behaviors appropriate within a framework of community expectations and tolerances, and so on. Nevertheless, they can provide students with an exciting and stimulating range of real-life situations. "A cow looks and certainly smells differently in the flesh than from in the dictionary. A common council or a legislature in action is a much more human institution than the textbook descriptions may suggest."* In their long experiences at school, students have very few opportunities actually to witness at firsthand people, objects, and processes other than those within the school confines.

In keeping with the concentric-circle sequencing of social studies topics in the elementary school, students may indeed witness cows and councils in the second or third grades. In junior high school, they may even have a transitory glimpse of local communities in state geography or history courses; too often this is the sum total of firsthand experiences for the majority of students. It seems to be tacitly assumed that written facts, concepts, and generalizations are what students in secondary school social studies should have and will have, regardless of their interests and inclinations.

---

*Clifford L. Lord, *Teaching History with Community Resources*, 2d ed. (New York: Teachers College Press, 1967), p. vi.

Students need to experience more than the theory taught to them within the confines of the classroom. It would seem that they need a repertoire of "people models" with whom to interact in addition to their teachers, so often stereotyped as middle-of-the-road, traditional, conforming persons. In short, students need to undertake their own inquiry, to observe, interact, and work with a host of people operating in different community settings, whether specialized agencies (social work, urban redevelopment) or general community functions (city council).*

The Philadelphia Parkway School is often cited as an exemplary model where the city is the campus and over fifty commercial and governmental agencies are used as centers of activity for students. Many other alternative schools incorporating community-based programs have been springing up throughout the United States, although they have not enjoyed the same degree of publicity. However, collectively, the total number is still very low. It seems certain that the majority of American students will continue to be educated in traditional schools, but, if due regard is given to the inclusion of local community studies, they may still be able to enjoy and participate in many activities comparable with those used in alternative schools.

The current focus on inquiry teaching in social studies, as indicated throughout this book, is, in our opinion, a sound reason for a greater emphasis upon local community studies. A teacher who thinks that leading students through a predetermined sequence within a social science discipline to arrive at solutions is inquiry teaching should skip the next two paragraphs! To a large degree, nationally produced social studies projects appear to have been based on this premise. Leading academicians in specific social science disciplines have carefully prescribed both the content (concepts and generalizations) and the learning processes (scientific steps of inquiry) through which the students are to progress.

True inquiry teaching surely has an interdisciplinary focus. Topics that have meaning for students and those that are worthy of being investigated do not necessarily fit into neat subject boundaries. Neither do human activities in the world outside the classroom. Consequently, a social studies topic can and should be studied in a community setting so that a range of points of view can be examined, although the major emphasis may be economic, sociological, or even historical.† As a parenthetical remark, agencies examining the deleterious effects of man upon the ecosystem are using this wide-ranging inquiry approach. In California schools, an interdisciplinary en-

---

*The present emphasis on career education suggests a similar range of educational experiences, even though a more distinct vocational motive appears to be implied.

†Chapter 3, Simulations, reveals the importance of multifaceted approaches to topics if they are to provide authentic and realistic learning situations for students.

vironmental education curriculum entitled "Ekistics" has recently been formulated and implemented.

Furthermore, free-ranging inquiry topics focusing on a specific community activity allow students more scope for individual initiative in selecting data, persons, and organizations with whom to pursue their topics. Inquiry learning should not be and cannot be confined to a forty-five-minute time slot in Room 105. Although there are all sorts of difficulties involved in securing lengthy time slots for students to be away from the school, such trips can be arranged. The project need not always be carried on within the formal school hours. Often self-generated inquiry by students will spill over into many hours of their own leisure time, both on weekdays and weekends.

Mention should also be made of the positive group and interpersonal experiences acquired in local community studies. Students have opportunities to work closely in small action groups, as well as individually. They are confronted with many opportunities to interview, discuss, and debate points of interest with outside individuals and groups. Most important, they may begin to understand something more about themselves, their strengths and weaknesses, likes and dislikes, and even potential career dispositions.

Most teachers would readily agree that the general public's expectations of schools are often unrealistic and rarely fulfilled. One has only to witness the frequency of school board levy rejections to realize that a higher level of public-relations activities is needed to improve the school image. Local community studies can in many instances foster this development. Parents, citizens, and taxpayers generally like to know what is going on in the secondary schools. What could be more flattering to local residents than to be encouraged to participate in such activities as guest speakers or to act as on-site spokesmen and guides for visiting students?

Some illustrations of local community studies

Five major assumptions of the author need to be made explicit before any tentative list of topics can be made.

First, it is assumed that a local community study is undertaken either for the purpose of introducing a national or international topic (for example, a Social Distance Scale could be used with local residents before commencing a unit on social class) or as an integration exercise that consolidates a wide range of concepts and generalizations (for example, observing the voting behavior of residents in an election of local government officials). A local community study is not undertaken merely to fill the time slot prior to Thanksgiving or Christmas vacation, nor is it an administrative device to cover the lack of a suitable teacher replacement.

Second, it is assumed that because local community studies are involved with real-life people and processes, it is not possible to compartmentalize them as a part of history or geography or any of the other social sciences. An interdisciplinary focus is central to all local community studies. In fact, on occasion it might be very useful to analyze an issue in terms of an even wider focus, namely the humanities (fine arts, music, literature), history, and the other social sciences.

Third, to engender true inquiry learning, it is vital that students have an active role in the planning, implementation, and appraisal of any local community study. The initial theme or issue may come from the suggestion of a student, a number of students, or a committee specially selected for this purpose. Likewise, the implementation of the study might be carried out by a series of action groups either under the direction of a committee or as independent specialist groups. In this situation, the social studies teacher merely acts as facilitator, resource guide, and perhaps figurehead for arranging official interviews, visits, and surveys.

Fourth, it is assumed that local community studies can vary greatly in terms of scope, depth, and level of personal involvement. For example, surveys tend to be noninvolved observations, merely systematic recordings of specific people and objects and their interactions. Yet, as soon as these recordings are classified and categorized, subjective values are involved, both procedural and content-oriented. It would be difficult for students working on a local community study not to move from detached impersonal observations to the level of values. Many might become so immersed in the study that cooperative actions with community members would be initiated. This could take the form of participation with existing agencies or the taking on of a social activist role (see chapter 2 on role playing).

Finally, it should be recognized that local community studies can only be effectively planned and implemented if students and teacher are willing to undertake a considerable amount of researching, both for information and for useful resource personnel. Furthermore, a study can only come about in the traditional school program if administrators and fellow teachers are willing to assist with scheduling, community public relations, financial outlays, and other potential obstacles.

A tentative list of problems and issues that might be utilized in local community studies

1. An examination of the reasons for the settlement of the local community. Why did people come to live here originally? What problems have people in the community faced through the years? For what reasons has the community thrived?
2. A study of variations in retail prices in different socioeconomic sections of the community.
3. An examination of the effects of the passing or rejection of next month's school levy. Should concerted action be taken? What steps, if any, are needed?

4. A study of the effects of the lack of a qualified orthodontist in the local shopping center. Is such a service needed? What moves need to be taken to facilitate the creation of this service?
5. An examination of the extent of poverty in the local community. Is it a problem of great magnitude? If so, what are the chief causes and avenues for alleviation?
6. An examination of the feasibility of converting the Old Road Mill into a local museum. Is there a need for such a facility? What procedures are required to achieve this end?
7. An examination of the types, number, and variety of stores that have evolved in the community since the beginning of the century. What patterns are evident? How have they been related to changing occupational patterns?
8. An examination of the attitudes of older residents toward current plans for public and commercial buildings in the community.
9. A study of the need for an abortion clinic. Is there sufficient demand for such a service? What are the probable desirable and undesirable effects upon the community if a clinic is established?
10. An examination of the feasibility of building a pedestrian bridge over Interstate 71. What justification is there for the financial outlay? What are alternative plans?
11. A study of the desirability of having the proposed $100,000,000 chemical plant located adjacent to the community. What are the short- and long-term advantages and disadvantages? What immediate moves should be made?
12. An examination of the causes of the steep increase in car stealing and petty theft in the local community during the past year. What are the causes? What measures should be taken?
13. An examination of the cause of the polluted condition of the local river. What short-term measures can be taken? Should stringent long-term safeguards be implemented?
14. A study of local folklore. What have been the sources of folklore? What does it tell us about life in the community through the years?

Example A

To examine the prices of basic toiletry items in selected drugstores. Do prices vary in different parts of the city? Why do they vary?

A few weeks ago some tenth-grade economics students were discussing in their lunch hour the large number of drugstores located near their homes. The conversation drifted to the number of times they visited drugstores in any given week and the kinds of toiletries and other goods they often needed to purchase. When specific toiletry items were mentioned by individual students, it came as a surprise to them all that the prices varied considerably.

The issue of price variations among drugstores was raised by one of the students at their next economics class meeting. Their economics teacher didn't miss the opportunity to take up the issue. Here was a fantastic example of price differentials related to factors other than the textbook equation of supply and demand! At first the students in the class were eager to swap anecdotes about what toiletry items they had recently purchased and to make comparisons about price variations. Then the discussion began to revolve around the kinds of action that they might take. Should they concentrate on ascertaining price differences on a representative list of standard toiletry items? Should they consider the clientele of each drugstore in their search for reasons of price differences? Should they find out whether the local residents were aware of price differences among selected drugstores? It was soon realized that the starting point would have to be the price differences on selected commodity items, and so a plan of action for the next three weeks was drawn up.

Week 1. During the week the economics teacher tried to pin the students down to some basic sample survey principles when considering the commodity items to be compared. Checklists of a large number of toiletry items were compiled. Different students were then allocated the tasks of checking the availability of the items and the range of standard sizes and packaging available. The teacher brought in comparative data on commodity items used in consumer price index series, as well as reference books on sampling theory and techniques. By the end of the week, the students had eliminated a number of commodity items and had selected what they considered to be a representative sample. They had surveyed and mapped all drugstores within a five-mile radius of their school, and each student had been allocated five items to check out over the weekend. All had been warned about the necessity for tact in carrying out their survey. They were to obtain the prices of the commodities as unobtrusively as possible and not in any way to broach the topic of seemingly high or low prices with the drugstore operators, even though it might prove to be tempting!

Week 2. This started off at a frantic pace as students reported back with their data and the process of collation began. Large charts were drawn up depicting sample toiletry prices at specific drugstores. It soon became apparent that there were considerable differences, but the pattern of these price variations was quite complicated. Some commodity lines, especially toothpastes and toothbrushes, had the least variations among drugstores, while cosmetics and pain relievers varied enormously. The study offered a fruitful opportunity for the economics teacher to highlight these elasticities and inelasticities of demand. Discussions were initiated on why drugstores could apparently raise some commodity prices but were careful to keep others relatively low.

More important, the collated data revealed that price variations among drugstores seemed to be related in some way to varying socioeconomic levels in different parts of the city. Although the group had no socioeconomic indices, the higher prices seemed to have an inverse relationship to socioeconomic residential levels. It was a useful opportunity for the teacher to delve into socioeconomic indices with the class and also to initiate the idea that perhaps a public opinion poll could reveal whether residents were aware of and/or concerned about price variations on toiletry items.

Week 3. Most of the economics class periods during this week were spent in devising an appropriate public opinion poll. All the pitfalls of devising suitable questionnaires were presented, together with basic principles of interviewing and sampling. At last a brief but concise questionnaire was completed and tried out on some parents and friends. Ambiguities in the wording of some items were noted and rectified. The sample population to be surveyed was carefully plotted, and the tasks of interviewing were allocated to various students.

It took several weeks for students to complete their interviewing, as most were only able to do it on weekends. In due course, after various door-knocking frustrations and revisitations, students successfully completed their task, and the results were tabulated and collated. Rather unexpectedly, the results revealed that residents were vaguely aware of differences in prices but were more concerned with personal service and convenience than with monetary differences. The students decided that was where their study should stop. Apparently they, with relatively meager incomes, were more sensitive to price variations than the community at large!

Commentary on example A

The study proved to be extremely interesting for the students involved, though they were puzzled and somewhat disappointed by the apathy of the general public toward price variations. But the value of the exercise was in the inquiry processes that occurred. Students developed specific skills in sampling, interviewing, and data analysis almost incidentally as they went about their task of pursuing price differences. A number of stimulating discussions were generated in which hitherto unresponsive students became deeply involved. For the teacher and for a great number of students, the exercise was both rewarding and satisfying.

Example B

To examine the effects of the passing or rejection of next month's school levy. Should concerted action be taken? What steps, if any, are needed?

For the past four months, Mr. Davies had been responsible for teaching Problems of Democracy (POD) to three twelfth-grade classes and an elective in sociology to two other twelfth-grade classes. During this time, the classes had explored major concepts in both political science and sociology, with special emphasis on such concepts as pressure groups and status, reference groups, and peer groups. One day in the faculty lounge, Mr. Davies became involved in a discussion with other faculty about the possible repercussions if next month's school levy did not pass. Then a thought suddenly struck him . . . he checked out his idea with the school principal and then, having obtained approval, went into action.

Mr. Davies started the sessions of each of his POD and sociology classes the next day with a discussion of the future of Greenhall High School, its academic and athletic accomplishments, and its standing in the community. In particular, he was careful to remind them of the developments that were planned for the next two years—a new football stadium, a computer console for use both by students and faculty, a senior students' lounge with a smoking room section and a quiet study section. Then came the punch line. "Well, you guys, I guess you realize that we have no hope of getting any of these things. The school levy is going to be presented next month but there is little chance that it is going to be passed and so . . . ." The initial student response was silence, then murmurs followed by angry mutters. It wasn't long before the students were busily thinking about what could be done. How could they ensure that the school levy would be passed? The student groups swung into action as follows:

Week 1. At first, only the more vocal students showed a lot of concern. The following day in class, they presented short papers explaining the urgency of the situation and exhorted other class members to participate. Their most effective presentations were short tape-recordings by the school principal, board chairman, and school superintendent, who explained the likely effects on the students if the levy was not passed. This was all the students needed! The five classes had a lunchtime meeting in which action groups were decided upon and organized. It was decided that these would be:

1. An action group to ascertain what influential residents were likely to be in favor of the levy.
2. An action group to ascertain what influential residents were likely to be against the levy.
3. An action group to investigate who was eligible to vote next month and to locate on a map the catchment area for voters.
4. An action group to review the most urgent amenities needed at Greenhall High School in the next two years and to provide detailed descriptions of their potential value to students and faculty.
5. An action group to consider forms of advertising to be used, including comparative data on levies in similar school districts.

The various action groups started collecting all their information. This involved interviewing influential community members; looking through educational journals in the library to obtain comparative data; having talks with the art and media faculty about types of advertising that could be used; and arranging a dance the next Saturday to raise funds for their operating costs.

Week 2. The first few days of the second week turned out to be feedback and general evaluation sessions. Several lunchtime meetings were held in which students provided information and outlined tentative promotional ventures. By the middle of the week, a coordinated offensive was put into action:

1. An open night was provided at the school, during which interested citizens and parents were shown the current school activities together with proposed plans for future developments.
2. Leaflets were distributed to every eligible voter in the community.
3. The local radio station allocated fifteen minutes of prime listening time for a student forum to express their opinions about the forthcoming levy.

4. A roster of drivers for the voting day was organized.
5. Pickets and pamphlet vendors were organized on a roster basis outside the voting booth.

The day of reckoning came the following week, when a record turnout of eighty-four percent of the eligible voters registered their votes. The result was a narrow but decisive defeat of the school levy, 630 to 587!

Commentary on example B

It could be argued that school levies are not topics within the domain of social studies teaching and that social action by students is not to be desired. If so, students will continue to be bored, disillusioned, and discontented with typical school programs that teach theoretical concepts but never give them a chance to view the processes at work in the real world, much less allow them the opportunity to participate. So long as board members and other officials are aware of these student projects, it would seem that such a community study must achieve nothing but good. It allows endless opportunities for students to apply various political and sociological principles. Further, it provides numerous occasions for students both to interact and to work with community citizens who are cooperatively striving for the same goal. It could well lead to a better understanding by students of the responsibilities that they and their parents enjoy within their local community. In this particular study, students learned to face up to failure even though tremendous effort was expended on their part. The reality shock of the final result brought home most vividly the effects of power—the power of informal and formal pressure groups that they apparently had not been able to dissuade from voting against the levy.

The above examples represent a range of potential topics for local community studies as envisaged by *one* person in a particular school system with particular kinds of students, administrative personnel, and community relationships. Obviously, the direction, style, and depth of local community studies will vary enormously with each individual teacher.

Whether you embark upon such undertakings depends upon the degree to which you consider it important to view man and his activities in real world situations and feel that the goal of helping students to become talented and insightful citizens who can build and support a community at the grass roots level is valid.* Community studies not only provide practical situations in which theoretical information from the social sciences can be reexamined and integrated; they also provide students with insights about their personal roles in society. Most present-day social studies writers no longer treat this

---

*Donald W. Oliver and Victoria Steinitz, *Mobility or Community: The Hard Choice of the New Professional* (Cambridge: Harvard University Graduate School of Education, 1970), p. 3.

form of social training in terms of glittering democratic ideals. Yet they all emphasize the need for modern youth to acquire a sense of belonging, a sense of community.

Even if you accept the ideas expressed in the above paragraph (and there are many educators who either don't believe in them or think they can't be accomplished at the present time), what about the resources you are going to use to carry out these local community studies? One can almost hear the readers' rumblings:

"How can we get information about our local community? It's not important enough to have had any books or articles written about it. There are no historic relics. There's nothing unique or unusual about this community—just where do I start?"

Resources for local community studies

Acquiring and exploring local community resources can be very time-consuming, but once one starts searching, the scope of the possibilities that open up is amazing.

As with most teaching activities, after you have undertaken one community study, subsequent repetitions become easier to organize and are often more successful, until you get to the point where the topic becomes boring. Local community studies undertaken once or twice a year over a period of several years make it increasingly easy for a teacher to accumulate a resource bank, provided that the data previously collected are carefully stored and cataloged and that well-written reports, summaries, and papers are included as an integral part of each study.

The resources available for a local community study can be classified in a variety of ways, in terms of individual persons, groups, printed materials, and artifacts or in terms of location (whether the resources are viewed in the classroom or in the community itself). The first classification will be used in the following pages, but several comments need to be made about the latter alternative.

There is a definite advantage to using the classroom as a setting for some of the activities in a local community study. Apart from being a headquarters base for the various student working committees, the classroom can and should be used for other activities. On occasions, notable personnel representing particular industries or associations will come to the school in the role of guest speakers. In this instance, the school classroom provides a more effective forum for open discussion and debate than a noisy factory or office. Certain movable artifacts, including specimen kits on loan from museums and societies, are often more appropriately examined in the classroom. Sometimes commercially produced multimedia kits may contain sections appropriate to a local community study, such as the 1930s multimedia kit produced by the Ontario Institute for Research Studies.* These kits could be used in the classroom.

In most studies, however, the majority of the investigations will be carried out by students in the field. This may be done either formally or informally; in hour sessions or half-day sessions; in school time or nonschool time; in large groups, small groups, or individually; as observers or participators—the range and scope is limited only by the initiative and resourcefulness of the teacher and his students. Examples that come to mind range from highly structured field trips to informal camping hikes, attendance by students at public meetings as reporters, or student service as aides in a nursing home on a Saturday morning. No "dos" and "don'ts" about student behavior, manners, and courtesies have been included in this chapter, but obviously one could wax eloquent for many pages on these subjects.† Instead, let us look in some detail at the range of resources available for local community studies.

People in specific occupations

The local community for social studies teachers is chiefly a residential one because most other kinds of community are not readily accessible to the students. However, there is usually a sprinkling of residents who reside and work within the same locality.

What resource personnel do you seek out? We have all come into contact with the terse, surly factory foreman or the loquacious, beaming politician. Are these the people we really want? It would seem that for most local community studies, there are two main categories of resource personnel. There are a select few who are well known for their general knowledge of and interest in the local community. Often these people have held the same positions for a considerable period and have been involved over the years in most of the community action. In this category, one normally finds the local newspaper editor, head librarian, city council chairman, and county clerk. The second category consists of personnel who may not have lived in the community for a long period and may not be well known, but who possess specific skills and knowledge about the industry of which they are specialized members. Some examples would include banker, labor union secretary, supermarket manager, and farmer. Both categories of personnel have useful contributions to make and may, in various ways, enrich and broaden the interests of the students.

---

*David Stansfield, *The 1930's Multi-Media Kit* (Toronto: Ontario Institute for Studies in Education, 1970). In chapter 6 of this book guidelines are clearly set out for teachers and/or students to produce their own multimedia units.

†For example, see Leonard S. Kenworthy, *Guide To Social Studies Teaching* (Belmont, Calif.: Wadsworth, 1970), pp. 187–190, 370–377, and Edward G. Olsen, *School And Community*, 2d ed. (Englewood Cliffs, N.J.: Prentice Hall, 1954), pp. 111–205.

People now retired, but previously in specific occupations

These are the local "delights," the Civil War buff and the collector of sailing ship models, who have time to explain and reminisce about their particular hobbies or interests.* Then there are the octogenarians who can describe in remarkable detail the social, economic, and political activities of the local community in years gone by. These people are the ones who give color to local community studies and who, if they are carefully sought out (and kept to the topic), can be very useful sources of information. One highly promising way of capitalizing on the experiences of older community members is to record on audiotape or videotape their recollections of former times. A collection of such recorded remembrances can bring life to the study of history, and can provide students with firsthand experience in collecting and analyzing primary data. The Foxfire project, carried out by students in Rabun Gap, Georgia, is an excellent example of this kind of local community study. The project involved the students' recording by tape and photography the reflections and insights of their elderly neighbors and relatives. The findings, reported in the *Foxfire Books*, provide a fascinating glimpse into the lives of people living in an Appalachian mountain community.†

Groups, associations, and organizations

Local associations are often available and willing to provide specific information to students. An examination of the yellow pages in the telephone directory will reveal that they run the whole gamut, including religious, recreational, sporting, business, cultural, political, and social welfare groups. Again, discretion must be used by teachers and students in only contacting groups that have information specifically related to the topic under study. Also, students need to be aware of indirect (and sometimes blatant) propaganda maneuvers by these organizations!

Some examples of specific associations often found in a local community include the following:

Business

Association of Real Estate Builders
Better Business Bureau
Convention Bureau
Junior Chamber of Commerce
Bar Association
Chamber of Commerce
Hotel and Motel Association
Local industries

---

*Clifford L. Lord, *Teaching History with Community Resources,* 2d ed. (New York: Teachers College Press, 1967), pp. 10–17.

†The *Foxfire Books* are published by Doubleday & Company, Inc., Garden City, N.Y., under the Anchor Books imprint. Many of the articles in the *Foxfire Books* first appeared in *Foxfire Magazine*, which was put together by students at the Rabun Gap-Nacoochee School in Georiga under the guidance of their teacher, Eliot Wigginton.

Recreational

B'nai B'rith
Police Athletic League
YWCA
Local park and recreational association
YMCA

Social Welfare

Alcoholics Anonymous
Daughters of American National Council
Good Samaritan Alcoholic Rehabilitation
Leukemia society
The Nature Conservancy
Planned Parenthood
Service clubs (Rotary, Kiwanis Lions, etc.)
American Association of University Women
Earth Day Association
Hearing and speech center
Mental health center
Parent-Teacher Association
Salvation Army
Society for the Prevention of Cruelty to Animals
Volunteers of America

Religious

Christian Center
Council of Churches
Specific denominations, sects, and organizations
Church Women United
National Council of Community Churches

Political

Democratic state executive committee
Interward political council
Republican state headquarters
Educators' political action committee
League of Women Voters

Cultural and Educational

Antique automobile museum
Art gallery
Colleges and universities
Libraries
Natural history museum
Railway museum
Aquarium
Center of science and industry
Historical museum
Municipal orchestra
Planetarium
Zoo

Materials and artifacts

Newspapers Newspapers are often an important source of information about a local community, both for present-day happenings and historical events. The best source is the local newspaper, which is often "the diary of the community, recording events as they take place and in considerable detail."* However, nearby city newspapers often contain local community supplements, flashback columns and, most important, special centenary issues.

*Lord, *Teaching History with Community Resources*, p. 29.

Usually all these newspapers are readily available from either the head offices of the newspapers, or from libraries and historical societies.* Depending upon the interests of the students (and especially the exigencies of storage space availability), a search of the community can often bring rewarding results. Parents and friends searching through attics may find all sorts of historic newspaper editions and sometimes are willing to donate to schools complete sets going back many years.

Documents and reports The satisfaction that students gain from working with primary data has been noted by many social studies educators and is elaborated in some detail in chapter 4. In the local community, a wealth of documents are available, although head offices in larger centers may have to be visited to actually pick up the data.

Data from government offices include:
1. Census data on population and industries
2. Federal and state studies pertaining to economic or sociological topics
3. Data on water supply, sewerage, and health services
4. Land deeds
5. Court records
6. Vital statistics (births, deaths, marriages)
7. City directories
8. Official reports, e.g., annual reports by the superintendent of schools

Data from private firms include:
1. Ledgers and journals
2. Annual reports
3. Booklets on the historical growth of a particular company

However, a caveat needs to be stated. Students should only embark on the examination of documents and reports if they have a specific objective in mind. Otherwise the exercise becomes an interesting but wasteful use of student time. The availability of relatively inexpensive forms of photocopying enables important documents to be reproduced in their original form and with a minimum of time and effort.

Photographs and films In a local community, a whole wealth of photographs are available—historical and current, of good and poor quality, relevant and nonrelevant.

The historical photographs can be very useful for depicting social customs and town life. They are usually available as discards from newspaper offices,

---

*For example, the Ohio Historical Society Museum has a very comprehensive collection of printed materials (newspapers and books) and artifacts.

business firms, and professional photographers. If asked, parents and local citizens will often provide schools with literally thousands of old photographs. The major problem is culling out the few really useful ones. Many schools now have photographic facilities where small photographs can be enlarged to a size suitable for teaching.

Recent photographs, produced from high-quality photographic equipment, are often of a far superior quality. These may include eye-level views as well as oblique and vertical air photographs and mosaics. Air photographs, when used in conjunction with stereoscopes, provide students with spectacular three-dimensional views of their local community. Unfortunately, recent photographs are more expensive to purchase, eye-level ones being available from newspaper offices and professional photographers, while vertical and oblique air photographs are available from lands and survey departments and private aerial mapping firms.

Films are even more difficult to procure and, of course, their cost is often prohibitive. Amateur student camera clubs can sometimes combine their expertise with the special needs of the social studies classes, for mutual advantage.

One of the major advantages of both photographs and films is that they can be used to show scenes at different time periods, especially before and after major changes have occurred. Consequently, local community enthusiasts have to be continually on the alert for changes that are imminent so that they can record the present situation for posterity. Such instances might include the demolition of a historic landmark, the pulling up of the railroad tracks that run right down the middle of the main street, or even the replacement of an old school building!

Recordings Photographs provide authentic visual records of events; tape recordings provide authentic auditory evidence. For example, a tape recording of the reminiscences of a notable local resident might be of great value, as might the recording of local folk songs, important public meetings, or even sounds of a past era. It is up to the students to record the sounds of objects or persons that might be unavailable in the near future. Modern technology makes it relatively easy to obtain good-quality reproductions of tapes from radio stations or from private and public companies. As the result of the development of projectors that synchronize either slides and audiotape or 8mm film and audiotape, it is now possible to reproduce high-quality records of past and present-day events.

Books Nonfiction books written specifically about a local community are relatively rare. Nevertheless, both indirect and direct references are often available. Volumes of state history and biographical sketches usually contain passing references to a local community and its members. In some instances, specific studies of a local community or segment thereof, have been produced, such as the history of a local college, company, or church.

Most local libraries have general biographical volumes, including the *Dictionary of American Biography, Who's Who in America, Who Was Who In America*. Specific local community studies may have to be searched out elsewhere, as in historical societies or in private libraries. Yet it is surprising how many "finds" (together with numerous worthless items) can be obtained by making concerted appeals to local residents.

Diaries, letters, and sketches Although a whole range of these resources might be available in neighboring museums and libraries, it is unlikely that many would be very applicable to local community studies, especially considering the time needed to search them out. Furthermore, it is unlikely that hunts for these resources would reveal anything of very great significance. If by chance a very rare and valuable item were discovered, the school wouldn't have the heating, lighting, and humidity controls to store it safely! Nevertheless, some students might develop a special interest in these resource items and, provided that they have the time to spend, should be encouraged.

Miscellaneous personal items For specific school displays in conjunction with a local community study, parents and citizens are often willing to lend a miscellaneous array of personal items, sometimes of considerable historical interest. Such a display might contain samples of tools, utensils, weapons, crockery, or even clothing and toys pertaining to particular groups.

Local museums and historical societies often have a great number of items that can be viewed by students. In some instances, museums provide boxes of contemporary and historic artifacts for loans to schools for short periods of time. However, most teachers (and custodians) would be rather reticent, if not appalled, about the idea of collecting miscellaneous personal items for permanent storage!

Resources of the physical and human environment Preceding pages have made reference to a wide number of persons, printed matter, and artifacts that can be examined by students in context or even brought to the classroom. However, specific mention has not been made of the environment as a whole.

One of the big advantages of local community studies is that students can view the interaction of people within a specific physical environment. They learn to appreciate the benefits of locating towns in river valleys, the need for proximity to rivers for water supply, and the differential effects of soil fertility on the types of land use practiced.

Then, of course, there are the more indirect interrelationships of the physical environment and the human environment. To what degree does the town follow the natural contours of the land? Are there natural or manmade barriers that may impede the growth of the town in the future? Are there any buildings in the community that now serve a function different from the original one? Are there any derelict offices, houses, factories? If so, why?

Even though these observations of the environment might start out as merely observation, mapping, and tabulation exercises, obviously students will want to take up certain issues more closely. For example, they may embark upon the value issue of whether the physical environment has been used appropriately in their local community or whether sufficient conservation methods are at present being used.

The realities of the local community are potentially available to all students as a very positive aid and supplement to the largely theoretical activities undertaken in schools. It is up to enlightened teachers to make good use of these resources.

Some precautions

Before we dismiss all learning experiences other than local community studies as being inappropriate and obsolete, a few precautions are in order. We are assuming that at regular points in time in social studies courses it is both appropriate and effective to undertake local community studies, either as an introductory stimulus/springboard to a theme or topic or as a culminating, integrative exercise. A steady diet of local community studies might become just as nauseating as regular programs to many secondary school students. But on occasions, it would seem that they provide students with realistic firsthand experiences that can be extremely valuable.

This does not mean that vicariously presented alternatives, such as 16mm and 8mm films, filmstrips, or slides, should not be used. As indicated in chapter 6, well-produced audiovisual presentations can be very effective, especially if particular points of view are emphasized.

To some students, local community studies might have too wide a focus, so that they cannot see past an array of undigested, unrelated facts. Training over a period of time is often required so that students can adjust to purposeful searching for relevant material.

Local community studies don't just happen on a sunny afternoon! Very careful planning is required by the teacher(s) to ascertain the resources available, the personnel to be contacted, travel details to be arranged, fields of emphasis, follow-up activities, and reference materials, just to mention a few. In particular, attention needs to be directed to teacher responsibilities and liabilities for student travel. School districts vary considerably with regard to provisions for student travel insurance and general teacher liabilities. It is necessary to check these out very carefully before embarking upon any community excursion. Care must also be taken to ensure that students are aware of their responsibilities. Tact and diplomacy with community personnel is an obvious but often forgotten social skill. If handled adroitly, however, community excursions offer tremendous opportunities for improved public relations between the school and its neighborhood.

Very few book publishers consider specific community studies to be profitable ventures, and so most teachers have to literally dig out their own sources of information and personnel with whom to contact. This is very time-consuming, although the final rewards in terms of student response are usually more than compensating.

Local community studies need to be judiciously placed in social studies courses so that students can see the realities of people and the social interactions and processes at work. A few words of caution, however, may be in order: too often community studies can become narrow, provincial interpretations. Sometimes superficial glances at the community create the impression for students that all local veterans were prominent generals and that local historical relics rank closely with those in Williamsburg!

Students are not the only group that gains from community studies. Interested community residents, workers, and parents are often only too willing to assist with such projects and thereby gain more insight into the workings of the local secondary school. Few would deny that such interaction is desirable and should be fostered. On the other hand, some teachers, especially senior teachers and administrators, might fear that increased outside interest will lead to increased community/parent control. There is indeed a fine line between encouraging and fostering parent-community interest and involvement, on the one hand, and upholding the professional statuses and responsibilities of the teachers and administrators on the other. Furthermore, some participants in community ventures inadvertently or deliberately become involved in veritable hornets' nests—controversial issues that may sectionalize a community. Unfortunately, one or two extreme actions by students can incur the wrath of the entire community in a remarkably short time.

Summary

Present-day high-school students tend to lead highly individualistic and materialistic lives, yet seem to be yearning for something else. Could it be that many lack a sense of community? Persons can belong to many communities; the residential and occupational community are the most important. Even though there is a decreasing likelihood that these two communities will be spatially contiguous, they are the most readily accessible to social studies teachers. In particular, the local residential community is proximate to many students and may often contain subcommunities based upon occupational, religious, sporting, and social interests.

Local community studies appear to have been traditionally ignored in many secondary-school social studies programs. It seems to be implicitly assumed that once students in the second grade of elementary school have studied their local community, they should aspire to wider and wider horizons. Even the high-quality social studies programs and activities that evolved from the national projects in the 1960s provided minimal local community studies. The predominant emphasis has been on single-discipline studies of specific concepts and generalizations.

Yet there are numerous reasons why local community studies should form an integral part of any social studies curriculum. Such studies can provide illustrations and practical insights about theoretical concepts; they allow students to interact with community residents and workers and, in so doing, help them to find themselves; they allow wide-ranging inquiry studies, which become interdisciplinary and often self-generating; and, in many instances, they provide opportunities for local community residents to learn about and appreciate the functions and activities of the schools to which they are financially committed. It can be argued that these advantages outweigh such disadvantages as the teacher energy and time expended in planning and implementing studies and the danger of students becoming involved in issues that might incur the wrath of community members.

Specific examples are often the best way of illustrating the strengths and characteristics of a particular teaching technique. Within the chapter a listing of potentially useful issues was included, followed by the presentation of two detailed examples. The first example illustrated a survey study that proved to be very successful, while the second example focussed on a community participation project that provided a wide range of learning experiences for the participants, even though the final outcome was unsuccessful.

For many teachers, not knowing where to start is a major problem. Resources for local community studies are more readily available than may be popularly known. In the latter part of the chapter, descriptions of these resources were given. The resources listed were: personnel and groups; printed materials, photographs, films, and tape recordings; miscellaneous personal items; and the totality of the physical and human environments.

Bibliography

Bacon, Phillip, ed. *Focus on Geography: Key Concepts and Teaching Strategies.* Washington, D.C.: National Council of Social Studies, 1970.

This fortieth yearbook of the NCSS provides some useful material on inquiry models in part I and teaching and learning applications in part II, even though there are no specific chapters on local community studies.

Banks, James A., ed. *Teaching Ethnic Studies*. Washington, D.C.: National Council on Social Studies, 1973.

This forty-third yearbook of the NCSS contains some useful background material on racism, cultural pluralism, and social justice.

Bowman, James; Freeman, Larry; Olson, Paul A.; and Pieper, Jan. *Of Education and Human Community*. Lincoln: University of Nebraska Press, 1971.
This book contains papers presented by leaders in experimental education. Of note are chapters by James S. Coleman, Jerome S. Bruner, and John Bremer (Philadelphia Parkway School).

"Career Education and Social Studies." *Social Education* 37 (1973): 484–531.
The entire issue is devoted to the topic of career education. In particular, John P. Marchak's "*Career Education: What's Happening Across the Nation*" has some useful pointers for local community studies.

Fraser, Dorothy McClure, and West, Edith. *Social Studies in Secondary Schools*. New York: Ronald, 1961.
Although this book is now rather dated, the chapter on community resources is very useful.

Gross, Richard E., and Zeleny, Leslie D. *Educating Citizens for Democracy*. New York: Oxford University Press, 1958.
This book contains interesting chapters on the community and community problems, even though it is not a recent publication.

High School Geography Project. *The Local Community: A Handbook For Teachers*. New York: Macmillan, 1971.
This book is not sold as an integral part of the six HSGP units. However, it does contain some very useful hints for community studies with a geographical orientation.

Kenworthy, Leonard S. *Guide to Social Studies Teaching*. Belmont, Calif.: Wadsworth, 1970.
This book contains useful but largely superficial comments about various aspects of community studies.

Lord, Clifford L. *Teaching History With Community Resources*. 2d ed. New York: Teachers College Press, 1967.
This is one of a series of books on specific states and cities. Chapters that are especially valuable include those dealing with research in community resources, field trips, and building community resources.

Mehlinger, Howard D., and Patrick, John J. *American Political Behavior*. Boston: Ginn, 1972.
This project material contains useful case studies of communities and illustrates how they can be incorporated into lessons to teach specific political science concepts.

Metcalf, Lawrence E., ed. *Values Education: Rationale, Strategies and Procedures*. Washington, D.C.: National Council on Social Studies, 1971.
This forty-first yearbook of the NCSS does not provide specific material on community studies but does include some useful chapters on teaching strategies for value analysis.

Oliver, Donald W., and Fred M. Newmann. *Public Issues/Harvard Social Studies Project*. Columbus: Zerox Corporation, 1967.
Of the many titles available, especially useful and powerfully presented are "Community Change," "Municipal Politics," and "Social Action."

Oliver, Donald W., and Steinitz, Victoria. *Mobility or Community: the Hard Choice of the New Professional*. Cambridge; Harvard University Graduate School of Education, 1970.

Olsen, Edward G. *School and Community*. 2d ed. Englewood Cliffs, N.J.: Prentice Hall, 1954.

This book was originally printed in 1945, but it is still one of the most comprehensive available and includes a wealth of material on planning community experiences and community materials.

Inquiry-oriented teaching can be greatly enhanced by the proper use of audiovisual aids. A broad range of useful media is available to the social studies teacher, and it is the intent of this chapter (1) to consider ways in which the use of audiovisual materials and other media can be supportive of inquiry-oriented instruction; (2) to identify sources of commercially produced materials; and (3) to suggest procedures by which teachers can create audiovisual materials of their own.

Chapter 6

Media

Inquiry-oriented teaching emphasizes media as an integral part of the instructional process. Media experiences should be coordinated with the curriculum and designed to (1) promote the acquisition of procedural skills, (2) allow students to practice individual and group decision making, (3) challenge belief systems, and (4) develop skills that are transferable to a wide range of situations. The purely illustrative use of media is secondary to their use in posing situations that motivate students to engage willingly in problem solving.

Inquiry-based audiovisual materials set up problems that are of genuine concern to students—problems that contradict common beliefs, that raise questions, that cause students to recognize and investigate inconsistencies in their thinking.

Audiovisual materials should be selected to motivate students to ask questions and pursue solutions to problems. Needle-sort decks and computer-based simulations, for example, are largely autoinstructional; by themselves, they create a learning environment. Working as individuals or in groups, students might use the material from Education Systems Research, "Who Came to the First U.S. Congress? A Data Bank for Inquiry," to explore basic questions about the ninety-five members of the first Congress: "How many of the members had also been members of the Continental Congress?" How many members had been delegates to the Constitutional Convention?" How many had been born in the same states that sent them to Congress?" Students could then go on to develop correlations, test hypotheses, and construct research designs on such matters as the location of the United States capital, the funding of the national debt, and the creation of the national bank. In the same way, students can interact as individuals with a computer-based unit, such as LIFE DECISIONS, to trace career and educational patterns and to examine their own potentialities in a supportive environment.

Social-studies media, properly used, will stimulate interest in many social-studies topics, and often will allow teachers to act as creators of their own audiovisual materials. Teachers who work side by side with students to design instructional materials will find that the number of students reached by instruction increases, that individuals and groups become self-directed and autonomous, and that the teaching-learning process becomes more enjoyable. Teacher-student teams and student production groups can simultaneously carry on a number of activities.

For example, using the topic "Life during the Fifties," one team, acting as anthropologists or cultural historians, might collect "cultural artifacts" to create a "1950s Box." Another production group might document the political atmosphere of the decade with collections of annotated audiotapes of various political personalities, political cartoons, campaign buttons, etc. Still another team could collect histories from their families, acquaintances, and others who remember the 1950s and then analyze and illustrate the impact of the decade's culture on various people.

This chapter emphasizes teacher and student involvement in the creation and use of audiovisual materials. The pool of media ideas is planned to guide the teacher who wishes to involve students in production, to investigate the several media, and to design novel media experiences.

A word of caution: Do not pick a medium and then create a lesson around it; rather, design the lesson plan and then select the medium that will best complement that plan and its objectives.

Slides, filmstrips, and photographs

Student- or teacher-prepared "still" picture shows are an economical means of bringing the outside world into the classroom. Slides, filmstrips, and photographic prints can be used to condense time, isolate experiences and scenes, bring past events and distant places into the classroom, illustrate several sides of a controversial question, display steps in a process, and illustrate a quality common to a set of diverse situations.

When pictures of events occurring over a period of, say, two weeks, are shown within the confines of a class period, time has been condensed. Photographs that illustrate such topics as the phases of a political campaign, a fight by citizens to prevent destruction of a historic building, the path of a bill through Congress, or events of a past era are examples of the concentration of time by the camera.

Photographs showing the points of view of others and dealing with controversial topics move the media-oriented teacher into the realm of problem-centered instruction. For example, such controversial topics as the treatment of the poor, abortion, race relations, and sex education can all be treated by the camera-equipped teacher or student.

Slides

Slides are a more flexible medium than filmstrips because of the ease with which slides can be edited and the slide trays or magazines updated by deleting slides or adding new ones. In addition, the teacher can select certain groups of scenes for projection or change the projection sequence. However, what is usually an advantage can sometimes be a disadvantage. Slides can get out of order or be lost, and this usually means the teacher must put some limits on individual student use of the slide carrier or of individual slides. Also, if slide shows use recorded narratives with magnetic cues, the audio portion is usually recorded on reel-to-reel tape recorders, which are a little more complicated to use than the cassette machines that accompany sound-cued slide shows and filmstrips.

For slides that do not use recorded, magnetically cued narratives, individualized instruction is possible with tabletop slide viewers. For individuals to use slides that have taped narratives with magnetic cues, a rather bulky projector must be set up to project on a screen or the wall; and a tape recorder and, perhaps, a tape-slide synchronizer must be moved. For individualization of instruction with this type of slide presentation, a well-defined physical space must be set aside in which slide projectors and tape recorders can be used by individuals or small groups.

Filmstrips

Set in a permanent instructional sequence, filmstrips are ideal for presenting topics or events that will not require reinterpretation in the near future. Historical events, life in other cultures, ethnic neighborhoods, or cultural changes over the centuries are examples of topics best adapted to filmstrip presentation. (Topics such as current events, pollution, and local politics are best handled by slides, which can be edited. If parts of a filmstrip become dated, the teacher has only the options of either masking out frames or skipping over them quickly. Either procedure distracts a class.)

Filmstrips also allow individualization of instruction. There are a number of inexpensive, compact, portable filmstrip viewers on the market, and several of them have integral cassette tape players for audio accompaniment. A student who misses a filmstrip presentation, wishes to review the filmstrip, or has it assigned for enrichment can use the viewer at his or her seat or in some other designated place without disturbing instruction of the rest of the class.

Photographs

When a display must emcompass more than one picture at a time, still photographs are superior to both slides and filmstrips. It would be difficult to use slides in, say, a sociological exercise on stereotypes where ethnic names accompany photographs of faces shown simultaneously or in an unfolding sequence.

Among the disadvantages of photographic prints, the typical photograph is too small for use before a class. It must either be enlarged to a usable size, probably at least 12″ × 18″ (commercial cost, about $4.00 from a 3″ × 5″ photo), or shown on an opaque projector. Use of an opaque projector negates the value of photographs, as they must then be shown singly rather than as part of a display. If the school has a photo lab, 3″ × 5″ print can be blown up to 12″ × 18″ for about $.75, or a slide can be made from the photo for about $.10.

A sample still-picture exercise

The problems of the old and poor in our society form a valuable topic for study. The audiovisual presentation shown in Figures 6.1 and 6.2 could lead to an exploration of how people perceive and categorize others and of questions of social status, as well as of the problems of the elderly. Would Mr. Taub be right if he classed Lylah Tiffany with "some of them not even belong to live in a decent house . . . they are nothing, just trouble"? Where might Lylah Tiffany stand in her social relations with Mr. Taub? How do you think Lylah Tiffany ended up in the Columbus Hotel? Did she lead a productive life, or was she a drain on society? This topic would also be very suitable for a film (see "A Sample 8mm Film Exercise").

Teachers who may want to produce their own slides, filmstrips, and photographs (as well as motion pictures) will find material in the following sections that will help them in these projects.

Producing slides, filmstrips, and photographs

Ask your students, "How many of you own a camera?" or "How many of you have access to a camera?" In many schools, 60–75 percent of the students own cameras, and another 15–20 percent have access to them. Where the incidence of ownership or access is low, the teacher has other means available to acquaint students with the process of documenting the environment via photographic prints and slides. A camera such as the **see** is available for $2.60 from Selective Educational Equipment, Inc.,* which also merchandises a packaged instructional kit complete with **see**-cameras, developing kit, sample project material, and an excellent introduction to picture taking and film developing and printing, *Camera Cookbook*.

Slides A full-frame 35mm camera is best for school use. A range-finder 35mm camera is small, economical, simple to use, and versatile. A single-lens reflex 35mm camera is even more versatile, and quite possibly easier to use than a range-finder camera, but it is a good deal more expensive. If a 35mm camera is not available, any camera using Kodak 126 or 110 Instamatic cartridges or 127 roll film can be used; the slides are fully compatible in the same projector with no adjustments. To add emphasis to slide presentations, a device can be purchased that will synchronize a tape-recorded narrative with a slide show.

---

*Addresses of companies will be found in the Bibliography.

Figure 6.1. Lylah Tiffany

I'm originally from Ohio, where a good many of our best presidents came from. My father was a famous family in his line, but it was a line that would not get famous universally, because people don't use flour mills, do they . . . in everyday life and that's what he invented, flour mills.

In the past I did have a ten-year stay in vaudeville doing a bicycle act with my first husband. So . . . when I was offered a part in this play, *All the Way Home*, an actress part, which I'd never done before (I was eighty-one when I made my debut). So I did develop a stage presence and I was all right on the stage for *All the Way Home* for a solid year. I was in it an entire year and then Susskind made a picture of it a couple years later and he got me for that same part. And it was on television the year after that, yet he got me in the same part, so I acquired a little bit of notoriety; well, you might not call it that because actually it didn't extend over a whole life, though it could have if I hadn't got sick, with the emphysema.

I'm perfectly satisfied all by myself if I could only get a place that I can breathe in. I can't breathe where I am. Do you smell any fresh air in here? My God! And got an alley there right next to the house, about that close . . . and everybody throws their dog dirt out the windows and if I open the window wide that's what I smell. So I have to keep the door open in the hall to keep any air and that air is polluted too, but not quite so bad. So I want to get in a place where I will be comfortable and I don't want anything, I don't require anything. All I want is cleanliness and health and I'm strong enough, even though I'm about ninety-one years old, to live about twelve years yet, but I won't do it in this place. I can't.

Figure 6.2. Mr. Taub

The one day I'm going to be the happiest when I get out from here, ALIVE! I can't take it no more. I never had no trouble before. I used to work, I finished my eight-hour work whatever it was; I was working hard all my life. I didn't care what I was doing, long I'm making a dollar. I used to be doing all kinds of jobs. So when I went in this business . . . well, I was very sick and I couldn't do any other job. I used to work outside, fourteen winters. My fingers got froze. I was cleaning windows, my fingers got froze, my toes, my ears, I got so sick I couldn't do it no more. So I had a few dollars. This guy came along, one of my friends in the same business, he told me about an investment broker who had a place for sale. So I had a few dollars. I put it in. And I going to be sorry the rest of my life. Only what I draw here, I have my two kids, my wife to support. I'm making $125 a week. And I risk my life every minute on the hour, while I'm here. You have a lot of aggravation, lotta trouble with these people, some of them not even belong to live in a decent house. The most of them, they are on dope, or they are drinking, and they are nothing, just trouble.

I was born in Europe. All my life I was discriminated and when I was about nineteen years old they put me up in the concentration camp. When the war was ended, I survived, I came to America. Little by little, after so many years hard work, I saved up some money and I run into this business. But I think I was better off that time than I am today. But one day I be free, I gonna be outa here one day, I hope in life, I gonna get rid of the building.

Photographs (Fig. 6.1, 6.2) courtesy of Laurence Salzmann, from *Neighbors on the Block: Life in Single Room Occupancy Hotels*. An exhibit portfolio by the New York State Council on the Arts for the New York Museums Collaborative. Produced by the Visual Arts Program, New York State Council on the Arts, 250 West 57th Street, New York, NY 10019. Allan Schoener, general ed.

Two processing alternatives are open to teachers creating slide pictures: the film may be sent out for processing, or the teacher may process the exposed film and mount the pictures as slides. Teachers who decide to process their own slides will need (1) a film developing tank, (2) chemicals, (3) slide mounts, (4) 16-ounce dark bottles, and (5) a timer. This equipment may be purchased at any camera shop and is relatively inexpensive; the entire cost of a camera and all supplies is within the reach of any teacher's pocketbook. The following list gives the approximate cost of the equipment that will be needed for slide processing.

Kodak Instamatic X-15F 126 for slides and photographs

Camera	$19.50
Chemicals (kit)	19.75
Slide mounts (100)	3.50
Dark bottles	3.00
Developing tank	13.50
Timer	25.00
	$84.25

Twelve rolls of Ektachrome film can be developed with a color processing kit at a cost of approximately $.10 per slide, compared to the $.20 per slide charged by commercial laboratories. There are drawbacks to developing your own slides rather than having them commercially produced, however. The chemicals are caustic and have a useful life of only about two months, and it takes approximately one and one-half hours to develop and mount twenty slides. The developing and mounting process can, however, be handled by a secondary school student after some instruction. Only a limited workspace is needed for slide processing.

Filmstrips Filmstrip production follows the same general pattern as slide production. The only differences are that a half-frame 35mm camera (a camera that takes a picture one half the width of a standard 35mm frame) is used, and the processed film is kept in a continuous strip rather than cut apart and mounted in frames. Be aware that camera shops and camera brochures may refer to the half-frame camera as full-frame and the standard 35mm as double-frame.

Photographs Black-and-white prints are fairly inexpensive to produce, but they require additional equipment and a darkened area in which to develop prints. Explaining the processes involved is beyond the scope of this chapter. Several inexpensive books ($1.00-$1.95) dealing with picture taking, developing, and printing are available from Eastman Kodak.

On the next page is a brief list of equipment that you will need if you wish to produce your own black-and-white photographs.

Item	Cost
35mm enlarger	$150.00*
Chemical trays	10.00
Print dryer	20.00
Chemicals	10.00
Developing equipment (see section on "Slides")	13.50
Total	$203.50

There is an inexpensive alternative method: Selective Educational Equipment, Inc., markets three types of contact paper that can be used to make unenlarged prints directly from negatives with the sun as a light source. Blueprint paper (enough to make 400 prints) costs $2.50; repro-negative, $4.50 for 200 prints; and studio proof paper, $5.00 for 200 prints. The same company sells a simple enlarger for $17.50 and an enlarger kit for $45.00.

8mm films

An 8mm movie camera is small, unobtrusive, and perfect for making action records. The camera fits easily into a glove compartment, a purse, or an attaché case.

The 8mm camera is the only visual recording device capable of making single-concept film loops, in particular, teacher- or student-produced film loops that deal with contemporary problems.

Projected 8mm film provides a large screen image that can be combined with other instructional techniques. For example, the film sequence could present an open-ended role-playing episode or a value dilemma, which students could carry to a conclusion at the end of the film. Or the teacher could design an instructional film using episodes in which the film is stopped at several decision points to allow the student audience to vote on what paths the action should take. Live actors, audio tapes, transparencies, and slides could be integrated to produce a multimedia environment that would provide actors, film, adjunct media, and audience interaction.

Still picture exercises similar to those discussed in "Slides, Filmstrips, and Photographs" can be translated into action on 8mm film. Topics such as poverty, cultural divergency, occupations, and aging are natural subjects for the hand-held camera.

A sample 8mm film exercise

A study of aging would provide a good initial production experience, as people at different stages of life are readily available. If relentless enough, the teacher can gain access to private and city-, county-, and state-managed "retirement homes."

*Enlargers are available that will make prints from many different sizes of negatives. The price, of course, varies with the versatility of the enlarger.

The film could use a chronological format either to follow the aging process naturally or to manipulate time using "cutaways" (changing scenes to give the impression that long or short intervals of time have passed). The camera could first repeatedly cut from active sequences involving a newborn, a toddler, and an adolescent to longer, more composed sequences involving older persons. Time of day or year might vary so that, for example, younger persons are filmed in the mornings, adults in the afternoon, and the aged in the evening. Clocks, calendars, and types of clothing could be inserted as time clues. Once the first view of aging is established, the remaining half of the film could reverse the image. Younger individuals could be featured in the composed sequences and fast cutaways used to depict episodes in the lives of active, older persons, to combat the negative idea that the elderly are passive, asleep in life.

Producing 8mm films

A simple Super 8 camera costs $60.00, a Sylvania "Sun Gun" costs $9.95, and a fifty-foot Super 8 cartridge costs $3.95—a total investment of $73.90. Send exposed cartridges to Eastman Kodak and ask that they be returned as film loop cartridges. Another alternative is to have the film returned on reels so that it may be edited by either deletion or addition of scenes. Edited footage is then returned to the processor, where it is mounted in film loop cartridges. Write to Eastman Kodak or query a local film processor on current processing and cartridge-loading costs.

The first step is to make a decision on how much time will be allotted to each scene. A fully exposed, fifty-foot Super 8 cartridge contains three minutes of possible film-story time. Using the foregoing example of aging, this three-minute film story could be broken up into visual sequences of shots of toddlers, adolescents, adults, active retired persons, and geriatric patients.

Rhythm is important. Figure that you have twenty shots of nine seconds' duration each to work with. Divide these nine-second units into smaller units, such as three units of three seconds each, or into four- and five-second sections. Eastman Kodak recommends that shorter and more numerous shots be used for exciting sequences, and that fewer and longer shots be used to record sentimental, sad, or dreamy events. Combining visual rhythm with "cutaway" technique and some creative flair will produce an 8mm film tailored to support classroom instruction.

Audio experiences

Well-planned audio lessons compel listeners to participate, form mental images, and create self-made, internal experiences. Using audio recording equipment, students can produce radio drama; exchange audio visits with classes in other cities, states, and nations; interview public figures; or perhaps set up contacts with individuals or groups living in a tornado belt, an area of volcanic activity, or a city where the Olympics or a world's fair is being held.

Two sample audio exercises

A one-act play *Do Not Spit at Random* is a one-act street play written by the Hangchow Stage Group to support the patriotic health movement. It is quite effective when taped by student actors and then played through a radio via an AM (audio modulation) or FM (frequency modulation) broadcast microphone, piped into the room through the school's intercom system, or played back on a tape player. While this play obviously fits into any course dealing with modern China, it could also be used to kick off a discussion of man's impact on the environment or of personal freedom versus social responsibility.

DO NOT SPIT AT RANDOM

by Fang Tzu

TIME: The early 1960s
PLACE: Street corner of Hangchow, People's Republic of China
Characters:
Young Pioneer (Hsiao-Ying)
Passer-By (ch'em Jung-fa)
One of the Crowd
Crowd
People's Police
Mother

(*A young girl Pioneer with a megaphone comes out from a crowd in the street or from among the audience in a theater.*)

Young Pioneer — Dear uncles and aunts, please do not spit at random. Spitting at random on the ground is a most deplorable habit. It helps to spread germs and disease, and so may affect our health harmfully. Dear uncles and aunts, if you want to spit, please do so into a cuspidor. If there is no cuspidor at hand, then spit into a handkerchief.

Passer-by — (*Walks across stage with a briefcase, makes noise as if going to spit. Spits phlegm on the ground.*)

. . . .

The YOUNG PIONEER confronts the PASSER-BY and requests that he wipe up the spittle, noting that spittle spreads disease.

. . . .

One of the Crowd — (*Speaks from the crowd or from the audience in a theater.*) Rub the spittle away quick!

Narrator — (*A large crowd gathers around the passer-by.*)

Passer-by — (*irritated*). Hmm. You want me to squat there and rub away the spittle? But I have no time for that. Besides, I am not used to doing that sort of thing. (*Prepares to go.*)

Young Pioneer: Uncle, uncle, don't go. I haven't finished with you yet.

. . . .

The PASSER-BY tells the YOUNG PIONEER that he must leave for home and has no time to carry on a conversation. The crowd criticizes the PASSER-BY and the PEOPLE'S POLICE arrives. The YOUNG PIONEER'S MOTHER arrives and identifies the PASSER-BY as an accountant at her mill.

. . . .

People's Police: Good, thank you. (*Addressing the passer-by.*) I think there's only one way now.

Narrator: (*Draws a circle round the spittle on the ground with a piece of chalk and is about to write down the name of the passer-by and the unit to which he belongs*).

Passer-by: (*frightened*). Comrade, don't! Don't write down the name of my unit! (*Addressing the crowd.*) Comrades and my young friend, please pardon me this once. You may write my name there, but please do not write the name of our mill too. Our mill has already signed a patriotic health pact.

People's Police: Yet you break the pact?

Passer-by: All right, I'll clean it, I'll clean it. I promise not to do the same thing again.

. . . .

The PASSER-BY squats, wipes up the spittle, and the crowd disperses. The PEOPLE'S POLICE congratulates the YOUNG PIONEER'S MOTHER and notes that when disease is largely wiped out the nation will be prosperous and stronger. The YOUNG PIONEER'S MOTHER asks the YOUNG PIONEER to come home for dinner. The YOUNG PIONEER replies that she must wait until relief arrives. The mother leaves the YOUNG PIONEER to carry out her duties, saying only that the meal would have to be warmed anyway.

. . . .

Young Pioneer: (*Speaking through megaphone and coming toward crowd in the street or toward audience in theater*). Dear uncles and aunts, please do not spit at random. Spitting at random is a most deplorable habit. . . .*

**Do Not Spit at Random* and other contemporary plays from the People's Republic of China may be obtained from China Books and Periodicals: *West:* 2929 24th St., San Francisco, California 94110; *Central:* 900 W. Armitage Ave., Chicago, Illinois 60614; *East:* 125 5th Ave., New York, N.Y. 10003.

DO NOT SPIT AT RANDOM is also available in: Curriculum Bulletin 1969–70 Series, No. 12. Social Studies Grade 9. World Studies: Eastern Civilization—Regional Studies. Course of Study and Related Learning Activities. Revised edition. Bureau of Curriculum Development, Board of Education of the City of New York, Publications Sales Office, 110 Livingston St., Brooklyn, N.Y. 11201. $7.50.

Following the broadcast, the teacher should ask questions that stimulate students to recall detail and sequence, and to understand the play. Why do the Chinese Communists put on this play? Why is a Young Pioneer used in the play? Would you be a Young Pioneer if you were Chinese? Explain. How are the Communist Chinese able to keep a tight control over the activities of their people? What are some of the arguments and social pressures used to make the Passer-By clean up the spit? If you were the Passer-By, what would you do? Why? How does this play help us to understand the people and the culture of the Chinese?*

An audio exercise with visual support In some cases it is desirable to present material simultaneously through both visual and audio communication channels. In real life, visual images often have verbal accompaniment. The two together—are part of the entire "happening" and each helps to explain the meaning of the other. Language is used to provide clues to the meaning of symbols.

Cooper's Helper is a multimedia presentation produced by the Federal Mediation and Conciliation Service. It uses photography and recorded dialogue in a visual/verbal strategy designed to explore the nature of conflict and conflict resolution through arbitration. One of its strong points is that it shows how chance occurrences and quick, rash judgments can lead to confrontations that cannot be resolved without the aid of a disinterested third party.

COOPER'S HELPER

Camera shots	*Sound*	*Dialogue and picture clues*
1. FMCS Plaque	Theme up	(1)
2. Bargaining table with men around it	Theme down	(2) *First narrator:* Labor and management are partners in the economic growth and development of our country. Across the bargaining table or in joint committee sessions many of the problems of working together are discussed and solved. Enlightened labor-management relations grow from a spirit of mutual responsibility and joint decision making.

*Questions drawn from Curriculum Bulletin 1969–70 Series No. 12, Board of Education of the City of New York.

3. Two men in argument		(3)
4. Man on strike with placard		But frequently the common problems are not explored through sound joint deliberation. Instead, differences may be allowed to explode into threats, violent arguments and harsh charge and counter charge. (4)

. . . .

McKay, the chief steward, has been promised by Powers that Cooper will be assigned a helper to assist him in setting up his machine. The assigned helper does not arrive on time, and Powers instructs Cooper to begin by setting up the machine while waiting for the helper. McKay walks through the shop and sees Cooper setting up the machine by himself. McKay rushes to the management section and storms into Ed Price's office. An argument starts over Cooper's helper and Price orders McKay to leave the office and get back to work.

. . . .

	music sneak	*McKay:* Sure, I'll go back to work. I can't disobey one of your dictatorial orders like that. I can see there is only one way to get these things straight and organized around this joint . . . And when the boys hit the bricks, don't say I didn't warn you: (40)
40. C.U. of Price scratching his head and looking at paper with a frown	Harsh music up and out	*Second narrator:* What developed between Ed Price and Max McKay is not a pretty nor a pleasant thing to see. This looks like the end of that beautiful morning for Ed Price, and maybe some others, too.
41. Letter board. "Let's discuss together"		*First narrator:* (41) Now let us take a look at this situation. *Let's discuss together* the nature and meaning of this difficult turn of events. Let's try to find ways that could have avoided this crisis and explosion. (42)
42. FMCS Plaque	Theme music fade	
END		

Presentation of audio instruction

Records and magnetic tapes, reel-to-reel and cassette, are the audio hardware most familiar to teachers. There are, however, audio channels that center class attention on the presentation rather than the hardware and allow the teacher more creative leeway. Audio presentations can use telephone lines via a Spokesman or its equivalent, table radios by means of an FM or AM broadcast microphone or, in some cases, the school's intercommunication network.

Spokesman Spokesman is a telephone device, consisting of a small, portable device that amplifies both incoming and outgoing signals. To use it in a classroom, the teacher dials the number of a person the class is to talk to, makes the initial contact, and then places the handset on the Spokesman's cradle. From that point on teacher and students may ask questions of the respondent from any place in the room within range of the amplifier. The respondent's incoming answers will be amplified so they can be heard throughout the room. When two devices are operating, one at each end of the conversation, the class can carry on conversations and question-answer sessions with a number of people on the other end. Classes at distant points can exchange audio visits. Interviews may be held. For example, a student or teacher might make an appointment to interview the mayor, police chief, or members of the city council, and prior to the interview or talk, might describe the setting in detail—for example, the police station or the council chambers. Following this, the on-site person can ask questions and moderate the discussion. Properly controlled, this procedure can be used with twenty to thirty people at each end of the phone line.

Local telephone companies can provide details on the availability and the cost of a Spokesman or of similar devices available for purchase by schools. Comparable two-way telephone amplifiers cost about $13.95 in kit form and $20.00–$25.00 assembled.

AM and FM wireless broadcast microphones Authentic live or prerecorded radio broadcasts can be made in the social studies classroom, using wireless broadcast microphones available through companies such as Lafayette Radio or Allied Radio/Radio Shack, Inc. Wireless broadcast AM and FM microphones range in price from $5.95 to $11.95. A broadcast microphone is effective at distances of up to 200 feet. Another similar apparatus, called an AM oscillator, broadcasts over electrical lines and ranges in price from approximately $4.95 for a kit to $24.95 assembled.

Broadcasts can originate in an adjacent room and be picked up on an AM or FM radio, depending on the microphone used. Radio presentations can originate live, with students or teachers broadcasting from a remote room into their classroom, or they can be prerecorded, with the presentation recorded on magnetic tape and then played over the microphone during class sessions.

The school's central communication system can be used in much the same manner as AM or FM broadcast microphones. However, this usage would monopolize the intercom, and instead of directing attention to a radio, it would center attention on a wall-mounted speaker that blurts out messages at odd times during the day.

The decision to use live or recorded presentations is a matter of teacher judgment. With the exception of Spokesman, it is suggested that recorded experiences be used because sessions can be edited, students who participate can then listen to the recording and observe reactions in the classroom. One presentation can be used with classes that meet at different times.

Videotape

Videotapes have been used in the classroom to preview activities, record the stages of a process, bring the outside world into the classroom, share experiences with other classes and schools, record student participation in school activities, evaluate and record student performances, record class sessions for use by absentees, educate teachers, and inform parents about the social studies program.* This is a wide spectrum of activities, in which the portable videotape machine carries out the functions of a movie camera. While initial equipment cost is high, the tape product is produced quickly and inexpensively.

Unique characteristics of television

Television has two characteristics that set it apart from all other media. First, videotape can provide participants with almost immediate feedback on their activities, with the machinery an integral part of the setting. Second, an exposed monitor is used, simultaneous feedback between viewer and monitor can modify both the direction and the quality of viewer behavior and monitor image.

Sociodramas, simulations, and gaming situations are perfect videotape material. Used properly, these strategies require that students assess their own contributions and recognize and apply the concepts and processes that occur during instruction. Only videotape can provide a complete or selected overview of classroom activities, with virtually no time loss between activity and review. Visual evidence of types of competition and cooperation, the effects of decisions, interconnections within a social situation or system, the

---

*R. Murray Thomas, "Videotapes: Diverse Functions for Social Studies Videotapes," in R. Murray Thomas and Dale L. Brubaker, *Teaching Elementary Social Studies: Readings* (Belmont, Calif.: Wadsworth, 1972).

essential elements of a historical sequence, or an assessment of skills learned and those still needed can be provided via videotape. In such situations as open-ended role playing, where it is desirable if not necessary to resolve a problem situation, videotape can gather and review clues to possible solutions that might otherwise have been lost.

Teachers may also benefit from videotape playback. Theodore Parsons' *Guided Self Analysis for Professional Development* (GSA) makes use of the full power of videotape.* This anthropological look at teaching behavior allows the teacher to analyze both verbal and nonverbal communication and gives suggestions on means of modifying behavior. A good introduction to GSA is provided by the schedule "Classroom Questions," which, along with five other schedules, may be obtained from Parsons (see Bibliography) at $18 per schedule.

Videotape has several advantages over film. It allows instant replay—no time lag between taping and the finished tape—and sound is automatically synchronized with the visual flow. Thirty minutes of half-inch black-and-white videotape costs about $12.50, as compared to around $90.00 for a half hour of processed unedited Super 8 film with sound, and it can be reused at least eighty times before a deterioration in visual or audio equality is apparent. If a mistake is suspected, the tape can be rewound and played back on the monitor. If there is an error, the scene can be shot over.

Porta-paks are ideal for documenting the environment. They are portable, unobtrusive, and simple to operate. Students have initiated, written, taped, and presented rather sophisticated dramatizations and documentaries.

An experiment was held in Newburgh, New York, under the auspices of New York's Center for Understanding Media with a grant from the Ford Foundation. Experiment in Community Communications Operation (ECCO) let 115 students, ages 10 to 20, make their own television programs with portable equipment. The results were broadcast over cable television. Participants videotaped city council meetings, created parodies of late-night talk shows, interviewed local celebrities, made documentaries on air pollution and drug abuse, and recorded how Walter Cronkite put together his CBS news show. Subject matter and method of treatment were wide open.

Akai, Sony, Panasonic, JVC, and other manufacturers have reduced portable television equipment to a size that can be handled by a student in the middle grades. Color portables are now available, and new half-inch videotape machines use a standard tape, making black-and-white tapes interchangeable.

There are drawbacks, of course, to videotaping with porta-paks. The equipment is expensive (a Sony Video Rover costs $1,850.00), and most

*Flander's Interaction Analysis has been used to classify and evaluate teaching behavior; however, this system deals with verbal interaction and needs only an audio record of behavior.

equipment weighs in excess of twenty pounds, compared to Super 8's two or three pounds. Also, videotape is more difficult to edit than film.

The second unique characteristic of television is the ability of videotape to provide two-way instant feedback between a performer and a television monitor. According to an article in a popular magazine Philip Morton, a faculty member at the School of the Art Institute of Chicago, "insists that videotape is not product but process . . . when not recording, the video camera shows your image on the monitor scope simultaneously—in what Morton calls 'no time'—but from a completely different angle, which is oddly upsetting; what's happening is not two different actions but a single one in which the image feeds back to the performer and vice versa, and that instant feedback will subtly but inevitably alter the behavior, and perhaps even the nature, of whoever is watching. Morton believes that the identity crises so familiar to today's generation may never occur at all to a generation that's used to having itself fed back as information at a very early age."*

What can be done with this concept of "no time" in the classroom? Students could watch themselves perform such activities as folk dances and modify their future activities if they began to vary from the original. In role-playing situations, students could observe their behavior on the monitor and vary it in a direction that would resolve the problem situation. An image of themselves "acting out" and a look at classmates' reactions to this could go far toward modifying the behavior of troublemakers. Teachers should also consider training the camera on themselves during the course of instruction, to provide them with the opportunity to view themselves as students see them and to modify their teaching behavior accordingly.

Disadvantages of television

At its best, television can open new creative horizons for the teacher; at its worst, it might lead to magnification of all the abuses current in the use of 16mm sound films for teaching—innocuous content, repetition of previous instruction, subject matter out of sequence with the curriculum, ideological bias, and an emphasis on passive rather than active learning.

Enlightened and creative classroom instruction should lead students to the point where they willingly go outside for additional experiences. Bringing the full range of outside watching experiences into the classroom defeats this purpose by filling up instructional time with what should be outside experience. The possibility of developing individuals capable of rational decision making is reduced where there is a massive effort to bring packaged experience into the classroom. Classroom television, particularly teacher-created television, should have goals other than packaging materials for

---

*"Shoot and Show," *Playboy* 19 (May, 1972): 191.

Figure 6.3

LINCOLN RECOVERING RAPIDLY

AUSTRIA AND SERBIA TO ARBITRATE

U.S., CHINA, RUSSIA TEAM FOR MARS EFFORT

ONE CHILD PER FAMILY NOW LAW OF THE LAND

passive learning. Television should emphasize active learning experiences, such as interviewing, preparing documentaries, analysis of behavior through instant replay, and analysis of classroom behavior.

Broadsides and newspaper headlines

Imagine being able to produce front pages cheaply and efficiently with banners such as those in Figure 6.3. The first banner could be used to promote student thought about and investigation of the "great man" theory of history. After supplying every student with a newspaper headline, the teacher could use questions as the basis for future study. What would the Reconstruction period under President Lincoln have been like? Do the students think he would have had the same problems as President Johnson? How long would Reconstruction have lasted under President Lincoln? What measures would Lincoln have taken to counteract the erosion of Negro rights and the polarization of North and South? These questions could lead into a consideration of the relationship between president and Congress, the different "styles" of

Lincoln and Johnson, the charisma that surrounds some people, and whether a strong president with congressional support would have taken steps that would have eventually affected contemporary race relations and sectional politics.

The second headline could lead to an investigation of the causes of war or even speculation on the effect of chance on history, while the third banner could bring on a discussion of international cooperation and "great power" politics. The last headline could be used as a springboard into population study or as a vehicle to challenge students' beliefs on such questions as population control versus individual freedom and "right to life" versus the freedom to choose abortion.

Broadside and newspaper headline production

The availability of low-cost offset-printing masters and the increasing availability of equipment to produce offset masters opens up a new technique to the social studies teacher. Offset is a printing process implemented in either of two ways. The first method uses a heavy sheet of paper as the printing medium in an offset press. Copy is typed directly on this master, which is given to a printer, who prints copies directly from the master. In the second process, a photo master is made of the material to be printed, and this photo-offset master is then used in an offset press to produce multiple copies. For producing broadsides and front pages, the second method is preferred because the photographic process may be used to reduce or expand copy and reproduce valuable out-of-copyright material. It allows the teacher more flexibility in the use of different typefaces and graphics, which may be attached to the original. Authentic-looking 8½″ × 11″ or 11″ × 13″ newspaper stock can be used. The first method is slightly cheaper and can be used to save money when producing straight printed materials with no variation in print size or style.

To produce a front page, the teacher needs clear white paper; transfer type letters, stencils, or a lettering pen and India ink; a ruler; a sharp pencil (one that writes in a light blue, which will not photograph); and white correction liquid or correction tape. In this process the size of the original can be photographically reduced, and the teacher will find it much easier to work on an oversize original than on a piece of paper the same size as the final copy. Also, the process only picks up blacks and whites unless a halftone plate is specified—grays above a certain value print as black. This allows the producer a great deal of leeway in setting up guidelines in blue, and erasing or correcting errors by using white block-out liquid or white correction tape.

The production process is fairly simple. Take an oversize sheet of white paper, say 12″ × 15″, and rule in blue lines, to locate the headlines and typed news stories. Type in the news stories, using the blue lines as guides. When this is done, use transfer type, stencils, or pen and ink to add display letters for the headline, newspaper name and location, and the date. This entire process takes less than an hour, even for a fairly detailed broadside. The master plate is then made from this original. This usually costs between $.25 to $1.25 at a school, or approximately $6.00 for a master and 100 copies at a commercial printer's shop.

Artifacts and material remains

Introducing artifacts and other indicators of history into the classroom allows students to deal directly with materials used as source data by anthropologists and cultural historians. This will help students to develop a sense of time, examine the methodologies of anthropology and history, explore the meanings of culture and cultural transmission, and confront the problem of why people in past and present cultures adopted certain lifestyles and value systems.

Artifacts, material remains, oral traditions, pictorial data, and written records are the five sources used by archeologists and historians to recreate and investigate the past. Artifacts are objects created by man for ornamental, magical, or functional use. The artifacts of our society are objects such as earrings, cuff links, a contemporary crucifix or menorah, an electric saw, or a hand calculator. Material remains are such things as the bones of prehistoric or historic man, bones of the creatures he ate, fibers or seeds of the plants he used, and even the outlines of the postholes and posts that supported his dwellings. Oral traditions are folk tales and folk songs in the vernacular. In the United States "the hat-in-the-mud tale" and "Short in the Saddle" are examples of folk tales, while songs such as "On Red River Shore" and "The Boston Burglar" are definitely folk songs. Pictorial data are signs of man's attempts both to communicate with others and to document his environment through pictures drawn or carved on various substances. Cave paintings, Amerindian paintings on skin, and early film cartoons are examples of pictorial data. Written records are too well known to need special explanation.

Examples of artifact exercises

Artifacts and material remains can be used alone in the classroom or combined with secondary-source archeological data or with practical experience in archeological field work.

Be cautious, however, when introducing them. Many students, even those in the upper levels of high schools, lack a chronological sense and have a limited time perspective. Therefore, when using these evidences of history in the classroom, provide experiences that allow students to conceptualize the word "past." Build a temporal reference point or series of points for them to use as they work with these objects.

One way to pave the way for introducing artifacts is to help the students determine what the term "past" means. Use the blackboard to list the things they have done prior to class: "*got up*," "*had* breakfast," "*went* to school." What do the *italicized* words express? Have the students write down what they have done so far that day; then have them turn the paper over and list what they have done in the week leading up to this class. Discuss the notion that the time before "now" is the "past." Next, have the class brainstorm for ideas on how to investigate and recreate the past. Books, newspapers, pictures, antiques, old records, television, and radio are the most common sources named.

A simple exercise can follow this introduction. Prior to class, select a small group of students to fill a wastebasket with artifacts and material remains that typify American society and/or events that occurred within the room and school over the past week or month (posters, bulletin-board material, gum wrappers, aspirin boxes, bottle caps, plastic bottles, newspapers, paper boxes, magazines, and so on). Arrange the class in a circle and dump the wastebasket contents in the center. Ask students to list the articles they can identify, and, possibly, have them categorize as they write. Ask questions like "Can you use this evidence to tell me what has happened in this room today?" "Yesterday?" "For the past week?" "Month?" "What can you tell me about the society that left these artifacts?" "How did you reach that conclusion?" "Can you point out evidence to support that statement?"

Students should be presented with at least one more general type of experience before exposing them to situations that deal with long time periods and the artifacts of unknown cultures. Visit a junkyard—go by yourself or, preferably, take some student volunteers. Pick up articles that show their history on labels—for example, pop bottles, cans, empty jars, medicine tins. Try to find a number of examples of each general type of article to get those that bear outward signs of different ages. Before leaving, collect a number of objects that appear to have been there a very long time. Back in the classroom, set up an observation table. Have teams of students arrange the articles chronologically from newest to oldest. Once this is done, discuss the arrangement. Is the order logical? How can they tell? What criteria were used for ordering (rust, wear, surface erosion, dates)?

As an alternative to this exercise, have students (with parental permission) bring in souvenirs or other articles from their homes. Expect to see such things as theater programs, war memorabilia, pressed flowers, and stereopticon cards. Put the articles on an observation table and order the objects in the same way as in the previous exercise. Deal with one article at a time by having students discuss and determine its age. Require students to state the rationale for the dating. Then open the class up for a game session where each student either formulates hypotheses about an event or the circumstances associated with an article or writes a story about the object. The student to whom the article belongs can tell the other students how accurate they were, thus reinforcing the idea of attempting to learn about the past by the study of objects.

Next, consider allowing students to handle an object of great age. Ancient coins, some dating as far back as 2,500 years, can be purchased for two or three dollars or borrowed from a local museum or collector. As students look at and feel the coins, talk about the milieu in which they were minted, bringing important events of the age; use anecdotes and, perhaps, read heroic verse and folk tales.

Archeological uses of artifacts

The January 1966 issue of *Scientific American* contained an article by Betty J. Meggers and Clifford Evans of the Smithsonian Institution that added a new dimension to the controversy over who first discovered the New World. A synopsis of this article was written by John A. Osmunson in the January 3, 1966 *New York Times*. Teachers are urged to read and use both articles.*

Meggers and Evans speculate that the Japanese landed in the New World in approximately 3000 B.C. The process used by the authors to arrive at this conclusion can be extremely interesting to teachers introducing archeological concepts and research techniques into the secondary curriculum. The article opens up the question of what the word "discovery" means. The Japanese were probably caught in a storm and swept along by ocean currents. Can this accident be called a discovery of the New World? Also, can it be called a discovery if the Japanese never returned home to report it? Even if they had, their exploits could not have been recorded—the Japanese had not yet developed writing. These questions on the nature of discovery can serve as a prelude to the introduction of the artifactual evidence used by Meggers and Evans.

Artifact 1 in Figure 6.4 was found near the town of Valdivia, Ecuador, in 1961. The pottery fragment was dated between 2300 and 3000 B.C. Meggers and Evans noted that "at a time as early as [that] this form of [pot] rim is rare anywhere in the world except Japan. There it occurs on pottery of the prehistoric Jomon period." Students should at this point be led to speculate on the possibility of a cultural link between Japan and Ecuador. This brings in the concept of cultural transmission. Questions such as "Are they sure it isn't a fake?" "Were other pieces of pottery found?" "Did they have rims?" can be expected from students. (The Valdivian artifact was found by Emilio Estrada, an amateur archeologist. Between 1961 and 1966, a number of pottery shards with the same general characteristics were found on the site.)

Artifacts 2A, 2B, 3A, and 3B (Fig. 6.4) should now be introduced. Shards 2B and 3B were also found at the Valdivian site; 2A and 3A are of Japanese

*Both articles and photographs of the artifacts described and illustrated are reproduced in Curriculum Bulletin 1967–68 Series No. 2[d], Social Studies Grade 6. Our World: Early Civilizations. Course of Study and Related Learning Activities. Preliminary Materials. Bureau of Curriculum Development, Board of Education of the City of New York, pp. 135–37.

Figure 6.4

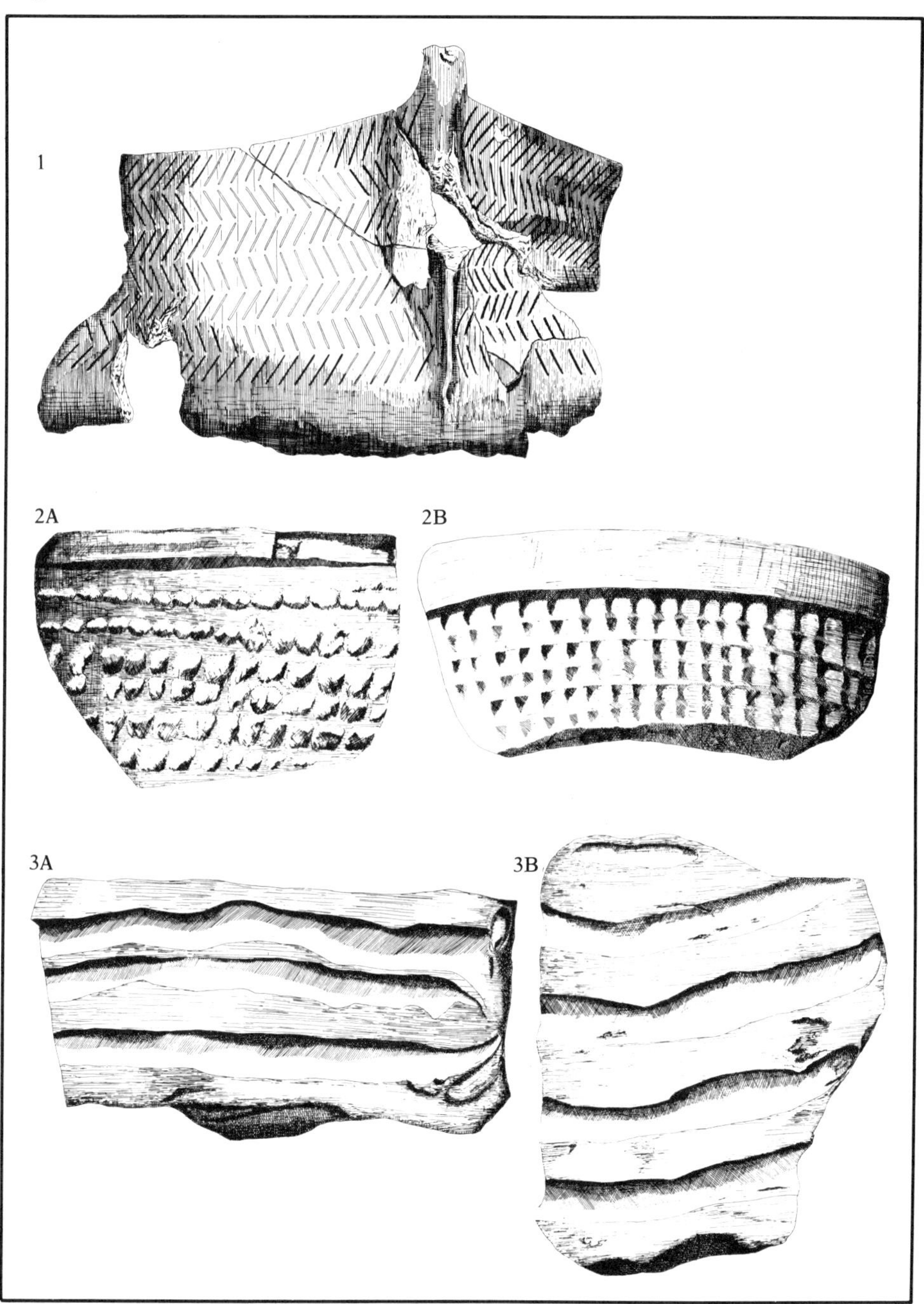

Drawings by Jerome R. Heckmann, 102 Miller Avenue, Buffalo, NY 14222.

origin. To start discussion, the teacher might ask, "Can you see any similarities in the decoration on these shards?" or "How do you think they made those grooves?" As discussion opens up, the instructor might insert a question such as, "What can you guess about the people that made this pottery?" At this point, introduce the article from the *New York Times* and the three criteria Meggers and Evans used to build their "airtight" case. First, pottery of the Valdivian style was produced in Japan before it occurred in Ecuador, and the Valdivian pottery is established as the oldest found in the New World. Second, the evolution of Valdivian-style pottery can be traced in prehistoric Japan but not in Ecuador. Third, the Valdivian style is decorative rather than functional, and so necessity did not force the simultaneous development of Valdivian-style pottery in Japan and Ecuador. Are these criteria enough for the researchers to conclude they have an "airtight" case? Osmunson states that " . . . this work presents evidence that New World and Old World cultures did not necessarily develop along parallel lines by accident, but might have had direct influences upon one another's growth." What does Osmunson mean when he says that?

Before becoming too involved in the use of artifacts and material remains, it would be a good idea for the teacher to (1) examine the two national projects in anthropology, the Anthropology Curriculum Study Project and the University of Georgia Anthropology Curriculum Project; (2) read John M. Good's treatment of the Kensington Stone in *The Shaping of Western Society: An Inquiry Approach;* and (possibly) (3) view classroom episodes in which Edwin Fenton initiates discussion on "frames of reference," the nature of evidence, and the establishment of authenticity.*

Teacher- and student-produced artifacts

The social studies teacher and students can build a package of artifacts, record rare artifacts and material remains on film, or reproduce three-dimensional objects in terra cotta, clay, or plaster of paris. To build a package of artifacts, objects from the immediate environment (posters, plastic bottles, stamps, bottle caps, a transistor radio, coins), from recent history (medicine and soft-drink bottles, advertising material, stereopticon cards and perhaps a viewer, 78 RPM records, paper silhouettes, bow ties, engravings and tinted prints, beanies), or ancient times (coins, shards, clay figures, beads, cloth

---

*Thomas R. Henry, "The Riddle of the Kensington Stone," *Saturday Evening Post*, 221 (August 21, 1948), p. 25, reprinted in John M. Good, *The Shaping of Western Society: An Inquiry Approach* (Holt Social Studies Curriculum, Edwin Fenton, ed.), New York: Holt, Rinehart and Winston, 1968, pp. 23-28.

Holt, Rinehart and Winston, Inc.: "How the Historian Classifies Information," No. 1; "How the Historian Proves Hypotheses," No. 2; "How the Historian Decides What is Fact," No. 3; "How the Historian Asks a Question," No. 4; "How the Historian Deals with Mind Set," No. 5.

fragments, eating utensils) can be located and arranged into coherent packages. When building such kits, it may be necessary to use reproductions or photographs of rare and valuable items.

Many items of potential use to the social studies teacher are housed in public and private collections. Most of these artifacts and material remains can be recorded photographically and used in the classroom. A word of caution, however: ask permission to photograph these objects. This is particularly important when using a flash attachment, as certain fabrics, paintings, and prints and old photographs can be damaged by the intense incandescent light. Ask, also, if it would be possible to have the glass cases opened while you take pictures and whether the institution has a copy stand and, perhaps, a copying camera. If the cases are open while you are taking pictures, particularly when using a flash attachment, there will be no reflected lights showing up on finished prints or slides. If a copy stand is available, you can photograph rare books, unusual pictures, and original texts. In most cases, a museum that has this apparatus will have a technician or staff member who can provide instruction in its use or even do the copying. Even without a resource person, duplicating in this fashion is a simple process of focusing, setting a needle to match the pointer on a light meter, and releasing a shutter.

Reproducing artifacts is a somewhat more complicated process. The first rule for the teacher interested in reproducing artifacts is to get on good terms with an art teacher or a local amateur or professional potter.

Terra Cotta Terra cotta is a hard, brown-red earthenware used in making pottery, figurines, and ornamental building tile. It is worked moist and left unglazed. The teacher should consider receiving instruction in its use or doing some intensive reading before attempting to use it for reproducing artifacts.

Clay Clay is much easier to work with than terra cotta. Various types of clay abound in the United States, and virtually all of them can be used for reproducing shards, whole pottery, and various types of statuary. As a class project, students could "mine" clay from deposits in the area and refine it at home or in class. Refining clay consists of picking out chunks of matter that do not belong, adding water until the clay becomes semiliquid, and pouring the mixture through a screen to take out large particles. What comes through the screen is a creamy mixture called slurry that might be blue, gray, or any of several shades of brown. The slurry is allowed to settle, and excess water is poured off or allowed to evaporate. When the clay is thick enough to be formed into balls or ropes, the process of reproduction can begin.

Reproducing coiled clay Amerindian pots is a classroom experience in which students of all ability levels can participate. As the first step in production, students should knead and then roll the clay out into ropes. These ropes should then be coiled into cylindrical shapes that approximate the size and form of the finished object. Students then should use wet hands to unite the rings of clay and to attach bottoms to the pots. To blend the rings, they should start at the bottom, work around the pot in *one direction*, and keep the hands wet. The idea is not to obliterate the rings, but to unite the rings so that there are no gaps between them and the object is strengthened.

When the pot has been worked to the point where its form is final, it should be fired. Dig a pit, start a hardwood fire, and keep adding to it until a bed of coals fills the pit. Dig holes in the bed of coals that are slightly larger than the pots, fill the pots with glowing embers, put them in the pit, and cover them with the leftover coals. Leave the pots to bake for several hours or until most of the heat is dissipated. Uncover them, and you will have approximations of early coiled pottery. When working outdoors is not practicable, ask the art or shop teacher to fire the clay pots or simply let them air dry.

A word of caution: the project should not stop with making the pottery. Students should speculate on the people who made this type of utensil. At what stage was their culture? In what other ways might they exhibit adaptation to their environment? What other kinds of local materials might they have used? Are there other types of household goods, tools, or weapons that could be reproduced? What other cultures can be explored, using a parallel method?

Latex Molds and Sand Casts Artifacts of many types can be reproduced from molds. Here again the teacher is urged to confer with people who have some expertise in making flexible latex molds (possibly someone who retails arts and crafts materials) or in producing sand castings (the school shop teacher).

In making latex mold castings, several thin coats of liquid latex are brushed over a three-dimensional object, and the coating is peeled off in one piece, forming a mold. This mold is then filled with plaster of paris, liquid plastic, or a commercial casting product. When the medium is fully set, the casting is removed and finalized with an authentic finish.

Sand casting requires a two-part mold for reproducing a 360-degree object or a frame for duplicating one face of such things as bottles, embossed tiles, or statuary. The piece to be duplicated is inserted or pressed into wet sand to produce a mold, and then a casting medium is poured in, allowed to harden, and removed from the sand. The second method, using a frame that holds sand for the purpose of casting one face of an object, is much more adaptable to classroom use than 360-degree casting. Assemble a frame with four sides, about 2″ to 5″ in depth, and attach a bottom. Fill the frame with moist sand and press an object into the sand. For practice use your hand or a bottle of interesting shape. Fill the indentation with plaster of paris and let it dry. Remove the casting, brush it gently, let it dry for forty-eight hours, and give it a coat of shellac or spray it with a clear finish. If you are successful in this preliminary casting, go on to reproducing other articles. Be careful in choosing the objects you reproduce. Some finishes do not stand up well under contact with moisture. Check with someone familiar with types of finished surfaces, or test them yourself before making a mold from a valuable object.

Transparencies

Transparencies can be used to present current events, pose problem situations, act as springboards to discussing complex areas of values, or work with the "structures" of the several disciplines. A large screen image allows the instructor to point out specific areas to the class by marking directly on the transparency or by using a pointer directed at the screen. The teacher can easily isolate sections of the transparency by blocking light with opaque paper. Transparencies can also be readily used in combination with other media to form multimedia presentations.

Transparencies are inexpensive when compared to other audiovisual materials. They are easily packed and moved from room to room, and can be produced at home or school. Transparencies are particularly valuable when the teacher uses them for more than simply illustrating or describing phenomena.

A sample transparency exercise—CHANGING DOLLARS*

This activity is designed to simulate the economic responses of people to a fluctuating currency. The game displays how people react when they see their cash resources lose value during inflationary periods and gain value during deflationary times. The impact of inflation and deflation on currency and on persons with fixed incomes and people with expanding incomes is determined.

Strategy Divide the class into four-member groups. Each group will consist of a banker, a buyer, an accountant, and an economic forecaster. These roles can either be assigned by the teacher or determined by members of the groups. In each group the *banker* manages all economic resources and supervises all sales; the *buyer* visits other groups to seek out the best deals and to purchase properties from bankers; the *accountant* keeps a running tally of the group's resources and the changes in the value of the holdings due to inflation or deflation; and the *economic forecaster* keeps the group informed of changes in the value of the dollar (by interpreting the "Changing Dollar Value" projected from a transparency) and estimates future changes by examining previous trends.

The goal of the game is to accumulate the greatest possible cash value in assets during a forty-minute time period. During the game, the value of the

---

*Donald R. Hetzner and Ronald Tietz, *Changing Dollars* (Provo, Utah: Student Education Material, 1973).

Figure 6.5

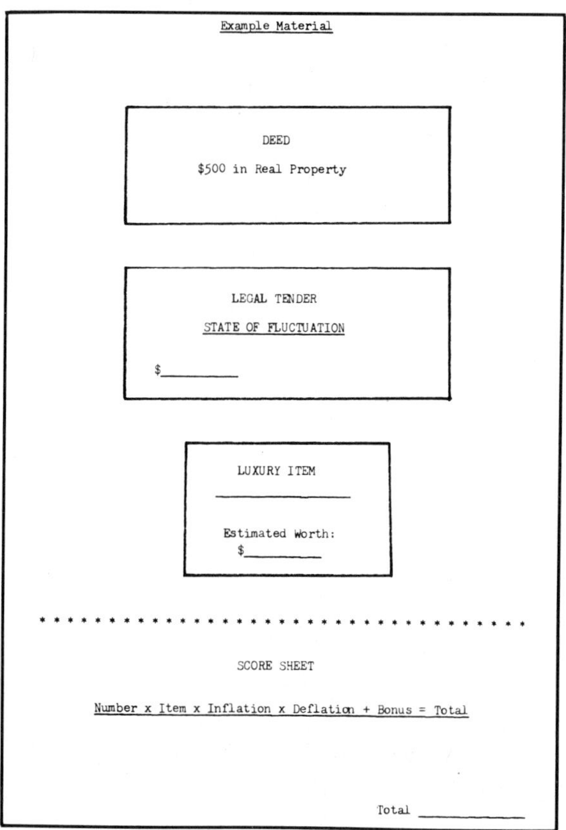

dollar fluctuates as a result of inflation or deflation. Information on the fluctuation of the dollar is given simultaneously to all groups and is preprogrammed on the "Changing Dollar Value" transparency. Each group tries to adjust its economic activity to make the greatest possible financial gains.

Materials Each group receives the following resources (see Figure 6.5).

1. $5000 in simulation money (produced by teacher).
2. Five deeds of property worth $500 each (produced by teacher), which can be sold at higher or lower prices at the will of the group.
3. Five cards detailing luxury items that are worth any amount for which the group can sell them. Examples: a color television, a sixteen-foot motorboat, a diamond ring, a stereo set, silver flatware. (Cards are produced by the teacher. Care should be taken that every group starts out with five luxury items that are approximately the same in estimated value.)
4. One scoring sheet.

To commence play Each group should meet for ten minutes at the beginning of the game to assign roles and secretly discuss strategies that will be used to counteract fluctuations in the dollar. The teacher or game director meanwhile should prepare the "Changing Dollar Value" transparency for projection (see Fig. 6.6). After the ten-minute strategy session ends, active play begins. One line of the transparency at a time should be exposed to view, according to a preset time schedule: 00 = the beginning of the game, 02 = two minutes after the game has commenced, 15 = fifteen minutes after the game has begun, and so on. Students buy and sell, using cash as a means of exchange—no trading is allowed. Any deed or luxury item may change hands more than once. All buying and selling should end promptly at the end of forty minutes. Scores should then be tabulated. The group with the greatest dollar value in assets wins.

Scoring To stimulate buying and selling, each group will be awarded a $100 bonus for each deed of property that they possess at the termination of the game that was not theirs at the start of the game. They will also be awarded a $50 bonus for each luxury item that was not originally theirs.

All transactions must be in cash. Only cash inflates or deflates. All other assets will be scored at the original value of the dollar.

Example of Scoring:

Number	×	*Item*	×	*Inflation*	×	*Deflation*	+	*Bonus*	=	*Total*
8	×	$100	×	50%					=	$ 400
7	×	deeds					+	$150	=	$4,200
3	×	luxury items					+	$150	=	$ 150
									Total	$4,750

Application To test students' abilities to apply the principles involved in this activity, have them conduct interviews with neighbors or relatives who are retired. Particular attention should be paid to documenting how people living on fixed incomes budget their money for such items as food, clothing, entertainment, and savings. Students should relate their experiences to such questions as:

1. From what major source do many, if not most, elderly draw their incomes?
2. How do inflation and deflation affect retired persons?
3. What are the special problems of living on a fixed income?

Students can also contact the Bureau of Labor Statistics for their city or area and collect and graph primary data for use in making and testing hypotheses on inflation and deflation.

PLATE A

CHANGING DOLLAR VALUES

00	BEGIN	
02	DEFLATION	$1.00 = 1.10
05	"	$1.00 = 1.20
15	INFLATION	$1.00 = 1.08
20	"	$1.00 = .97
28	"	$1.00 = .85
30	"	$1.00 = .72
33	"	$1.00 = .65
35	"	$1.00 = .62
38	"	$1.00 = .58
39	"	$1.00 = .50
40	STOP	

Figure 6.6

PLATE B

CHANGING DOLLAR VALUES

00	BEGIN	
03	INFLATION	$1.00 = .95
05	"	$1.00 = .75
09	"	$1.00 = .71
15	"	$1.00 = .65
22	"	$1.00 = .55
28	DEFLATION	$1.00 = .70
29	DEFLATION	$1.00 = .75
35	INFLATION	$1.00 = .68
37	"	$1.00 = .59
39	"	$1.00 = .50
40	STOP	

Transparency production

Graphs, charts, and line drawings Most teachers probably were first introduced to teacher-prepared transparencies in the form of clear acetate film and a grease pencil. This is perfectly all right when the transparency is only to be used once or is not to be used by any great number of people. To extend life expectancy, use India ink or a felt-tip marker in place of the grease pencil; then spray the working side with a clear matte finish, such as DelCote or Krylon.

When a number of teachers in a school or school system will utilize the same transparency, a method of producing multiple copies is needed. The easiest way is to draw up an original in black ink on white paper and run this, together with a heat-process transparency master, through a 3M or Standard copier. Where this equipment or the necessary materials are not available, a simple, inexpensive process can be used instead. Take a duplicating master, preferably one that prints black, and draw or write on it in the usual way. Lock the completed master into the copier and set the pressure down to a few points above zero. Take as many sheets of frosted acetate as you need transparencies and run them through the machine one at a time, dull side up. As soon as the transparencies are completely dry, spray them with DelCote or Krylon. This process is particularly good when it is necessary to add features to succeeding transparencies. After each run, the master can be taken from the machine; another set of features is added to it, it is replaced in the machine, and another set of more highly detailed transparencies is produced. Time-series transparencies, such as those showing United States historical growth or maps for inquiry-oriented exercises can be made by this method.

Color-lift transparencies Four methods of producing color-lift transparencies are available to the teacher.

1. Color pictures can be sent to regional centers operated by the 3M Company. This produces the most professional-appearing job but is the most expensive. A list of mailing addresses and prices can be obtained by writing to 3M Company.
2. The hot-iron method, using maglar film, produces a color transparency with sharp lines and good color at a cost of approximately $1 for enough maglar film to cover 178 square inches. Sealamin sells for $15 in 200′ × 11½″ rolls. Information on maglar laminating film and its cost can be obtained from Seal, Inc.
3. Probably the most convenient and inexpensive method is the use of clear plastic adhesive. One dollar will buy enough plastic adhesive to cover 800 square inches. It is found in hardware and variety stores under the trade names Contact and Zip-Quilt.
4. Transparencies may be made by using frosted acetate and rubber cement. The materials for this process are always available in school, and it is the

least expensive method, but it is least satisfactory in terms of projection quality.

Maglar laminating film process—To lift color pictures using this process, the teacher needs maglar laminating film, an assortment of pictures printed on clay-base paper, an iron, newsprint, a plastic tray or dishpan, one or two sponges, and liquid soap. To find out if the picture is on clay-base paper, rub the picture with a wet finger; a white material will rub off if the paper is clay based. Color pages in *Time, Newsweek,* and *Sports Illustrated* are printed on clay-base paper.

Cut the picture to a satisfactory size and place it face up on a sheet of newsprint. Cut a piece of maglar laminating film to a size that will leave a 1″ border all around the picture; then place the film over the picture with the glossy side up. Cover the picture and laminating film with a sheet of newsprint and press it with the iron for ten to twenty seconds. During the pressing process, check to be sure that the air bubbles are coming out. When all air pockets are ironed out, remove the newspaper from the transparency in this way: place the transparency in a pan of soapy water and allow it to soak for ten to fifteen minutes. Carefully test one corner of the transparency; the paper should fall off, leaving the color embedded in the adhesive. If the paper does not come off easily, allow the transparency to soak for a few more minutes. Use a wet, soft sponge to wash the excess clay off the back, and hang the transparency up to dry. When it is dry, check to be sure that all of the clay has been washed away. (Excess clay shows as white spots.) If some clay remains, return the transparency to the soap bath and go over it again with the sponge. When it is completely dry, spray the back with a matte finish spray fixative and mount it in a cardboard frame.

Plastic adhesive color lifts—Plastic adhesive color lifts require no heat source and no machinery, and lift color from clay-base paper with less difficulty than the maglar film or rubber cement processes. The only materials needed are clear adhesive plastic, such as Contact, pictures on clay-base paper, a dishpan, liquid detergent, and matte finish spray.

Cut a piece of plastic, allowing a 1″ border all around the picture. Peel the backing from the plastic, and lay it on a flat surface with the adhesive side up. Place the picture face down on the adhesive. Turn the transparency over and rub the plastic with your fingers until there is complete contact between the adhesive plastic and the picture. Place the picture in a warm detergent bath, and follow the same procedure used with the maglar laminating film.

Frosted acetate and rubber cement process—To color lift with this process, the teacher needs frosted acetate, rubber cement, pictures on clay-base paper, a dishpan, and liquid detergent.

First cut the frosted acetate so that there will be a 1″ border around the picture, and place it on a flat surface with the frosted side up. Cover the frosted side with a thin, even layer of rubber cement. Place the picture face down on the adhesive, turn the transparency over, and follow the rubbing procedure used with the clear plastic adhesive. Continue rubbing until there is a firm bond between the picture and the adhesive. Place the transparency in a warm detergent bath and let it soak. From this point on, follow the same procedure used with the maglar film and clear adhesive plastic.

Needle-sort data decks

Social studies teachers and students can use preconstructed needle-sort data banks and produce needle-sort decks containing all types of social, political, economic, historical, and demographic data. Students can then engage in data retrieval and the processes of cross-classifying and correlating historical facts. Moreover, the needle-sort deck can serve as an introduction to the data-processing techniques that are a basic part of contemporary life.

Needle-sort decks promote active student participation in the inquiry process.* The student must state a problem, pose a question or series of questions, and then translate these questions into data-bank operations. To be successful in manipulating the data bank, the student must define the problem, hypothesize on relationships, operationalize these hypotheses, and then physically work with the data contained in the bank.

Mitchell P. Lichtenberg of Education Systems Research notes that needle-sort decks are extremely flexible instructional materials. They and the materials that surround them do not possess a linear structure (requiring beginnings and endings); therefore, teachers and students are offered unlimited points of entry into the materials. Thus, data banks can be used to teach a single concept (like intergenerational mobility in ESR WARD 23); to help students conduct research on original source material; to structure work for a day, a week, or a month; and to instruct individuals, small groups, or entire classes. Teachers should also consider the do-it-yourself idea. Students will obtain a depth knowledge of the materials by making decisions about systematizing and ordering data and producing a product of use to others. Sociological surveys, geographic data, local history, ecological issues, and current events are just a few of the sources from which needle-sort decks can be created by teachers and students.

A few cautions. Needle-sort decks should not be equated with computers, nor should they be confused with games and simulations. Completed decks are collections of source data—vehicles for actively involving students in inquiry and research. Needle-sort data decks are not self-explanatory—the questions and hypotheses posed by the user supply the meaning. No knowledge of data processing or quantitative research is necessary to use a data

---

*I am indebted to Mitchell P. Lichtenberg for his permission to use comments from his correspondence with me during the development of this section and sample materials from ESR's brochures and data banks.

bank—it can answer the simplest or the most complex question, depending on how the user sets up the design.

A sample exercise

Each card in a needle-sort deck represents a single individual or item. The number of cards depends on the size of the institution or group to be studied. A deck that stores data on members of the United States House of Representatives would contain 437 cards, while one containing profiles of United States senators would have 100 cards. Data on individuals or items are coded on punched holes along the edges of the card.

To work with a commercial deck, the student refers to either a key or code book, picks out a characteristic of interest, and inserts the needle sorter in the hole associated with the characteristic. When the sorter is lifted, cards with punched holes drop from the deck. These cards represent individuals or items that have the selected characteristic.

Figures 6.7 and 6.8 are taken from *Who Came to the First U.S. Congress? A Data Bank for Inquiry*. This data bank contains ninety-five cards, each representing an individual attending the first United States Congress. Key characteristics, such as prior political experience, voting behavior, age, occupation, and education of the legislators, are code-punched along the perimeter of the cards. The data bank contains diary excerpts, portions of the 1789 New York Street Directory and street map, descriptions of eight pieces of legislation, and a map of the topography, population distribution, and congressional districts of the United States in 1789. Research problems and a brief analytical study by a colonial historian complete the data bank.

Figure 6.7 displays the key sheet used for interpreting the punches on the ninety-five cards. Figure 6.8 is a sample problem used in ESR's brochure on *Who Came to the First U.S Congress?*

Producing needle-sort decks

Needle-sort cards can be purchased from manufacturers of business forms and from retail office supply firms; however, the most efficient way to get into data bank production is to contact Education Systems Research and request information on their data banks and the Do-It-Yourself Data Bank. The Do-It-Yourself kit contains 300 blank cards, a demonstration kit, sorting needles, and instructions. A special hand punch that makes V-shaped holes is needed. A regular round-hole punch or a scissors can be used, but either one is tedious to use for a large number of cards. The special punch can be purchased from McBee Systems, a division of Litton Automated Business Systems. McBee also retails a card sorter that consists of a wooden handle and a replaceable pointed rod. The sorter is attractive and well designed, but the teacher wishing to experiment at minimum cost will find that a small shish kebab skewer or a piece of wire coat hanger will do the job.

Figure 6.7*

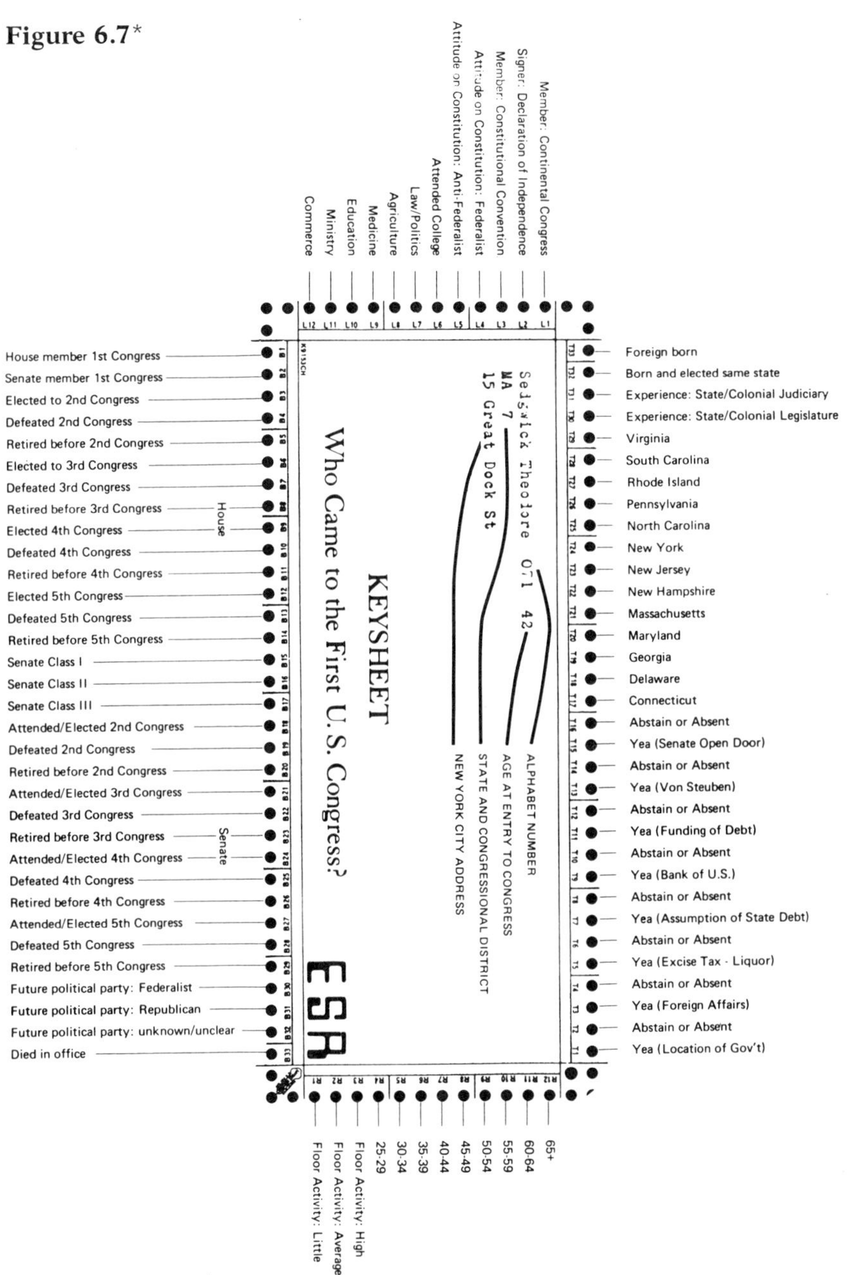

*Figures 6.7 and 6.8 from Ronald L. Boucher and Mitchell P. Lichtenberg, *Who Came to the First U.S. Congress? A Data Bank for Inquiry* (Shrewsbury, Mass.: Education Systems Research, 1972). © 1972 by Mitchell P. Lichtenberg.

Figure 6.8

A Research Design

Good research depends upon careful planning. The example below presents one method of conducting your investigations. The example starts with a hypothesis which must be tested. Then several steps outline a procedure to test the hypothesis. Finally the hypothesis is rewritten to fit the facts.

HYPOTHESIS:

"Senators who came from Northern states were much better educated than Senators who came from Southern states."

PICK OUT THE KEY WORDS:

"Senators who came from Northern states were much better educated than Senators who came from Southern states."

DEFINE THE KEY WORDS:

Senators = all Senators in the DATA BANK

Educated = Attended College [L-6]

Much better = more than a simple majority

Northern states = Massachusetts, Rhode Island, New York, New Hampshire, New Jersey, Pennsylvania, and Delaware.

Southern states = the remaining states in the DATA BANK

SET UP A DATA CHART AND SORT FOR THE DATA:

	North	South
Number of Senators who attended college.	9	7
Total number of Senators	17	12

DECIDE HOW YOU WILL COMPARE YOUR DATA:

Will you use raw numbers: "Of 17 Northern senators, 9 attended college."

Will you use a percentage: "53% of Northern senators attended college." [9 divided by 17]

DOES YOUR HYPOTHESIS FIT THE FACTS?

Why not work through the rest of this problem and draw your own conclusion.

An enterprising teacher can, with some luck, get needle-sort cards free. Approach a company that uses needle-sort cards for billing and inventory and ask for used cards that are no longer needed. These cards can be patched, using inexpensive repair tabs manufactured by McBee Systems. The particularly fortunate teacher might locate a company that is shifting from the McBee system to computerized data processing. In that case the teacher might acquire a lifetime supply of cards.

With used cards or new imprinted cards, the teacher has two choices: (1) to adapt the coding scheme on the face of the cards or (2) to turn the cards over and print his or her own format. Printing the backs of needle-sort cards requires only a few minutes. A master is made by drawing or typing on a mimeograph stencil, and the cards are then run through the mimeograph machine with the reverse side up. When making the master, be sure to follow the guidelines on the sides of the stencil so the printing section will meet the cards properly as they go through the machine. Set the mimeograph pressure and feed control for card stock.

Interactive computer-based instruction

Only the computer has the speed and data-storage capacity necessary to carry out the sophisticated problem-solving exercises needed in the study of complex social phenomena. In the social studies classroom, the time-share computer can perform data manipulation and statistical testing and, most importantly, simulate historical and contemporary social processes.

Social studies teachers can expect to see interactive computing used in their classrooms or in conjunction with the school's guidance office in the near future. A great deal of this computer-based instruction will be not only interactive but also autoinstructional. This will be made possible by increased availability and lower cost of terminals; the design of sophisticated yet easy-to-learn languages such as BASIC, NEW BASIC, and APL (*A Pro*gramming *L*anguage); and the development of inexpensive computer-based simulations.

Students using computer-based simulation games work at the "talking typewriters" that have become familiar sights in mathematics and science classrooms. This type of computer terminal resembles a typewriter and is tied to a large central computer via a phone line. Some terminals are the size and weight of a portable electric typewriter and can be carried from room to room with ease. The terminal acts as a device by which the operator transmits alphanumeric data to the remote computer, which in turn responds by sending back alphanumeric data that are typed out on a roll of paper by the terminal. An alternative type of terminal uses a cathode-ray tube to transmit and display data. The central computer services a number of terminals by scanning all operating terminals and making and returning calculations in fractions of a second.

A number of individuals and groups have been actively producing various types of computer-based and computer-assisted instructional units for the social studies. Richard Duke and Barton Burkhalter have designed METROPOLIS, a simulation based on the interaction between the political system of a contemporary city and a space allocation pattern within the urban area. In Westchester, New York, the Board of Cooperative Educational Services (B.O.C.E.S.), in conjunction with IBM, has produced the SUMERIAN GAME and SIERRA LEONE; information and on-site demonstrations can be arranged by contacting the B.O.C.E.S. center. Huntington II, now located in the College of Engineering, State University of New York at Stony Brook, has programmed several social studies simulations, all distributed by Digital Equipment Corporation. The Career Development Project at the State University of New York at Buffalo has produced two computer-based units that have been successfully tested in western New York State: LIFE DECISIONS, a simulation game written and programmed by Donald R. Hetzner, and WHO DOES WHAT? a computer-based pedagogical game by Paul R. Lohnes.

A sample computer-based simulation game

Career and educational choices—determinants of what path a person will take through life—are intense in their personal impact and provide excellent material on which to base a simulation.

LIFE DECISIONS was developed to provide social studies teachers, guidance counselors, and secondary students with a future-oriented simulation experience that emphasizes decision-making practice and exposure to information on career and educational development processes. It was also designed as an exemplar of a possible class of curriculum units that could be chained together to provide a coherent, autoinstructional career-guidance sequence for secondary schools.

LIFE DECISIONS begins by asking the student to "build a man." The player designates personal characteristics, such as mental abilities, life goals, values, and probable educational attainments, for the hypothetical man. Taking the part of the man, the student next selects a life-style goal from eight general types of "life-styles" offered and guides himself or herself through a series of life decisions. The player competes at every step against a table of expected outcomes of decisions, based on research that details how personal characteristics affect the outcomes of decisions, and a chance factor that is present at every decision point. A manual, written to save terminal typing time and to render the simulation autoinstructional, informs the student about the details of contacting the computer, the chance factor, and how the game is scored; and it provides seven "presentations" that give detailed explanations of the nature of particular decisions.

LIFE DECISIONS is not presently designed to "build a woman." Predicting the future career patterns of women is highly unreliable at this time. The assumption of LIFE DECISIONS is that many women's career decisions will begin to parallel those of men in the near future. Therefore, the simulation asks females to role-play and "build a man." As soon as more reliable data are pulled together, LIFE DECISIONS will be programmed to "build a woman"—or, perhaps, build a person."

The answers are typed as numerical data after question marks. The player turns to the manual when PRESENTATION appears, reads the corresponding section, and then depresses the carriage return key, thus continuing the simulation. The game is a dynamic process; the only lags in the man-machine interface occur when students read a presentation; even then, the terminal is on and ready to respond to the carriage return key. At all other times player and computer are in a cybernetic loop in which the actions of one affect the responses of the other. Research indicates that students attain a great deal of personal involvement with the hypothetical man and that student excitement during the LIFE DECISIONS simulation is quite high; unlike most computer-based units, learning in this particular simulation is active rather than passive.

The following extracts display the language and nature of a typical protocol. What is printed here represents approximately five minutes out of the forty to forty-five minutes that it takes to go through a run of LIFE DECISIONS. The terminal types everything in uppercase. Remember, there is a manual that goes along with the simulation to transmit instructions and tables.

```
LIFE DECISIONS

YOU ARE GOING TO BUILD A MAN. THIS MAN WILL
GO THROUGH LIFE MAKING DECISIONS. EACH DECI-
SION HE MAKES WILL AFFECT HIM LATER IN LIFE.
AT TIMES MAKING TOO FIRM A DECISION EARLY IN
LIFE WILL NOT PAY OFF WELL LATER.
.
.
.
HIS HAPPINESS IN LIFE WILL DEPEND ON HOW WELL
YOU GUIDE HIM THROUGH A SERIES OF DECISIONS.
.
.
.
LOOK CLOSELY AT THE SET OF CHARACTERISTICS
YOU GAVE YOURSELF. MEMORIZE THEM. THE
WAY YOU CONSTRUCTED YOURSELF DETERMINES
THE WAY YOU SHOULD MAKE DECISIONS. YOU
```

```
HAVE ESTABLISHED THE BOUNDARIES OF YOUR
ABILITIES AND ORIENTATIONS TOWARD LIFE.
CERTAIN AREAS OF CHOICE ARE OPEN TO YOU WHILE
OTHER AREAS ARE PARTIALLY OR TOTALLY
CLOSED.

PRESENTATION THREE
.
.
.
YOUR FIRST TASK AS AN EIGHTH GRADER IS TO
MAKE UP YOUR MIND ABOUT WHAT HIGH SCHOOL
CURRICULUM TO FOLLOW. NOW, WHICH CURRI-
CULUM TYPE WILL YOU TAKE UP? (1) VOCATIONAL
--THING ORIENTED, (2) COLLEGE--THING ORI-
ENTED, (3) VOCATIONAL--PEOPLE ORIENTED,
(4) COLLEGE--PEOPLE ORIENTED.
? 1      (Pupil typed this "1")
A VERY GOOD CHOICE. 12 POINTS.
KEEP IN MIND THAT YOU HAVE COMMITTED YOUR-
SELF, FOR THE DURATION OF THE GAME, TO
WORKING TOWARD A DEFINITE LIFE STYLE, MAKE
YOUR DECISIONS ACCORDINGLY. YOUR NEXT DECI-
SIONS REVOLVES AROUND CHOOSING COURSES FOR
HIGH SCHOOL.
.
.
.
LET US EXAMINE TAKING PART IN EXTRACURRICU-
LAR ACTIVITIES.  USUALLY, BEING ACTIVE IN
SCHOOL, CHURCH AND OTHER GROUPS WILL BENE-
FIT A STUDENT.  THERE ARE CASES, HOWEVER,
WHERE TOO MUCH TIME CAN BE SPENT ON THESE
ACTIVITIES....DECIDE HOW YOU WILL DIVIDE
YOUR TIME BETWEEN HOMEWORK AND AFTER
SCHOOL ''FUN'' ACTIVITIES.
.
.
.
THE LOGIC IS SOMEWHAT THE SAME WHEN WORK-
ING FOR PAY IS CONSIDERED.  YOU HAVE ONLY A
LIMITED NUMBER OF FREE HOURS EVERY DAY.
YOU MUST DIVIDE YOUR TIME TO GET THE MOST
OUT OF WORK AND SCHOOL.  ASSUME THAT IF YOU
```

```
HOLD A JOB YOU WILL NOT TAKE PART IN EXTRA-
CURRICULAR ACTIVITIES.  NOW, FIRST OF ALL,
ARE YOU GOING TO HOLD A JOB DURING THE
SCHOOL YEAR?
.
.
.
WILL YOU ENTER THE SERVICE AS AN ENLISTED MAN
'1', OR AS AN OFFICER '2'?
? 1      (Pupil typed this "1")
.
.
.
YOU WERE CRITICALLY WOUNDED AND ARE NOW
PERMANENTLY DISABLED.
.
.
.
FINAL GAME SCORE = 53.10
```

So disastrous an end is rarely arrived at in the simulation, but it does represent a reasonable probability of such an event occurring. There is an effort to have the branches of the game tree correspond to the contingencies of real life, even though some of the junctures might be too "realistic" for some people. It is estimated that various combinations of personal characteristics, selection of life-style, and environmental press (the chance factor) result in a simulation with at least 200,000 permutations.

Producing computer-based instructional units

Programming a computer-based data bank, test, or simulation game is not a highly technical task, particularly if natural language sequences are used. BASIC, the variations on BASIC, and *A P*rogramming *L*anguage (APL) are quite straightforward; the beginner can set up simple programs with about fifteen minutes of instruction or an hour's reading. To begin fairly sophisticated programming in BASIC, the teacher needs to know only seven statements:

(1) PRINT "   "; (2) IF   THEN   ; (3) GO   TO   : (4) INPUT; (5) PRINT "SCORE =   "; (6) FILE   ; and (7) READ FILE

APL, an IBM proprietary language, uses synonymous statements.

The procedures for getting started in do-it-yourself computer programming are somewhat different from those noted for other instructional media. Contact a commercial computer time vendor or educational time-share system, arrange for a demonstration, and write to the Bureau of Research, Department of Health, Education and Welfare, to request copies of *The Career Development Project, Final Report, Parts 1 and 2*. A commercial or educational time vendor can arrange a "hands-on" demonstration and can supply on-site advice and programming manuals to get the teacher started. Parts 1 and 2 of *The Career Development Project, Final Report,* provide basic theoretical discussions of pedagogical and simulation games, discuss programming, and give the entire program and a sample printout for WHO DOES WHAT?: A CAREER GAME. Consult the Bibliography for the names of time vendors and the full citation for *The Career Development Project, Final Report*.

Summary

Student and teacher involvement in the production of inquiry-oriented audiovisual materials has a number of welcome effects. In particular, classroom climate undergoes positive changes. Students suggest high-interest topics, practice decision making, developing self-sufficiency, solve problems, and talk out problems without fear. "Hands-on" experiences help to create the learning atmosphere striven for by the inquiry teacher.

Bibliography

General media references

Article

Schneider, D. O. "Instructional Media: Guidelines for Selecting Media," *Social Education* 36 (1972) pp. 799–802.

Books

Kemp, J. E. *Planning and Producing Audiovisual Materials*. 2d ed. San Francisco: Chandler, 1968.

Wittich, W. A., and Schuller, C. F. *Instructional Technology: Its Nature and Use*. 5th ed. New York: Harper & Row, 1973.

———in collaboration with Jay C. Smith and David W. Hessler. *Student Production Guide* (a supplement to *Instructional Technology: Its Nature and Use)*. New York: Harper & Row, 1973.

Catalogs

Educators Progress Service, Randolph, Wisconsin 53956:
Educators Guide to Free Curriculum Materials
Educators Guide to Free Films
Educators Guide to Free Social Studies Materials
Educators Guide to Free Tapes, Scripts and Transcriptions

Social Studies School Service, 10000 Culver Blvd., Culver City, CA 90230. Request the yearly catalog.

Journal

"Instructional Media and the Social Studies," Donald O. Schneider (ed.) *Social Education*, 40 (1976) pp. 262–88.

Still picture production and use

Articles

Bentley, M. "How to Publish Your Own Slide Tape Presentation," in *Learning Resources:* A Supplement to *Audiovisual Instruction* 19 (March 1974) pp. 10–12.

Brown, L. E. "Another Look at an Old Medium—Using Pictures in Social Studies," *Audiovisual Instruction* 14 (November 1969) pp. 72–73.

Caterino, S. J. "Student Involvement in Making Visual Perception Materials," *Audiovisual Instruction* 14 (November 1969) pp. 74–75.

Criscoe, B. "The Camera as an Aid in Historical Research," *Audiovisual Instruction* 20 (October 1975) p. 42

Cumba, J. "Photography: A Key to Learning," *Audiovisual Instruction* 14 (November 1969) pp. 66–67.

Irwin, V. "School Daze Primer: Slide Show Project," *School and Community* 41 (March 1975) pp. 22–23.

Jacoby, S. "Photo Frenzy in the Classroom," *Audiovisual Instruction* 14 (October 1969) pp. 37–39.

Lukas, T. "Inexpensive, Easy to Build Slide-Tape Programmer," *Audiovisual Instruction* 20 (November 1975) pp. 46–48.

Pendered, N. C. "Field Trips Vicariously? Slide Tape Presentation," *Man/Society/Technology* 34 (September 1975) pp. 14–15.

Booklet

Elements of Visual Literacy. Rochester, NY: Eastman Kodak Company, 1968.

Kits

Draw Your Own Filmstrip and Slide Kit. Grossman Publishers, 44 W. 56th St., New York, NY 10019.

Selective Educational Equipment Inc., 3 Bridge St., Newton, MA 02195. Produces photography instructional kits and contact paper.

Media presentations

Effective Visual Presentations. Rochester, NY: Eastman Kodak Co., 1969. Slide/tape.

How Does a Picture Mean? Rochester, NY: Eastman Kodak Co., 1968. Filmstrip.

Organization

Federal Mediation and Conciliation Service, 2100 K St. NW, Washington, DC 20427.

8mm film production and use

Articles

Brasso, R. "Making Student Filmmaking Work," *Media & Methods* 10 (January 1974) p. 27ff.

Rich, C. L. "Super 8: It's Now a Real Consideration for Filmmakers," in *Learning Resources:* A Supplement to *Audiovisual Instruction* 19 (March 1974) pp. 15–16.

Media presentations

Children Make Movies. McGraw-Hill Book Co., 330 West 42nd St., New York, NY 10036. 16mm black/white sound film. 10 minutes.

The 8mm Film: Its Emerging Role in Education. Du Art Film Laboratories, Inc., 245 W. 55th St., New York, NY 10019. 16mm color, sound film. 28 minutes.

International Film Bureau, 322 S. Michigan Avenue, Chicago, IL 60604. Ask for information on their instructional film series.

Super 8—A Unique Communication System. Eastman Kodak Co., Motion Picture and Educational Markets Division, 343 State St., Rochester, NY 14650. Color, slide-tape presentation. 30 minutes.

Audio production and use

Articles

Nelson, C. L., and Klavon, A. J., "Extend Your School to the Community and the University: Conference Phone," *Agricultural Education Magazine* 47 (October 1974) p. 80.

Booklets

Creative Teaching with Tape. 3M Company, Visual Products Division, St. Paul, MN 55119.

Taylor, Sanford E. *Listening*. Bulletin No. 29. Department of Classroom Teachers, American Educational Research Association, National Education Association, 1201 16th St., N.W., Washington, DC 20036.

Media presentation

The Tape Recorder. Iowa University. 16mm sound/black and white film. 6 minutes.

Videotape production and use

Articles

Clawson, E. U., and Moore, D. M., "Videocassettes: A New Dimension in Social Studies Education," *Social Education* 38 (1974) pp. 212–13.

Kahn, L. "VTR in the Classroom; or, How I Learned to Stop Worrying and Start Saving Cardboard Boxes," *Media & Methods* 11 (April 1975) pp. 40–41.

LeBaron, J. "Television: Production for K-12," in *Audiovisual Instruction* 19 (January 1974) pp. 4–6.
McGrady, S. "Smile, You're on Classroom Camera," *Nation's Schools* 92 (October 1973) pp. 44–46.
McLean, A. C. "Uses of Follow-up: Television in the Classroom," *English Language Teaching* 29 (July 1975) pp. 303–309.
Neumann, R. C. "Student Producers or How to Get Off the Ground and on the Air," *Audiovisual Instruction* 20 (September 1975) pp. 47–48.

Media

Examples in the Secondary School. National Association of Educational Broadcasters (NAEB). 16mm black/white film. 30 minutes.
Preparing the Television Lesson. NAEB, 16mm black/white film. 30 minutes.
Promising Practices. NAEB. 16mm black/white film. 30 minutes.
The Role of the Classroom Teacher. NAEB. 16mm black/white film. 30 minutes.
What Television Brings to the Classroom. NAEB. 16mm black/white film. 30 minutes.

Schedule

Parsons, Theodore. *Guided Self Analysis for Professional Development*. Department of Anthropology, University of California, Berkeley, CA 94720.

Broadside and newspaper headline production and use

Lettering equipment

Carters Ink Co., 239 First St., Cambridge, MA 02142.
Dietzgen Co., 2425 No. Sheffield Ave., Chicago, IL 60614.
Dri-Flo Pen Co., P.O. Box C, Detroit, MI 48213.

Letters

Instantype, Inc., 6553 W. Sunset Blvd., Los Angeles, CA 90028 (Instantype).
Quik Stik Company, P.O. Box 3796, Baltimore, MD 21217 (Quik Stik Letters).

Shading material and graphic tape

Craft-tint Manufacturing Co., 18501 Euclid Ave., Cleveland, OH 44112. (Craft-Tone.)
Para-tone, Inc., 5227 So. Dansher, Countryside, IL 60525. (Zip-a-Tone.)

Artifacts use

Article

McCurdy, R. "I Dig!" *Grade Teacher* 87 (March 1970) pp. 120-23.

Curriculum projects

American Anthropological Association, Anthropology Curriculum Study Project, Grades 9 and 10 (July 1969), Social Science Educational Consortium, Inc. (SSEC), Boulder, CO 80302 ($.50), CMA92.

Anthropology Curriculum Project, University of Georgia, 105 Fain Hall, Athens, GA 30601.

Anthropology Curriculum Study Project, published as *Patterns in Human History*, Macmillan Company, 866 Third Avenue, New York, NY 10022.

University of Georgia; Anthropology Curriculum Project, Grades 1–7 (February, 1969), SSEC ($.95), CMA88.

Simulations

"Culture Contact." Abt Associates, Inc., 55 Wheeler Street, Cambridge, MA 02138 ($30).

"Dig." INTERACT, P.O. Box 262, Lakeside, CA 92040 ($10).

Transparency production and use

Article

Lundy, L. L. "How to Make Your Own Transparencies," *Industrial Education* 64 (September 1975) p. 65.

Materials

Charles Beseler Company, 219 S. 18th St., East Orange, NJ 07018.

Eastman Kodak Company, 343 State St., Rochester, NY 14650.

Keuffel and Esser Company, 20 Wippany Rd., Hoboken, NJ 07960.

Labelon Corporation, 10 Chapin St., Canandaigua, NY 14424.

National Adhesive Products, Inc., 19600 St. Clair Avenue, Cleveland, OH 44101.

Ozalid Division, General Aniline and Film Corporation, 140 W. 51st St., New York, NY 10020.

Seal, Inc., Roosevelt Dr. and B Street, Derby, CT 06418.

Tecnifax Corporation, 195 Appleton Street, Holyoke, MA 01040.

3M Company, 3M Center, St. Paul, MN 55119.

Needle-sort data deck production and use

DO IT YOURSELF! Education Systems Research, P.O. Box 157, Shrewsbury, MA 01545 ($17.50).

McBee Systems, 600 Washington Ave., Carlstadt, NJ 07072.

Computer program production and use

Articles

Heines, J. M. "Everything You Always Wanted to Know About Computers . . . You Can Teach Yourself," *Educational Technology* 15 (May 1975) pp. 47–50.

Hetzner, D. "Life Decisions: A Computer Based Simulation Game for Social Studies Classrooms," *The Social Science Record* 10 (Spring 1973) pp. 35–37.

Computer time vendors

All of the following companies have offices in major cities. If they are not listed in the local phone directory, contact a company listed in the Yellow Pages under "Data Processing Service."

General Electric Information Services (division of the General Electric Company).

IBM Corporation

National Cash Register Co.

On-Line Systems, Inc.

Service Bureau Co. (division of Control Data Corporation).

Software Distribution Center, Digital Equipment Corporation, 146 Main St., Maynard, MA 01754. $.25 for information on computer-based units programmed in BASIC. $3 per program complete with punched paper tape, teacher's manual, and student manual.

Organization

Board of Cooperative Educational Services (B.O.C.E.S.), Westchester County, Yorktown Heights, NY 10598.

Reports

Lohnes, P. R. *The Career Development Project, Final Report*. Grant No. OEG-2-70-0001-(508), Office of Education, Bureau of Research, Department of Health, Education and Welfare, 1971.

Hetzner, D., and Lohnes, P. R. *The Career Development Project, Final Report, Part 2*, 1972.

Perhaps the greatest frustration for inquiry-oriented social studies teachers is trying to assess students' growth. Most of us have learned forms of evaluation that emphasize factual recall and the parroting of content; we have a hard time shifting our focus to inquiry-oriented evaluation. This chapter develops a rationale for a sound program of evaluation to help teachers faced with this difficulty. It provides numerous examples of evaluation techniques designed for use in inquiry-oriented classes.

Chapter 7

Assessing what has been learned

The purpose of this chapter is to offer suggestions for improving evaluation. Emphasis is placed on practical techniques that should be readily adaptable by you for immediate use in the classroom. There are numerous suggestions and examples for the techniques presented. Lists of sources are also included, if you desire additional information.

Evaluation and measurement

Teachers in the schools regularly perform tasks of evaluation and measurement. As you perform these tasks, you will be more effective if you clearly understand their meaning. Ahmann and Glock define them as follows:

> Educational evaluation is a process in which a teacher commonly uses information derived from many sources in order to arrive at judgments.
>
> Educational measurement is the process that attempts to obtain a quantified representation of the degree to which a trait is possessed by a pupil.*

From these definitions you can see that evaluation and measurement are closely related; measurement provides information for evaluation. For example, when a physical education teacher measures to see how far a student has broad jumped, information is gained to assist in evaluating whether the student is able to make a longer jump.

The basic purpose of evaluation in social studies instruction is to give both the teacher and the student information that will help them to decide what they should do next. The difficulty is that measurement techniques used by the social studies teacher to evaluate a student are not as accurate as those used by the physical education teacher who measures the distance of a broad jump. In the social studies we look for changes in behavior with respect

---

*J. Stanley Ahmann and Marvin D. Glock, *Evaluating Pupil Growth*, 2d ed. (Boston: Allyn & Bacon, 1963), pp. 11–13.

to knowledge, skills, and attitudes—changes that are usually quite difficult to measure.* Therefore, it is most important to use a wide variety of measurement techniques and to use care in their construction.

Objectives and evaluation

Some teachers never develop any objectives. They proceed to teach with the notion that they have to "cover the material." Other teachers plan lessons around objectives that are inadequate. In both cases guides for instruction and evaluation are missing. The result can be a discrepancy between what teachers hope their students will learn and what the students actually do learn. When this happens, evaluation is bogged down in confusion.

Behavioral objectives

The idea for behavioral objectives grows out of the definition of learning, the change in behavior that comes about as a result of experience. The purpose of behavioral objectives is to make clear what is to be learned as a result of instruction. If teachers hope to get students to learn something—that is, if they hope to achieve certain changes in student behavior—they they should write objectives that precisely state the changes that are expected. If behavioral objectives are used properly, confusion and vagueness about what is expected of students are eliminated as causes of failure. Teachers can concentrate on whether the failure was the fault of the student (maybe caused by inattention) or the fault of the teacher (maybe inappropriate materials were used).

Objectives that state that the student is "to know," "to understand," or "to appreciate" are too vague. Students do not get clear ideas of what is expected of them. What are students supposed *to do to demonstrate* that they know, understand, or appreciate? Properly worded behavioral objectives can eliminate this vagueness and sharpen the entire instructional process.

Many educators agree that behavioral objectives should be written to include each of the following elements:

1. The *person* who is to perform the particular learning behavior (e.g., the student, the learner, a small group, a committee).
2. The *specific behavior* required to demonstrate accomplishment of the objective (e.g., to write, to name, to construct, to locate).
3. The *learning outcome* or product by which accomplishment of the objective can be evaluated (e.g., a statement of fact, a generalization, a contour map, a simple grid system).
4. The *conditions* under which the behavior is to be performed (e.g., with the aid of an atlas, using data from the 1970 census).

---

*For a good discussion of this point see Edgar B. Wesley and Stanley P. Wronski, *Teaching Secondary Social Studies in a World Society* (Lexington, Mass.: Heath, 1973), pp. 287–289.

5. The *criterion* or standard used to evaluate accomplishment of the performance (e.g., correct to the nearest mile, four out of five correct).*

The following behavioral objectives use these five elements.

1. Given casualty figures for all the wars in which the United States has been involved, the student translates this information into a bar graph correct to the nearest hundred.
2. Given an outline map of Africa, the student will correctly locate four of the five following countries: Senegal, Kenya, Liberia, Zambia, and Ethiopia.
3. Given case studies and readings on social control, the student will correctly classify eight of ten statements into categories of laws, mores, and folkways.
4. Given primary source material (letters, diaries, autobiographies) written by pioneers headed toward the western territories, the student will list four reasons why people moved west.
5. Given six different newspaper accounts of various historical events, the student will correctly identify four different propaganda techniques.

Instructional objectives

As you try your hand at writing behavioral objectives that incorporate all five elements, you will quickly discover that it is difficult. Most of the difficulty has to do with the last two elements, conditions and criterion. This has caused several social studies educators to take a closer look at the whole process of writing and using behavioral objectives. Keller applauds the goal of using all five elements but goes on to state, "many teachers waste so much time anguishing over the wording of objectives that they leave little time for developing imaginative activities."† Ehman, Mehlinger, and Patrick argue that the elements of conditions (or, as they say, performance) and criterion are too often arbitrary and restrictive. While they believe, as does Keller, that these two elements can be of value, their opinion is that objectives without these elements can be quite useful to the teacher.‡

We agree with these opinions. The social studies teacher with five classes of thirty to thirty-five students and two different preparations is hard pressed

---

*Ambrose A. Cleggs, Jr., "Developing and Using Behavioral Objectives in Geography," *Focus on Geography: Key Concepts and Teaching Strategies,* ed. Philip Bacas. 40th Yearbook (Washington, D.C.: NCSS, 1970), p. 292. See also James A. Banks with Ambrose A. Cleggs, Jr., *Teaching Strategies for the Social Studies: Inquiry, Valuing and Decision Making* (Reading, Mass: Addison-Wesley, 1973), p. 523.

†Clair W. Keller, *Involving Students in the New Social Studies* (Boston: Little, Brown, 1974), p. 24.

‡Lee Ehman, Howard Mehlinger, and John Patrick, *Toward Effective Instruction in Secondary Social Studies* (Boston: Houghton Mifflin, 1974), pp. 88–89.

to find the time to adequately prepare for classes. That teacher is not going to bother to write objectives if the process is too difficult and time-consuming. If the choice is between not writing objectives at all or writing them without the elements of conditions and criterion, we opt for the shorter, simpler instructional objectives. You can see from the following examples that such instructional objectives are stated with sufficient clarity for both student and teacher to understand what is expected.

1. The student will list five executive powers given by the United States Constitution.
2. The student will summarize the three main points of the Senator's speech.
3. The student will construct a bar graph showing the United States' population growth over the last seventy years.
4. The student will identify three irrelevant claims made in the article.
5. The student will formulate a hypothesis to explain why there is a trend for black people living in northern cities to move to the South.
6. The student will voluntarily express opinions on political issues.
7. The student will demonstrate a problem-solving attitude.
8. The student will express a rationale about the role of a parent in a family.
9. The student will demonstrate a willingness to change an opinion when confronted with new evidence.
10. The student will define terms when needed in the course of solving a problem.
11. The student will point out the frame of reference of the author of a statement.
12. The student will judge if the conclusion of an article is warranted by the evidence presented in the article.

To help you write better instructional objectives, we emphasize the following suggestions:

1. Objectives are to be written *prior to instruction*. The purpose of using objectives is to clarify, to make more precise, and to give direction to instructional activities. That purpose is defeated if you wait until instructional activity is underway and then draw objectives from what is taking place in your classes. Of course, after writing initial instructional objectives you may want to alter the list in light of what has happened in class.
2. Each objective must have a strong *action verb*. List, measure, select, categorize, hypothesize, revise, rank, choose, participate, prepare, translate, locate, etc., are good action verbs for objectives.
3. State the objective in terms of the *product of learning, not the process of learning*. "The student will gain knowledge of economic terms," for example, seems to describe what will be going on during class rather than what

the student will be expected to do as a consequence of class activity. A better instructional objective would be, "The student will define the economic terms profit, loss, production, consumption, and distribution."

4. State the objective in terms of *student behavior and not content*. Teachers are understandably concerned about the content of what they are teaching. They sometimes confuse the content with the student behavior they hope to achieve. "The class will study the causes and events leading to United States' entry into World War I," for example, is primarily a description of the content to be covered in class. As a consequence of studying this content, students might be expected to meet these instructional objectives:

   The student will list the causes for the United States' entry into World War I.

   The student will arrange in proper chronological sequence the events leading to the United States' entry into World War I.
5. There should not be more than *one behavior* to each instructional objectives. A poor objective would be, "the student will know three criteria for determining the reliability of a source and apply them." To know the three criteria should be the basis of one objective. To apply the criteria should be the basis of a second, separate objective.

Advantages of instructional objectives Using instructional objectives does not guarantee success in instruction; however, the use of properly written instructions will help.

1. to more systematically organize instructional activities. Therefore, learnings beyond the acquisition of factual information are more likely to be identified and emphasized. Frequently neglected skills receive greater emphasis.
2. to give direction to the student that facilitates learning.
3. to ensure that the appropriate materials and equipment will be on hand when they are needed.
4. to organize subject matter in a logical manner, such as from the relatively simple to the more complex.
5. to check the tendency of the teacher to lecture for personal satisfaction rather than to help students learn.
6. to guide the teacher in devising appropriate tests for evaluating student progress.

Disadvantages of instructional objectives As with advantages, the things listed here do not automatically occur if instructional objectives are used. Nevertheless, the possibility exists that the teacher may find some of these things happening.

1. Adhering to a previously written set of instructional objectives may cause the teacher to ignore unplanned but significant learnings.

2. Because it is more difficult to write instructional objectives for higher cognitive and affective learnings, lower-level and even trivial learnings may be emphasized.
3. Commitment to the achievement of the learnings expressed in instructional objectives may discourage the teacher from capitalizing on student interest to achieve other worthwhile learnings.
4. Writing precise instructional objectives dealing with separate steps in a process may lead the teacher to ignore the need to learn the steps in combination to master the overall process. A student may be able to demonstrate at separate times his mastery of the individual steps of problem-solving but may not be able to successfully use them in combination to solve problems.
5. Instructional objectives are difficult and time-consuming to write and there is no proof that explicit objectives are really as useful as their proponents claim.*

Sources of instructional objectives As you begin to write and collect instructional objectives to guide your instructional efforts, you will need (1) sources that will give you ideas for different levels and kinds of objectives and (2) sources or collections of instructional objectives already developed to cut down some of the time and effort you would otherwise have to put into generating objectives.

Here are some things you may find helpful.

1. Look at your own teaching situation first. Your classroom experiences, your school's curriculum syllabus, and what other teachers are doing will provide ideas.
2. Some states have elaborate recommended curriculum guides that are good sources.
3. Check the professional literature. The following publications contain lists of skills that suggest instructional objectives, samples of objectives, and additional information concerning their construction and use:

Armstrong, Robert J., *et al. The Development and Evaluation of Behavioral Objectives.* Worthington, Ohio: Charles A. Jones, 1970.

Berg, Harry D., ed. *Evaluation in the Social Studies*. 35th Yearbook. Washington, D.C.: NCSS, 1965.

Carpenter, Helen McCracken, ed. *Skill Development in the Social Studies*. 33rd Yearbook. Washington, D.C.: NCSS, 1963.

Fraenkel, Jack R. *Helping Students Think and Value: Strategies for Teaching the Social Studies*. Englewood Cliffs, N.J.: Prentice-Hall, 1973.

Fraser, Dorothy McClure, ed. *Social Studies Curriculum Development: Prospects and Problems*. 39th Yearbook. Washington, D.C.: NCSS, 1969.

Gronlund, Norman E. *Stating Behavioral Objectives for Classroom Instruction*. New York: Macmillan, 1970.

*June R. Chapin and Richard E. Gross, *Teaching Social Studies Skills* (Boston: Little, Brown, 1973), p. 16.

Instructional Objectives Exchange, P.O. Box 24095, Los Angeles, California, 90024. A paperback for social studies can be purchased from "IOX."

Mager, Robert F. *Preparing Instructional Objectives*. New York: Harper & Row, 1970.

Morse, Horace T., and McCune, George H. *Selected Test Items for Testing of Social Studies Skills and Critical Thinking*. Revised by Lester E. Brown, and Ellen Cook. Bulletin 15, Fifth Edition. Washington, D.C.: NCSS, 1971.

Popham, W. James, and Eva T. Baker. *Establishing Instructional Goals*. Englewood Cliffs, N.J.: Prentice Hall, 1970. Can be purchased with filmstrip and audiotape from Vimcet Associates, Inc., P.O. Box 24714, Los Angeles, California, 90024.

4. The taxonomies are probably the most valuable tools for helping you write a broad range of instructional objectives. Benjamin S. Bloom and associates developed a taxonomy for classifying cognitive objectives. David R. Krathwohl and associates did the same for affective objectives. These two taxonomies are quite complete, with explanation, sample objectives, and sample test items for each level of the taxonomies. However, to make the best use of them requires more time for study than the average classroom teacher has. Therefore, simplified taxonomies are presented in Tables 7.1 and 7.2.

Table 7.1
*Major categories of the cognitive taxonomy and examples of instructional objectives.**

1. *Knowledge*. The student will be able to recall or recognize previously learned information. The information may range from the simple and concrete, such as recalling a date, to the more complex and abstract, such as recalling complicated theory. All that is required is the remembering of knowledge.

   Ideas for Objectives. Name the members of the Supreme Court. List the steps of the scientific method. Define the term reparations. Appropriate verbs: identify, define, recall, list, name, state, match, recognize, indicate, tell, describe, locate, label, repeat.

2. *Comprehension*. The student will be able to demonstrate that he understands a communication. This can be done by translating or interpreting the communication or by determining its implications or consequences. While comprehension is a higher level in the cognitive taxonomy than knowledge, it is the lowest level of understanding.

   Ideas for Objectives. Give an example of racial discrimination. Predict from the Senator's speech how he will vote. Summarize the information contained in the

---

chart. Appropriate verbs: explain, describe, translate, interpret, predict, infer, summarize, distinguish, paraphrase, restate in your own words, determine the implications, estimate, give an example.

3. *Application*. The student will be able to correctly use previously learned knowledge and skills in new situations. This includes the ability to apply concepts and generalizations.

   Ideas for Objectives. Demonstrate the correct procedure of writing a research paper. Apply a generalization about social results of the industrial revolution to a contemporary world situation. Use the concept containment to explain United States foreign policy toward North Korea. Appropriate verbs: demonstrate, use, employ, apply, utilize, solve, explain, prepare, develop, measure, construct, make, perform, present.

4. *Analysis*. The student will be able to break down material into its component parts. This may be done to identify the separate parts, to clarify the relationship between various parts, or to recognize the organizational structure of the material.

   Ideas for Objectives. Distinguish between relevant and irrelevant information used to support an argument. Recognize bias in an article. Select data which support the hypothesis. Appropriate verbs: recognize, identify, differentiate, distinguish, analyze, select, outline, detect, arrange, categorize.

5. *Synthesis*. The student will be able to arrange parts into a new pattern or structure. This could be to put together a new hypothesis or plan.

   Ideas for Objectives. Formulate an appropriate hypothesis to explain the rise of the crime rate in suburban areas. Devise a strategy to investigate the problem of growing unemployment. Develop a scheme for classifying wars. Appropriate verbs: plan, propose, develop, create, formulate, hypothesize, revise, organize, categorize, combine, produce, devise.

6. *Evaluation*. The student will be able to judge the value of ideas, materials, or methods for a given purpose. Evaluation is on the basis of internal evidence (for example, determine if an argument is free of logical fallacies) or on the basis of external criteria (for example, determine if a certain course of action would serve better than another to achieve a desired outcome).

   Ideas for Objectives. Determine if the evidence is sufficient to support the hypothesis. Rank according to reliability accounts of the episode. Compare the merits of proposals for alleviating unemployment. Appropriate verbs: choose, determine, select, rank, assess, evaluate, judge, approve, appraise, decide, compare.

Table 7.2
*Major categories of the affective taxonomy and examples of instructional objectives.**

1. *Receiving*. The student is willing to notice or to be aware of what is going on. The willingness to be aware may be so slight that the teacher must capture the student's attention, or the willingness may be so keen that the student independently selects certain things to pay attention to.

   Ideas for Objectives. Pays attention during class role-playing episode. Listens to others with respect during class discussion. Is aware of political pressure groups. Is aware of social discrimination toward Chicanos. Appropriate verbs: aware, listens, attention, prefer, choose, select, observe, recognize, realize.

2. *Responding*. The student's awareness or attention has become such that the student reacts with active participation. The reaction may range from merely complying with directions to acting independently of others to doing something with a sense of satisfaction.

   Ideas for Objectives. Completes homework assignment. Willing to work with others. Contributes to group discussions. Volunteers news about political events. Makes an effort to eliminate bias toward Chicanos from speeches. Appropriate verbs: comply, volunteer, display an interest, contribute, participate, enjoy.

3. *Valuing*. The student accepts a value (attitude or belief). The degree of acceptance may vary from being quite tentative to having a firm commitment or even to having a strong sense of conviction. The key characteristic is that the student acts consistently with a belief without being told to do so.

   Ideas for Objectives. Demonstrates a desire to be well informed about social issues. Assumes responsibility for efficient working of the group. Expresses a position on political issues. Tries to convince others not to discriminate against Chicanos. Appropriate verbs: demonstrate, assume responsibility, work to improve, initiate, propose, invite, studies.

4. *Organization*. The student gradually builds a value system, a philosophy of life. This includes seeing how a value relates to those already held, organizing values into a system, and changing the sytem as new values are included.

   Ideas for Objectives. Derives ideas for a philosophy of life from readings. Develops a rationale for the role of an individual in a family. Judges people on terms of their behavior rather than on the basis of groups to which they belong. The student's new attitude of opposition to discrimination against Chicanos extends to opposition of discrimination against the aged, women, and other groups. Appropriate verbs: accept, derive, develop, establish, recognize, judge, alter, combine, organize.

---

5. *Characterization by a Value or a Value Complex*. The student has internalized personal values to the extent and for the length of time that behavior reflects the value system in a regular and predictable manner. The student's overall behavior and philosophy of life are consistent with one another.

   Ideas for Objectives. Willing to change an opinion when confronted with new evidence. Displays respect for the dignity of the individual. Has so eliminated bias toward Chicanos from personal behavior that a different, new way of acting is carried out unconsciously. Appropriate verbs: display, develop, act, practice, change, demonstrate.

It is important to emphasize that the taxonomies are merely sources for objectives in the same way as lists of skills and curriculum guides are. Don't worry if you can't think of an objective for a particular category of a taxonomy or if you can't determine to which category one of your objectives belongs. The value of the taxonomies is that they remind and help us to plan for learning outcomes beyond those at the lower cognitive levels of knowledge and comprehension. They are not meant to be restrictive.

Constructing objective test questions

Some general suggestions

Benefits gained by using instructional objectives are lost if evaluation isn't based on the best efforts to measure student learning. Because most teachers rely heavily on teacher-made tests, it is essential that they include well-constructed questions. The following suggestions will help you construct better objective questions of all kinds.

1. Be sure there are an adequate number and variety of questions included in the test to cover each of the objectives for the unit of instruction being tested. A good idea is to draw up a simple table of specifications. A variety of schemes for such tables can be found by checking any of the works listed in this chapter's bibliography, but the scheme shown in Table 7.3 should be adequate for most teachers.
2. Construct the test over a period of time. A good test cannot be constructed in a hurry. Good questions require ingenuity; take the time to mull over various possible questions to get the best one. Periodically check your questions and make revisions.
3. Include elaborate and clear instructions for each section of the test. Clearly explain what the student is to do for each group of questions used in the test. The purpose of the test is to find out what the student has learned, and that purpose will not be achieved if the student is confused in the process of completing the test.
4. In your instructions to students, encourage them to go through the test first answering easy questions. Then they should take more time with the more difficult questions.

Table 7.3
Questions for various types of objectives

Topic—New Deal and the Depression	Recall	Comprehension	Analysis	Synthesis	Evaluation	Total
1. Background of the New Deal	10	5	5			20
2. The Hundred Days	10	5	5			20
3. Struggle for Economic Recovery	10	5	5			20
4. Climax of the New Deal	5	5	5	5		20
5. Evaluation of the New Deal	5		5	5	5	20
Total	40	20	25	10	5	100

5. Encourage students to consider their answers carefully and to be willing to change answers. Studies indicate that students improve their scores by being willing to change answers.*
6. Be sure to avoid mistakes in grammar, punctuation, and spelling. Going through the process of typing and duplicating helps to eliminate these kinds of errors, in addition to making certain each student has an easily readable test.
7. To test student skills, the data used in the questions must be new and unfamiliar to the student to avoid the possibility of the student's answering correctly by merely recalling material from instructional activity.
8. Avoid trivial and trick questions. There is nothing worthwhile to be gained by asking students to recall trivial information or to use information that they had little reason to expect would be included on the test. Also, it is of no value to word questions in such a way that the student is confused about what the question asks. For example, avoid using double negatives.
9. Be sure each question has an answer that is clearly correct.

*Sidney Archer and Ralph Pippert, "Don't Change the Answers," *Clearing House,* 37 (September 1962): 39–41.

10. Avoid questions that provide answers to other questions.
11. Avoid vague, ambiguous questions.
12. Don't use the words "always," "never," "all," "none," "every." They usually indicate the wrong answer in multiple-choice questions and are usually false statements in True-False questions. Correct answers are given away by the use of the qualifiers "frequently," "often," "usually," "seldom," "occasionally."
13. Avoid using the wording of the text in the construction of questions. Subject matter from the text should be avoided except in questions calling for recall or recognition of knowledge.
14. Group similar type questions together instead of mixing different type questions throughout the test.
15. Have all students take the same test.
16. Construct the test so that there will be plenty of time for the students to complete the test. This is especially true if the test contains questions designed to test skills. It takes time to think. By imposing an unrealistic time limit, you will increase the student's anxiety, which interferes with test performance.

Multiple-choice test questions

Multiple-choice type questions are especially useful for social studies, which, unlike mathematics and the physical sciences, does not have a lot of precisely accurate or definitely true areas of knowledge. Multiple-choice questions can be used to test a wide variety of skills, in addition to testing knowledge. This type of question has a relatively high degree of reliability because the chance of successfully guessing the right answer is less than in true-false or matching style questions. While they are time-consuming to construct, good, carefully thought out multiple-choice questions can be filed and used repeatedly.

1. In what year did President Monroe proclaim the Monroe Doctrine?

   a. 1803
   b. 1816
   √c. 1823
   d. 1848

In discussing multiple-choice questions, there are three parts; the stem, the answer, and the distractors or foils. In the first example the question forms the stem; options "a," "b," and "d" are the foils; in this example option "c" is the answer.

2. The provisions of the Compromise of 1850 which were most favorable to the South were those which concerned:

   √a. runaway slaves
   b. the admission of a state
   c. slavery in the District of Columbia
   d. slavery in newly acquired territories

Berg uses the above as an example of how multiple-choice items can be used to test important social studies skills.* The variety of uses for multiple-choice questions is demonstrated in the following section, Examples of Multiple-Choice Questions.

In addition to the general suggestions for constructing test questions listed above, you should keep these points in mind for constructing multiple-choice questions.

1. Use clear, precise language in all three parts of the question; stem, foils, and answers.
2. Eliminate all unnecessary words or phrases.
3. To make certain that the question is clear and makes sense to the student, avoid using long, complex sentences for the stem.
4. Use at least four options for the foils and answers.
5. Don't use foils that are absurdly wrong.
6. Make sure that only one of the options can be the answer. The foils should be constructed to challenge the unsure student, but they should not in any way be possibly correct answers.
7. Be sure the answer is so clearly correct that there will be no difference of opinion.
8. Don't construct the question so that the student selects incorrect information as the correct answer. For example, avoid questions worded like this:

   "Which one of the following is *not* a reason for the United States entry into World War I?"

9. Avoid the use in answers of such options as "none of the above" or "all of the above."
10. Place the answers in a random manner so students cannot select correct answers by discovering a pattern of correct responses.
11. Avoid accidental clues. Test-wise students get clues to the right answers by checking to see if the stem ends with "a" or "an," if one option is much longer or shorter than the other, if one option is of a different kind than the others, or if the answer is tipped off by the stem of another question.

Examples of multiple-choice questions The following examples indicate the wide variety of uses you can make of multiple-choice questions. The first four examples that follow are questions dealing with the use of data in various forms.

---

*Harry D. Berg, ed., *Evaluation in the Social Studies,* 35th Yearbook. (Washington, D.C.: NCSS, 1965), pp. 51–52.

Interpreting tabular data

Areas	Population 1860	1880	1900
New England	3,135,283	4,010,529	5,592,017
Middle Atlantic	7,458,985	10,496,878	15,454,678
East North Central	6,926,884	11,206,668	15,985,581
South Atlantic	5,364,703	7,597,197	10,443,480

1. According to the above figures the only correct statement among the following is:
   a. All sections more than doubled in population between 1860 and 1900.
   b. New England had its greatest gain in population between 1860 and 1880.
   c. The South Atlantic had its smallest gain in population between 1880 and 1900.
   √ d. Of all areas listed between 1860 and 1900, East North Central had the greatest gain in population.

Interpreting graphs

Index of Department Store Sales: 1920-1950
In Million Dollars of Sales
Index 1944 = 100

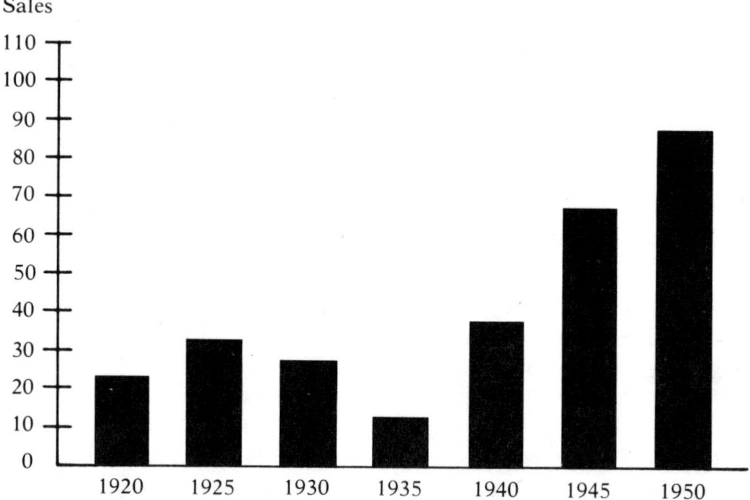

2. On the basis of the above information, which of the following statements is most likely to be correct?
   a. The information is not accurate because it reflects the impact of inflation.
   √ b. World War II had the effect of stimulating department store sales.
   c. The depression brought a sharp decline in department store sales.
   d. Between 1930 and 1950 department store sales steadily increased.

Interpreting cartoons

QUADRENNIAL HEROES

Shanks in the *Buffalo Evening News*, 1972. Reprinted by permission of the Buffalo Evening News, Inc.

3. Which of the following statements correctly states the meaning of the above cartoon?
   a. Operation of the railroads forces high rates of taxation.
   b. The ties of many taxpayers to railroads prevent the political parties from lowering taxes.
   c. Political parties are more concerned with the efficient running of the railroads than they are with the taxpayers.
   √d. Presidential elections cause political parties to be concerned about the taxpayer.

Reading maps

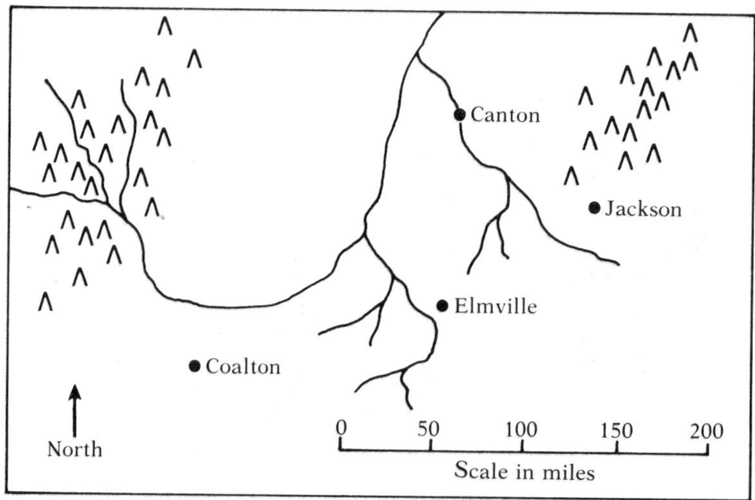

4. Select the statement that is correct, according to the above map.
   a. The town of Jackson is west of Coalton.
   b. Elmville is farther from Jackson than is Coalton.
   √ c. Canton is 100 miles north of Elmville.
   d. Jackson is 150 miles west of Elmville.

The next six examples deal with several of the critical thinking skills that are important in the social studies but are often neglected in teacher-made tests.

Determining reliable sources

1. To determine if General Robert E. Lee felt his subordinate officers were responsible for his loss at Gettysburg, which would be the most reliable source?
   √a. An account of the battle found in Lee's diary.
   b. A newswriter's account in a Confederate newspaper.
   c. An account written to commemorate the men who fought in the battle.
   d. An account written in an American history textbook.

Distinguishing fact from opinion

2. Which of the following is a statement of fact rather than opinion?
   a. The participation of the federal government in local government affairs always leads to undesirable federal controls.
   b. The Democratic Party was responsible for getting us into two World Wars.
   c. The American form of government is the best yet devised by man.
   √d. The birth rate in the United States declined during the Great Depression.

Recognizing frame of reference

3. Read the statements of the four men and then answer the question that follows.

Art: I grew up during hard times and with no help from anyone. I learned to get ahead by hard work and always had a good job, even when engineers and other educated people were out of work.

Bob: I've lived on the farm all my life and do not pretend to have all the answers. But, I do know that darn few boys from the farm are involved in college demonstrations. They are too busy earning their way through college.

Karl: A tragic waste that too few of us think about is underemployment. That occurs when a person, through lack of adequate training, is employed at a job that requires less skill than that person is capable of. The degree to which people are underemployed is the degree to which we waste a great deal of our productive capacities as a nation.

Paul: One of my biggest regrets is not having taken greater advantage of my opportunities when I was in college. My grandfather sent me, and I looked upon it as a good vacation. Maybe if I would not have had it so easy I would have appreciated college more.

Which one of the men's statements seems to indicate he would be most in favor of federal subsidies to help reduce the cost of a student attending college?

a. Art √c. Karl
b. Bob d. Paul

Recognizing assumptions

4. Read the following selection and then indicate which one of the assumptions was made by the writer.

The Soviet Union's efforts to gain missile superiority over the United States will not have the hoped-for results. Even with missile superiority the Soviets could not successfully blackmail this country. With missile sites scattered around the world and under the seas the United States would absorb an initial attack and still retaliate with a terrible blow.

√a. The Soviet Union would not be able to knock out United States missile sites around the world.
b. The United States would win any nuclear war with the Soviet Union.
c. The Soviet Union wants nuclear war with the United States.
d. The United States wants nuclear war with the Soviet Union.

Recognizing bias

5. Which of the statements is biased?
a. The average American male is taller and heavier than the average Chinese male.
b. More Americans were killed in auto accidents in the last five years than American troops in all of World War I.
c. There appears to be good reason to believe that cigarette smoking is harmful.
√d. A vote for increased military expenditures is a vote for war.

Recognizing value conflict

6. Read the comments by Sue and Ann and select the response that correctly indicates the value conflict expressed in their statements.

   Sue: I read in the paper that a policeman said he could have obtained a confession from a robbery suspect he had captured if he could have had time to question the suspect alone. Instead, the questioning was held up until the suspect talked to his lawyer. As a result, the policeman said, the suspect will not confess. No wonder we can't convict criminals!

   Ann: I don't know. Some guy who has done nothing could be picked up by the police. They might ask him all sorts of things, and being confused, scared, and without advice, he might say lots of things that would make a jury think he might be guilty. . . .

   a. Individual rights versus protection of the innocent.
   b. Trial by jury versus individual rights.
   √c. Police power versus protection of the innocent.
   d. Public safety versus police power.

The third group of examples indicates how multiple-choice items can be used to assess some of the critical thinking skills involved in the problem-solving process that is central to the inquiry approach to social studies.

Recognizing the problem

1. Read the comments by Ed and Walt and select the question that states the problem that needs to be studied if their disagreement is to be resolved.

   Ed: Yes, I am opposed to federal aid to education whether at the public school or college level. Equality of opportunity has always been an American ideal, and one of the few guarantees of that ideal left today is the fact that local school boards and trustees of private colleges can still make decisions in light of local needs and interests. That kind of freedom fosters equality of opportunity. Federal funds inevitably bring federal controls. Once the federal government gets control of local education, it will want a national curriculum for the schools and a national university system, both of which will serve national interests rather than be concerned with the needs of the individual.

   Walt: Some things are happening that make me disagree with you. The best schools, at least for getting into college, are in the suburbs. So, if you happen to live in the suburbs your chances of going to college are greater. Also, capable children of parents who have not attended college often do not enter college because of lack of funds. What we need are federal subsidies for inner-city schools and for students with insufficient funds to attend college.

   √a. Should federal funds be used to create greater educational opportunity?
   b. Should federal funds be used for inner-city schools?
   c. Is education a means to greater equality of opportunity?
   d. Is equality of educational opportunity desirable?

Recognizing the need for evidence

2. For which of the following statements would it be easiest to gather evidence to prove the statement correct?
   a. If the United States and China became involved in a war, the Soviet Union would not intervene.
   b. Few Communist party members actually believe strict Marxist ideology.
   c. Most Americans cheat when paying federal income tax.
   √d. The United Nations owns only a small portion of the property in New York City on which its buildings are located.

Determining if a statement supports a hypothesis

3. Select the statement that would cause you to doubt the following hypothesis.

   The mayor will be reelected because his strong rule has helped the city avoid having its problems become as serious as they are in most other cities.

   a. The mayor's intervention prevented a teachers' strike.
   b. The mayor made a special plea to the state legislature for funds to speed construction of city throughways.
   √c. The federal government is going to investigate hiring practices in the city's construction industry because minority groups are not being hired often enough.
   d. The mayor prevented the movement of the city's professional football team to another city by announcing plans to construct a municipal stadium.

Recognizing the feasibility of solutions

4. Which of the following alternative courses of action offers a feasible solution to the problem?

   Problem: What should be the governmental arrangement for Berlin so that the city may be unified?

   a. Place the entire city under the administration of the present East German authorities.
   b. Place the entire city under the administration of the present West German authorities.
   c. Place Berlin under the administration of a 33 government tribunal.
   √d. Make Berlin an independent free city.

The fourth group of examples shows how multiple-choice questions can be used to assess student skills in working with concepts and generalizations.

Forming a concept

1. Milwaukee is in the midwest near Chicago.
   To get to Indianapolis, drive west from Columbus for about 3½ hours.
   The Grand Canyon has a latitude of 36.2N and a longitude of 112.8W.
   Buffalo is 275 miles east of Detroit.

   The above statements could be categorized under the label:

   a. Direction c. Distribution
   √b. Location d. Region

Applying a concept

2. Read the following statement, and select the concept with which it is most closely related.

   A child is supported and protected by his family, but when he is grown to adulthood, he is expected to support himself and to protect the interests of others.

   √a. Role
   b. Sanction
   c. Citizenship
   d. Cultural change

Applying a generalization

3. Assuming that the following generalization is valid, select the one course of action out of the four stated that would probably decrease inflation.

   Generalization: If the federal government practices deficit spending under conditions of full employment, then inflation is likely to result.

   a. Increase the pay of government employees.
   b. Increase federal funds for highway construction.
   c. Reduce federal taxes on luxury items.
   √d. Reduce the number of men in the armed forces.

The fifth group of examples demonstrates how a large number of critical skills can be assessed with the use of a single reading.

Selection X

Enough is enough! How long are we to tolerate indecision and ineptness in our foreign policy? We all know that behind the world's trouble spot lies Russia whose final goal is world domination. Are we to allow ourselves to be involved in a series of indecisive Koreas? Korea ranks as the fourth most costly war in our history with over 118,000 casualties. Is this to be repeated in Indo-China, Iran, Germany or any other spot to be picked by Russia? Our policy of containment merely allows our real enemy time to build up a superior power while we squander ours. We now have a superiority of resources, production, atomic bombs and in many other strategic fields. We must face the test of world communism squarely, and if action is taken now, we can prevent the inevitable war that will surely come on Russia's own terms. "Can we endure another Pearl Harbor in this atomic age?" You may ask, "How do we know that quick action now will succeed?" An analysis of the current situation is very revealing. Russia took a severe beating in the last war, in which she lost from 8 to 10 million people and most of her Western lands were ravaged. Her transportation system is highly inadequate. In fact, over two-thirds of Russia, from Vladivostok to Moscow, is connected with only a double-tracked railroad. In many other parts during certain seasons the roads became impassable.

We must also keep in mind that the government of Russia is a dictatorship and does not have the support of her people. In fact, only six to seven million out of a population of over 210 million people are members of the Communist Party. The enforced low standard of living and the terrorizing secret police make the people ready for a change. There is a mad scramble for power among the leaders of the power-mad Presidium. The existence of slave-labor camps, annual purges, daily mass escapes through the iron curtain, and the underground movements prove that popular unrest is rampant.

To the above facts we must add that it is madness to think that we can bargain with the present rulers of Russia. As Russia builds up her strength, we may lose the initiative. Let me remind skeptics who do not believe that we could deliver a substantial blow against the Soviet Union of a happening in the last war. Most people believed that it would cost the allies over 1,000,000 casualties to force Japan out of the war. As we all know, the atomic bomb changed all that.

A similar quick strike will succeed against Russia, and the time is ripe. Delay is fatal. We Americans, once we have the facts, will see the task ahead, will roll up our sleeves and do the job. We must prevent the inevitable.*

1. Selection X best supports the thesis of
   1. isolationism.
   √2. preventive war.
   3. good common sense.
   4. capitalistic imperialism.

2. The selection makes all but one of the following assumptions:
   1. War with Russia is inevitable.
   √2. Our allies will support us.
   3. Russian morale is low.
   4. Negotiation is not possible with the Russians.

3. The selection
   √1. implies that the United Nations is a failure.
   2. is consistent with the principles of the United Nations charter.
   3. implies this action would strengthen the United Nations.
   4. implies this action would receive the support of the members in the United Nations.

4. In a critical analysis of the facts presented, one can say that they
   1. are impartially selected.
   2. are not related to the conclusion.
   3. adequately support the conclusion reached.
   √4. are insufficient to support the conclusion reached.

5. The additional information that the average age of the Russians is quite low, that the Communists have been in power since 1917, and that the government controls all the media of communication (schools, press, radio)
   √1. challenges several assertions made.
   2. supports several assertions made in the argument.
   3. is irrelevant to the argument.
   4. refutes the conclusion drawn.

---

*"Selection X" and the questions pertaining to it from Hymen M. Chausow, "Evaluation of Critical Thinking in the Social Studies," in *Evaluation in Social Studies*, ed. Harry D. Berg. 35th Yearbook. (Washington, D.C.: NCSS, 1965), pp. 86–88. Reprinted with permission of the National Council for the Social Studies and Hymen Chausow.

6. The President of the United States, the Secretary of the Air Force, and the Commanding General of the 10th Air Force (includes Chicago), all admit that the Russians are capable of striking Chicago and that some bombers will get through despite anything we do. The Russians have the atom bomb. This additional information
   1. is pure propaganda.
   2. refutes the conclusion reached.
   √3. provides important data to consider in accepting or rejecting the argument.
   4. is not related to the argument.
7. To take the initiative against the Kremlin by a sudden strike would probably have all of the following effects except
   √1. strengthening of the United Nations.
   2. losing the support of our allies.
   3. provoking retaliation by Russian armed forces.
   4. causing us to be condemned by world public opinion.
8. The American success in blocking Russian expansion in Greece, Turkey, Berlin, Iran, and Europe-in-general
   1. supports the argument presented.
   2. is not related to the argument.
   √3. challenges statements made in the argument.
   4. refutes the conclusion reached.
9. Communist ideology maintains that capitalism contains the seeds of its own destruction. Their doctrine calls for strategic withdrawal. This additional information
   1. supports the conclusion reached.
   2. is a false interpretation of communistic ideology and tactics.
   3. is not related to the argument.
   √4. challenges the assumption that war with Russia is inevitable.
10. With reference to the struggle for power in the Presidium, this selection presents
    √1. no evidence.
    2. adequate evidence.
    3. unrelated evidence.
    4. reliable sources.
11. The lack of adequate transportation facilities has led the Soviet Government to establish approximately seven decentralized economic and political regions. This information
    1. is irrelevant to the original conclusion reached.
    2. makes a sudden knockout blow against the Soviet Union impossible.
    √3. suggests that a sudden knockout of the Soviet Union might prove more difficult than is implied in the selection.
    4. does not affect the conclusion reached.
12. Most experts believe that it will take us at least ten years to build up enough power in Europe to prevent the Russians from overrunning it. This additional information
    1. has no relationship to the conclusion reached.

2. refutes the conclusion reached.
3. supports the conclusion reached.
√4. raises important questions.

13. The additional information provided in some of the above questions may lead one to believe that the conclusion stated in the selection is
    1. proved.
    2. unaffected.
    √3. unwarranted.
    4. warranted.

Matching questions

This style of question has limitations because it cannot be readily used for testing cognitive objectives above the knowledge level. Furthermore, it is time-consuming for students to complete. The following example demonstrates several suggestions for constructing matching questions.

1. Place the elements of the question in the left-hand column and the responses in the right-hand column. For example:

___Montesquieu	a. *Candide*
___Rousseau	b. *Concerning Man*
___Voltaire	c. *Leviathan*
___Adam Smith	d. *Principia*
___Thomas Hobbes	e. *Social Contract*
	f. *The Spirit of Laws*
	g. *Wealth of Nations*

2. Don't use more than ten elements in one question.
3. Provide several more responses than elements.
4. Construct the question so that the elements and responses are homogeneous. That is, match authors with works, causes with effects, or dates with events. Don't mix different kinds of matches in one question.
5. Precise instructions are particularly important for matching questions.
6. Be certain all elements have a correct response.
7. Space test questions so that all elements and responses to a matching question are on a single page.

Completion questions

There are two kinds of completion questions commonly used: (1) a statement in which one or more key terms are left blank and (2) a question to which a word, date, name, or phrase is the answer. Completion questions are good for testing recall as opposed to recognition of information, but they are difficult to construct for higher cognitive level questions. Also, they are difficult to construct in a manner that avoids the possibility that students will give correct but unexpected answers. Following the examples are suggestions for the construction of completion questions.

1. The Industrial Revolution began in the English ______ industry.
2. What was the name of the case which established the right of the Supreme Court to declare a law of Congress unconstitutional?

Suggestions for completion questions:

1. Keep the number of blanks in the question to a minimum. Too many blanks can cause the question to lose its meaning for the student.
2. Avoid letting the syntax of the question give a clue to the answer. For example, be careful in using "a" or "an" before a blank.
3. Avoid calling for an answer at the beginning of the question. Organize the question so the blank appears near the end.
4. Strive to construct questions so that only one answer is correct and so that students aren't likely to discover unexpected correct answers.
5. Word the question so the student knows what kind of answer is required—place, person, date, term.
6. Strive for questions that require a single word answer.

True-false questions

Although commonly used by teachers, the use of true-false questions by social studies teachers should be discouraged. As Wesley and Wronski point out, if a statement is unquestionably true or false, it is often of little importance, or it can be more satisfactorily tested by means other than true-false questions. Significant social studies content is rarely completely true or false. For example, is this statement true or false: "The cause of the American Revolution was taxation without representation"? It is more misleading than it is true or false.* Another reason for opposing the use of true-false questions is that the student has a 50-50 chance of a correct response on each question merely by random guessing. The teacher is left wondering if the student knew the answer or merely guessed it.

Other types of objective questions

Your choice of the kind of test question to use is limited only by your ability to create questions that yield useful results. Following are examples of question styles other than the more regularly used multiple-choice, matching, completion, and true-false questions.

Arrangement

1. Arrange the following events in proper chronological order, using 1 for the first event to occur, and so on, through 4 for the last event to occur.

   These events led to World War II:
   __German attack on Poland

---

*Edgar B. Wesley and Stanley P. Wronski, *Teaching Secondary Social Studies in a World Society* (Lexington, Mass: Heath, 1973), pp. 306–307.

___Stalin-Hitler nonaggression pact
___Munich Conference
___German reoccupation of the Rhineland

Chronological order

2. In the space before each event in Column I place A, B, or C from Column II to indicate the time during which the event took place.

Column I	*Column II*
___U-2 Affair	A. 1940–1949
___Hungarian Revolution	B. 1950–1959
___The Truman Doctrine	C. 1960–1969
___Lebanon Landing	
___Berlin Wall built	
___Guatemalan Revolution	
___Berlin Airlift	
___Cease-fire in Korea	
___Bay of Pigs Incident	

Free response

3. In a short paragraph explain President Truman's Point Four Program.
4. Briefly explain and give an example of balance-of-power diplomacy.
5. On the following outline map indicate the Confederate States by writing their names in the appropriate places.

6. Using the following data, construct a bar graph to show the increase in the per capita share of the public debt during World War II.

Year	*Per Capita Share of Public Debt*
1945	$1,848
1944	1,452
1943	999
1942	537
1941	367

(You will note that free-response questions can be of various kinds. In general, questions that require the student to construct something, such as a chart, a graph, or a map, are easier to use than questions that require the student to write an answer. You can write a free-response construction question in such a way that the student's response must be specific. However, it takes great care to write a free-response question that must be answered by a written explanation that is sure to be structured and to yield the information that you intend it to yield.)

Key list

7. Before each item list S for those you think should be classified as sources and Sec for those you think should be classified as secondary sources.

—1. *The Congressional Record.*
—2. *Years of Decisions*, President Truman's memoir.
—3. *A Thousand Days*, history of Kennedy's presidency.
—4. TV broadcast of President Ford's State of the Union Speech.
—5. A news correspondent's account of businessmen's reaction to a proposal for tax cuts.*

Item-analysis

The major purpose of testing should be to diagnose the level of achievement and the instructional needs of the students. An item analysis of test questions is a useful technique for making this diagnosis, and Clark suggests a relatively simple scheme for accomplishing this task (see Table 7.4). (1) Students' names are written at the head of columns, (2) test questions are listed on horizontal rows, and (3) the instructional objective that each question tested is also indicated. Then students' correct (+) and incorrect (−) responses are recorded. An examination of the chart will indicate the following things to the teacher.

---

*This question style was adapted from Horace T. Morse, and George H. McCune, *Selected Items for the Testing of Study Skills and Critical Thinking,* Bulletin No. 15 of the National Council for the Social Studies, Fourth Edition (Washington, D.C.: NCSS, 1964).

Table 7.4

Objective	Test item	Students: Sue	Ann	Jim	Sam
1	1	+	−	+	−
1	2	+	+	−	+
2	3	−	+	+	−
3	4	−	+	−	+
1	5	+	+	+	+
2	6	+	+	+	+
2	7	−	−	−	−
3	8	−	−	−	−

1. If a student answers correctly the questions that test attainment of a particular objective, then the student has achieved that objective.
2. If a student does not answer correctly a question that tests attainment of a particular objective, then that student has not achieved that objective.
3. If many students do not answer correctly the questions that test attainment of a particular objective, presumably instruction for that objective was not successful and should be redone.
4. If most students do answer a question correctly, presumably the instruction was successful.*

The results on the analysis should give you a better idea of what instructional activities need to be planned.

Advantages and disadvantages of objective test questions

In addition to the advantages and disadvantages for each kind of objective question already mentioned, several points should be made about objective questions in general. They offer advantages over essay tests. They can sample achievement of a wider range of instructional objectives because more questions can be asked during a test period. Scoring should be quicker and easier: quicker because students don't have the chance to include irrelevant material, as they do with "scatter-gun answers" to essay questions, and easier

*Adapted with permission of Macmillan Publishing Co., Inc., from *Teaching Social Studies in Secondary Schools: A Handbook* by Leonard H. Clark. Copyright © 1973 by Leonard H. Clark. (New York: Macmillan, 1973), pp. 137–38 and Figure 7.1.

because the questions, if properly constructed, have answers about which there is little difference of opinion.

A major limitation of objective questions is that they provide little opportunity for the student to plan and organize his own answer, to demonstrate divergent thinking, or to express his response in his own words. Though it has been mentioned previously, this statement bears repeating: Good objective questions require ingenuity, time, and effort to construct.

Using essay questions

It is unfortunate that essay questions are used so poorly in the schools because their proper use adds an important dimension to evaluation efforts. In this section suggestions and information are offered to help you write and use essay questions more effectively.

Advantages of essay questions

The advantages and disadvantages of essay questions are listed so frequently in educational literature that the tendency is to overlook them. However, the lists do contain valuable reminders that are worth reviewing. The most commonly mentioned advantages of essay questions are the following:

1. They are particularly well suited for testing students' abilities to collect and organize information.
2. They give students the freedom of expression necessary to exhibit the level and uniqueness of each student's understanding.
3. They enable the student to demonstrate the ability to effectively communicate within the parameters of a particular area of study or discipline.
4. They are more likely to place emphasis on testing student skills as opposed to testing recognition or recall of knowledge.
5. The time for the preparation of an essay test is usually less than for a test using objective questions.
6. They reduce the likelihood of the student's guessing correct answers.

Disadvantages of essay questions

Any social studies teacher who has been confronted with a stack of 150 essay tests that need to be graded knows that essay tests have disadvantages.

1. Scoring is unreliable. Different teachers will give the same essay answer different grades; the same teacher grading the same essay answer at a different time may grade the answer differently.
2. An essay question can focus on only a small portion of what has been studied during a unit of study.
3. Essay answers require a great deal of time to grade.

4. It is easy to write "essay questions" that are not really essay questions. A question that requires a student to "trace the coming of the Civil War" is not a true essay question, for it requires only listing in chronological sequence the events leading to the start of the Civil War.

Suggestions for writing essay questions

Good essay questions are not easy to write, but some of the following suggestions should be of help.

1. Be sure that the question is consistent with the instructional objectives established for the unit of study. Students soon learn to study for tests rather than instructional objectives if there is inconsistency between the two.
2. Be positive that an essay question is the best kind of question for what you are testing. As pointed out previously, the multiple-choice question is quite versatile. Many essay questions could be profitably replaced by the use of several multiple-choice questions.
3. Strive to state the essay question as simply and clearly as possible. To accomplish this, be sure that students understand what is expected when certain terms are used in essay questions. Some examples are:

   Explain—make clear. The reader assumes nothing. The writer must convince the reader by means of what is written that the subject is understood.

   Discuss—present both pro and con agruments. Answers should mention the various groups or individuals supporting each side of the argument and their reasons for that support. Answers to discussion questions should present all of the evidence pertinent to both sides of the argument.

   State—present the information called for as briefly and accurately as possible.

   Describe—narrate or give an account of an episode.

   Contrast—show the differences only and ignore the similarities.

   Compare—show similarities only and ignore the differences.

   Illustrate—give examples. For example: Give two illustrations of adverse effects on the United States created by Great Britain's entry into the Common Market.

4. In addition to using specific directions, such as those above, stating the essay question in the form of a problem can help students understand what is wanted. Avoid asking a question in such a form as "What is your opinion of a school principal banning a student newspaper?" Instead, state the essay as a problem: "Should a school principal have the right to censor student newspapers?" Improving the form of the question and using specific directions aid students to write better essay answers.
5. Once a tentative essay question has been written, try to anticipate what a student would write in response to that question. Try to put yourself in the student's shoes, and read the question from this standpoint. Try to limit your response to what the student could be reasonably expected to know. Quite often this will result in the realization that the question needs to be revised.

6. Remember that the essay question is better used to assess the student's depth of understanding rather than breadth of knowledge. Of course, knowledge is important in answering an essay question but not just for the sake of recalling isolated facts. Knowledge is a necessary ingredient, but the real goal of an essay question is to assess the student's ability to use knowledge in the process of utilizing intellectual skills.
7. Be sure to include in the instructions such information as how much time is available for each question, what the value of each question is, and if the student is to include an outline of each answer.
8. Have all students answer all questions presented. Because the essay question is so narrow in focus, some teachers may feel each student should have the opportunity to choose an essay question dealing with an area in which the student is well prepared rather than a question dealing with a less-familiar area. However, the practice of giving the student a choice does not seem to work to the student's benefit.* It is not realistic to think that a teacher can construct two equally difficult essay questions, and students are not good judges in selecting the essay questions on which they will do best. And, when the test is graded, which student did better—the one with a mediocre answer to a tough question or the one with a good answer to an easier question?

Open-book essay questions

Closely related to any discussion of essay questions is the issue of open-book examinations. If you want to present the student with a true essay question, then there is a lot to be said for the open-book approach. Essay questions are particularly good for testing student ability to collect and organize information and to effectively communicate about the effort. In essay questions the emphasis is not on recall of information but on the skill the student can demonstrate in using sources of information and information gathered from those sources. Therefore, present the student with cartoons, graphs, recordings, a film strip, textbooks, his class notes, an article, or any other pertinent source of information from which he will be expected to gather data for the purpose of answering the essay question.

An open-book essay test will provide the kind of school experience that has transfer or carry-over value into the life of the student in the real world. When a person buys a car or a home, chooses a college or a job, that person has to collect data from many sources to make a decision. When the time comes to make the decision reference can be made to the sources of data; the data don't have to be submitted to memory to be recalled at the time of decision making. Why should students never have the chance to test their decision-making abilities while they have selected information available for reference?

---

*Robert L. Ebel, *Essentials of Educational Measurement* (Englewood Cliffs, N.J.: Prentice-Hall, 1972), pp. 147–48.

Essay question examples

Conforming to a specific format is not important when writing essay questions. What matters is to effectively communicate to students what is expected of them.

1. To answer this essay question you may make use of the mimeographed excerpt from Brinton's *Anatomy of a Revolution*, your class notes for the film, "Cuba—The Forgotten Revolution," your study notes for the article, "Revolution and Counter Revolution," from the *Encyclopedia of the Social Sciences*, and your class notes.

   You have the entire period to read and analyze the question, work with your sources, create an outline of your tentative answer, write your answer, proofread, and state your answer in final form.

   Question. On the basis of the information with which you have to work, what generalizations can you formulate to explain the conditions that give rise to major revolutions? Be sure to explain why you think your generalizations are warranted.

This example is the open-book variety of essay question. Rather than focusing on the recall of knowledge, the example requires the student to demonstrate the ability to perform a number of skills at the heart of the inquiry process. Can the student analyze different kinds of sources of information? perceive the relationships presented in the accounts of several episodes? formulate hypotheses? work with concepts? successfully test his hypotheses against the available information? draw from information to synthesize generalizations?

The second example assumes that the student has engaged in class discussions on the topic of overpopulation, read about the topic, and worked with relevant charts, maps, and tables of statistics.

2. You have the entire period to read and analyze the question, to prepare an outline of your answer, and to write your answer. Both the outline and answer are to be turned in.

   Question. Should the federal government in the effort to deal with the problem of overpopulation impose penalties, such as additional income tax payments, for families with more than two children? Be sure to fully discuss both sides of the issue.

For this essay question to test skills as well as mastery of knowledge, the problematic situation of the question must be a new and novel one for the student. If the problem is unfamiliar, the student is then faced with the need to formulate a hypothesis, check that hypothesis against pertinent knowledge, draw a conclusion that is warranted by the evidence, and effectively communicate what the answer is and why it is the answer. If the student is familiar, however, with this particular problem, the problem may be correctly answered on the basis of recall.

Preparing students to take essay tests

A common practice is for social studies teachers to tell their students to expect an essay question on one of the first tests of the year. Then, even if teachers follow all of the "do's" and "don'ts" of essay test construction, they probably will be disappointed in their students' performances and will be heard to exclaim that their students "just can't write essays." The suggestion that students need to be taught how to write a good essay answer will usually provoke the response, "They are supposed to do that in English class."

Well, that is not entirely true. In their English classes students do learn something about answering essay questions; but in social studies, as in every subject matter area, there are special emphases that are at the heart of writing good essay answers in that area. The ability to communicate effectively using the language and the conventions of social studies is a learning goal that no social studies teacher should ignore or assume to be the responsibility of the English teacher.

What should you do to prepare your students to write good essay answers? First, give each student a handout on answering essay questions, then discuss it with each student. The handout should be divided into three main sections:

A. Interpreting the question
B. Answering the question
C. Writing the answer

Interpreting the question The students should be told to read the question carefully and to analyze its key words. At this point it would be a good idea to include explanations of what is meant by such words as explain, discuss, and state. In addition, students should be taught to answer questions logically. One of the best ways to do this is to teach students to prepare brief outlines of their prospective answers.

Answering the question Students should be made aware of the functions of the three parts of any good essay answer: introduction, main body, and conclusion. The topic sentence of the introductory paragraph should be a statement of the writer's position. This should be followed by an indication of the major points to be covered. The main body should consist of the substantive arguments and details of evidence. The substance of the main body obviously should be related to the question and should be as accurate and complete as possible. The conclusion should summarize or reemphasize the major point of the essay answer. The conclusion ties together all that has been written. It is too important to be left out because of the pressure of time that results from poor planning.

Students should be reminded that essay questions are *not* invitations to make general statements without supporting evidence. General statements must be supported with facts that are relevant, adequate, and correct. Also, events should be located in time and place, the more exact the time and place, the better. If books, articles, speeches, and the like are mentioned, then they must also mention the authors, when and why they wrote the articles, what they said, and what the value was of what they said. The point is to get students to recognize that their job is to pack into their answers all of the *pertinent* information that they possibly can. To do this, the student will have to allot time carefully and master the art of saying much that is significant in a few words.

Writing the answer This section of the handout should make the student aware of the requirement to write clearly and according to the conventions of good grammar. Striving for a smooth flow of ideas, adequate vocabulary, accurate use of words, correct paragraphing, correct sentence structure, and correct spelling should be emphasized.

Practice

After your students understand the directions and suggestions of the material about writing an essay, give them a practice run in writing an answer to an essay question. The most beneficial portion of this activity comes after the students have written their first essay. A good essay question does not have *one right answer*, but any correct answer must be written in a proper way. To help your students realize this, have them as a class reach consensus as to what would be an outline of a good answer to the question. To accomplish this, initiate class interaction with the following kinds of questions.

> "Bob, what is the purpose of an introduction to an essay?"
> "Ann, do you agree with Bob?"
> "Carol, what about you?"
> "Everybody agree with Bob, Ann, and Carol?"
> "Okay, if we were going to make an outline of an answer for this essay question, what should we put on the blackboard as a good outline statement for the introduction of the essay?"
> "Ed, what would you say? Use what you wrote in your essay."
> "Sue, would you change Ed's statement?"
> "George, who do you agree with, Sue or Ed?"
> "Everybody agree with Sue and George? Any other changes? You all think this is a good introductory statement, and you're willing to stick with it?"

By drawing students into a class discussion in this manner, they usually respond eagerly and go on to develop an entire outline of an essay answer. By being active participants in the process of developing the final outline, they get a feel for what they need to do when they plan their individual essays.

After studying the handout on essay writing and after participating in a practice writing session and review, students may still need some help to become accomplished essay writers. Usually the two skills in which students most need help are those of recognizing and accumulating the necessary information from various sources and, once they have gathered the information, of organizing the information in a manner that best meets the requirements of the essay question.

To help students become more skillful at recognizing and accumulating information, give them plenty of practice. Confront them with such sources as readings, cartoons, graphs, charts, records, films, etc., and have them translate, interpret, extrapolate, analyze, and evaluate these sources. Engage them in such exercises as reading two articles, each advocating a different solution to a common problem, and then consulting graphs, charts, tables, and maps to gather data that will enable them to make a judgment about which of the two readings seems to propose the most feasible solution to the problem.

To help students become more skilled in organizing the information they have accumulated, impose some artificial but useful writing conditions. Give students an essay question, but tell them that their answers must be in outline form only and that they can use only the amount of paper you give them. Do not impose a time limit. The goal is to get your students to achieve tight, logical organization. Thus, to require an outline and limited paper are useful conditions: to impose a condition of limited time adds pressure that interferes with students' reflections. Tightly organized, thoughtful answers to good essay questions require time.

It takes time to prepare students to write good essay answers. However, the results will be rewarding if you are willing to prepare and discuss a handout on essay writing, to give students a chance to write some practice answers, to have the class participate in reviewing the practice answers, and to give students ample practice in developing the skills necessary for good essay writing. Students can write good essays, but they need help in developing their skills to do so.

At this point it might be well to make a few suggestions about administering essay tests. It is a good idea to give students one essay question at a time on a fairly regular basis, rather than to give them groups of three or four essay questions at one time. Writing essays is something students need to do on a regular basis if they are to make the greatest progress in their writing skills. Also, students should have time to think, so that they can do their best work. The average class period is not long enough to allow students to write three or four essays without subjecting the students to unrealistic time pressure. Students need time to study the question, to develop an outline, to read what has been written, and to make desired revisions. In addition, the burden for the teacher grading the answers is reduced if the questions are spread out over regular intervals.

Grading essay answers

Grading essay answers is time-consuming and difficult, but the task will be done more satisfactorily if these suggestions are followed.

1. At the time the essay question is constructed, write the criteria for grading the answer. What interpretations, theories, and ideas should be included? How much credit should be granted for the various parts of the essay?
2. Read a few essay answers first on a trial basis to make sure your expectations are realistic and to get a feel for what the students have done.
3. Have the students put their names on the backs of their papers so the answers can be graded with a minimum of prejudice. (The "A" students may not have written the best papers this time around.)
4. If more than one essay question has been assigned, read all answers to question 1 first, then read all answers to question 2, and so on.
5. Give separate grades for social studies skill and for the mechanics of writing.
6. To achieve consistency in grading, place the answers in piles according to their grades, all "A's" in one pile, all "B's" in another pile, and so on. After the first reading, go through the piles and compare all of the "A's." One or two of the answers in a pile may not match with the others.
7. Make detailed and numerous comments about strengths and weaknesses.
8. Grade, return, and discuss the answers with the class as soon as possible. Students are highly interested and motivated when the time comes to review their test answers. Cash in on this. Often teachers consider going over the previous day's test as a less-than-economical use of teaching time. Nothing could be further from the truth. The time spent doing this will be quite profitable for both you and the students.
9. Be willing to take time to discuss answers with individual students. It is time-consuming to deal with questions peculiar to individual student's papers, but you can accomplish a great deal by taking that time.

Techniques of evaluation other than testing

No matter how often a student is tested, tests alone will not give the teacher all of the information needed for complete assessment of what has or has not been learned. This is especially true if your teaching makes use of case studies, simulations, community studies, and the other instructional activities presented throughout the previous chapters. Using these activities in the inquiry approach means that you are teaching knowledge, skills, and attitudes. Testing may adequately assess student learning in many areas of knowledge, but it will adequately assess learning of only a limited area of skills and a few kinds of attitudes. When using a simulation, for example, you will need to use a rating sheet or a checklist to determine if a student has developed such skills as recognizing the central issue or distinguishing fact from opinion. To determine if the use of a case study has affected a student's attitudes, you will need to use such means as Likert scales, the semantic differential, or a projective technique.

Because teachers know that testing alone is not adequate, they supplement testing with observations of student behavior. The trouble is that many teachers fail to observe students in a directed manner. Consequently, teachers have only that information that they can recall from memory and that has been gathered haphazardly. By using proper techniques teachers can direct observations to gain information selected and recorded for a purpose. Rating sheets, checklists, anecdotal records, and conferences may be used to assess both skills and attitudes. Several of these techniques can be used by the student for self-evaluation and peer-evaluation. Likert scales, the semantic differential, and projective techniques are helpful for assessing attitudes and values.

Rating sheets

Rating sheets are easy to construct, and they can be constructed to rate a wide range of skills and attitudes. First determine what you want to rate, and then develop a continuum or scale along which you can rate the behaviors.

The examples in Figures 7.1 and 7.2 indicate the versatility of rating sheets. A single student can be rated (Examples 1, 3, and 4), a group of students can be rated (Example 2), skills can be rated (Examples 1 and 3), interests can be rated (Example 4), rating can be made by the teacher (Examples 1, 2, and 3), and ratings can be made by the student (Examples 1, 2, 3, and 4).

Two concerns teachers have about rating sheets are how to find the time to use them and how to use them best. The following suggestions will help you deal with these concerns.

1. For some activities you will want to rate all students, but there are times when it is more efficient to rate only those students who would be most likely to benefit from extra evaluation.
2. Class discussions could focus on the ratings of students compiled by other students. During panel discussions, role-playing, oral reports, and debates the students not involved in the presentation could compile ratings of those participating. After the presentations have been completed, a class discussion of student performances based on peer-evaluation could be a valuable learning experience.
3. These discussions can be enriched if participating students are given time to rate themselves. The comparison of self-evaluations and peer-evaluations will capture the students' interest.

Figure 7.1

Example 1

Rating sheet for discussion skills

Name ______________________ Topic ______________________

Class ______________________ Date ______________________

1. Recognizes the central issue of the discussion

1	2	3	4
Unsatisfactory	Fair	Good	Excellent

2. Recognizes the need to define terms

1	2	3	4
Never	Seldom	Usually	Always

3. Distinguishes between fact and opinion

1	2	3	4
Never	Seldom	Usually	Always

Example 2

Rating sheet for panel discussion

Panel members

______________________ Topic ______________________

______________________ Date ______________________

______________________ Class ______________________

____

1. Preparation

1	2	3	4
Unsatisfactory	Fair	Good	Excellent

2. Presentation of the main problem

1	2	3	4
Unsatisfactory	Fair	Good	Excellent

3. Presentation of possible solutions

1	2	3	4
Unsatisfactory	Fair	Good	Excellent

Figure 7.2

Example 3
Rating sheet for discussion (audience)

Name ______________________ Topic ______________________
Class ______________________ Date ______________________

1. Did you take good notes?	1	2	3	4
	Unsatisfactory	Fair	Good	Excellent
2. Did you understand the main topic?	1	2	3	4
	Unsatisfactory	Fair	Good	Excellent
3. Did you understand the terms used?	1	2	3	4
	Never	Seldom	Usually	Always

Example 4
Rating sheet for student interests

Name ______________________ Date ______________________
Class ______________________

1. I read historical novels.	1	2	3	4
	Never	Seldom	Usually	Always
2. I read biographies.	1	2	3	4
	Never	Seldom	Usually	Always
3. I visit museums.	1	2	3	4
	Never	Seldom	Usually	Always

Checklists

The checklist is an evaluation technique that is quite similar to the rating sheet. It has the same versatility, in that it can be used to assess a variety of activities, can be used to gather various kinds of information, and can be used either by students or by the teacher. The major difference between the checklist and the rating sheet is that the checklist does not rank; it merely serves as a reminder that something did or did not take place or that something does or does not need improvement. Checklists enable rapid recording of a great deal of information about a student's performance.

Checklists and rating sheets are particularly useful for evaluating affective learnings. In the checklist in Figure 7.3, affective behaviors, such as will-

Figure 7.3

Example 1
Classroom discussion checklist

Name ______________________ Topic ______________________
Class ______________________ Date ______________________

	Bob	John	Sue	Jim	Carol	Ann	Sam	Dave
Skills students need to improve								
1. Recognizing a speaker's bias								
2. Distinguishing fact from opinion								
3. Presenting facts to support opinions								
Student attitudes								
1. Willing to freely participate								
2. Expresses political opinions								
3. Changes opinion when confronted with new evidence								

Example 2
Research paper checklist

Name ______________________ Date ______________________
Class ______________________

	Yes	No
1. Select and limit topic.		
2. Prepare working bibliography.		
3. Prepare preliminary outline.		

ingness to fully participate (responding), fully expressing political views (valuing), and changing opinion when confronted with new evidence (characterization), are much easier to assess through observation than by testing.

Classroom observation and anecdotal records

Rating sheets and checklists are good techniques for observing selected anticipated behaviors. However, rating sheets and checklists cannot anticipate *all* of the behavior that teachers will have opportunities to observe. Your efforts at student assessment will be improved if you record these unanticipated observations in a file of anecdotal records, rather than relying on your ability to recall what you have observed. Use of a file box and file cards is a handy way to maintain anecdotal records, and a good format follows.

Student ______Sam Smith______ Date ___10/1/75___

Class______World Cultures______

Episode: Sam did not enter into the dialogue of the debate. When asked questions, his answers were knowledgeable but brief.

Comment: His reluctance may have been caused by the argumentative nature of the debate. Perhaps he needs more opportunities to discuss issues in impersonal, analytical discussions.

These suggestions will help you improve the quality of your anecdotal records.

1. Record the episode as soon as possible after it has occurred. The greater the time lapse beteen the episode and the recording, the greater is the possibility of error in the memory of what actually occurred.
2. Use anecdotal records only for collecting information that you can't gain by some other evaluation technique. Most other evaluation techniques are more economical in terms of time and are usually more reliable.
3. Be sure to record important aspects of the environment or atmosphere of the episode so that your interpretation of the episode will be more accurate.
4. Beware of observer bias! What you may see as poor student preparation may really be the result of your inadequate directions. Also, you may unwittingly be less tolerant of one student than of another. You should consider the possibility of such bias before entering an episode in the anecdotal records.
5. Be sure to keep any explanatory comment separate from an objective description of the episode.
6. Don't overgeneralize. One or two recorded observations of a particular student's behavior may be more misleading than revealing. A good idea is to try to develop anecdotal records into a log or diary, so that observations are collected at fairly regular intervals and are recorded over a period of time. By taking the long view contained in the log, isolated incidents are put in proper perspective and significant trends are recognized. Assessment based upon observations becomes more accurate as more episodes are observed.
7. Remember that the purpose of anecdotal records is to objectively summarize an episode of student behavior. The goal is description, not judgment, as in the case of a rating sheet.

Simulations, role-playing, case studies, and value clarification

The instructional techniques of simulations, role-playing, case studies, and value clarification as advocated in previous chapters are major tools of the inquiry method of teaching social studies. As Wesley and Wronski point out, these instructional techniques can serve also as evaluation techniques.* During role-playing and simulation activities students assume the roles of others. By observing student actions you can gather much information about how much they understand and how they feel about whatever roles they have assumed. In much the same way, you can learn much about a student's understanding and attitudes from his or her work with a case study or during value clarification activity. The information you gather from observing students in these kinds of activities will be better if you use rating sheets, checklists, or anecdotal records to give direction to your observations.

Individual conference

The most rewarding evaluation technique is sitting down with a student to discuss tests, rating sheets, checklists, anecdotal records, and any other pertinent information. Discussing these together will help establish the student's current strengths and weaknesses as a learner. Each of you will become more aware of which activities should most appropriately come next.

The difficulty is finding the time to schedule a conference with each of your students. Conferences can often be worked in as the rest of the class is engaged in research or in preparing a written report. Steal time from a planning period. Squeeze in a conference before or after school. Don't be reluctant to use some regular class time for conferences. The advantages to be gained justify the time and effort.

Useful hints

These suggestions will help you observe and assess student performance.

1. Be unobtrusive. The best way to accomplish this is to make observing and recording performances a regular aspect of instructional activity rather than an occasional, unusual event. As the recording of observations becomes more familiar and less obtrusive to students the more natural will be their performances and the more reliable the information recorded.†
2. Use audiotape and videotape. When a student is given a rating sheet of his performance during a debate or similar activity, the meaning and impact of the evaluation is dramatically increased if the student has the opportunity to listen to himself on audiotape or to see himself on videotape.
3. Use the proper technique. If you know beforehand which behaviors should be demonstrated by the student, use a checklist, not an anecdotal card. If you want to assess behavior in addition to observing if it has or has not been performed, use a rating sheet, not a checklist. If you want to describe what happens, use an anecdotal card, not a rating list.

---

*Edgar B. Wesley and Stanley P. Wronski, *Teaching Secondary Social Studies in a World Society* (Lexington, Mass.: Heath, 1973), p. 315.

†Carl A. Cartwright and G. Phillip Cartwright, *Developing Observation Skills* (New York: McGraw-Hill, 1974), p. 57.

4. Beware of bias. It is easy to unwittingly give an undeserved high rating to a polite, bright student, rather than to a student who "rubs you wrong." Also, because you become accustomed to a student doing well at other times, it is easy to take it for granted that the behavior observed deserves a high rating.
5. Recognize the shortcomings of observation techniques. The records you accumulate by the use of rating sheets, checklists, and anecdotal records are neither complete nor fully accurate for a variety of reasons. Because of the numerous distractions in the usual classroom, many episodes of behavior go unobserved. Because the form you use for recorded observations and judgments is not comprehensive or flexible enough, what you actually record may be distorted to some degree from what you would like to record. Or, your records may be inaccurate due to simple clerical error.

Self-evaluation and peer-evaluation

Sprinkled throughout this section have been statements about student self- and peer-evaluation. Very little has been said about these practices in the literature of social studies education, and few classroom teachers employ these practices. This is unfortunate because there are good reasons for social studies teachers to make use of student self- and peer-evaluation.

In recent years social studies teachers have increasingly used simulations, role-playing, case studies, debates, panels, community surveys, media, games—in short, a wide range of materials and activities that require individual involvement and interaction by the student. The goals of this type of instruction include helping students to become more autonomous and skilled in knowing what they think and value, in the process of decision making, and in recognizing the consequences of their actions and values. With the establishment of these goals and the use of these activities, it is inconsistent to exclude students from a central role in the evaluation process.

There are other practical reasons for using self- and peer-evaluation in conjunction with student-involvement activities. As each student performs in a role-playing episode or participates in a discussion, no one knows that student's feelings and attitudes better than the student does. Similarly, during many activities involved students are the best judges of how well they use their skills. Why not give them the opportunity to assess themselves?

A somewhat similar argument may be made for peer-evaluation. Students view other students quite differently from the way the teacher, who is not a member of the student group, may view them. The teacher should make use of student opinions of their classmates' performances in collecting information for evaluation. In many cases students are more willing to accept—and more influenced by—what their peers have to say about their performances than by the teacher's comments.

With these reasons for using student self- and peer-evaluation to supplement the teacher's evaluation efforts, it is hard to understand why so little use is made of these practices, especially when it is easy to do so. The techniques described previously, such as checklists and rating sheets, are ideal for student use.

Assessing attitudes and values

Evaluation in the inquiry approach cannot ignore attitudes and values, and many of the techniques explained earlier can be adapted for assessment in the affective area. For example, if a student correctly identifies the current leader of West Germany's Christian Democrat Party in response to a multiple-choice question (knowledge level in the cognitive taxonomy), then the student is aware that West Germany has political parties (receiving level of the affective taxonomy). Assessment in the affective area, however, often requires techniques in addition to those used in the cognitive area. The following are practical techniques that have been found to be best suited for use in social studies classes.

Likert scales

To construct a Likert scale, select a list of positive and negative statements about a concept or issue. Do not include neutral statements. Have the students indicate how they feel about each statement—strongly agree, agree, undecided, disagree, strongly disagree.

Likert scale for racial attitudes

Directions: Indicate what your feeling is about each of the following statements by checking the appropriate space. Don't skip any statement. Your response should reflect your feeling about the statement, so don't worry about a right or wrong response.

SA = Strongly Agree
A = Agree
U = Undecided
D = Disagree
SD = Strongly Disagree

SA	A	U	D	SD	
___	___	___	___	___	1. Race should not be a factor in hiring someone for a job.
___	___	___	___	___	2. The people who live in a neighborhood should be allowed to decide who can or cannot live in their neighborhood.
___	___	___	___	___	3. Discrimination is a factor in minority groups being on welfare.

The information gathered will be more meaningful and easier to manage if it is put in the form of a score. To do this, first assign a value to each response as follows:

	Positive statement	Negative statement
Strongly agree	5	1
Agree	4	2
Undecided	3	3
Disagree	2	4
Strongly disagree	1	5

Next, tally the student's total score by adding together all values, including both positive and negative attitudes. The resulting score indicates the direction and intensity of the student's feelings. For example, if the complete scale in the example contained ten statements and a student's responses had values of 4, 5, 5, 3, 2, 5, 5, 4, 3, and 5, that student's score would be 41, which indicates a more intensively positive racial attitude than a score of 30 would.

Semantic differential

This technique is similar to the Likert scale, in that it is easy to construct, and it yields a score that indicates the intensity of the student's attitudes.

Semantic differential: attitudes toward labor unions

Directions: Indicate your feelings toward labor unions by reading each set of terms and quickly making a check mark in an appropriate column.

The center column is for a neutral response.

A response to the left of the center indicates agreement with the term on the left; the further to the left the response, the stronger the agreement with the term.

A reponse to the right of the center indicates agreement with the term on the right; the further to the right the response, the stronger the agreement.

Answer once but only once for each set of terms; don't skip a set!

The responses should reflect your feelings, so don't worry about right or wrong answers.

Labor unions

Good	___	___	___	___	___	Bad
Democratic	___	___	___	___	___	Undemocratic
Responsible	___	___	___	___	___	Irresponsible
Fair	___	___	___	___	___	Unfair
Strong	___	___	___	___	___	Weak

To arrive at a score for the student, assign values of 5, 4, 3, 2, and 1 as you work from the left, or positive, side to the right, or negative, side of the columns for each set of terms. Then tally a total for each student by adding together the values of the columns that have been checked. Using five sets of possible responses, as in the Labor Unions example, a score of 15 would be a neutral response. Scores over 15 and up to the maximum of 25 would indicate increasingly positive attitudes; scores under 15 down to the minimum of 5 would indicate increasingly negative attitudes. A score of 23 would indicate a more intensively positive attitude than a score of 17.

Projective techniques

The unfinished story The students are given an unfinished story. The story is about a soldier who is brave and ruthless in combat, always eager to attack the enemy. As a result, the soldier is awarded a medal for bravery of which he is very proud. One night he tells the other soldiers in his squad how proud he is and how eager he is to live up to the honor he has won. After the soldier leaves his friends, they discuss what he has said. The portion of the story given to the students does not include what is said in the soldiers' discussion; the students are asked to write an ending to the story in which they tell what they think the soldiers would be saying.

The unfinished story is a technique to provide a stimulus that will encourage a student to respond in an open manner, so that the response will reveal the student's feelings. For example, one student may reveal a strong feeling of patriotism by having the soldiers praise their comrade's bravery. Another student may express his feelings of pacifism by having an ending in which the soldiers criticize their comrade for his ruthlessness.

There are several techniques quite similar to that of the unfinished story.

The projective picture. The projective-picture technique presents the students with a picture. The students write about their reactions to the picture. A picture of a factory may provoke expressions of attitudes about pollution controls, unemployment, taxation, etc. A picture of a policeman arresting a youth might provoke expressions of attitudes about constitutional rights, law and order, etc.

Sentence completion In the technique of sentence completion, students are asked to complete a series of sentences. For example, asking them to complete the sentence, "Working with others in groups makes me __________," might provoke positive responses, such as "happy" or "more effective," or negative responses, such as "nervous" or "angry."

The critical incident In the critical-incident technique students are asked to write a brief description of an incident they have recently witnessed and whether they consider it to be good or bad. This technique could be used in conjunction with almost any issue (i.e., students could be asked to describe a recent example of good government, poor citizenship, effective action).

While projective techniques lack tight structure and do not allow scoring, as do the Likert scale and the semantic differential, they do offer certain advantages. The open structure allows students freedom to state their attitudes in terms of their unique experiences and reactions. Because they feel less obtrusive, students may express their feelings with greater candor.

The need for a variety of techniques

Presented earlier were discussions and examples of a number of evaluation techniques: rating sheets, checklists, anecdotal records, simulations, and individual conferences. All of these can and should be used for assessing attitudes and values. These techniques—along with Likert scales, the semantic differential, the unfinished story, projective pictures, sentence completions, and the critical incident—provide you with a number of assessment techniques. It is important to remember that a single technique cannot comprehensively assess a student's attitude toward an issue. True, each technique generates some information about a student's attitudes, but information gained from a single technique gives only a partial description of how a student feels. The numerical scores gained from the use of a Likert scale or the semantic differential are nothing more than a convenient way to manage information about attitudes. In addition, it should be remembered that students are not always honest when responding to these techniques. Some will seek to mask their true feelings; others will respond according to what they think is wanted. For these reasons it is important to conduct the assessment of attitudes according to these guidelines:

1. Regularly use a variety of assessment techniques.
2. Check for consistency in students' responses. An inconsistent pattern often indicates that the student is not responding candidly.
3. Respect the right of students to believe what they wish.
4. Directions should always emphasize that there are no right or wrong answers.
5. Do not use data gained from the assessment of attitudes and values as a basis for grading.

Pitfalls to avoid

As a means of emphasizing some of the ideas underlying the material on student evaluation that has been presented, several traditional pitfalls are explained in the hope that you will avoid them in your evaluation efforts. Unit testing is a common and unfortunate practice. In too many social studies classrooms, evaluation is reduced to giving a test every four or five weeks with a few quizzes tossed in here and there. This approach encourages cramming for tests, mistrust for the teacher who is responsible for the unexpected quiz, and the belief that students need learn nothing during the course except what is required for the unit test and the quizzes. Evaluation should be a continuous, ongoing, integral phase of the learning process and should make use of a variety of techniques.

When evaluation is limited to unit testing, it is easy for the test itself to become an end for teaching. Symptoms of this pitfall are apparent when the teacher tells the class, "You had better pay attention because this will be on the test," or when one student tells another, "Oh, I can't fail this grading period because I've done so well on the tests so far that I can fail all the rest and still have a passing average." In such situations as these it is clear that teaching and learning as perceived by the student are geared to no higher level than merely "passing the test." Tests should serve as only one of a variety of techniques aimed at gathering information to help judge how well teaching and learning have progressed toward the goals of instruction.

Teaching only for the purpose of having students pass a test is especially distressing when it is accompanied by the pitfall of testing for only recall of knowledge. The notion is widespread, particularly in social studies class rooms, that students should learn to recall a host of names, dates, places, and terms. One prominent textbook for prospective social studies teachers even lists names and dates in American history that are considered essential for all students to learn! To reduce testing to the level of requiring only the recall of names and dates is to ignore a more useful function of testing. Teacher-made tests can and should be constructed so that they will help to determine the student's development of attitudes and of the skills of inquiry as well as the acquisition of knowledge.

Another pitfall is the belief that objective style tests are somehow "more fair" to the student than essay tests. No test is truly objective. The teacher chooses the question type, selects the material to be covered, decides if the students can use notes or not, determines the worth of different questions and sections of the test, and judges if certain knowledge is too obscure to be included in the test. Obviously the test is subjectively constructed, even though it may be objectively graded. Just because a question can be correctly answered by a simple "yes" or "no" doesn't mean the question is a fair question.

Closely related to the preceding pitfall is the belief that commercial standardized tests are somehow better than teacher-made tests. It may be that you want to compare your students with national norms. If so, a commercial standardized test is called for because a teacher-made test cannot yield national norms. Except for this limited use, however, commercial tests have little to offer the classroom teacher. A check of test reviews reveals that standardized social studies tests are usually achievement tests of rather low quality that focus on a narrow range of knowledge and skills. For these reasons, plus the fact that it would be virtually impossible to find a standardized test that would match a particular unit of study in an inquiry class, the value of standardized tests does not warrant the expense of their purchase.

Another pitfall to avoid is the belief that to use a full evaluation approach (including tests, rating sheets, checklists, anecdotal records, conferences, and student self- and peer-evaluation to assess students' knowledge, skills, and attitudes) is to invite parental criticism of being subjective, unfair, and just plain nosey. A clearly explained rationale for the use of a wide variety of evaluation techniques and sound use of those techniques should effectively meet such criticism. Even the most anxious parent will usually agree to a richer concept of evaluation when the rationale and techniques are explained.

In conclusion, you should not forget that at the heart of evaluation is teacher judgment. Your judgment permeates all aspects of your evaluation efforts, and good judgment depends upon having good information. The two most serious difficulties you as a social studies teacher have in obtaining good information are (1) the techniques for gathering information are not precise and (2) you must seek information about such a wide range of concerns. For these reasons, we hope this chapter will help and encourage you to use a variety of techniques as you gather information to make judgments about your students.

Bibliography

Ahmann, J. Stanley, and Glock, Marvin D. *Evaluating Pupil Growth*, 2d Ed. Boston: Allyn & Bacon, 1963.

A classic textbook on evaluation. Many ideas for the social studies teacher.

Banks, James A., with Cleggs, Ambrose A., Jr. *Teaching Strategies for the Social Studies: Inquiry, Valuing and Decision Making*. Reading, Mass.: Addison-Wesley, 1973.

Excellent section on behavioral objectives.

Berg, Harry D., ed. *Evaluation in Social Studies.* Thirty-fifth Yearbook of the National Council for the Social Studies. Washington, D.C.: NCSS, 1965.

An indispensible guide for evaluation in the social studies. Good examples of test items.

Bloom, Benjamin S., ed. *Taxonomy of Educational Objectives: The Classification of Educational Goals, Handbook I. Cognitive Domain.* New York: McKay, 1956.

Detailed instructions and plenty of examples for developing cognitive objectives and test items.

Bloom, Benjamin S.; Hastings, J. Thomas; and Madaus, George F. *Handbook on Formative and Summative Evaluation of Learning*. New York: McGraw-Hill, 1971.

A readable and useful source with a separate chapter devoted to evaluation in secondary social studies.

Buros, Oscar K., ed. *The Seventh Mental Measurements Yearbook.* 2 vols. Highland Park, N.J.: Gryphon Press, 1972.

Contains critical reviews, descriptions and other useful information about standardized tests.

Cartwright, Carol A., and Cartwright, G. Phillip. *Developing Observation Skills*. New York: McGraw-Hill, 1974.

Presents many suggestions and examples for rating sheets, checklists and anecdotal records.

Chase, Clinton I. *Measurement for Educational Evaluation*. Reading, Mass.: Addison-Wesley, 1974.

An easy to read, thorough treatment.

Clark, Leonard H. *Teaching Social Studies in Secondary Schools: A Handbook*. New York: Macmillan, 1973.

Chapter 7 contains practical suggestions for testing and evaluation.

Ebel, Robert L. *Essentials of Educational Measurement.* Englewood Cliffs, N.J.: Prentice-Hall, 1972.

A comprehensive text with many examples.

Fraenkel, Jack R. *Helping Students Think and Value: Strategies for Teaching the Social Studies*. Englewood Cliffs, N.J.: Prentice-Hall, 1973.

Presents excellent treatment of the different purposes of evaluation and numerous examples.

Gronlund, Norman E. *Stating Behavioral Objectives for Classroom Instruction.* New York: Macmillan, 1971.

A lucid treatment of behavioral objectives—a good first step for improving evaluation.

Krathwohl, David R., ed. *Taxonomy of Educational Objectives: The Classification of Educational Goals, Handbook II. Affective Domain.* New York: McKay, 1964.

The best source on assessment of affective objectives.

Lindeman, Richard H. *Educational Measurement*. Keystones of Education Series. Glenview, Ill.: Scott, Foresman, 1967.

A brief but thorough treatment of most aspects of measurement.

Morse, Horace T., and McCune, George H. *Selected Items for the Testing of Study Skills and Critical Thinking*. Revised by Brown, Lester E. and Cook, Ellen. Bulletin No. 15, Fifth Edition. Washington, D.C.: NCSS, 1971.

An outstanding reference with pages of examples.

Popham, W. James. *Educational Evaluation*. Englewood Cliffs, N.J.: Prentice-Hall, 1975.

A thorough and practical guide for important evaluation issues.

Popham, W. James, and Eva T. Baker. *Establishing Instructional Goals*. Englewood Cliffs, N.J.: Prentice-Hall, 1970.

Can be purchased with filmstrip and audiotape from Vimcet Associates, Inc., P.O. Box 24714, Los Angeles, California, 90024.

Sanders, Norris M. *Classroom Questions—What Kinds?* New York: Harper & Row, 1966.

Using Bloom's cognitive taxonomy as a base, Sanders presents examples of questions for various cognitive levels.

Scannell, Dale P., and Tracy, D. B. *Testing and Measurement In The Classroom*. Boston: Houghton Mifflin, 1975.

Presents many practical suggestions and examples.

The quality of inquiry-oriented teaching to a large extent depends upon the students' access to a broad range of appropriate data. Seldom does a standard textbook provide information sufficient for dealing thoroughly with significant problems or issues. As a result, teachers usually find it necessary to provide supplementary materials or to direct their students to appropriate sources. This chapter should prove helpful by identifying a wide variety of resources that are easily accessible and appropriate.

Chapter 8

Resources for social studies teachers

Social studies teachers face the continuing problem of keeping abreast of new materials and ideas in their field. The beginning teacher finds close ties with teacher educators, social scientists, and historians severed once he or she enters the high school classroom. Veteran teachers may find catching up on recent trends difficult and time-consuming, for heavy teaching loads limit their access to new ideas; there is only limited professional discussion with colleagues, and most teachers are fortunate to attend one professional meeting per year.

In many school systems there are supervisors and coordinators who attempt to keep the classroom teacher up to date. There are also divisions in state departments of education to keep teachers up to date through representatives of social studies education bureaus and the creation of curriculum information networks. Colleges and universities sponsor summer workshops and graduate programs. However, even with all of the persons and agencies and their efforts, keeping up to date professionally is a difficult task for individual social studies teachers. The earlier chapters of this book present one means for teachers to develop understandings of current instructional strategies and to select and develop materials and skills to implement these strategies. Another method of staying alive professionally is to keep in touch with various organizations that produce and disseminate materials and information about emerging ideas for social studies teachers. One of the major characteristics of innovative teachers is their extensive use of cosmopolite information sources. An informational network for the teacher might include membership in various professional organizations, subscriptions to journals and newsletters, and mailings of special-interest groups; the exact nature of the network would, of course, depend upon the interests and needs of the individual.

The purpose of this chapter is to identify and explain some of the agencies and organizations that teachers can utilize in keeping up to date and in obtaining materials for improving instruction. The following list of agencies and organizations represents a spectrum of interests; however, it is important to realize that, while this list is extensive, it is by no means exhaustive. Those selected tend to have a long-standing interest in keeping teachers up to date, a commitment to improving social studies education, and a willingness to provide inexpensive materials to classroom teachers. All of the costs, memberships, subscriptions, and fees listed for the various agencies and organizations are subject to change.

Subject area(s)

Sources of free and inexpensive materials

African-American Institute
833 United Nations Plaza
New York, NY 10017

Africa
Area studies

The AAI exists to facilitate and improve teaching about Africa in elementary and secondary schools through its publications, materials collections, and provisions for in-service education and conferences; the School Services Division will provide various types of assistance to local school systems. The purpose: to further African development and to strengthen African-American understanding.

Africa Reports, a bimonthly current events magazine that also includes teaching ideas, is available from the Institute; the subscription cost is $9 per year. The Institute also sponsors the Educators to Africa Association, which provides study seminars in Africa for American educators. It will send many free bibliographies, teaching ideas and materials, and background articles to teachers on its mailing list.

American Association for the Advancement of Slavic Studies
190 West 19th Avenue
Ohio State University
Columbus, OH 43210

Area studies

The Association has recently produced two helpful aids for secondary teachers. One is an audiovisual guide that lists Slavic studies films, filmstrips, and records, and describes rental procedures. The other is a catalog of social studies textbooks, *A Guide to High School Materials for Soviet Studies*, which describes the secondary social studies materials in this area. Both publications are available from the Ohio State office for a nominal charge.

American Civil Liberties Union
22 East 40th Street
New York, NY 10016

Nationally and locally ACLU members participate in the defense of civil liberties; the ACLU also provides a series of related books, pamphlets, and reports like *The Rights of Teachers, The Rights of Students, Cops and Rebels*, "The Case Against the Death Penalty," and a variety of magazine reprints, all of which could be utilized in social studies instruction. Members of the ACLU also receive *Civil Liberties*, the national newspaper. The basic membership fee is $15; however, teachers can obtain many materials without becoming members of the organization.

Law, civics/ government

Political science

Public issues

American Friends of the Middle East, Inc.
1717 Massachusetts Avenue, N.W., Suite 100
Washington, DC 20036

The AFME Information Services exists to provide materials on the Middle East and North Africa for use in social studies classes; maps, booklets, pictures, historical surveys, bibliographies, books, and films are just some of the available materials. In addition to developing materials, the AFME serves as a clearinghouse for materials developed by other publishers and related agencies; the Information Services operates its publication program on a cost basis, so many of its materials are offered at less than suggested prices. *AFME Reports* is a quarterly newsletter reporting on and describing educational materials and opportunities as well as AFME organizational developments. A free sample copy is available upon request; the subscription fee is $2 per year. A free overview of all AFME materials is also available.

Area studies

Middle East

The American Museum of Natural History
79th Street at Central Park West
New York, NY 10024

The Museum's Division of Photography can supply an extensive slide library to classroom teachers. There are many individual photographs of artifacts and ruins, along with scenes of archeological digs. Also available are slide series summarizing many of the recent anthropological and archeological exhibits at the Museum. Catalogs are sent upon request.

Anthropology

American Newspaper Publishers Association Foundation
P.O. Box 17407, Dulles International Airport
Washington, DC 20041

Multi-disciplinary
Newspapers

This industry-sponsored association has developed many publications on educational uses of the newspaper. Teachers can obtain lesson plans and guides to use in integrating newspapers into the traditional objectives of their social studies curriculum; one of these guides is *The Newspaper in the American History Classroom*. For additional information contact the Foundation.

The American Universities Field Staff, Inc.
3 Lebanon Street
Hanover, NH 03755

Area studies
World affairs

The AUFS is a nonprofit membership organization devoted to the enlargement of American understanding of significant developments in foreign countries. American Universities Field Staff publishes the *Fieldstaff Reports*, pamphlets concerned with changing political, economic, and social structures of Asia, Africa, Latin America, and Europe. The pamphlets also provide studies of some of the major international issues of today. *Fieldstaff Portfolios on Population* were created for use in urban and environmental studies and in other contexts. *Fieldstaff Perspectives* is a series of books that attempts to provide an understanding of non-Western cultures. Additional information about AUFS materials and current prices are available upon request.

An individual membership in AUFS is $12 per year; it includes the following: *Common Ground*, a quarterly journal that presents topical analyses and reports on foreign countries; four issues of *Points on Common Ground*, a supplementary newsletter to the journal; and special price reductions for other general AUFS materials.

Antidefamation League of B'nai B'rith
315 Lexington Avenue
New York, NY 10016

Civics/government
Problems of democracy
Public issues

The League is concerned with combating discrimination against minorities and promoting intercultural understanding and cooperation among religious faiths in America. It provides films, pamphlets, and books dealing with prejudice, civil rights, education, human relations, extremism, and totalitarianism. These materials are relatively inexpensive and are appropriate for classroom use. A free publications catalog is available. The League also offers consultant services through its thirty regional offices and its many local chapters.

The Asia Society
112 East 64th Street
New York, NY 10021

Area studies

Asia studies

Non-Western history

The Society, a nonprofit educational organization dedicated to deepening American understanding of Asia and to stimulating intellectual exchange between the two areas, publishes a handsome bimonthly newsletter, *Asia,* which teachers of Asian studies, non-Western history, etc., should find both interesting and helpful. The newsletter provides information about the Society and staff reports of sponsored activities, reviews of books and other materials pertaining to Asia and America, highlights of recent exhibitions of Asian art, and summaries of other related events. The charge for the newsletter is $6 per year. Teachers may also join the Society; there are various membership rates based on one's age, occupation, and proximity to the New York office.

Association on American Indian Affairs
432 Park Avenue South
New York, NY 10016

American history

American Indians

The Association on American Indian Affairs is a national citizen organization supported entirely by members and contributors that assists Indian and Alaskan native communities in their efforts to achieve full economic, social, and civil equality. The Association has developed several bibliographies for secondary teachers and publishes the newsletter, *Indian Affairs;* there is a $3 annual subscription fee. The Association can also provide educational consultant service.

Atlantic Information Centre for Teachers
1616 H Street, N.W.
Washington, DC 20006

Area studies

World affairs

The Atlantic Information Centre is a nonprofit international educational project to encourage the study of world affairs in schools and colleges. It acts as a clearinghouse on methodologies and curricula in world affairs teaching, and facilitates contact between social studies teachers in Europe and the United States through workshops, seminars, and conferences. The Centre publishes *Crisis Paper,* an *ad hoc* series of papers that summarizes world press reactions to international crises. These summaries, prepared by the London-based staff, are airmailed to the United States and arrive within ten days of an international event. At least six issues per year are published; individual subscriptions are $8, and quantity discount rates are available. Other AICT publications include *The World and The School,* a thematic review of international affairs for social studies teachers, published three times per year; *World Survey*, a monthly monograph on a country or subject of international importance; and bibliographies of teaching aids.

Bureau of the Census
Social and Economic Statistic Administration
United States Department of Commerce
Washington, DC 20233

Public issues
Sociology
Urban studies

The Bureau of the Census can provide a variety of material abstracted from the 1970 census for use by social studies teachers and students. The *Census Portrait* series contains data about each of the fifty states from the most recent census. The *We The Americans* series presents census data analyzed topically; the following topics are included in this series: black Americans, housing, women, education, work, the elderly, young marrieds, cities and suburbs, Indians, youth, Asian-Americans, and immigrants. Both of these inexpensive series provide much data to use in inquiry-oriented social studies classrooms. The current Bureau of the Census catalog includes information about costs and how to obtain these and other census-related materials.

Bureau of Indian Affairs
Department of the Interior
Washington, DC 20242

American history
American Indians

The Bureau publishes many types of bibliographies and materials describing Indian life, customs, and crafts; information about Indian museums, pen pals, films, picture collections, music, food, ceremonies, and contemporary Indian problems is available. Although the Bureau cannot supply multiple copies of its publications, these are in the public domain and can be reproduced locally in sufficient quantities for classroom use.

Center for History of the American Indian
The Newberry Library
60 West Walton Street
Chicago, IL 60610

American history
American Indians

The Center was created to further the study of American Indians. While much of the Center's work is related to scholarship in this area, the newsletter, *Meeting Ground*, would be of help to teachers wanting to incorporate new information about American Indians into their social studies classes.

Center for International Programs and Comparative Studies
The State Education Department
99 Washington Avenue
Albany, NY 12210

Anthropology

Area studies

Non-Western cultures

Having a special interest in societies and cultures of Asia, Africa, and Latin America, regions of the world often neglected in American education, the Center has develped several programs to improve the teaching about non-Western cultures in both the social sciences and the humanities. The Center serves as a clearinghouse for teachers in the fields of non-Western area studies, global education, and overseas opportunities. It also develops related bibliographies, and curriculum materials about other societies for use by secondary social studies teachers. *ISIS*, a nine-issue-per-year journal, is available at $20.

Center for War/Peace Studies
218 East 18th Street
New York, NY 10003

Political science

Public issues

The Center, the major program of the New York Friends Group, seeks to promote rational and informed exploration of alternatives for improving the human condition. It works with students, teachers, schools, and related agencies to foster the examination of critical social issues. The Center assists teachers in adapting new curriculum materials and methodologies for classroom use, sponsors several curriculum-development pilot projects, and publishes a number of books and materials related to social studies education. *Intercom*, the Center's quarterly publication for teachers, contains new materials and ideas ready for classroom use; *War/Peace Report*, a bimonthly publication, features substantive articles on global problems. Current and back issues of these two publications are available. *Intercom* is $1 per issue; *War/Peace Report* is $8 per year. Pamphlets describing the overall program of the Center and its affiliates and the free or inexpensive publications are available.

Citizens' Advisory Committee on Environmental Quality
1700 Pennsylvania Avenue, N.W.
Washington, DC 20006

Environment

As part of their major goal of obtaining the participation of a well-informed and energetic citizenry, this citizens' committee of advisers to the President and the Council on Environmental Quality has published several materials pertaining to this national problem. Their materials document the seriousness of environmental problems while also describing actions citizens can undertake, and they report various case studies of citizen environmental action that has been effective. Sample materials and publication lists are available from the Committee; all publications can be obtained from the Superintendent of Documents, U.S. Government Printing Office.

Constitutional Rights Foundation
609 South Grand Avenue, Suite 1012
Los Angeles, CA 90017

Law

Political science

Public issues

The CRF has attempted to involve young people in community affairs through study of and actual participation in the legal system; it has also developed a variety of social studies materials. *The Bill of Rights Newsletter* is published semiannually; each issue focuses on a legal or constitutional topic with appropriate background articles and teaching ideas. The annual subscription fee is $3. Back issues and classroom sets of materials can also be obtained. The CRF also provides a series of low-cost role-playing episodes and simulations pertaining to law-related education. Two books, *The Bill of Rights: A Source Book* and *The Bill of Rights: A Handbook*, offer legal information and teaching techniques to assist teachers in incorporating this subject into their social studies courses.

Consumers Union
256 Washington Street
Mount Vernon, NY 10550

Consumer education

The purposes of the nonprofit, independent Consumers Union are: (1) to provide consumers with information and counsel on consumer goods and services, (2) to give information on all matters relating to the expenditure of family income, and (3) to foster cooperation among groups seeking to create and maintain decent living standards. *Consumer Reports*, a monthly magazine of consumer issues and information, including product ratings and reports, is available for $11 per year. *Teaching Tools for Consumers Reports* provides several lesson plans based on the current issue of *Consumer Reports;* there is no charge for this teaching aid. Reprints of articles that appeared in previous issues can be obtained; the CU will send samples of all of its materials. Special subscription rates for classroom orders of *Consumer Reports* are available.

Educational Research Council of America
Rockefeller Building
Cleveland, OH 44113

Curriculum development

The Educational Research Council, in addition to sponsoring curriculum development projects, publishes a social science newsletter for secondary teachers, *You, Too.* This newsletter, published monthly during the school year, contains ideas and suggestions for teaching secondary social studies along with a topical article and related teaching strategies. The annual subscription fee is $5.

Education Development Center, Inc.
55 Chapel Street
Newton, MA 02160

Curriculum development

The EDC, a publicly supported nonprofit corporation engaged in educational research and development, has developed *Man: A Course of Study*, and has incorporated a variety of additional curriculum development and dissemination activities into its ongoing efforts for educational improvement in social studies and other curricular areas. The general newsletter, *EDC News*, describes the wide-ranging activities of the Center, surveys current efforts in social studies curriculum development, and contains descriptions of professional opportunities for teachers. In addition to the general newsletter, individual EDC projects like *Exploring Human Nature* publish separate newsletters. The Center will provide further information about these two newsletters as well as all of its other activities.

Educators' Guide to Free Social Studies Materials
Educators' Progress Service
Randolph, WI 53956

Multi-disciplinary

This annual publication lists and describes an extensive amount of free instructional materials for social studies teachers; the necessary ordering information for all of the audio and print resources is included. The cost of this guide is currently $10.50.

ERIC Clearinghouse for Social Studies/Social Science Education
855 Broadway
Boulder, CO 80302

Multi-disciplinary

ERIC ChESS is a federally supported information clearinghouse for identifying, creating, and disseminating social studies education resources. Those materials identified by the clearinghouse are added to the national ERIC system and stored on microfiche; ERIC microfiche collections are available in the libraries of most larger colleges and universities. *Resources in Education* (RIE) is the annotated index to all of these materials. The center publishes a periodic newsletter, *Keeping Up*, which describes new resources added to the ERIC system and professional developments in social studies; also available is a topical newsletter, *Looking At . . .*, which is devoted to specific topics and ERIC resources—future studies, women, international education. These two newsletters are presently included as separate sections in the newsletter from the Social Science Education Consortium. The social studies clearinghouse staff writes regular columns for *Social Education* and *People Watching*, as well as occasional columns for other journals. ERIC ChESS also publishes a variety of social studies materials in conjunction with other related agencies. A description of ERIC ChESS, a guide to using the ERIC system, and a catalog of materials and prices are available upon request.

Facts on File
119 East 57th Street
New York, NY 10019

Multi-disciplinary

Public issues

This news reference service provides an extensive amount of indexed news and editorials from the nation's press. Facts on File publishes a weekly *News Digest*, summarizing national and international events, and *Editorials on File*, appearing twice monthly, which contains editorials from over 140 North American newspapers. Also available are several annual current events reference books. A sample packet of Facts on File materials and information about subscription procedures and publications prices are available from the New York office.

The Foreign Policy Association
345 East 46th Street
New York, NY 10017

Political science

Problems of democracy

Public issues

A private, nonpartisan organization, the Foreign Policy Association seeks to create informed, thoughtful, and articulate public opinion on major foreign policy issues through publications and cooperative programs with many other national and local world affairs organizations. The FPA publishes a number of materials appropriate for secondary social studies. *The Headline Series*, five issues per year, provides timely analyses of major foreign policy issues by foreign policy experts; back issues are available. *The Great Decisions* booket, published each January, contains impartial discussion materials on major foreign policy issues. *New Dimensions*, a series of books, presents a variety of methods for teachers to use in enriching their teaching about world affairs, such as simulations, interpreting the newspaper in the classroom, and teaching about war and war prevention. Information about these and other publications and about prices will be supplied upon request.

Institute for World Order
1140 Avenue of the Americas
New York, NY 10036

Problems of democracy

Public issues

The Institute for World Order—formerly the World Law Fund—is a pioneer organization in peace and world order studies; it supports a wide range of activities designed to lead toward the development of a just and peaceful world order. This publicly supported organization reaches secondary social studies teachers through its school program, books, pamphlets, reprints, audiovisual materials, and games and simulations designed to foster understanding and analysis of world affairs. National and regional teacher training workshops are developed in cooperation with interested educational institutions. *Progress Report* covers recent developments within the IWO and related areas; *Ways and Means of Teaching about World Order* features ready-to-use classroom materials for the social studies classroom. These two newsletters are free to persons on the Institute's mailing list. Additional information about the remainder of the IWO's resources is available.

InterCulture Associates
Box 22
Thompson, CT 06277

Anthropology

InterCulture Associates publishes a free newsletter, *InterCulture News*, during the school year. The focus of this free newsletter is on the materials developed by InterCulture Associates, but there are also articles about, and teaching strategies for, intercultural and international education, plus articles of general educational interest and bibliographies.

Joint Council on Economic Education
1212 Avenue of the Americas
New York, NY 10036

Economics

The JCEE is an independent, nonprofit, nonpartisan, educational organization that seeks to encourage, improve, coordinate, and service the economic education movement. The Joint Council does its vital work for economic education in seven principal areas: affiliated councils, college economic centers, teacher training programs, college and university programs, curriculum development, teacher-pupil materials, and career preparation; it also serves as a clearinghouse. The JCEE publishes periodic checklists, annotated bibliographies of economic education curriculum materials, evaluation guides, the *Journal of Economic Education*, and *Progress in Economic Education*, a newsletter for elementary and secondary social studies teachers. The newsletter is free to those persons on the Joint Council mailing list. A sample of other JCEE materials and price information is available upon request.

The Latin American Service
304 Colorado Building
Washington, DC 20005

Area studies

Latin America

The Latin American Service is exclusively devoted to reporting trends and events in Latin America by summarizing news stories from the area, providing access to Latin American books, magazines, and newspapers, and serving as a clearinghouse for other related Latin American materials and information. A weekly publication, *The Times of the Americas*, a national newspaper about all of Latin America, is available for $8 per year.

League of Women Voters of the United States
1730 M Street, N.W.
Washington, DC 20036

Political science

Problems of democracy

Public issues

Through a variety of programs, the League seeks to increase informed citizen participation in all levels of government. Many of its inexpensive publications could be used by social studies teachers and students. Current pamphlet topics include: environmental quality, land use, human resources, international relations, representative government, and effective citizen participation in government. For $10.00 a year one can obtain a copy of all new League publications; for $7.50 each, one can obtain *Time for Action* and *Report from the Hill*, two publications for keeping up on current legislation and the League's positions; for $2.00, one can obtain the newsletter, *The National Voter*, which features short articles about selected national issues. In addition to the national headquarters, city chapters throughout the country can also provide materials for the social studies classroom.

Lincoln Filene Center
Tufts University
Medford, MA 02155

Multi-disciplinary

The Lincoln Filene Center has produced an extensive amount of student and teacher materials for secondary social studies; citizenship, policy making, urban problems, economics, American history, law, and international relations are just some of the topics for which they have created materials. The Center also produces current affairs materials for *Newsweek* and for other commercial publishers; they can provide intergroup relations materials and training sessions.

Most of the materials are inexpensive, particularly those available directly from the Center; information about the costs of all materials can be obtained by writing.

<u>Media Mix</u>
Clarentian Publications
221 West Madison Street
Chicago, IL 60602

Media

Media Mix is an eight-issues-per-year newsletter that contains ideas and resources on media and communication; the editor is Jeffrey Schrank. In each issue, films, books, radio, records, television, and periodicals are briefly surveyed and reviewed; ideas for organizing a teaching unit about a selected media topic or problem are also included. Many of the suggestions and materials could be used in values clarification lessons. The annual subscription rate for this newsletter, packed with interesting teaching ideas and aids, is $7.

The Middle East Institute
1761 N Street, N.W.
Washington, DC 20036

Area studies

Middle East

The Institute attempts to promote a better understanding between the peoples of the Middle East and the United States; each year it sponsors conferences, seminars, study groups, exhibits, and a limited publications program. An Information Service answers queries from Institute members and the general public; the Film Library lends its growing collection of films on the contemporary Middle East to teachers, at quite modest rentals. The Institute also serves as a clearinghouse for Middle East information and materials. The annual membership fee, $13, includes the *Middle East Journal* and *Middle East Monitor*, a bimonthly newsletter.

The National Archives and Records Service
General Services Administration
Washington, DC 20408

American history

The National Archives, the national storehouse of historical documents, is probably best known for its exhibition area, where the Declaration of Independence, Constitution, and Bill of Rights are on display for tourists, and for its maintenance of presidential libraries. However, the National Archives has also preserved thousands of other historical documents, prints, photographs, and films; printed facsimiles of many of the most important documents are available at a nominal cost. Some archival materials have been collected into thematic packets of primary source materials for use in the study of American history. Brochures containing complete descriptions of currently available materials and prices are available.

National Assessment for Educational Progress
700 Lincoln Tower
1860 Lincoln
Denver, CO 80203

Multi-disciplinary

The NAEP, a project sponsored by the Education Commission of the States, has developed procedures to measure levels of educational attainment in 10 curriculum areas among various age groups in American society; social studies and citizenship are two of these curriculum areas. The project, working with professional educators and community representatives, has developed goals, objectives, and test items in these areas and has administered them to samples of the nine-year-old, thirteen-year-old, seventeen-year-old, and adult populations. Periodic reports of the NAEP assessment of student and adult performance are available. Copies of the social studies and citizenship goals and objectives and samples of the test items can also be obtained. General information is contained in the free *NAEP Newsletter.*

National Association for the Advancement of Colored People
1790 Broadway
New York, NY 10019

Civics/government

Law

Problems of democracy

Public issues

For six decades the NAACP has fought racial bias through national and state legislation and litigation; newer civil rights programs have centered on providing community services. The NAACP, as a part of its overall program to eliminate racial bias, has published a series of pamphlets and reprints that describe current civil rights programs, historical developments in the civil rights struggle, and civil rights leaders. The official organ, *The Crisis*, is available at $3.50 per year; the $6.00 membership fee includes a year's subscription.

National Center for Law-Focused Education
Law in American Society Foundation
33 North LaSalle Street, Suite 1700
Chicago, IL 60602

Law

Political science

The LASF is a leadership training and curriculum development center for law-related education. The Foundation's goals are to work toward adequately informing American youth about the role and function of law in America and to check the increased alienation of youth toward the American system of constitutional government.

The Foundation sponsors teacher education and curriculum development projects, facilitates information dissemination, and attempts to assess the impact of law-related educational projects. Interdisciplinary teacher training institutes are conducted in Chicago each summer and throughout the year at several major universities. The *Teacher Education Handbook* series provides a summary of the staff development activities of the Foundation. A resource center has been established in Chicago to further the dissemination of law-related materials, films, games, and articles. The Center publishes *Law in American Society*, a quarterly journal devoted to law-focused education; it contains articles on substantive legal issues and teaching ideas. There is no charge for this publication.

National Committee on United States–China Relations
777 United Nations Plaza, 9B
New York, NY 10017

Area studies

China

Since its creation in 1966, the National Committee, believing that increased public knowledge and discussion of China are essential to the effective conduct of American foreign policy, has conducted an extensive information and education program to encourage public interest in, and understanding of, China and its relations with the United States. The Committee sponsors conferences, workshops, and symposia on current themes in Sino-American relations; an extensive roster of specialists is available through a speakers bureau. Typical school service programs include films, materials, evaluation assistance, and in-service programs for teachers. Curriculum guides, resource units, background materials, and audio tapes are currently available. Particularly valuable is *China: A Resource and Curriculum Guide,* a comprehensive annotated bibliography of materials available to educators interested in china. *Notes from the National Committee*, a quarterly newsletter containing information about United States-China relations and National Committee activities and new materials on China is also available. A voluntary contribution of $2 is requested to cover the cost of the newsletter.

National Organization for Women
5 South Wabash, Suite 1615
Chicago, IL 60603

Problems of democracy

Public issues

Women's studies

The NOW Committee to Promote Women's Studies publishes *The News Sheet*, an occasional newsletter that contains an extensive amount of materials and ideas for incorporating women into the social studies curriculum and for dealing with sexism wherever it exists in the school. Briefly annotated bibliographies of trade and text books, descriptions of various women's studies programs, curriculum materials, information about journals and magazines, and general information about the women's movement are also included in this free newsletter.

National Wildlife Federation
1412 Sixteenth Street, N.W.
Washington, DC 20036

Environment

The National Wildlife Federation is a private educational organization that seeks to stimulate proper public attitude and appreciation regarding the wise use and management of all natural resources. The Federation will provide a variety of teacher and student materials for use in environmental education; a sampler of these materials is free upon request. Nominal charges are made on quantity orders. Federation membership dues, including a subscription to the magazine *Wildlife*, are $6.50 per year.

Organization of American States
Nineteenth and Constitution Avenue, N.W.
Washington, DC 20006

Area studies
Latin America

The Department of Publications and Conferences of the OAS publishes an extensive amount of informational and technical materials covering various phases of activities in the American nations, their backgrounds and achievements, and the official records of the OAS and its various agencies. All materials and costs are described in the current catalog of publications.

Overseas Development Council
1717 Massachusetts Avenue, N.W. #501
Washington, DC 20036

Area studies
World affairs

The ODC is an independent nonprofit organization seeking to increase American understanding of the problems faced by developing countries and the importance of those countries to the United States. The Council publishes materials for use by scholars and the general public. Two publications series that are appropriate for secondary social studies are the *Development Paper Series*, pamphlets describing major current development issues, and the *Communique Series*, short articles summarizing important issues in the development field. Both series are inexpensive; for $12 teachers can obtain all ODC publications during the membership year. Another valuable publication especially for teachers is *Focusing on Global Poverty and Development: A Resource Book for Teachers*, a 630-page compendium of background essays, teaching strategies, and student resources for integrating global development studies into existing social studies programs. The cost of this teacher resource is $12; it is not included in the yearly publications fee described above.

The Population Institute
110 Maryland Avenue, N.E.
Washington, DC 20002

Environment

Problems of democracy

Public issues

The Population Institute serves as a clearinghouse for materials on population education. It can provide bibliographies of commercially available teacher and student resources, descriptions of materials obtainable from other population education interest groups, pictures, and posters, and the *Population Activist's Handbook*, an action-oriented workbook describing strategies for those who seek to change American attitudes toward population growth. One section of the *Handbook* describes ways for secondary students to promote population policy discussions in the schools. The Institute will provide descriptions of other specific materials and services.

Public Affairs Committee
381 Park Avenue South
New York, NY 10016

Multi-disciplinary

Public issues

The Public Affairs Committee was founded to create new methods for educating Americans on current social and economic problems; the *Public Affairs Pamphlets* were the results of this action. These timely, concise, inexpensive booklets cover such areas as social and economic issues, family life, health and science, race relations, and consumerism. Approximately 200 titles are now in print (selected pamphlets are available in Spanish); about 15 new titles are published each year. For a fee of $4.50 per year, a teacher can receive a copy of all new pamphlets. Descriptions of special packets of related pamphlets, descriptions of films and filmstrips, and information about how to obtain back issues, the complete pamphlet library, and discounts for quantity orders are in the current free catalog.

Public Education Religion Studies Center
Wright State University
Dayton, OH 45431

Religion

The purpose of PERSC is to encourage and facilitate increased and improved teaching about religion within constitutional bounds in elementary and secondary public schools. The natural inclusion of study about religion within regular curricular offerings is emphasized. The goal is a lucid understanding of religion and the relation of religion to mankind's history. The Center provides for staff development, serves as a curriculum materials resource center and clearinghouse, sponsors research, provides consultants to interested groups, and publishes a quarterly newsletter. The PERSC will provide a substantial packet of sample curriculum materials, relevant pamphlets, bibliographies, and reprints to interested teachers at no charge.

Resources for the Future, Inc.
1755 Massachusetts Avenue, N.W.
Washington, DC 20036

Environment

Resources for the Future is a nonprofit organization dedicated to the development, conservation, and use of natural resources and improvement of the quality of the environment. It publishes materials covering the following areas: natural resources and economic development, environmental studies, water resources, marine resources, land use, energy and nonfuel minerals, urban and regional studies, and Latin American studies. Also published is a free, three-times-a-year newsletter, *Resources*, containing articles related to the concerns listed.

The Robert A. Taft Institute of Government
420 Lexington Avenue
New York, NY 10017

Civics/ government

Political science

The Taft Institute is a national nonpartisan organization seeking to stimulate an understanding of the processes and problems of American government, to inspire more active citizen participation in government at all levels, and to advance the study of political science. The Institute sponsors a series of annual nationwide summer workshops to help teachers acquire academic training in political science and realistic experiences in practical politics. In these workshops political scientists and politicians share their experiences and insights with classroom teachers. The Institute will send information about the location of upcoming institutes and application procedures.

SANE
318 Massachusetts Avenue, N.E.
Washington, DC 20002

Problems of democracy

Public issues

SANE, a citizens' organization for a sane world, seeks to create informed public opinion about the dangers of the military industrial state and to bring pressure on elected representatives to reorder national priorities. The organization can provide inexpensive materials about military spending, arms control and disarmament, American foreign policy, chemical and biological warfare, and changing attitudes toward war and peace. Also available are social action kits that describe ways for interested citizens to help the organization reach its goals. *SANE World*, a monthly newsletter, is available for $3 per year.

Service Center for Teachers of Asian Studies
Ohio State University
29 West Woodruff Avenue
Columbus, OH 43210

Asia

The Service Center, part of the Committee on Secondary Education of the Association for Asian Studies, publishes a periodic newsletter, *Focus*, which features a variety of articles, bibliographies of materials for teachers and students, descriptions of professional growth opportunities for teachers, and lists of resources for teachers of Asian studies, non-Western cultures, world history, etc. The yearly subscription fee for the newsletter is $2.

Social Science Education Consortium
855 Broadway
Boulder, CO 80302

Multidisciplinary

The Consortium, a group of educators and social scientists concerned about the improvement of social education, carries on a comprehensive program. Included in its activities are national and regional conferences, workshops and training sessions, and an extensive publications program. The Consortium's newsletter, *Newsletter*, contains descriptions of current activities of the SSEC and of professional developments and opportunities in social studies education, topical articles by Consortium members and other social science educators, and descriptions of new curriculum developments. The newsletter is free.

The SSEC also publishes the *Data Book*, an annually updated analytical guide to over 200 different social studies curriculum materials, and several other guides to various kinds of instructional resources for social studies education. The Consortium has also published materials about political science education, values education, teaching concepts, environmental education, and educational change. *Profiles of Promise*, containing newsy, brief descriptions of innovative social studies teaching practices, is available on a subscription basis. A current publications catalog describing all SSEC materials and prices is available.

Social Studies Development Center
Indiana University
513 North Park
Bloomington, IN 47401

Curriculum development

The SSDC, initially organized to develop *American Political Behavior*, continues to research, develop, and disseminate new resources and techniques for improving social studies education. A high school political science course and a global studies program for the middle grades are being developed. The Center can provide consultants and workshop programs through the Coordinator for School Social Studies, as well as social studies resources from its extensive collection of research reports, curriculum materials, and professional journals. Samples of curriculum materials under development can be obtained, usually at no cost. *News and Notes on the Social Sciences*, a free newsletter, is published three times per year.

Teachers Guides to Television
Post Office Box 564
Lenox Hill Station
New York, NY 10021

Media

Each issue of *Teachers Guides to Television* contains previews of selected television programs of educational value, along with a series of teaching suggestions and bibliographies of related books and films. All of these materials facilitate the use of television to enrich social studies teaching. There is also a topical article in each issue; recent examples are, "The Intelligent Parents' and Teachers' Guide to TV," "Watching Television with Your Child," and "Teaching Values: To Preserve, Protect and Defend." In addition, there is a complete listing of all upcoming television programs of educational value and bulletin-board materials. The *Guides* are published in October and February; the prepaid subscription rate is $3.25 per year.

United Nations Association of the United States of America
345 East 46th Street
New York, NY 10017

Area studies

Public issues

The UNA-USA is an independent, nonprofit, nonpartisan organization working through 175 chapters and 150 affiliated organizations for a more effective United Nations. The Association can provide inexpensive materials describing current UN activities, background materials for students, portfolios of teaching materials and ideas, visual aids, and UN Day kits. The *Inter Dependent*, UNA's monthly tabloid covering international issues and related developments in Washington, costs $3 per year for eleven issues. Each issue contains background articles, summaries of current developments, and teaching suggestions. The Association will provide a sampler of materials upon request and information about membership fees.

United States Committee for UNICEF
331 East 38th Street
New York, NY 10016

Area studies

Multi-disciplinary

As a nongovernmental, nonprofit organization, the Committee works to inform Americans about the needs of the world's children and to seek private financial support for UNICEF's programs. The Committee also produces inexpensive educational materials for schools, including display materials; slides, films, and filmstrips; books and records; teacher resource kits; and various bibliographies of materials for teaching intercultural understanding. Samples of some of these materials, which are described in the Committee's annual catalog, are available at no charge. *UNICEF News* is a quarterly magazine featuring articles related to UNICEF's worldwide programs for children; a four-issue-per-year subscription is $3.50. There are also local UNICEF committees in many of the larger cities throughout the nation.

Youth Education for Citizenship
American Bar Association
1155 East 60th Street
Chicago, IL 60637

Civics/government

Law

Political science

Sponsored by the Bar Association, YEFC seeks to stimulate the creation of law-related citizenship education programs in schools throughout the United States by providing consulting services to schools, coordinating the efforts of existing law education programs, serving as a clearinghouse, and supporting research and development through its full-time staff of lawyers and educators. The following materials are currently available from the organization: *Directory of Law-Related Educational Activities, Bibliography of Law-Related Curriculum Materials, Reflections on Law-Related Education,* and *Help: What to Do, Where to Go?* There is no charge for single copies of these materials, and additional materials and guides are being developed.

Zero Population Growth, Inc.
4080 Fabian Way
Palo Alto, CA 94303

Environment
Public issues

Zero Population Growth (ZPG) is a national organization seeking to stabilize population growth in the United States; it holds that such stabilization is a vital step in creating a quality life in a quality environment for all. It seeks to achieve public awareness and understanding of population issues through both the formal and nonformal sectors of American education. It has developed many types of bibliographies on the population growth issues: audiovisual materials, population-related organizations, secondary school resources, birth control, and curriculum materials; posters, pamphlets, and teaching units are also available. Membership dues in the organization include a subscription to *ZPG National Reporter*, an action newsletter, and *Equilibrium*, a quarterly journal; teachers can also subscribe to either publication without joining the organization. A packet of sample materials is available upon request.

Professional organizations

American Economic Association
1313 Twenty-First Avenue South
Nashville, TN 37212

The AEA publishes two quarterly journals, *American Economic Review* and *Journal of Economic Literature*. These journals, plus related books, guides, and other publications, may be of interest to economics teachers. Annual membership dues are $23; however, any of the publications may be obtained separately by nonmembers.

American Historical Association
400 A Street, S.E.
Washington, DC 20003

The AHA, the professional organization of American historians, provides a number of materials for improving precollegiate instruction in American history. The *AHA Pamphlet* series of concise, narrative, critical essays on selected areas of United States, European, and Asian history is an excellent aid for secondary teachers in keeping up to date on new historical interpretations. *Discussions on Teaching,* another pamphlet service, covers questions of interpretation, methods, and approaches suitable for the secondary classroom. The Association can also provide back issues of the *Service Center for Teachers of History* pamphlets. The price per pamphlet is $1. A complete list of pamphlets will be sent upon request.

American Political Science Association
1527 New Hampshire Avenue, N.W.
Washington, DC 20036

The Division of Educational Affairs of the APSA, the professional organization of political scientists, publishes *DEA News*, a periodic newsletter that is available free of charge upon request. Each issue contains information about the teaching of political science at both the precollegiate and collegiate levels, evaluations of existing curriculum materials, descriptions of the activities of current curriculum development projects, discussions of the effectiveness of particular teaching strategies, and descriptions of opportunities for professional growth. The APSA's Committee on Pre-Collegiate Education and the Political Science Education project has published a directory of educational resources that describes current curriculum development projects, publications, and other related activities for the improvement of political science teaching at the high school level.

American Psychological Association
1200 Seventeenth Street, N.W.
Washington, DC 20036

The APA's Clearinghouse on Precollege Psychology and Behavioral Science publishes a free newsletter, *Periodically*, from September through May. The newsletter is part of the Clearinghouse's efforts to gather and disseminate information on the teaching of high-school-level psychology and elementary-level behavioral science. Each issue of *Periodically* contains brief reviews of related textbook and supplementary materials, information about professional opportunities for teachers, professional developments, and a lesson plan ready for classroom use. Also available is *The Psychology Teacher's Resource Book*, a relatively inexpensive guidebook for teachers. Affiliate membership in the APA division on the teaching of psychology is open to interested secondary teachers; affiliate dues are $2 per year. This membership status will allow teachers to obtain APA materials at discount prices and the *APA Monitor,* a general newsletter.

American Sociological Association
1722 N Street, N.W.
Washington, DC 20036

Seeking to improve instruction and research in sociology, the ASA publishes several journals, including the bimonthly *American Sociological Review*, $15 per year, and *Footnotes*, a newsletter, $10 per year. A brochure describing all publications is available on request. Most publications are sent to ASA members. Membership dues are based on income.

Association for Supervision and Curriculum Development
1701 K Street, N.W.
Washington, DC 20006

While ASCD directs its activities and publications to all areas of curriculum development and supervision, it can be a resource for social studies in particular. Books and pamphlets describing new trends in social studies are available, in addition to yearbooks; special issues of *Educational Leadership*, the Association's journal; and audio cassettes dealing with more general curriculum and supervision trends. Subscription price of the journal is $8 a year; a comprehensive membership is $30 a year; individual books, pamphlets, and cassettes have various prices. The most recent catalog describes these materials and includes prices and ordering information.

Association of American Geographers
1710 Sixteenth Street, N.W.
Washington, DC 20009

The AAG, the sponsor of the High School Geography Project, provides several services and publications for improving the study and teaching of geography. Consultant services and research reviews can be provided. The Association sponsors the typical roster of professional literature: *AAG Newsletter*, and two journals, *Annals* and *The Professional Geographer*, plus books, guides, and miscellaneous publications. Regular membership dues are $25 per year; however, other types of memberships can be obtained.

Council of Anthropology and Education
American Anthropological Association
1703 New Hampshire Avenue, N.W.
Washington, DC 20009

Through membership in the Council, classroom teachers can keep in touch with what anthropologists are doing and become part of a network of persons interested in both anthropology and education. Members receive the *CAE Quarterly*, a journal of papers and articles, plus bibliographies, course descriptions, and professional announcements. Yearly CAE membership is $7.50.

National Council for Geographic Education
115 North Marion Street
Oak Park, IL 60301

One of the main goals of the National Council for Geographic Education is to provide materials and guidelines for geography, social studies, earth science, conservation, and environmental education to teachers in the elementary and secondary schools. The Council provides a list of publications, which focus on research and curriculum development, evaluation, teaching techniques, and teacher reference materials in geographic education. Sets of color slides selected from the collections of widely-traveled geographers are also available. The *Instructional Activities Series* has been developed to meet two identified needs: (1) the need for teachers to obtain resource materials at low cost, (2) the need for materials relevant to real classroom situations. The activities, which are divided into elementary and secondary sections, include the following topics: city planning, urban problems, the environment, population, and conflict resolution. There is a $.50 charge for each of the activities.

Perspectives is the newsletter published by NCGE to keep teachers informed about professional activities and to provide information about public and private programs related to geographic education. The *Journal of Geography* contains articles on geography and the teaching of geography. The NCGE also publishes a topical national yearbook. The cost of regular membership ranges from $12 to $16, depending upon the applicant's salary level.

National Council for the Social Studies
1201 Sixteenth Street, N.W.
Washington, DC 20036

The NCSS is the primary professional organization of social studies educators at every level of education. The Council sponsors an annual national convention and several regional conferences. There are also state and local affiliates of the national organization. In addition to yearly meetings, the Council sponsors a multi-purpose publications program. *Social Education*, the official journal of the NCSS, published seven times per year, contains information, commentary, and innovative viewpoints in social studies education. Many of the articles in the journal are focused on certain topical issues. Recent topical issues have included moral development, consumerism, social studies in alternative schools, teaching about the American Revolution, and career education. Back issues of the journal are available. *The Social Studies Professional*, a periodic newsletter, usually contains information about social studies curriculum resources, professional opportunities, and activities of the NCSS. In the Council's annual yearbook, noted social studies educators deal with significant areas of concern. Each volume usually contains both theoretical treatments of the topic and classroom applications. Recent yearbooks have been: *Teaching American History, Teaching Ethnic Studies, Teaching about Life in the City, Values Education*, and *Focus on Geography*. Back issues of each yearbook are available.

The three resources described above are available to regular members of the NCSS; a regular membership is currently $15 per year. In addition to the journal, newsletter, and yearbook, the Council also publishes topical bulletins, a how-to-do-it series that describes various teaching procedures, and other materials of interest to social studies educators. Copies of all publications issued during the membership year are sent to those who hold a comprehensive membership, $25 per year.

National Education Association
1201 Sixteenth Street, N.W.
Washington, DC 20036

Print and media materials pertaining to law enforcement and juvenile justice, sex-role stereotyping, and human relations are just some of the NEA materials that might be appropriate for the social studies classroom; other curriculum materials are available. Both members and nonmembers can obtain any of the NEA materials; however, members are entitled to special price discounts. The annual catalog, published by the Publications Sales Section, describes currently available publications of the NEA and affiliated organizations.

The Society for History Education
California State University, Long Beach
Long Beach, CA 90840

The Society is the only professional organization devoted solely to the improvement of the teaching of history in the secondary school and university classroom. Its publication, *The History Teacher*, serves to keep teachers abreast of new techniques and innovative programs in both secondary schools and colleges. Textbooks, readers, and media materials are evaluated in each issue of the quarterly journal; also appearing in each issue are summaries of trends in historical scholarship. The Society also produces and distributes audiovisual materials, maintains a reprint file, and sponsors national and regional history education workshops. The annual membership fee is $8.

United Federation of Teachers
260 Park Avenue South
New York, NY 10010

The UFT publishes study guides that would be helpful to high school social studies teachers; among these are a series of curriculum outlines of the history of various ethnic groups. Certain issues of *New York Teacher* magazine contain resource units for use in the social studies classroom. Brochures describing these and other social studies materials will be sent upon request.

Magazines and journals

	American Heritage
Subject area(s):	American history
Contents:	Articles, illustrations, book reviews
Publication schedule:	6 issues per year
Subscription rate:	$24
Publisher:	American Heritage Subscription Office 383 West Center Street Marion, OH 43302

	Atlas World Press Review
Subject area(s):	Public issues, world history
Contents:	Articles, cartoons, and editorials, translated from the world press
Publication schedule:	Monthly
Subscription rate:	$14
Publisher:	World Press Company 230 Park Avenue New York, NY 10017

	High School Behavioral Science
Subject area(s):	Anthropology, psychology, sociology
Contents:	Articles, course descriptions, teaching materials and methods, book and media reviews
Publication schedule:	2 issues per year
Subscription rate:	$6
Publisher:	Human Science Press Periodicals 72 Fifth Avenue New York, NY 10011

Current

Subject area(s):	American history, political science, public issues, world history
Contents:	Background articles on current affairs
Publication schedule:	10 issues per year
Subscription rate:	$15
Publisher:	Heldref Publications 4000 Albemarle Street, N.W. Washington, DC 20016

Current History

Subject area(s):	Area studies, world history
Contents:	Background articles on current affairs
Publication schedule:	11 issues per year
Subscription rate:	$13.50
Publisher:	Current History, Inc. Box 4647 4225 Main Street Philadelphia, PA 19127

Focus

Subject area(s):	Geography
Contents:	Background articles on world geography
Publication schedule:	6 issues per year
Subscription rate:	$7
Publisher:	The American Geographical Society Broadway at 156th Street New York, NY 10032

The History and Social Science Teacher

Subject area(s): World history, social science

Contents: Articles, teaching materials and methods, reviews of books and media

Publication schedule: 4 issues per year

Subscription rate: $8

Publisher: The Ontario History and Social Science Teachers' Association
469 Briar Hill Road
Toronto, Ontario M5N 1M8

The History Teacher

Subject area(s): American history

Contents: Articles, teaching materials and methods, books and media reviews

Publication schedule: 4 issues per year

Subscription rate: $8

Publisher: Department of History
California State University, Long Beach
6101 East Seventh Street
Long Beach, CA 90840

Human Behavior

Subject area(s): Social sciences

Contents: Articles, research reports, book and media reviews

Publication schedule: Monthly

Subscription rate: $14 per year

Publisher: Human Behavior, Subscription Department
P.O. Box 2810
Boulder, CO 80302

Journal of Economic Education

Subject area(s):	Economics
Contents:	Articles, teaching materials and methods, book and media reviews
Publication schedule:	2 issues per year
Subscription rate:	$4
Publisher:	Joint Council on Economic Education 1212 Avenue of the Americas New York, NY 10036

Mankind

Subject area(s):	World history
Contents:	Articles, illustrations
Publication schedule:	6 issues per year
Subscription rate:	$6
Publisher:	Raymond F. Locke 8060 Melrose Avenue Los Angeles, CA 90046

Media & Methods

Subject area(s):	All areas
Contents:	Articles, teaching materials and methods, extensive media reviews
Publication schedule:	9 issues per year
Subscription rate:	$9
Publisher:	Media & Methods North American Building 401 North Broad Street Philadelphia, PA 19108

People Watching

Subject area(s):	Psychology, sociology
Contents:	Articles, teaching materials and methods, book and media reviews
Publication schedule:	2 issues per year
Subscription rate:	$5
Publisher:	Behavioral Publications, Inc. 72 Fifth Avenue New York, NY 10011

Psychology Today

Subject area(s):	Psychology, sociology
Contents:	Articles, research reports, book and media reviews
Publication schedule:	Monthly
Subscription rate:	$12
Publisher:	Psychology Today P.O. Box 2990 Boulder, CO 80302

Simulation/Gaming

Subject area(s):	All areas
Contents:	Articles, teaching materials and methods, simulation reviews, professional activities
Publication schedule:	6 issues per year
Subscription rate:	$6
Publisher:	Simulation/Gaming Box 3039, University Moscow, ID 83843

Skeptic

Subject area(s):	Public issues
Contents:	Articles plus teacher's guide
Publication schedule:	6 issues per year
Subscription rate:	$6
Publisher:	Forum for Contemporary History, Inc. 812 Anacapa Street Santa Barbara, CA 93101

Social Education

Subject area(s):	All areas
Contents:	Articles, teaching materials and methods, book and media reviews, professional activities
Publication schedule:	7 issues per year
Subscription rate:	$15
Publisher:	National Council for the Social Studies 1515 Wilson Boulevard Arlington, VA 22209

Social Policy

Subject area(s):	Social issues
Contents:	Topical articles, book and media reviews
Publication schedule:	5 issues per year
Subscription rate:	$10
Publisher:	Social Policy Suite 500 184 Fifth Avenue New York, NY 10010

The Social Studies

Subject area(s):	All areas
Contents:	Articles, teaching materials and methods, book and media reviews
Publication schedule:	6 issues per year
Subscription rate:	$9
Publisher:	Heldref Publications 4000 Albemarle Street, N.W. Washington, DC 20016

Society

Subject area(s):	Sociology
Contents:	Articles, research reports, book and media reviews
Publication schedule:	10 issues per year
Subscription rate:	$9.75
Publisher:	Society Box A Rutgers—The State University New Brunswick, NJ 08903

Teaching Political Science

Subject area(s):	Political science
Contents:	Articles, course descriptions, teaching materials and methods, book and media reviews
Publication schedule:	2 issues per year
Subscription rate:	$8
Publisher:	Sage Publications, Inc. 275 South Beverly Drive Beverly Hills, CA 90212

Teaching Sociology

Subject area(s):	Sociology
Contents:	Articles, course descriptions, teaching materials and methods, book and media reviews
Publication schedule:	2 issues per year
Subscription rate:	$8
Publisher:	Sage Publications, Inc. 275 South Beverly Drive Beverly Hills, CA 90212

Social studies curriculum projects

As part of a large-scale national effort to promote overall improvement in education, the federal government in the mid-1960s supported a variety of curriculum development projects in the social studies. Curriculum developers, which included social scientists, historians, and social studies educators, combined their talents to produce, evaluate, and disseminate new materials for virtually every area within the social studies. Those initial projects, plus later ones, are listed in this section; an overview of each project is included. Information about the projects and samples of materials can be obtained from the appropriate publisher or development center.

American Political Behavior
High School Curriculum Center in Government
Indiana University

Subject(s): Political science

Grade level(s): 9–12

Material(s): Text, audiovisuals, worksheets and tests, simulations, films, teacher's guide

Source: Ginn and Company
191 Spring Street
Lexington, MA 02173

Analysis of Public Issues
Utah State University

Subject(s): Public issues

Grade level(s): 9–12

Material(s): Text, booklets, audiovisuals, teacher's guide

Source: Houghton Mifflin Company
1 Beacon Street
Boston, MA 02107

Anthropology Curriculum Project
University of Georgia

Subject(s): Anthropology

Grade level(s): K–12

Material(s): Texts, workbooks and tests, audiovisuals, teacher's guide

Source: Anthropology Curriculum Project
University of Georgia
107 Dudley Hall
Athens, GA 30601

Asian Studies Inquiry Program
University of California at Berkeley

Subject(s): Area studies

Grade level(s): 10–12

Material(s): Booklets, teacher's guide

Source: Field Educational Publications, Inc.
2400 Hanover Street
Palo Alto, CA 94304

Basic Legal Concepts
The Cornell Law Program

Subject(s): Law

Grade level(s): 7–12

Material(s): Texts, teacher's guides

Source: Ginn and Company
191 Spring Street
Lexington, MA 02173

Committee on Civic Education
University of California at Los Angeles

Subject(s): Civics/government

Grade level(s): 7–12

Material(s): Texts, teacher's guide

Source: Ginn and Company
191 Spring Street
Lexington, MA 02173

Comparing Political Experiences
Social Studies Development Center
Indiana University

Subject(s): Political science

Grade level(s): 9–12

Material(s):	Text, audiovisuals, simulations, tests, teacher's guide
Source:	Social Studies Development Center 513 North Park Bloomington, IN 47401

Economics in Society
San Jose State College

Subject(s):	Economics
Grade level(s):	12
Material(s):	Texts, teacher's guide
Source:	Addison-Wesley Publishing Company, Inc. 2725 Sand Hill Road Menlo Park, CA 94025

Ethnic Heritage Curriculum Project
Social Science Education Consortium

Subject(s):	Ethnic studies
Grade level(s):	K–12
Material(s):	Sample curriculum materials, resource bibliographies, teaching strategies, curriculum materials evaluations
Source:	Social Science Education Consortium 855 Broadway Boulder, CO 80302

Exploring Human Nature
Education Development Center, Inc.

Subject(s):	Interdisciplinary
Grade level(s):	10–12
Material(s):	Texts, films, simulations, materials for experiments, teacher's guide
Source:	Education Development Center, Inc. 55 Chapel Street Newton, MA 02160

From Subject to Citizen
Education Development Center, Inc.

Subject(s):	American history
Grade level(s):	8–9

Material(s): Texts, audiovisuals, worksheets, simulations, role-play cards, primary source material, tests, teacher's guides

Source: Denoyer-Geppert Company
5235 Ravenswood Avenue
Chicago, IL 60640

Geography in an Urban Age
High School Geography Project

Subject(s): Geography

Grade level(s): 10

Material(s): Texts, audiovisuals, simulations, teacher's guides

Source: Macmillan Publishing Company, Inc., School Division
866 Third Avenue
New York, NY 10022

Global Studies for Middle Grades
Mid-America Program for Global Perspectives in Education
Social Studies Development Center
Indiana University

Subject(s): Global studies, interdisciplinary

Grade level(s): 7–12

Material(s): Units, simulations, bibliographies

Source: Social Studies Development Center
513 North Park
Bloomington, IN 47401

Issues in Religion
The Religion-Social Studies Curriculum Project
Florida State University

Subject(s): Religion, American history, world history

Grade level(s): 9–12

Material(s): Texts, teacher's guides

Source: Addison-Wesley Publishing Company, Inc.
2725 Sand Hill Road
Menlo Park, CA 94025

Japanese American Curriculum Project

Subject(s): Ethnic studies

Grade level(s): K–12

Material(s): Texts, trade books, activity kits, audiovisuals, periodicals

Source: Japanese American Curriculum Project
P.O. Box 367
San Mateo, CA 94401

Justice in Urban America
Law in American Society Foundation

Subject(s): Law

Grade level(s): 9

Material(s): Texts, teacher's guide

Source: Houghton Mifflin Company
1 Beacon Street
Boston, MA 02107

Lincoln Filene Center for Citizenship and Public Affairs
Tufts University

Subject(s): Political science

Grade level(s): K–12

Material(s): Resource materials, audiovisuals, bibliographies, films, teacher's guides

Source: Lincoln Filene Center for Citizenship and Public Affairs
Tufts University
Medford, MA 02155

Manpower and Economics Education:
Opportunities in American Life
Ohio University

Subject(s): Economics

Grade level(s): 8–10

Material(s): Text, teacher's guide

Source: Joint Council on Economic Education
1212 Avenue of the Americas
New York, NY 10036

Patterns in Human History
Anthropology Curriculum Study Project

Subject(s):	Anthropology
Grade level(s):	9–10
Material(s):	Multimedia kits, teacher's guides
Source:	Macmillan, Inc. 866 Third Avenue New York, NY 10022

People and Change: A Mosaic of World History
World History Project
Indiana University

Subject(s):	World history
Grade level(s):	9–12
Material(s):	Texts, audiovisuals, simulations, tests, teacher's guides
Source:	Ginn and Company 191 Spring Street Lexington, MA 02173

People and Technology
Education Development Center

Subject(s):	Technology
Grade level(s):	5–7
Material(s):	Texts, artifacts, films, audiovisuals, tests
Source:	Education Development Center 55 Chapel Street Newton, MA 02160

Project Social Studies
University of Minnesota

Subject(s):	Interdisciplinary
Grade level(s):	K–12
Material(s):	Texts, artifacts, audiovisuals, trade books, teacher's guides
Source:	Selective Educational Equipment, Inc. 3 Bridge Street Newton, MA 02195

Religion in Human Culture
World Religion Curriculum Development Center

Subject(s):	Religion, world history
Grade level(s):	9–12
Material(s):	Texts, audiovisuals, teacher's guide
Source:	World Religion Curriculum Development Center 6425 West 33rd Street St. Louis Park, MN 55426

Schools Council Integrated Studies

Subject(s):	Multidisciplinary
Grade level(s):	5–9
Material(s):	Resource packs including primary source materials, teacher's guides
Source:	Oxford University Press 70 Wynford Drive Don Mills M3C 1J9 Toronto, Ontario, Canada

Slow Learner Project
Carnegie-Mellon University

Subject(s):	American history, urban studies
Grade level(s):	8–9
Material(s):	Texts, workbooks and tests, audiovisuals, teacher's guide
Source:	Holt, Rinehart and Winston, Inc. 383 Madison Avenue New York, NY 10017

Social Studies Curriculum Project
Carnegie-Mellon University

Subject(s):	American history, economics, area studies, political science, world history
Grade level(s):	9–12
Material(s):	Texts, audiovisuals, tests, teacher's guide

Source: Holt, Rinehart and Winston, Inc.
383 Madison Avenue
New York, NY 10017

Social Studies Project
Harvard University

Subject(s): Public issues

Grade level(s): 7–12

Material(s): Texts, tests, teacher's guides

Source: American Education Publications
Education Center
Columbus, OH 43216

Sociological Resources for the Social Studies

Subject(s): Sociology

Grade level(s): 10–12

Material(s): Texts, readings, audiovisuals, teacher's guides

Source: Allyn & Bacon, Inc.
Rockleigh, NJ 07647

Units in American History
Amherst College, The Committee on the Study of History

Subject(s): American history

Grade level(s): 11

Material(s): Texts, teacher's guides

Source: Addison-Wesley Publishing Company
2725 Sand Hill Road
Menlo Park, CA 94205

World Studies Inquiry Series
University of California at Berkeley

Subject(s): Area studies

Grade level(s): 7–12

Material(s): Texts, teacher's guides

Source: Field Educational Publications, Inc.
2400 Hanover Street
Palo Alto, CA 94304

Media

Slides

American Library Color Slides Company, Inc., 305 East 45th Street, New York, NY 10017

American Museum of Natural History, Central Park West at 79th Street, New York, NY 10024

Eastman Kodak Company, Motion Picture and Educational Markets Division, 343 State Street, Rochester, NY 14650

Educational Development Center, Inc., 55 Chapel Street, Newton, MA 02160

Meston's Travels, Inc., 3801 North Piedras, El Paso, TX 79930

Metropolitan Museum of Art, Fifth Avenue at 82nd Street, New York, NY 10028

Museum of Modern Art, 11 West 53rd Street, New York, NY 10019

Sandak, Inc., 4 East 48th Street, New York, NY 10017

Society for Visual Education, Inc., 1345 West Diversey Parkway, Chicago, IL 60614

Filmstrips

Guidance Associates, Pleasantville, NY 10570

Scholastic Magazines and Book Service, 906 Sylvan Avenue, Englewood Cliffs, NJ 07632

Index—R. R. Bowker Company, 1180 Avenue of the Americas, New York, NY 10036 (the major source guide for filmstrips—compiled by the National Information Center for Educational Media at the University of Southern California. The current price is $34. The guide is updated at regular intervals by supplements.)

Flat pictures

Audio Visual Enterprises, 911 Laguna Road, Pasadena, CA 91105

Creative Educational Society, 515 North Front Street, Mankato, MN 56001

Documentary Photo Aids, Inc., P.O. Box 2620, Sarasota, FL 33578

Informative Classroom Picture Publishers, Inc., 31 Ottawa Avenue, N.W., Grand Rapids, MI 49501

International Communications Foundation, 870 Monterey Pass Road, Monterey Park, CA 97154

National Geographic Society, School Service Division, 16th and M Streets, N.W., Washington, DC 20036

Society for Visual Education, Inc., 1345 West Diversey Parkway, Chicago, IL 60614

United Nations, Public Inquiries Unit, Department of Public Information, New York, NY 10017

Index—Catherine M. Williams. *Learning from Pictures.* 2d ed. 1968. Association for Educational Communications and Technology, 1201 16th Street, N.W., Washington, DC 20036 (an index of sources of flat pictures, $4.50)

8mm films

Hubbard Scientific, 2855 Shermer Road, Northbrook, IL 60062
International Film Foundation, 475 Fifth Avenue, New York, NY 10017
National Audiovisual Center. *U.S. Government Films.* Washington, DC
National Film Board of Canada, 670 Fifth Avenue, New York, NY 10019
Thorne Films, Inc. *The 8mm Documents Project.* 1229 University Avenue, Boulder, CO 80302

Indices

Index of 8mm Motion Cartridges. R. R. Bowker Company, 1180 Avenue of the Americas, New York, NY 10036 ($39.50)
National Center for Educational Media. *Index to 8mm Motion Cartridges.* University of Southern California, 1969
Service Press. *Guide to Government Loan Films.* Alexandria, Service Press, 1971–1972
Syracuse University Audio Visual Center. *Instructional Materials for Teaching Audio Visual Courses.* 3d ed.
Technicolor Corporation, Commercial and Educational Division. *Silent Film Loop Source Dictionary.* 6th ed. 1300 Trawley Drive, Costa Mesa, CA 92627

Audio equipment

Allied Radio Corporation, 100 North Western Avenue, Chicago, IL 60612
Lafayette Radio Electronics, Mail Order and Sales Center, 111 Jericho Turnpike, Syosset, Long Island, NY 11791
Radio Shack. Located in many cities.

Records

Audio Cardalog, Box 989, Larchmont, NY 11058 ($30 [annual])
Caedmon Records, 461 Eighth Avenue, New York, NY 10001
Capitol Records Distributing Corporation, 175 North Vine Street, Hollywood, CA 90028
Columbia Records, Educational Division, 51 West 52nd Street, New York, NY 10019
Decca Records, Educational Division, 50 West 57th Street, New York, NY 10019
Educational Record Sales, 157 Columbus Street, New York, NY 10007
EMC Corporation, Educational Materials Division, 180 E. 6th Street, St. Paul, MN 55101

Enrichment Materials, Inc. (a division of Scholastic), 50 West 44th Street, New York, NY 10036
Enrichment Teaching Materials, Inc., 71 E. 23rd Street, New York, NY 10010
Epic Records, 51 West 52nd Street, New York, NY 10019
Folkways Records and Service Corporation, 50 West 44th Street, New York, NY 10036
Ginn and Company, 191 Spring Street, Lexington, MA 02173
Harcourt Brace Jovanovich, 757 Third Avenue, New York, NY 10017
London Records, 539 West 25th Street, New York, NY 10001
National Council of Teachers of English, 1111 Kenyon Road, Urbana, IL 61801
Walt Disney Educational Materials Company, 800 Sonora Avenue, Glendale, CA 91201

Tape recordings

Academic Recording Institute, P.O. Box 22961, Houston, TX 77027
Associated Educational Materials Company, Inc., 14 Glenwood Avenue, Raleigh, NC 27602
Educational Activities, Inc., P.O. Box 392, Freeport, NY 11743
Educational Development Laboratories, Inc., Huntington, NY 11743
EMC Corporation, Educational Materials Division, 180 East 6th Street, St. Paul, MN 55101
Imperial International Learning Corporation, P.O. Box 548, Kankakee, IL 60901
National Association of Educational Broadcasters, 1346 Connecticut Avenue, N.W., Washington, DC 20036
National Tape Repository, Bureau of Audio-Visual Instruction, Stadium Building, 348, University of Colorado, Boulder, CO 80907
Spoken Arts, Inc., 319 North Avenue, New Rochelle, NY 10801
Vital History Cassettes, Grolier Educational Corporation, 845 Third Avenue, New York, NY 10622
World Tapes for Education, Box 9211, Dallas, TX 75215

Video equipment

Ampex, 2201 Lunt, Elk Grove Village, IL 60007
Panasonic/Matsushita Electric Corporation, 23-05 44th Road, Long Island City, NY 11101
Shibaden Corporation of America, 58-25 Brooklyn-Queens Expressway, Woodside, NY 11377
Sony Corporation, 47-47 Van Dam Street, Long Island City, NY 11101

Television

ABC, 1330 Avenue of the Americas, New York, NY 10019
Adler Educational System Division, Litton Systems, Inc., 72 East Main Street, New Rochelle, NY 10801
Association for Educational Communications and Technology, 1201 Sixteenth Street, N.W., Washington, DC 20036
CBS, 51 West 52nd Street, New York, NY 10019
Children's Television Workshop, 1 Lincoln Plaza, New York, NY 10023
Committee on Television, American Council on Education, 1785 Massachusetts Avenue, N.W., Washington, DC 20036
Great Plains Regional Instructional Library, University of Nebraska, Lincoln, NB 68508
National Association of Educational Broadcasters, 1346 Connecticut Avenue, N.W., Washington, DC 20036
NBC, 30 Rockefeller Plaza, New York, NY 10020
NET Film Service, Indiana University, Bloomington, IN 47401
PBS, 955 L'Enfant Plaza North, S.W., Washington, DC 20006
RCA Victor Division, Front and Cooper Streets, Camden, NJ 08102

Reprints

Jackdaws, Grossman Publishers, 44 West 56th Street, New York, NY 10019
Springboards, Noble & Noble Publishers, Inc., 1 Dag Hammarskjold Plaza, New York, NY 10017
The 1930's Box, Ontario Institute for Studies in Education, 109 Bloor Street, West, Toronto, Ontario, Canada ($100)

Artifacts

Alva Museum Replicas, Inc., 30-30 Northern Boulevard, Long Island City, NY 11101
Educational Communications Systems, Inc., 145 Witherspoon Street, Princeton, NJ 08540
Hubbard Scientific Company, 2855 Shermer Road, Northbrook, IL 60062
Inter-Culture Associates, Box 277, Thompson, CT 06277

Transparencies

Allyn & Bacon, Inc., AV Department, 470 Atlantic Avenue, Boston, MA 02210
Black Box Collotype Studios, Inc., 4840 West Belmont Avenue, Chicago, IL 60641
John Colburn Associates, Inc., 1122 Central Avenue, P.O. Box 236, Wilmette, IL 60091
Creative Visuals Division, Games Industries Inc., P.O. Box 1911, Big Spring, TX 79720

Encyclopaedia Britannica Educational Corporation, 425 North Michigan Avenue, Chicago, IL 60611
Hammond Inc., 515 Valley Street, Maplewood, NJ 07040
The Instructo Corporation, Paoli, PA 19301
Keuffel and Esser Company, 20 Wippany Road, Hoboken, NJ 07960
Ozalid Division, General Aniline and Film Corporation, 140 West 51st Street, New York, NY 10020
3M Company, Visual Products Division, 3M Center, St. Paul, MN 55119
Visual Materials, Inc., 2549 Middlefield Road, Redwood City, CA 94063
Index—R. R. Bowker Company, 1180 Avenue of the Americas, New York, NY 10036 (lists over 18,000 transparencies; $22.50)

Needle-sort decks

EDUCATION SYSTEMS RESEARCH, P.O. Box 157, Shrewsbury, MA 01545, produces the following:

Ward Twenty-three, Pittsburgh, Pennsylvania 1870–1900, $59.50
Hazelwood's Landowners, 1870, $4.75
Who Came to the First U.S. Congress? $27.50
U.S. Southern Leadership 1850–1880, $59.50
Southern Congressmen on the Eve of the Civil War, $27.50
Southerners in a Reconstruction Congress, $27.50
The Deep South and the Border: A Case Study, $17.50
Community in Colonial Massachusetts, $59.50
URB 60 & 70, Forthcoming
Suburbia, Forthcoming
The Agricultural Frontier, 1875, Forthcoming

Embassies

Most embassies are eager to provide a host of free or inexpensive materials about their countries; these materials include pamphlets, maps, posters, travel brochures, information sheets, press releases, and newspapers. Some embassies can provide various audiovisual materials, including films for classroom use. While embassy materials are created to present a favorable image of each country, these materials can be used as sources to provide an extra dimension to social studies teaching.

Afghanistan
Embassy of Afghanistan
2341 Wyoming Avenue, N.W.
Washington, DC 20008

Algeria
Embassy of the Democratic and Popular Republic of Algeria
2118 Kalorama Road, N.W.
Washington, DC 20008

Argentina
Embassy of the Argentine Republic
1600 New Hampshire Avenue, N.W.
Washington, DC 20009

Australia
Embassy of Australia
1601 Massachusetts Avenue, N.W.
Washington, DC 20036

Austria
Embassy of Austria
2343 Massachusetts Avenue, N.W.
Washington, DC 20008

Bahamas
Embassy of The Commonwealth of The Bahamas
Suite 865
600 New Hampshire Avenue, N.W.
Washington, DC 20037

Bangladesh
Embassy of the People's Republic of Bangladesh
Brighton Hotel
2123 California Street
Washington, DC 20008

Barbados
Embassy of Barbados
2144 Wyoming Avenue, N.W.
Washington, DC 20008

Belgium
Embassy of Belgium
3330 Garfield Street, N.W.
Washington, DC 20008

Bolivia
Embassy of Bolivia
Suite 600
1625 Massachusetts Avenue, N.W.
Washington, DC 20036

Botswana
Embassy of the Republic of Botswana
4301 Connecticut Avenue, N.W.
Washington, DC 20008

Brazil
Brazilian Embassy
3006 Massachusetts Avenue, N.W.
Washington, DC 20008

Bulgaria
Embassy of the People's Republic of Bulgaria
2100 16th Street, N.W.
Washington, DC 20009

Burma
Embassy of the Socialist Republic of the Union of Burma
2300 S Street, N.W.
Washington, DC 20008

Burundi
Embassy of the Republic of Burundi
2717 Connecticut Avenue, N.W.
Washington, DC 20009

Cambodia (See Khmer Republic)

Cameroon
Embassy of the United Republic of Cameroon
2349 Massachusetts Avenue, N.W.
Washington, DC 20008

Canada
Embassy of Canada
1746 Massachusetts Avenue, N.W.
Washington, DC 20036

Central African Republic
Embassy of Central African Republic
1618 22nd Street, N.W.
Washington, DC 20008

Ceylon (See Sri Lanka)

Chad
Embassy of the Republic of Chad
1132 New Hampshire Avenue, N.W.
Washington, DC 20037

Chile
Embassy of Chile
1732 Massachusetts Avenue, N.W.
Washington, DC 20036

China
Chinese Embassy
2311 Massachusetts Avenue, N.W.
Washington, DC 20008

Colombia
Embassy of Colombia
2118 Leroy Place, N.W.
Washington, DC 20008

Congo (See Zaire)

Costa Rica
Embassy of Costa Rica
2112 S Street, N.W.
Washington, DC 20008

Cyprus
Embassy of Cyprus
2211 R Street, N.W.
Washington, DC 20008

Czechoslovakia
Embassy of the Czechoslovak Socialist Republic
3900 Linnean Avenue, N.W.
Washington, DC 20008

Dahomey
Embassy of the Republic of Dahomey
2737 Cathedral Avenue, N.W.
Washington, DC 20008

Denmark
Embassy of Denmark
3200 Whitehaven Street, N.W.
Washington, DC 20008

Dominican Republic
Embassy of the Dominican Republic
1715 22nd Street, N.W.
Washington, DC 20008

Ecuador
Embassy of Ecuador
2535 15th Street, N.W.
Washington, DC 20009

Egypt
Embassy of the Arab Republic of Egypt
2310 Decatur Place, N.W.
Washington, DC 20008

El Salvador
Embassy of El Salvador
2308 California Street, N.W.
Washington, DC 20008

Estonia
Legation of Estonia
9 Rockefeller Plaza
New York, NY 10020

Ethiopia
Embassy of Ethiopia
2134 Kalorama Road, N.W.
Washington, DC 20008

Fiji
Embassy of Fiji
Suite 520
1629 K Street, N.W.
Washington, DC 20006

Finland
Embassy of Finland
1900 24th Street, N.W.
Washington, DC 20008

France
Embassy of France
2535 Belmont Road, N.W.
Washington, DC 20008

Gabon
Embassy of the Gabonese Republic
2210 R Street, N.W.
Washington, DC 20008

German Democratic Republic
Embassy of the German Democratic Republic
1717 Massachusetts Avenue, N.W.
Washington, DC 20036

Germany, Federal Republic of
Embassy of the Federal Republic of Germany
4645 Reservoir Road, N.W.
Washington, DC 20007

Ghana
Embassy of Ghana
2460 16th Street, N.W.
Washington, DC 20009

Great Britain
British Embassy
3100 Massachusetts Avenue, N.W.
Washington, DC 20008

Greece
Embassy of Greece
2221 Massachusetts Avenue, N.W.
Washington, DC 20008

Grenada
Embassy of Grenada
(temp.) Care of the Mission of Grenada to the United Nations
866 Second Avenue, Suite 502
New York, NY 10017

Guatemala
Embassy of Guatemala
2220 R Street, N.W.
Washington, DC 20008

Guinea
Embassy of the Republic of Guinea
2112 Leroy Place, N.W.
Washington, DC 20008

Guyana
Embassy of Guyana
2490 Tracy Place, N.W.
Washington, DC 20008

Haiti
Embassy of Haiti
4400 17th Street, N.W.
Washington, DC 20011

Honduras
Embassy of Honduras
4715 16th Street, N.W.
Washington, DC 20011

Hungary
Embassy of the Hungarian People's Republic
2437 15th Street, N.W.
Washington, DC 20009

Iceland
Embassy of Iceland
2022 Connecticut Avenue, N.W.
Washington, DC 20008

India
Embassy of India
2107 Massachusetts Avenue, N.W.
Washington, DC 20008

Indonesia
Embassy of the Republic of Indonesia
2020 Massachusetts Avenue, N.W.
Washington, DC 20036

Iran
Imperial Embassy of Iran
3005 Massachusetts Avenue, N.W.
Washington, DC 20008

Ireland
Embassy of Ireland
2234 Massachusetts Avenue, N.W.
Washington, DC 20008

Israel
Embassy of Israel
1621 22nd Street, N.W.
Washington, DC 20008

Italy
Embassy of Italy
1601 Fuller Street, N.W.
Washington, DC 20009

Ivory Coast
Embassy of the Republic of Ivory Coast
2424 Massachusetts Avenue, N.W.
Washington, DC 20008

Jamaica
Embassy of Jamaica
1666 Connecticut Avenue, N.W.
Washington, DC 20009

Japan
Embassy of Japan
2520 Massachusetts Avenue, N.W.
Washington, DC 20008

Jordan
Embassy of the Hashemite Kingdom of Jordan
2319 Wyoming Avenue, N.W.
Washington, DC 20008

Kenya
Embassy of Kenya
2249 R Street, N.W.
Washington, DC 20008

Khmer Republic
Embassy of the Khmer Republic
4500 16th Street, N.W.
Washington, DC 20011

Korea
Embassy of Korea
2370 Massachusetts Avenue, N.W.
Washington, DC 20008

Kuwait
Embassy of the State of Kuwait
2940 Tilden Street, N.W.
Washington, DC 20008

Laos
Embassy of Laos
222 S Street, N.W.
Washington, DC 20008

Latvia
Legation of Latvia
4325 17th Street, N.W.
Washington, DC 20011

Lebanon
Embassy of Lebanon
2560 28th Street, N.W.
Washington, DC 20008

Lesotho
Embassy of the Kingdom of Lesotho
Caravel Building
1601 Connecticut Avenue, N.W.
Suite 300
Washington, DC 20009

Liberia
Embassy of the Republic of Liberia
5201 16th Street, N.W.
Washington, DC 20011

Libya
Embassy of the Libyan Arab Republic
2344 Massachusetts Avenue, N.W.
Washington, DC 20008

Lithuania
Legation of Lithuania
2622 16th Street, N.W.
Washington, DC 20009

Luxembourg
Embassy of Luxembourg
2210 Massachusetts Avenue, N.W.
Washington, DC 20008

Madagascar
Embassy of Madagascar
2374 Massachusetts Avenue, N.W.
Washington, DC 20008

Malawi
Malawi Embassy
2362 Massachusetts Avenue, N.W.
Washington, DC 20008

Malaysia
Embassy of Malaysia
2401 Massachusetts Avenue, N.W.
Washington, DC 20008

Mali
Embassy of the Republic of Mali
2130 R Street, N.W.
Washington, DC 20008

Malta
Embassy of Malta
2017 Connecticut Avenue, N.W.
Washington, DC 20008

Mauritania
Embassy of the Islamic Republic of Mauritania
2129 Leroy Place, N.W.
Washington, DC 20008

Mauritius
Embassy of Mauritius
Suite 134, 4301 Connecticut Avenue, N.W.
Washington, DC 20008

Mexico
Embassy of Mexico
2829 16th Street, N.W.
Washington, DC 20009

Morocco
Embassy of Morocco
1601 21st Street, N.W.
Washington, DC 20009

Nepal
Royal Nepalese Embassy
2131 Leroy Place, N.W.
Washington, DC 20008

Netherlands
Embassy of the Netherlands
4200 Linnean Avenue, N.W.
Washington, DC 20008

New Zealand
Embassy of New Zealand
19 Observatory Circle, N.W.
Washington, DC 20008

Nicaragua
Embassy of Nicaragua
1627 New Hampshire Avenue, N.W.
Washington, DC 20009

Niger
Embassy of the Republic of Niger
2204 R Street, N.W.
Washington, DC 20008

Nigeria
Embassy of Nigeria
2201 M Street, N.W.
Washington, DC 20037

Norway
Embassy of Norway
3401 Massachusetts Avenue, N.W.
Washington, DC 20007

Oman
Embassy of the Sultanate of Oman
2342 Massachusetts Avenue, N.W.
Washington, DC 20008

Pakistan
Embassy of Pakistan
2315 Massachusetts Avenue, N.W.
Washington, DC 20008

Panama
Embassy of Panama
2862 McGill Terrace, N.W.
Washington, DC 20008

Paraguay
Embassy of Paraguay
2400 Massachusetts Avenue, N.W.
Washington, DC 20008

Peru
Embassy of Peru
1700 Massachusetts Avenue, N.W.
Washington, DC 20036

Philippines
Embassy of the Philippines
1617 Massachusetts Avenue, N.W.
Washington, DC 20036

Poland
Embassy of the Polish People's Republic
2640 16th Street, N.W.
Washington, DC 20009

Portugal
Embassy of Portugal
2125 Kalorama Road, N.W.
Washington, DC 20008

Qatar
Embassy of the State of Qatar
2721 Connecticut Avenue, N.W.
Washington, DC 20008

Romania
Embassy of the Socialist Republic of Romania
1607 23rd Street, N.W.
Washington, DC 20008

Rwanda
Embassy of the Republic of Rwanda
1714 New Hampshire Avenue, N.W.
Washington, DC 20009

Saudi Arabia
Embassy of Saudi Arabia
1520 18th Street, N.W.
Washington, DC 20036

Senegal
Embassy of the Republic of Senegal
2112 Wyoming Avenue, N.W.
Washington, DC 20008

Sierra Leone
Embassy of Sierra Leone
1701 19th Street, N.W.
Washington, DC 20009

Singapore
Embassy of the Republic of Singapore
1824 R Street, N.W.
Washington, DC 20009

Somalia
Embassy of the Somali Democratic Republic
Suite 710
600 New Hampshire Avenue, N.W.
Washington, DC 20037

South Africa
Embassy of South Africa
3051 Massachusetts Avenue, N.W.
Washington, DC 20008

Spain
Embassy of Spain
2700 15th Street, N.W.
Washington, DC 20009

Sri Lanka
Embassy of Sri Lanka
2148 Wyoming Avenue, N.W.
Washington, DC 20008

Sudan
Embassy of the Democratic Republic of the Sudan
Suite 400
600 New Hampshire Avenue, N.W.
Washington, DC 20037

Swaziland
Embassy of the Kingdom of Swaziland
4301 Connecticut Avenue, N.W.
Washington, DC 20008

Sweden
Royal Swedish Embassy
600 New Hampshire Avenue, N.W.
Washington, DC 20037

Switzerland
Embassy of Switzerland
2900 Cathedral Avenue, N.W.
Washington, DC 20008

Syria
Embassy of the Syrian Arab Republic
Suite 1120
600 New Hampshire Avenue, N.W.
Washington, DC 20007

Tanzania
Embassy of the United Republic of Tanzania
2010 Massachusetts Avenue, N.W.
Washington, DC 20036

Thailand
Embassy of Thailand
2300 Kalorama Road, N.W.
Washington, DC 20008

Togo
Embassy of the Republic of Togo
2208 Massachusetts Avenue, N.W.
Washington, DC 20008

Trinidad and Tobago
Embassy of Trinidad and Tobago
1708 Massachusetts Avenue, N.W.
Washington, DC 20036

Tunisia
Embassy of Tunisia
2408 Massachusetts Avenue, N.W.
Washington, DC 20008

Turkey
Embassy of the Republic of Turkey
1606 23rd Street, N.W.
Washington, DC 20008

Uganda
Embassy of the Republic of Uganda
5909 16th Street, N.W.
Washington, DC 20011

Union of Soviet Socialist Republics
Embassy of the Union of Soviet Socialist Republics
1125 16th Street, N.W.
Washington, DC 20036

United Arab Emirates
Embassy of the United Arab Emirates
Suite 740
600 New Hampshire Avenue, N.W.
Washington, DC 20037

Upper Volta
Embassy of the Republic of Upper Volta
5500 16th Street, N.W.
Washington, DC 20011

Uruguay
Embassy of Uruguay
1918 F Street, N.W.
Washington, DC 20006

Venezuela
Embassy of Venezuela
2445 Massachusetts Avenue, N.W.
Washington, DC 20008

Viet-Nam
Embassy of Viet-Nam
2251 R Street, N.W.
Washington, DC 20008

Yemen
Embassy of the Yemen Arab Republic
Suite 860
600 New Hampshire Avenue, N.W.
Washington, DC 20037

Yugoslavia
Embassy of the Socialist Federal Republic of Yugoslavia
2410 California Street, N.W.
Washington, DC 20008

Zaire
Embassy of the Republic of Zaire
1800 New Hampshire Avenue, N.W.
Washington, DC 20009

Zambia
Embassy of the Republic of Zambia
2419 Massachusetts Avenue, N.W.
Washington, DC 20008

Publishers

Harry N. Abrams, Inc.
110 E. 59th Street
New York, NY 10022

Addison-Wesley Publishing Co., Inc.
Reading, MA 01867

Aldine-Atherton, Inc.
529 S. Wabash Avenue
Chicago, IL 60605

Allyn & Bacon, Inc.
Rockleigh, NJ 07647

American Heritage Press
McGraw-Hill Book Co.
Princeton Road
Hightstown, NJ 08520

Appleton-Century-Crofts
440 Park Avenue, South
New York, NY 10016

Atheneum Publishers
122 E. 42nd Street
New York, NY 10017

Avon Books, The Hearst Corp.
959 Eighth Avenue
New York, NY 10019

Ballantine Books, Inc.
101 Fifth Avenue
New York, NY 10003

Bantam Books, Inc.
666 Fifth Avenue
New York, NY 10019

A. S. Barnes & Company
Box 421
Cranbury, NJ 08512

Barnes & Noble Books
Harper & Row, Publishers
10 E. 53rd Street
New York, NY 10022

Barron's Educational Series, Inc.
113 Crossways Park Drive
Woodbury, NY 11797

Basic Books, Inc., Publishers
404 Park Avenue, South
New York, NY 10016

Blaisdell Publishing Company
Xerox College Publishing
191 Spring Street
Lexington, MA 02173

The Bobbs-Merrill Company, Inc.
4300 W. 62nd Street
Indianapolis, IN 46268

George Braziller, Inc.
1 Park Avenue
New York, NY 10016

Cambridge University Press
32 E. 57th Street
New York, NY 10022

Collier Books
Macmillan, Inc.
866 Third Avenue
New York, NY 10022

Congressional Quarterly, Inc.
1735 K Street, N.W.
Washington, DC 20006

George F. Cram Co., Inc.
301 S. LaSalle Street
Indianapolis, IN 46206

Thomas Y. Crowell Company, Inc.
201 Park Avenue, South
New York, NY 10003

Dell Publishing Company, Inc.
750 Third Avenue
New York, NY 10017

Denoyer-Geppert Company
5235 Ravenswood Avenue
Chicago, IL 60640

The Dial Press and Delacorte Press
245 East 47th Street
New York, NY 10017

Dodd, Mead & Company
79 Madison Avenue
New York, NY 10016

Dorsey Press
1818 Ridge Road
Homewood, IL 60430

Doubleday & Company, Inc.
245 Park Avenue
New York, NY 10017

Encyclopaedia Britannica, Inc.
425 N. Michigan Avenue
Chicago, IL 60611

Farrar, Straus & Giroux, Inc.
19 Union Square, West
New York, NY 10003

Fawcett Publications, Inc.
Fawcett Place
Greenwich, CT 06830

Fearon Publishers, Inc.
6 Davis Drive
Belmont, CA 94002

Follett Corporation
1010 W. Washington Boulevard
Chicago, Illinois 60607

The Free Press
Macmillan, Inc.
866 Third Avenue
New York, NY 10022

Funk & Wagnalls Publishing Company, Inc.
666 Fifth Avenue
New York, NY 10019

General Learning Corporation
Morristown, New Jersey 07960

Ginn and Company
Xerox College Publishing
191 Spring Street
Lexington, MA 02173

Goodyear Publishing Company, Inc.
15113 Sunset Boulevard
Pacific Palisades, CA 90272

Grosset & Dunlap, Inc.
51 Madison Avenue
New York, NY 10010

Grove Press, Inc.
53 E. 11th Street
New York, NY 10003

Hammond Inc.
515 Valley Street
Maplewood, NJ 07040

Harcourt Brace Jovanovich, Inc.
757 Third Avenue
New York, NY 10017

Harper & Row, Publishers
10 E. 53rd Street
New York, NY 10022

Hayden Book Company, Inc.
50 Essex Street
Rochelle Park, NJ 07662

D. C. Heath and Company
Div. Raytheon Educ. Co.
125 Spring Street
Lexington, MA 02173

Herder and Herder, Inc.
232 Madison Avenue
New York, NY 10016

Holt, Rinehart & Winston
383 Madison Avenue
New York, NY 10017

Houghton Mifflin Company
110 Tremont Street
Boston, MA 02107

Intext Educational Publishers
Scranton, PA 18515

Richard D. Irwin, Inc.
1818 Ridge Road
Homewood, IL 60430

Alfred A. Knopf, Inc.
Random House
201 East 50th Street
New York, NY 10022

J. B. Lippincott Co.
East Washington Square
Philadelphia, PA 19105

Little, Brown & Company, Inc.
34 Beacon Street
Boston, MA 02106

Liveright
500 Fifth Avenue
New York, NY 10016

McCormick-Mathers Publishing Company
Division of Litton Educational Publishing Inc.
450 West 33rd Street
New York, NY 10001

McGraw-Hill Book & Education Services Group
1221 Avenue of the Americas
New York, NY 10020

David McKay Company, Inc.
750 Third Avenue
New York, NY 10017

Macmillan, Inc.
866 Third Avenue
New York, NY 10022

Charles E. Merrill Publishing Company
1300 Alum Creek Drive
Columbus, OH 43216

Modern Library, Inc.
201 E. 50th Street
New York, NY 10022

William Morrow & Company, Inc.
105 Madison Avenue
New York, NY 10016

Thomas Nelson, Inc.
407 Seventh Avenue, South
Nashville, TN 37203

The New American Library, Inc.
1301 Avenue of the Americas
New York, NY 10019

W. W. Norton & Company, Inc.
500 Fifth Avenue
New York, NY 10036

Oxford Book Company, Inc.
11 Park Place
New York, NY 10007

Oxford University Press, Inc.
200 Madison Avenue
New York, NY 10016

F. E. Peacock Publishers, Inc.
401 W. Irving Park Road
Itasca, IL 60143

Penguin Books
74 Fifth Avenue
New York, NY 10011

Pergamon Press, Inc.
Maxwell House
Fairview Park
Elmsford, NY 10523

Pocket Books
630 Fifth Avenue
New York, NY 10020

Popular Library Inc.
600 Third Avenue
New York, NY 10016

Praeger Publishers, Inc.
111 Fourth Avenue
New York, NY 10003

Prentice-Hall, Inc.
Englewood Cliffs, NJ 07632

G. P. Putnam's Sons
200 Madison Avenue
New York, NY 10016

Quadrangle/The New York Times Book Company
10 East 53rd Street
New York, NY 10022

Rand McNally & Company
8255 Central Park Avenue
Skokie, IL 60076

Random House, Inc.
201 E. 50th Street
New York, NY 10022

W. B. Saunders Company
West Washington Square
Philadelphia, PA 19105

Schocken Books, Inc.
200 Madison Avenue
New York, NY 10016

Science Research Associates, Inc.
1540 Page Mill Road
Palo Alto, CA 94304

Scott, Foresman & Company
1900 East Lake Avenue
Glenview, IL 60025

Charles Scribner's Sons
597 Fifth Avenue
New York, NY 10017

Sheed & Ward, Inc.
6700 Squibb Rd.
Mission, KS 66202

Silver Burdett Company
General Learning Press
250 James Street
Morristown, NJ 07960

Simon & Schuster, Inc.
630 Fifth Avenue
New York, NY 10020

Social Science Research Council
230 Park Avenue
New York, NY 10017

Time-Life Books
Rockefeller Center
New York, NY 10020

Van Nostrand Reinhold Company
450 W. 33rd Street
New York, NY 10001

Vantage Press, Inc.
516 W. 34th Street
New York, NY 10001

The Viking Press
625 Madison Avenue
New York, NY 10022

Vintage Books
201 E. 50th Street
New York, NY 10022

Wadsworth Publishing Company, Inc.
Belmont, CA 94002

John Wiley & Sons, Inc.
605 Third Avenue
New York, NY 10016

Xerox Education Division
1200 High Ridge Road
Stamford, CT 06905

The fact that this is only a selected list of resources for social studies teachers cannot be overemphasized. Other important resources are available, and new resources will continue to be developed. Also, the resources described herein are national in scope. Social studies teachers need to identify similar community and state agencies that can supply additional inexpensive resources for improving social studies instruction. They can then add these local sources to their wider professional communications network for keeping in touch with new ideas in social studies education.

Index

Abscissa, 191
Abt, Clark, 84(n)
Action sequence, in simulation, 103-104
Actions as clues to values, 52-53
Affective taxonomy; major categories and instructional objectives, 285-286(t)
Aggregate data, 154, 156-158
Ahmann, J. Stanley, 277
Allen, Cliff, 87
All-human simulations, 86
Alternatives, analyzing, 74
American College Testing Service, 161
Analysis
  bivariate, 191
  comparative, 150-151
  data, techniques, 172-195
Anecdotal records
  improving quality, 316
  for observing behaviors, 315-316
Anthropology Curriculum Study Project, 252
Artifacts
  archeological uses, 250-252
  cultural, 230
  defining, 248
  exercises with, 248-250
  personal, as resource, 222
  reproducing, 252-255
  sources, 373
  use of, 273-274
  Valdivian, 250, 251(f), 252
Assignment, random (*see* Sample)
Association
  among variables, 185-186
  negative, 189, 190(f)
  quantitative data to determine, 171
Associational analysis, 172, 185-195
Associations as resource, 218-219
Assumptions
  recognizing, 293
  verification, 162
Attitudes, assessing, 319-322
Audio lessons
  advantages, 237-238
  presentation, 242-243
  production and use, 272
  sample exercises, 238-241
  source materials, 371
  with visual support, 240-241
Audiovisual aids (*see also* Media)
  audio experiences, 237-243
  creation and use, 230
  8mm films, 236-237
  filmstrips, 231, 235
  photographs, 231-232, 233-234(f), 235-236
  selection, 229
  slides, 230-231, 232, 235
  source materials, 371
  still-picture exercise, 232, 233-234(f)
  still-picture production and use, 271
  videotape, 243-246
Average, 185

Beck, Clive, 51-52
Behavior
  daily, data sources, 155
  desirable, determining, 164
  experimental research, 159-161
  indirect measures, 154
  quantification, 151
  observable, indicators, 149-150
  values causing, 53
Behavioral objectives, 278-279
Bias
  in experimental research, 160
  in history study, 147
  in survey sampling, 152-153
Bivariate analysis, 191
Bivariate situation, 162-163, 185-186
Bloom, Benjamin S., 283
Board of Cooperative Educational Services (B.O.C.E.S.), 266
Boocock, Sarane, 84(n)
Broadcasts, 242-243
Broadsides, 246-248, 273
Burkhalter, Barton, 266

Cameras, 232, 235, 236
Cards, needle-sort (*see also* Data decks)
  obtaining, 262
  printing backs, 265
Career Development Project, Final Report, 270
Career education, emphasis on, 208(n)
Case studies
  analysis, teacher's role, 47-48
  classroom use, 14
  designing, 42-47

as evaluation technique, 316
presentation, 15
selecting materials, 17-18, 43-45
specific purposes, 17
types, 17-42
Case-study approach, 15-17
Causation
determining, 163
multiple, concept, 36
CHANGING DOLLARS, 255-258
Charts
for value comparisons, 65(f), 67(f)
transparencies, 259
values information, 64(f)
Checklists, 314-315
Children, stages of moral reasoning 70, 72
Citizens rights, studying, 18-20
Citizenship and local community studies, 215-216
Claims, value, 67-68
Clarification of values (*see* Value clarification)
Class, value conflicts among members, 20
Classroom
observation for evaluation, 315-317
use of case studies, 14, 16-17
use in local community study, 216-217
Coefficient of variability, 185
Cognitive taxonomy, major categories and instructional objectives, 283-284(t)
Coleman, James, 84(n)
Communication with numbers, 149, 150
Community
and controversial issues, 6
defined, 206
studies (*see* Local community studies)
types, 207
Comparative analysis, 150-151
Comparisons, personal, 163-164
Computer-based instruction, 265-270
program, production and use, 274-275
Concepts, operationalizing, 166
Conference as evaluation technique, 317
Content
analysis, 151, 153-154
learning, and simulations, 95
relation to inquiry, 8-9
selecting, 8-9
Contingency tables, 186-188
Cost factor in simulations use, 114
Crisscross diagrams, 188-190, 191(f)
Critical incident, 321
Critical skills, assessing, 296-299
Cross-plot, 190
Curriculum, teacher as designer, 1
Curriculum development projects, 362-369
Curves, Lorenz, 176, 178, 180, 181(f), 182(f), 183-184
Cynicism, avoiding, 10-11
Data
aggregate, 154, 156-157
analysis, techniques, 172-195
bank, computer-based, 269-270
checking relevancy and accuracy, 69
content analysis, 153-154
displays, as shortcuts, 148
economic, sources, 154-155
familiarization with sources, 169
from field studies, 155
gathering, 170
interpreting tabular, 290
for local community studies, 216-223
national, for content analysis, 154
personal, using, 142
quantitative (*see* Quantitative data)
from recorded public acts, 155-158
retrieval, 261
self-report, 155
sources, 200-203
Data decks
creation, 261
key sheet, 263(f)
production and use, 262, 265, 274
sample exercise, 262
sources, 374
Debriefing, postsimulation, 109-110, 111-112
Decisions
testing ability to make, 306
and values, 51
Definitional value claims, 67-68
Definitions in quantitative terms, 168
Dependent variable, 163
Development, stages of moral, 71(t)
Dewey, John, 70
Dilemmas
alternative, 73-74
moral, child's response, 70, 72-75
moral, defining, 69-70
Discussion strategy, developing, 46-47
Distribution
inequalities, visual display, 178
world resources, 178, 180, 183
Documents as resource, 24-26, 220
Doubt, resolving through inquiry, 2
Duke, Richard, 266

Economic system and human behavior, 154
Education Systems Research, 261
Education values, Kohlberg's theory, 72-73
Educational games, 87
Educational Testing Service, 160-161
Efficacy, sense of, 95
"EIAG" experimental learning model, 111-112
8mm films, 236-237, 272, 371
Embassies, list of, 375-382
Empathy, role-playing to build, 75-76, 95
Environment, physical-human, 222-223

Essay questions, 304-311
Essays, interpretive, for case studies, 22-24
Ethics, business, analyzing, 33-34
Evaluation
  of attitudes and values, 319-322
  basic purpose, 277-278
  of behavioral objectives, 278-279
  educational, defining, 277
  parental attitude toward, 323-324
  projective techniques, 321
  by self and by peers, 318
  of student, improving, 277
  and teacher judgment, 324
  techniques, need for variety, 322
  techniques other than testing, 311-318
Evans, Clifford, 250, 252
Event perception and frame of reference, 24
Evidence, 10
Exercises, quantitative data, 170, 171
Experiment in Community Communications Operation, 244
Experimental research
  criteria for evaluating, 160
  as data source, 159

Fact, distinguishing from opinion, 292
Feedback, instant, 243-244, 245
Feelings, discussion of, 75-76
Fenton, Edwin, 252
Field studies
  as data sources, 155
  in local community studies, 217
Films, local community, 220-221
Filmstrips
  classroom use, 231
  production, 235, 271
  source materials, 370
Flander's Interaction Analysis, 244(n)
Foxfire Books, 218(n)
Frame of reference
  of author, 33
  and perception of events, 24
Frankfurter, Justice Felix, 19
Front page, producing, 247-248

Galbraith, Ronald E., 73, 74
Games, 87-88
Generalizations, applying, 296
Glock, Marvin D., 277
Goals of social studies instruction, 4-5
Good, defining, 164
Good, John M., 252
Gordon, Alice Kaplan, 96-97, 113
Government
  beliefs about "good," 41(t)
  offices, data from, 220
Grade point averages as quantitative data, 167
Graphs (*see also* Lorenz curves)
  axes, 191-192
  bar, 173-175, 176(f)
  interpreting, 290
  histograms, 173-175, 176(f)
  line, 175-176, 177(f), 178(f), 179(f)
  pie, 173
  transparencies, 259
Group experiences and local community studies, 209
Group processes and simulations, 95
Guetzkow, Harold, 84(n)
Guided Self Analysis for Professional Development, 244

Harmin, Merrill, 55
Harper's Magazine, 163-164
Health statistics, 156
Historian, quantitative, 147-148
Historical conditions, data to describe, 170
Historical period, introducing study, 36
History and quantitative study, 146-149
Howe, Leland W., 55(n), 58
Human element, fear of eliminating, 145-146
Human-machine simulations, 86
Hypotheses, verification, 162-163, 295

Ideas, contradictory, introducing, 78-79
Incidents, value, 61-64
Independent variable, 163
Indicators, value, 64
Individuals
  categorizing, 141-143
  humanities vs. science-centered, 145
Inequality
  area of, 180
  visual demonstration, 178
Information sources, 7-8 (*see also* Data)
Inquiry
  advantages, 5
  approach, objections to, 5-11
  commitment to, 4-5
  defining, 2-3
  to develop student insights, 9
  evidence-conclusion relationship, 10
  levels of sophistication, 9-10
  limitations, 7
  skills, and case-study approach, 16-17
  and student behavior, 8
  student resistance to, 6-7
  teacher's role in, 3, 4
Inquiry learning
  evaluation, 276
  and individual initiative, 209
  promotion, 210
  and quantification, 140, 146, 195-196
  steps in, 161
Inquiry skills and simulations, 96
Inquiry teaching
  audiovisual aids, 228, 229

defining, 3-4
interdisciplinary focus, 208-209
and local community studies, 208
requirements, 161
using quantitative data, 165-172
Instructional materials
curriculum projects, 362-369
embassies, 375-382
free or inexpensive sources, 328-348
magazines and journals, 354-361
media, 370-374
professional organization sources, 349-353
publishers, 383-386
Instructional objectives, 279-288
Instrumental means, 52
Instrumental values, 52
Interaction
class, in answer-writing practice, 309
in simulation, 103-104
Interactive computing, 265
Interdisciplinary focus
of inquiry teaching, 208-209
of local community studies, 210
Interpersonal experiences, 209
Interview, public, 58
Issues, significant, complexity of, 30

Jewett, Robert E., 2
Jones, Thomas M., 73, 74
Journals, 354-361
Judgments, value, 52, 66-69

Kirschenbaum, Howard, 55(n), 58
Kohlberg, Lawrence, 70-72
Krathwohl, David R., 283

Languages, computer, 265
Learning
at different levels, 96
inquiry (*see* Inquiry learning)
situations, realistic, 208(n)
Library for resource material, 222
Lichtenberg, Mitchell P., 261
LIFE DECISIONS, 229, 266-269
Likert scales, 319-320
Literacy statistics, 156
Local community studies
benefits, 207-209, 224-225
defining, 206-207
examples, 211-215
overall benefits of, 224
possible problems and issues, 210-216
precautions, 223-224
purpose, 209-210
resources for, 216-223
and social studies, 204, 205, 206(f), 224-225
Location of simulations, 100, 115

Lorenz curves, 176, 178, 180, 181(f), 182(f), 183-184
Louis, Arthur M., 165

Magazines, 154, 354-361
Management factor in simulations, 114-115
Material remains, 248
Materials for case studies, 43-45
Mean, 185
Measurement, educational, defining, 277
Measures, statistical, 185
Media (*see also* Audiovisual aids)
artifacts and material remains, 248-255
broadsides and newspaper headlines, 246-247
computer-based instruction, 265-270
general references, 270-271
in instructional process, 229-230
needle-sort data decks, 261-265
transparencies, 255-261
Median, 185
Meggers, Betty J., 250, 252
METROPOLIS, 266
Microphones, 242-243
Mode, 185
Money, sources of data about, 154-155
Moral dilemmas
child's response to, 70, 72-75
defined, 69-70
Moral reasoning, 69-75
Moral values, 52
Morton, Philip, 245
Motion pictures, 236-237, 272, 371
Motivation and simulations, 95
Multimedia presentation, 240-241

Negative association, 189, 190(f)
New York Center for Understanding Media, 244
Newmann, Fred M., 18(n), 40
Newspaper headlines
classroom use, 246-247
production and use, 247-248, 273
Newspapers as resource, 219-220
1976 Yearbook of the National Council for the Social Studies, 61
Nominal variables
association of, 186-187
relationship between, 188-190, 191(f)
Nova Academic Games Project, 87
Number awareness in quantification, 167
Number manipulation, anxiety about, 144

Objectives
behavioral (*see* Behavioral objectives)
identifying, 42-43
instructional (*see* Instructional objectives)
questions for various, 287(t)
of simulation, 98, 101-102
Occupation statistics, 156

Offset printing, 247-248
Oliver, Donald, 18(n), 40
One-variable analysis, 172
Open-ended episode, 20-22, 44-45
Oral traditions, defining, 248
Ordering, rank, 57
Ordinal scales, 188-190, 191(f)
Ordinate, 191
Origin, 192
Osmunson, John A., 250, 252

Parents and evaluation, 323-324
Parkrose (Ore.) Senior High School, 87
Parsons, Theodore, 244
Patriotism, student perception of, 26
Peer group, influence on moral reasoning, 73
Peer-evaluation, 318
Philadelphia Parkway School, 208
Photographs
  of artifacts and material remains, 253
  disadvantages, 231-232
  local community, 220-221
  producing, 235-236, 271
  source materials, 370-371
Piaget, Jean, 70, 72
Pictorial data, defining, 248
Political action in local community study, 213-215
Porta-paks, 244-245
Pottery, reproducing, 253-254
Predicted condition, 186
Predictor variable, 186
Price indices, 154
Price variations, study of, 211-213
Private business, data from, 220
Probe questions, 73, 74
Problem solving and inquiry, 8-9
Problems
  dealing with, 30
  realistic attitude toward, 10
Processes and simulations, 83, 85, 98-100
Professional organizations, 349-353
Projective techniques of evaluation, 321
Propositional value claims, 67, 68
Publishers, 383-386

Quantification
  background reading, 197-199
  to define characteristics and concepts, 168
  definition, 143, 149
  and human element, 145-146
  skills, building, 167-172
  in social studies classroom, 195
  in study of history, 146-149
  teacher concerns, 144-146
  uses of, 149-151
Quantitative data
  benefits, 196
  commitment to use, 167
  from content analysis, 151, 153-154
  about daily behavior, 155-159
  defined, 149
  to determine association, 171
  developing file, 166
  drawbacks, 196
  economic, 154-155
  from experimental research, 159-161
  gathering, 170
  and inquiry learning, 161-162, 195
  and inquiry teaching, 165-172
  preparing students to use, 167-172
  and social studies, 140-141
  sources, 151-161, 165-166, 200-203
  from survey research, 151-153
  univariate analysis, 172
  and unwarranted statements, 170-171
  and values clarification, 163-165, 171
  to verify assumptions, 162
  to verify hypotheses, 162-163
  visual displays, 168-169
Quantitative thinking, introducing teachers to, 143
Questions
  arrangement, 300-301
  chronological order, 301
  completion, 299-300
  essay, 304-311
  free response, 301-302
  item analysis, 302-303
  key list, 302
  matching, 299
  multiple-choice, 288-299
  objective test, 303-304
  sequence, planning, 46-47
  true-false, 300

Racial problems, simulation, 88-93
RAILROAD GAME, 98-110
Random sampling, 152
Range, 185
Rank ordering, 57
Rank orders, comparative, 188-190, 191(f)
Raths, Louis E., 55
Rating sheets, 312, 313(f), 314(f)
Reality, classroom, and simulations, 95-96
Reasoning, moral, 69-75
Records, phonograph, sources, 371-372
Reform movements, introducing topic of, 33
Reprint sources, 373
Research
  content analysis, 153-154
  experimental, human behavior, 159-161
  proper procedures, determining, 169-170
  quantitative, selected readings, 199-200
  survey, 151-153
Resource distribution, visualization, 180, 182

Resources, 102-103, 326-387
Response, clarifying, 55-56
Rochin v. California, 18-19
Role identification, 100-101
Role-playing
  episode, 47
  as evaluation technique, 316-317
  in simulations, 86
Rules of operation, in simulation, 105-107

Sampling
  random, 152
  techniques, 151-152
Scattergram, 190
Scatterplots, 190-195
Schedule for simulation, 110-111
Scientific American, 250
Scoring procedures, simulation, 107-108
Selection, random (*see* Sampling)
Self-evaluation, 318
Self-report data, 155
Semantic differential, 320-321
Shaftel, Fannie R., 75-76
Shaftel, George, 75-76
SIERRA LEONE, 266
Simon, Sidney B., 55
Simulations
  advantages, 94-97
  cautions in use, 114-115
  classroom use, 110-112
  computer-based, 265-269
  definition, 84-86
  distributors and publishers, 130-133
  as evaluation technique, 316
  guides to, 133
  history, 84(n)
  journals and newsletters, 134
  measuring effectiveness, 96-97
  professional organizations, 133
  role of teacher in use, 112-113
  sources and descriptions, 116-134
  STARPOWER, 88, 93-94
  steps in designing, 97-98
  SUNSHINE, 88-93
  teacher supervision, 111-112
  as teaching tools, 82-84
  types, 84-88
Skepticism, developing student, 169-170
Slides
  classroom use, 230-231
  production, 232, 235, 271
  source materials, 370
Social problems, dealing with, 5-6
Social processes, 85
Social simulations, 86-87
Socioeconomic status, determining, 156
Solutions, determining feasibility, 295
Sources
  data, familiarization, 169
  determining reliable, 292
Spokesman, 242
Sports statistics as quantitative data, 167
Stadsklev, Ron, 111-112
Standard deviation, 185
Standards, values as, 52
STARPOWER, 88, 93-94
Statements, verifying, 170-171
Statistical analysis, simple forms, 185
Statistics, deliberate distortion, 169
Strategies, teacher as designer, 1
Strategy, developing discussion, 46-47
Students
  aggregate measures, 157-158
  avoiding cynicism, 10-11
  background for simulation, 110
  classroom behavior, 8
  creation of audiovisual aids, 230
  developing empathy, 95
  developing inquiry skills, 3-4, 16, 96
  developing insights, 9
  effect of simulation on, 114-115
  evaluating growth, 112
  grading achievement, 161
  improving evaluation, 277
  influence on curriculum, 1
  interviewing for value discussions, 77-79
  introducing artifacts, 248-250
  and local community studies, 207,
    215-216, 224-225
  motivation, 95
  need for "people models," 208
  negative reactions of, 6-7
  perception of patriotism, 26
  pitfalls in evaluation, 322-324
  preparing for essay tests, 308-310
  producing artifacts, 252-253
  and quantitative inquiry, 167-172
  ranking with standardized tests, 160
  sense of efficacy, 95
  suggestions in assessing performance, 317
Study, specialized, for quantification, 145
Success criteria in simulation, 107-108
SUMERIAN GAME, 266
SUNSHINE, 88-93
Survey research as data source, 151-153

Tape recordings, as resource, 221, 372
Taxonomy
  affective, 285-286(t)
  cognitive, 283-284(t)
  and instructional objectives, 283-286
Teacher
  benefits from videotape, 244
  in case-study analysis, 47-48
  community pressures, 6, 323-324
  concerns about quantification, 144-146
  creation of audiovisual aids, 230
  in discussion of feelings, 76
  and inquiry, 3, 4
  introducing to quantitative thinking, 143

judgment, and evaluation, 324
and local community studies, 223-224
preparing for quantitative inquiry, 165-167
producing artifacts, 252-253
resource materials, 326-387
in simulation use, 112-113
study guides, 353
supervising simulation, 111-112
in value discussions, 77-80
Teaching
defining inquiry-oriented, 3-4
inquiry (*see* Inquiry teaching)
test as end for, 322-323
Technological society and individual, 32
Television, source materials, 373 (*see also* Videotape)
Terminology
of quantification, 144
in simulations, 84-88
Terms, defining value, 67-68
Test
commercial vs. teacher-made, 323
constructing objective questions, 287-288
as end for teaching, 322-323
essay, 308-310
inadequacy of, 311-312
multiple-choice questions, 288-299
objectivity of, 323
scores, as quantitative data, 167
standardized, 160-161
Textbook
in inquiry-oriented class, 7-8
visuals, as data sources, 166, 168-169
Time
factor, in simulations use, 114
to introduce simulation, 110
span, covered by simulation, 100
Transparencies, 255
CHANGING DOLLARS, 255-258
color-lift, 259-261
production and use, 259, 274
sources, 373-374
Trends, ascertaining, 195
Two-variable analysis, 172

United Nations as data source, 156, 159
United States data, sources, 157, 201-202
Univariate analysis, 172
University of Georgia Anthropology Curriculum Project, 252

Value clarification
clarifying response, 55-56
as evaluation technique, 316
public interview, 58-59
and quantification, 163-165, 171
rank ordering, 57-58
teaching advantages, 60-61
value continuums, 60
value sheet, 56-57
values voting, 59-60
Value conflicts, 54-55
and case studies, 17
cause, 69
among class members, 20
recognizing, 294
types, 55
and war, 25-30
Values
allocation, determining, 165
assessing, 319-322
claims, 67-68
comparing and contrasting, 64-66, 67(f)
conflicting, illustrating, 40
continuums, 60
definition, 51
degrees of, 54
discussions, teacher's role, 77-80
education, Kohlberg's theory, 72-73
as emotional commitments, 51, 75
incident, 61-63
indicators, 52-55
information chart, 64
judgments, 52, 66-69
of others, identifying, 61-64
personal, 55-61
reasons for adopting, 53-54
sheet, 56-57
and social studies, 50-52, 55
as standards, 52
strategies in analyzing, 61
student clarification, 40-43
terms, defining, 67-68
voting, 59-60
Valuing, process of, 55
Variables
association, 185-186, 186(f), 187(f)
determining, 162-163
negative relationship, 194-195
nominal, relationship, 186-190, 191(f)
positive relationship, 192
unrelated, 193-194
Video equipment sources, 372
Videotape
advantages over film, 244, 245
disadvantages, 245-246
porta-paks, 244-245
production and use, 272-273
unique characteristics, 243-245
Visual displays
of quantitative data, 168, 172-195
reading, 168-169
Voting behavior as data source, 158-159

WHO DOES WHAT?: A CAREER GAME, 270
Words as value indicators, 53, 64

Zero point, 192